# B[barcode]N

MW01610107

# and New England

**Herbert Bailey Livesey**

**Prentice Hall Travel**

**New York • London • Toronto • Sydney • Tokyo • Singapore**

## THE AMERICAN EXPRESS ® TRAVEL GUIDES

Published in the United States by
Prentice Hall General Reference
15 Columbus Circle
New York, NY 10023

PRENTICE HALL is a registered
trademark and colophon is a
trademark of Prentice-Hall, Inc.

Edited, designed and produced by
Castle House Press, Llantrisant
Mid Glamorgan CF7 8EU
Wales

© American Express Publishing
Corporation Inc. 1994

All rights reserved, including the right
of reproduction in whole or in part in
any form

Contact Library of Congress for full
CIP data.

ISBN 0-671-86827-6

The editors thank Neil Hanson and
Alex Taylor of Lovell Johns, David
Haslam, Anna Holmes and Sylvia
Hughes-Williams for their help and
co-operation during the preparation
of this edition.

Some illustrations in this book were
first used in *The Mitchell Beazley
pocket guide to Architecture* by
Patrick Nuttgens (1980).

Although all reasonable care was
taken during the preparation of this
edition, the publisher, editors and
author cannot accept responsibility
for any consequences arising from its
use or from the information it
contains.

**FOR THE SERIES:**
**Series Editor:**
  David Townsend Jones
**Map Editor:** David Haslam
**Indexer:** Hilary Bird
**Gazetteer:** Anna Holmes
**Cover design:** Roger Walton Studio

**FOR THIS EDITION:**
**Edited on desktop by:**
  David Townsend Jones
**Art editor:**
  Eileen Townsend Jones
**Illustrator:**
  Sylvia Hughes-Williams
**Cover photo:** Tony Stone
  Worldwide/Jeremy Walker

**FOR MITCHELL BEAZLEY:**
**Art Director:** Andrew Sutterby
**Production:** Katy Sawyer
**Publisher:** Sarah Bennison

**PRODUCTION CREDITS:**
**Maps** by Lovell Johns,
  Oxford, England
**Typeset** in Garamond and
  News Gothic
**Desktop layout** in Corel
  Ventura Publisher
**Reproduction** by M & E
  Reproductions, Great Baddow,
  Essex, England
**Linotronic output** by Tradespools
  Limited, Frome, England

# Contents

## Boston

# New England

---

# Maps

# How to use this book

Few guidelines are needed to understand how this book works:

- For the general organization of the book, see CONTENTS on the pages preceding this one.
- Wherever appropriate, chapters and sections are arranged alphabetically, with headings appearing in **CAPITALS.**
- Often these headings are followed by location and practical information printed in *italics*.
- Subject headers, similar to those used in telephone directories, are printed in CAPITALS in the top corner of each page.
- If you still cannot find what you need, check in the comprehensive and exhaustively cross-referenced INDEX at the back of the book.
- Following the index, a LIST OF STREET NAMES provides map references for all streets, squares etc. mentioned in the book that fall within the area covered by the main Boston and Cambridge maps (color maps **7–12** at the back of the book).

## CROSS-REFERENCES
These are printed in SMALL CAPITALS, referring you to other sections or alphabetical entries in the book. Care has been taken to ensure that such cross-references are self-explanatory. Often, page references are also given, although their excessive use would be intrusive and ugly.

## FLOORS
Wherever we refer in this book to the "first floor," we mean the floor at ground level. "Ground floor" means the same thing.

---

## AUTHOR'S ACKNOWLEDGMENTS
Herbert Bailey Livesey would like to acknowledge the valuable assistance of Leslie Brokaw, who shared her knowledge and insights about the Boston/Cambridge area. He also thanks the Greater Boston Convention and Visitors Bureau for its ready assistance throughout his research for this book.

# Key to symbols

| | | | |
|---|---|---|---|
| ☎ | Telephone | MasterCard | MasterCard |
| Fx | Fax | VISA | Visa |
| ★ | Recommended sight | Garage | Garage |
| T | Rapid Transit station | ♿ | Facilities for disabled people |
| ⬅ | Parking | | |
| 🏛 | Building of architectural interest | Swimming pool | Swimming pool |
| | | Good view | Good view |
| 💲 | Free entrance | Gym/fitness facilities | Gym/fitness facilities |
| Entrance fee | Entrance fee payable | Sauna | Sauna |
| | | ♉ | Bar |
| ✗ | Guided tour | Refrigerator in room | Refrigerator in room |
| 🍴 | Cafeteria | Business center | Business center |
| ✲ | Special interest for children | Restaurant | Restaurant |
| | | Luxury restaurant | Luxury restaurant |
| Hotel | Hotel | ❂ | Good value (in its class) |
| Luxury hotel | Luxury hotel | | |
| AE | American Express | ♫ | Live music |
| Diners Club | Diners Club | Dancing | Dancing |

---

## PRICE CATEGORIES

| | | | |
|---|---|---|---|
| ☐ | Cheap | Expensive | Expensive |
| ☐ | Inexpensive | Very expensive | Very expensive |
| ☐ | Moderately priced | | |

Our price categories for hotels and restaurants are explained in the
WHERE TO STAY and EATING AND DRINKING chapters.

# About the author

After an early career in higher education culminating in the post of Director of Admissions at New York University, **Herbert Bailey Livesey** decided that he no longer wanted to get up early and wear suits. An exhibition of his sculptures had proved a modest critical success and a resounding financial flop, so he decided, with greater logic than might be apparent, to leave salaried employment for a full-time career in writing. A native New Yorker, he is the author of nine books on such subjects as education and sociology. *Tournament*, his only published novel, took as its backdrop the world of deep-sea game-fishing.

He has written four other books in this series, *New York* (1983), *Toronto, Montréal & Québec City* (1991), *Barcelona, Madrid & Seville* (1993) and its predecessor, *Spain* (1984). His work appears frequently in a variety of magazines, including *Travel and Leisure* and *Food and Wine*. He and his wife Joanne, a television executive, share four grown children and one very new granddaughter, Juliana. They live in a house north of New York City, overlooking the bay in which explorer Henry Hudson anchored his boat, the *Half Moon*, in 1609.

# A message from the editors

Months of concentrated work were dedicated to making this edition accurate and up to date when it went to press. But time and change are forever the enemies, and between editions we are very much assisted when you, the readers, write to tell us about any changes you discover.

Please keep on writing — but please also be aware that we have no control over restaurants, or whatever, that take it into their heads, after we publish, to move, or change their telephone number, or, even worse, close down. Some restaurants are prone to menu notices like the following genuine authenticated example: "These items may or may not be available at all times, and sometimes not at all and other times all the time." As to telephone numbers, everywhere on earth, telephone authorities seem to share a passion for changing their numbers like you and I change shirts.

My serious point is that we are striving to tailor the series to the very distinctive tastes and requirements of our discerning international readership, which is why your feedback is so valuable. I particularly want to thank all of you who wrote while we were preparing this edition. Time prevents our responding to most such letters, but they are all welcomed and frequently contribute to the process of preparing the next edition.

Please write to me at **Mitchell Beazley**, an imprint of Reed Illustrated Books, Michelin House, 81 Fulham Road, London SW3 6RB; or, in the US, c/o American Express Travel Guides, **Prentice Hall Travel**, 15 Columbus Circle, New York, NY 10023.

*David Townsend Jones, Series Editor, American Express Travel Guides*

# Boston
## and New England

# Around The Hub

Boston has had nearly four centuries to define itself and fashion its myths. In the process, inconvenient truths were discarded and virtues buffed to mirrored gleam. It is the "Cradle of Liberty," the intellectual center that was the "Athens of America," and the meritoriously humble "home of the bean and the cod." Never mind that Paul Revere actually whispered "The British regulars are out!" in alert ears. The surrogate shout of "The British are coming!" is so much more satisfying to a patriot's soul. And when Oliver Wendall Holmes referred to Boston's State House as "the hub of the solar system," the phrase was stripped down to the city's favorite nickname, "The Hub." That bit of chauvinistic bluster has been employed in pride or irony ever since about the de facto capital of the six northeastern states collectively known as New England.

What Boston is not is one of those cities on the cutting edge, where fashion and gold are all, and every waking hour is a challenge to the spirit. Rather, it belongs in that cadre of smaller, more livable American urban entities — Seattle, San Francisco, Minneapolis — where satisfaction is measured less by the accumulation of lucre and status than by the time available for friends, creative work and contemplation. Admittedly, it is afflicted with the same ills as any other city in the US: the deranged, the addicted and the homeless are present in similar proportions. Yet the streets of Boston are somehow cleaner, quieter, less threatening.

Visitors delight in its human scale and the residential character of even most of its central districts. Apartment dwellings are rarely more than a few stories high, and the tallest skyscrapers would all but disappear if transferred to midtown Manhattan. Apart from a few false steps, urban renewal has delivered what it promised: measured innovation, balanced by respect for neighborhoods and heritage. Half of Boston's workers walk to work, while the rest have the convenience of one of the cheapest, most comprehensive public transportation systems in the nation.

I shall enter no encomium upon Massachusetts; she needs none. Behold her, and judge for yourselves. There is Boston and Concord and Lexington and Bunker Hill; and there they will remain forever.
(Daniel Webster)

Tradition cleaves to Boston's institutions and monuments. After all, with its sister city, Cambridge, it boasts the oldest university in America, the oldest public school, the oldest library, the oldest African-American church, the oldest hotel, the oldest marathon, the oldest public park . . . And it is, in many respects, the birthplace of the oldest democratic republic on earth. The shades of the gifted men and women who made it so still touch the bricks and stones of these ancient lanes. Those visitors with the capacity to conjure a palpable past find being here very nearly an honor.

Such thoughts lend substance to the Bostonian image of sobriety and rectitude. So what might be surprising to first-time visitors is the city's spriteliness, its atmosphere of quest and curiosity. Credit that unexpected quality to the presence of more than 250,000 students who attend the 71 colleges and universities in the metropolitan area. Their bottomless capacity for inquiry fills the museums, bookstores and concert halls; their enthusiasms race through streets and coffeehouses and across playing fields and parks. No city can succumb to the frumpishness of old age when it is suffused each autumn with tens of thousands of fresh young minds and bodies.

## ALMOST AN ISLAND
Indians called the peninsula that became Boston, *Shawmut,* said to have meant "lively water" — a reference, perhaps, to the springs that sustained the first European settlers. In 1630, Shawmut was a bulb of hilly land connected to the mainland by a slender isthmus, approximately where the present Washington Street runs. At the end of the Revolutionary War, some landfill had been made, filling in the knob of waterfront, but the topographical profile remained much the same.

The prosperity of the 19th century and the vision of its merchant class were responsible for the city's appearance today. They lay behind the great projects that filled the mill pond between the North End and the Old West End, that pushed out the waterline to create the present Financial District, that made possible the Public Garden and then the Victorian residential neighborhood that retained its original watery name of Back Bay. Today, over 70 percent of the city, and much of neighboring Cambridge, are landfill.

In this great project, work was made for the refugees who fled from the Irish potato famine, and an untitled but monied aristocracy came into being. The descendants of the first settlers, known as Yankees, left the original village in the North End and moved to the south slope of Beacon Hill. About that time, persons unknown dubbed them the "Boston Brahmin," presumably a reference to the caste system of India. Irish and Germans took their place. As Back Bay developed, the wealthy and well-to-do moved on again. African-Americans, who had occupied the north slope of Beacon Hill, started filtering down to Roxbury and Dorchester. When South Boston, a thumb of land jutting into the Bay, began to take shape, the Irish flowed in. Their places in the North End were taken by still another wave of newcomers, the Italians.

Those are the ethnic identities that the neighborhoods retain today: Brahmin Beacon Hill and Back Bay, the Italian North End, Irish South Boston, and Black Roxbury. These are generalizations, of course, given the continuous arrivals of Asians, Eastern Europeans and Middle Easterners, but they bear enough truth to promote a variety of tribalism that can be both a source of pride and of divisiveness.

In 1910, one John Collins Bossidy delivered a half-mocking toast to what was perceived to be the order of social class in the city: "And this is good old Boston/The home of the bean and the cod/Where the Lowells talk to the Cabots/And the Cabots talk only to God." Even then, the sentiment was dated. By the end of the 19th century, Irish Catholics had accumulated sufficient numbers and political sophistication to wrest control from the descendants of the Puritan colonists. They have been

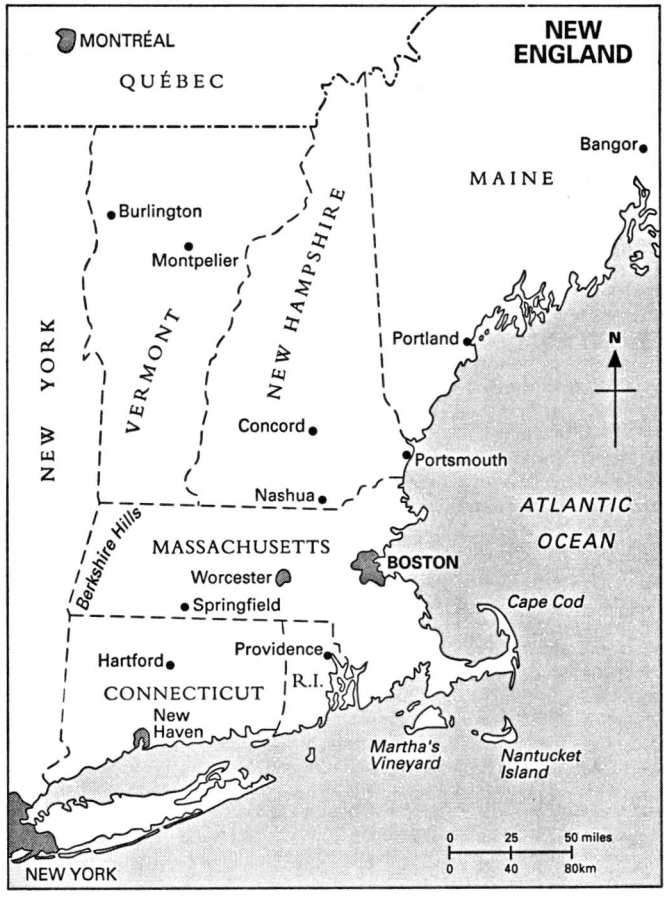

poking their fingers in Yankee eyes ever since. Albeit not quite obligatory, being of Irish ancestry has until now, at least, been a prime qualification for public office. Witness the parade of prominent politicians of the last hundred years: Fitzgerald, Curley, O'Neill, Kennedy, Kennedy, Kennedy, Flynn, and the man who apparently can continue as the powerful President of the State Senate as long as he wants, William Bulger.

Today, however, Irish-Americans are fewer in number, currently forming only 22 percent of the population. Nearly four out of every ten Bostonians are members of racial minority groups, and that doesn't take into account Hispanics, who can be of any race. Asians and Hispanics are stepping into the gaps left in the shrinking white population, while Italian-Americans understandably feel their time has come for a turn at the wheel. Now, candidates need to appeal broadly to the many components of the racial and ethnic mosaic that Boston has become — and they must find a way to tamp the subcutaneous bigotries that tribalism feeds.

## CAPITAL OF NEW ENGLAND

Given the regional prominence enjoyed by Boston due to its long history, relative size and intellectual resources, it often seems to cast a deep shadow over its neighbors. Yet the challenges it faces are only larger, not essentially different, than those of smaller cities throughout the region. Boston is, after all, simply the northern terminus of the amoebic urban sprawl that sweeps for hundreds of miles down the coast to Washington, DC, the megalopolis dubbed "Bowash" by anxious urbanologists.

What may be forgotten in this jittery serpents' nest of contemporary angst is the abundant calm and remarkable diversity of the larger New England that lies outside that frenetic corridor. Much of it is rural, agricultural, and not the least chic, apart from the ski resorts in its midst.

Forests and dairy farms surround inland villages with their omnipresent steepled churches. Beaches are interlaced with rocky inlets providing small boat anchorages all the way from the Canadian border to the affluent Connecticut suburbs at the rim of New York. Commercial fishing fleets also make port along that twisted coast and, though not the robust industry of old, shipbuilders still launch the product of their ancient craft. The Yankees of northern Vermont and New Hampshire continue to offer cautious taciturnity in response to the volubility of the city folk they encounter. And their pockets of tradition survive, as in the once-in-a-year town meetings that still govern some municipalities. Hard work, tolerance and independence of mind are still cherished values.

The people who call themselves New Englanders and the waters and lands they nurture will continue to gladden visitors and influence the nation far into the coming millennium.

# Boston

# Culture, history and background

## Boston and New England: a brief history

**DISCOVERY TO REVOLUTION**

Religious fervor and the profit motive uneasily joined hands in motivating the first migrations of European immigrants. Italian explorers in the employ of the French and English kings had pointed the way. In **1497**, Giovanni Caboto — "John Cabot" to Henry VII, who hired him — bumped into Cape Breton on his way to Asia. Twenty-seven years later, in **1524**, Giovanni da Verrazano was the first recorded European to explore the coast of what was to become British America. It was almost another century before the first attempts at colonization, in **1607** at Jamestown, Virginia and in **1620** at Plymouth, on the coast of the future Commonwealth of Massachusetts.

The 102 Pilgrims who landed at Plymouth were Calvinists, hounded out of England for refusing to recognize the ecclesiastical infallibility of the king. They intended to create a church that would incorporate their revisionism. Half of them died that winter, but the survivors' crops arrived in the next summer and another shipload of colonists landed that fall. In **1629** and '**30**, another 16 ships set sail from England. Their passengers and livestock were in sufficient numbers to establish settlements at 11 points around Massachusetts Bay.

The group that attempted to establish a toehold at Charles Towne, on the north side of the Charles River estuary, found clouds of rapacious mosquitoes and wells that produced only brackish water. Hearing of their plight, William Blackstone, an eccentric recluse who had lived alone for five years on the opposite Shawmut Peninsula, invited them to share his land and spring water. Eventually, his acreage was purchased as common ground, and the town that started to grow beside it was named Boston.

This group of colonists were Puritans, who, like the original 102, were at odds with the Church of England, but for different reasons. While they sought freedom of expression for themselves, they were harshly intolerant of those with views that varied even slightly from their own. Severe punishments and even execution were the lot of dissenters, the effect of which was to send colonists of differing persuasions fanning out across Massachusetts and down into Connecticut. One of these was the fiercely intelligent Anne Hutchinson, a natural leader exiled in **1637** as a heretic, for her outspoken conviction that people should be allowed to worship as they chose. She moved to New York, where she and her large family were murdered by Indians.

A divinity school was founded in **1636** in Cambridge, the new settlement north of the Charles. Two years later, John Harvard, a preacher, bequeathed half his estate to the school, including his library of over 300 books. In gratitude, the school was named after him. At the same time, one Roger Williams incurred the wrath of the theocracy by preaching the separation of church and state. He departed the Bay area to found Providence, in Rhode Island, which he intended to be an oasis of tolerance.

Despite hardships, both natural and self-imposed, the colonies grew, fed by births and steady immigration. By **1640**, more than 1,200 voyages had been made from England, making Boston one of the most prominent ports in the world in barely ten years. In Connecticut, the first written constitution in the New World established a popularly elected chamber of deputies.

Democracy and its explicit freedoms to do and say as one wished continued to flourish, paradoxically running parallel to the exclusionary policies of the Massachusetts Bay Colony. The unforgiving intolerance of that tyranny erupted in the predictable hysteria known as the Salem witch trials of **1691**, which resulted in the hanging of 19 men and women. That was, for all practical purposes, the final flameout of the theocratic form of government in America. New, more liberal ideas were flowering.

Europe's wars and rivalries came to the New World after William of Orange and his wife Mary ascended their British thrones in **1689** and promptly got into a squabble with France. It was to last, on and off, for almost 75 years. On the west side of the ocean, it pitted the British and their colonials against the French and their Indian allies. Yet growth continued despite periodic battles and massacres of civilian populations. Newspapers were published on a regular basis. By **1722**, Boston's population exceeded 10,000.

In **1756**, the defeat of an Anglo-American force in frontier Pennsylvania marked the start of the French and Indian War, an extension of the Seven Years War in Europe. By then, the British colonies strung along the Atlantic coast had a combined population of over 1.5 million, while the French, in far smaller numbers, were scattered over a long arc stretching from Québec down the Mississippi to New Orleans. The war ended in **1759**, when British General James Wolfe defeated the forces of the Marquis de Montcalm on the Plains of Abraham, west of Québec City. After the **1763** Treaty of Paris validated that victory, removing France from the North American continent, the American colonists began to take stock of their new circumstances. The French threat was gone. Many colonials had gained valuable military experience, including George Washington, a field-grade officer in General Braddock's army. Talk of union of the colonies intensified, while regard for their distant rulers declined.

Grumbling increased when duties were demanded by the Sugar and Stamp Acts imposed by England. The Stamp Act was swiftly repealed, only to be followed shortly by confiscatory taxes on tea, glass, newspapers and other documents. Insult was added by the Quartering Act, which stipulated that British troops be housed in private homes and inns when necessary, and their expenses paid by the colonies. Riots and protests ensued, often led by the radical Sons of Liberty organization.

More effective were boycotts of all British goods, which resulted in the withdrawal of all but one of the taxes in **1770**. George III kept the tax on tea, apparently to prove that he was willing to compromise but would not be intimidated.

On the evening of **March 5, 1770**, an angry and probably drunken mob of hundreds of Bostonians stormed up King St. in Boston with the vague purpose of harassing whichever representatives of the Crown might be present at the State House. A British soldier on guard took the brunt of the abuse. When a squad of men under Captain Thomas Preston arrived to rescue the threatened guard, retreat was cut off. The mob's taunts were followed by stones and clubs, and one of the soldiers struck by a missile fired his musket. His fellows joined him, and after a brief fusillade, a dozen or more of the colonials lay wounded; five of them died. Although the "Boston Massacre" was not the first of such incidents and hardly a massacre, radical leaders Sam Adams, John Adams and others made the most of its propaganda value. The troops were removed to Castle Island in the bay, but eventual armed rebellion seemed inevitable.

> I must study politics and war that my sons may have liberty to study
> . . . mathematics and philosophy, geography, natural history, naval
> architecture, navigation, commerce, and agriculture, in order to
> give their children a right to study painting, poetry, music, archi-
> tecture, statuary, tapestry, and porcelain.
>
> (John Adams)

In **1773**, after a gathering of thousands of protestors at the Old South Meeting House, a gang of about one hundred men, dressed as Indians, set off for Griffin's Wharf. They boarded three merchant ships and threw the cargoes of tea into the harbor. The British Parliament struck back with the punitive Intolerable Acts, which included the closing of the port and the stationing of 4,000 British troops in a city that then had a population of only 16,000. The effect was to rally other colonies to Boston's side.

Thousands of residents left the city over the next year, leaving it a virtual military garrison, with almost as many soldiers as civilians. British General Gage decided to halt the growing threat of rebellion by capturing munitions stored in Concord, west of Boston. The rebels got word of the plan. On the night of **April 18, 1775**, signal lanterns in the Old North Church alerted Paul Revere, William Dawes and Samuel Prescott that the British were crossing the bay on the way to Concord. They rode out to warn the militia.

Two prominent leaders of the rebellious colonials, John Hancock and Sam Adams, were in Lexington, a farm village 17 miles northwest of the city, on the road to Concord. Revere got there in time to warn Hancock and Adams. But in the misted morning hours of **April 19, 1775**, the 800 soldiers in the British column encountered 77 militiamen on the green at Lexington. Shots were exchanged, and when the smoke drifted off, 18 militiamen lay dead or wounded.

The British continued to Concord. On a hill above the village was a larger contingent of "Minutemen," militia members who had pledged to make themselves available on short notice. They challenged the British at Old North Bridge. The "shot heard 'round the world" was fired, and after the exchange that followed, the British withdrew. They had already marched over 20 miles in full equipment on an uncommonly hot April day. Now they returned to Boston, harried all the way by rebel snipers. The Revolution had begun.

Two months later, the rebel militia, now about 3,500 strong, had moved close to Boston, occupying Breed's and Bunker Hills, above Charles Towne. They were observed by Gage's forces stationed on Copp's Hill in the North End of Boston. Gage ordered bombardment of Charles Towne to suppress sniper fire prior to attacking the redoubts. The town disappeared in the resulting firestorm. Marching up Breed's Hill in parade ground order, the British were repulsed twice, but overran the American trenches on the third attempt. They lost 1,054 men in all, the rebels only 441 — a moral victory for the ill-trained militia. Gage was recalled to England in disgrace.

Stalemate prevailed over the next ten months. During that time, the brilliant American field commander Ethan Allen led his Vermont Green Mountain Boys against Fort Ticonderoga in upper New York. The cannon they captured were hauled hundreds of miles overland to Boston and presented to George Washington, now in command of the Continental Army. He emplaced his valuable new batteries on Dorchester Heights, pointing down at the British fleet. After due consideration, the British sailed out of Boston with all 8,900 troops, never to return. From then on, the war was fought primarily in the middle Atlantic region, especially New York and Virginia. It ended soon after French troops and naval forces were committed to the American side, when the army of Cornwallis was trapped at Yorktown, in Virginia. That was in **1781**, although confirmation did not come until the **1783** Treaty of Versailles.

### FEDERALISM AND THE NEXT REVOLUTION

Economic depression trampled the euphoria of victory. Dispossessed Massachusetts farmers led by Daniel Shay, a veteran of the Battle of Bunker Hill, attacked an arsenal in Springfield. They were repulsed, and "Shay's Rebellion" evaporated. But demands for a stronger central government than that permitted by the founding Articles of Confederation resulted in the far more lucid Constitution we find in force today.

Tensions over trade and maritime issues provoked the war of **1812** with Britain. New Englanders opposed the conflict, to the point of meeting in Connecticut to discuss the possibility of a separate union. It was not the first time that New England had taken an adversarial stance against the Southern states, which supported the war; nor would it be the last. While the slave trade had been made illegal, the institution itself continued in the South. New England, and Boston in particular, grew more avidly abolitionist. In **1829**, William Lloyd Garrison delivered his first fiery speech against slavery in the Park Street Church, on Boston Common.

In Ireland and parts of Europe, a decade of famine starting in **1840** provoked a flood of new immigration. Boston was a major port of entry, its population nearly tripling in only 25 years. By **1850**, it was the third largest city in the United States. Protestant Boston shuddered at the onslaught of impoverished followers of the Roman faith. But the influx coincided with the start of America's Industrial Revolution, which had also migrated from Europe, and cheap labor was required.

There was work to be had in Boston's most ambitious earthmoving project to date. New technologies, including railroads and steam-powered machinery, buttressed a proposal to fill in marshy Back Bay, a bulge in the Charles River that nearly cut off Boston from the mainland. The project began in **1852**, with new streets laid and houses built as soon as the landfill was stable. More than 600 acres were claimed from the river during the next 30 years.

Work was slowed by the **1861–65** Civil War, in which abolitionist New England fought on the side of the Union against the Confederacy. The first all-Black regiment was organized in Massachusetts and acquitted itself commendably in battle. With the end of the war, a second wave of immigration began, this time including Italians, Portuguese, Scandinavians and Eastern Europeans. They were less easily absorbed, in part because of the "Great Fire" of **1872**, which consumed 770 downtown buildings, aggravating already overcrowded housing conditions. Pressure began to rise for curtailment of immigration. Yet by **1900**, Boston's population had reached 560,892.

**ON TO THE NEW BOSTON**
The labor movement gathered momentum with the founding of the Industrial Workers of the World (IWW) in **1905**. Known as the "Wobblies," the union was particularly strong in the textile factories of New England. In **1912**, at the peak of its power, 10,000 textile workers joined the watershed "Bread and Roses" strike, which started in Lawrence, Massachusetts.

A star-crossed political dynasty began with the **1910** election of John F. Fitzgerald to the office of mayor of Boston. "Honey Fitz" was the grandfather of John, Robert and Edward Kennedy.

In **1921**, Nicola Sacco and Bartolomeo Vanzetti were convicted of a double murder in South Braintree, Massachusetts. The case aroused strong sentiments in the US and abroad, their supporters protesting that the self-described anarchists were the innocent victims of the "Red Scare" hysteria that followed the Russian Revolution. Despite repeated delays, the two were executed in **1927**. Intensified anti-foreigner sentiments inspired new federal legislation severely limiting future immigration. The tumultuous decade also saw female suffrage, Prohibition, the rise of organized crime, and a giddy prosperity that ended in the stock market crash of **1929**. The worst of the ensuing Depression was over by **1936**, but it did not end until **1939**, when the country began to prepare for war.

Boston did not experience great deprivation during World War II, apart from rationing, blackouts, and the perceived need to paint in gray the golden dome of the State House. By **1950**, Boston reached its peak population of 801,444. A decade later, the city's own John Fitzgerald Kennedy narrowly defeated Richard M. Nixon for the Presidency. He was Massachusetts' third native son to ascend to the office. Three years later he was assassinated in Dallas. Razing of the Scollay Square area began, to allow construction of the new Government Center. In **1968**, Robert F. Kennedy entered the presidential race, but he too was assassinated. In the same year, the daring new City Hall opened, the latest emblem of the widely trumpeted "New Boston."

With the end of the divisive Vietnam War and the Watergate scandal, as well as the heated local controversy over the forced busing of school-children to achieve racial integration, Bostonians joined other Americans in celebration of the national Bicentennial. It ended with a memorable concert by the Boston Pops orchestra punctuated with fireworks over the Charles River. In **1980**, the city celebrated its 350th anniversary.

The last decade of the century began on an optimistic note, with a major public works project intended to remove the blight of the elevated Central Artery and enhance access to the waterfront. A 14-lane express-way and a third tunnel to East Boston and the airport are scheduled to be completed by **2002**.

# Landmarks in Boston and New England history

**1620**    The second permanent British colony in North America was founded by Pilgrims from the *Mayflower* landing at Plymouth Rock.

**1625**    William Blackstone moved to what eventually became Boston Common and lived there as a hermit for five years.

**1626**    Settlement by Puritans at Salem on Cape Ann, north of the future Boston.

**1629**    White settlers established a village on the north shore of the Charles estuary. They found rapacious mosquitoes and a shortage of potable water.

**1630**    John Winthrop arrived with 11 ships carrying 900 Puritans, establishing eight outposts around Massachusetts Bay. William Black-stone invited them to share his land and water.

**1636**    A divinity school was founded in the settlement of Cambridge, north of the Charles River.

**1638**    John Harvard, a preacher, bequeathed half of his estate to the two-year-old divinity school. Roger Williams, persecuted for his dis-putes with the theocracy of the Bay area, left to found a colony in Rhode Island.

**1639**    Cambridge claimed the distinction of having the first operational printing press in British America.

**1660**    The combined population of the New England colonies now exceeded 30,000.

**1691**    The Salem witch trials: the final violent spasm of religious tyranny in New England.

**1704**    *The Boston News-Letter* was the first regularly published news-paper in the colonies.

**1761**    A disastrous fire destroyed much of downtown Boston.

**1763**   The French and Indian War ended with the Treaty of Paris. English sovereignty over most of North America was conceded.

**1765**   Grumbling over British rule escalated into sporadic riots and general unrest, prompted by punitive taxation.

**1770**   On March 5, British soldiers fired on a menacing mob, killing five in what was labeled the "Boston Massacre."

**1773**   George III refused to rescind the tea tax. Members of the rebellious Sons of Liberty disguised themselves as Indians and threw three boatloads of tea into Boston Harbor: the so-called Boston Tea Party.

**1775**   On April 18, Paul Revere and others rode out to warn the militia of hostile British troop movements. The next day, the Redcoats killed eight rebels at Lexington, and the Revolution began. Two months later, British troops attacked the Americans holding Breed's Hill in Charlestown. They won the battle, known in history as Bunker Hill, but took heavy casualties.

**1776**   On July 4, the Continental Congress adopted the Declaration of Independence. Patriot forces occupied Boston after the British withdrew to engage the Continental Army in New York.

**1780**   French troops and naval forces were committed to the American side.

**1781**   The army of Cornwallis was trapped at Yorktown, thus ending the war.

**1783**   The Treaty of Versailles confirmed American independence.

**1787**   A second major fire destroyed much of rebuilt Boston.

**1789**   Boston's population reached 18,000.

**1797**   John Adams of Boston became the second President.

**1812–14**   Another war with Britain. Peace treaty signed at Ghent.

**1816**   The first savings bank in the US opened in Boston.

**1825**   John Quincy Adams, son of the second president, was inaugurated in that office.

**1840s**   With the start of the Irish potato famine, the influx of European immigrants rose to flood proportions.

**1842**   A railroad connected Boston with Albany, New York.

**1850**   The population of Boston was 136,881, making it the third largest city in the US.

**1852**   Boston opened the first public library in the US. An ambitious landfill project began in Back Bay.

**1861–65**   The Civil War started. It was caused by growing differences between northern and southern states, notably the slavery issue. The abolitionist movement was strong in New England, which was on the side of the Union against the Confederacy.

**1868**   New waves of Italian, Scandinavian, Portuguese and Eastern European immigrants began to settle in and around Boston.

**1872**   Another "Great Fire" consumed 770 downtown buildings, adding to already severe problems of overcrowding. Pressure began to grow for curtailment of immigration.

**1897**   The first subway system in the US started operation with a tunnel along the eastern edge of the Boston Common.

**1900**   Boston's population was now 560,892.

**1919**    A 2.2-million-gallon tank of molasses crumpled in the North End, killing 21 people and injuring 150 others.

**1921**    In a highly controversial trial in Dedham, Massachusetts, the anarchists Sacco and Vanzetti were convicted of double murder.

**1929–30**    The Wall Street Crash and the start of the Great Depression.

**1941–45**    World War II.

**1950**    Boston reached its peak population of 801,444.

**1954**    The first nuclear-powered submarine was built in Groton, Connecticut.

**1960**    John Fitzgerald Kennedy was elected 35th President, the third from Massachusetts.

**1963**    Kennedy assassinated in Dallas.

**1966**    Edward W. Brooke of Massachusetts was the first African-American elected to the US Senate since the Reconstruction Period following the Civil War.

**1968**    Eugene McCarthy defeated President Johnson in the New Hampshire primary election. Robert F. Kennedy entered the race soon after, but was assassinated in California.

**1975–76**    American Bicentennial observances. Quincy Market was restored and re-opened.

**1980**    Boston celebrated its 350th anniversary.

**1985**    Vermont elected a foreign-born woman governor, Madeleine Kunin, a first.

**1990**    Boston's population reached 574,283, an increase after decades of decline.

**1993**    Thomas M. Merino was the first man to be elected mayor of Boston in 63 years who was not of Irish heritage.

# A Boston who's who

Boston cannot claim as native sons and daughters the legions of glitterati that spice the tabloids of New York and Los Angeles. But the "Athens of America" was birthplace to six presidents and enjoys a history rich in memorable characters active in statesmanship, scholarship and literature.

**Adams, John** *(1735-1826)*
George Washington's vice president was elected to the highest office on the new Federalist Party ticket in 1796. That triumph capped a distinguished and varied career that began in teaching after graduation from Harvard. On becoming a lawyer, he served contrary causes by arguing against taxation without representation and defending the British soldiers who shot civilians at the Boston Massacre. A signer of the Declaration of Independence, he subsequently became the first American ambassador to England. His single term as president foundered on his support of the Alien and Sedition Acts, which attempted to suppress dissent at a time when war with France loomed. It was a curious stance for a man who had inveighed against his former rulers for similar offenses. At a time when few men were fortunate enough to reach age 50, he lived to 90, dying on the same day as Thomas Jefferson. It was July 4, Independence Day.

**Adams, John Quincy** *(1767-1848)*
The sixth president was the son of the second, John, and Abigail Adams. He was as energetic in public service as his father, serving as representative to several European nations, as US senator, and as secretary of state to President James Monroe. He helped to formulate the "Monroe Doctrine," relating to the policy of nonintervention by foreign powers in the Western Hemisphere, and negotiated the ceding of Florida from Spain to the US. Destined to be a one-term president as was his father, he was defeated in 1828 by the popular Andrew Jackson. Three years later, he was elected to Congress and stayed for almost two decades. Adams was a vocal opponent of slavery and the Mexican War, the latter an exercise in expansionism that ranks as one of the least justifiable conflicts in American history.

**Adams, Samuel** *(1722-1803)*
The fiery Adams was on the forward edge of revolutionary fervor and, with his orations and pamphleteering, was as responsible as anyone for stoking the smoldering resentments of British rule. His flair for politics, perhaps inspired by his cousin John Adams, was discovered after his failures in business. He was a major figure in the formation of the radical Sons of Liberty and helped provoke the Boston Tea Party. Considered something of an extremist even by allies of similar views, he nonetheless moved from the lower chamber of the Massachusetts legislature to member of the Continental Congress to signer of the Declaration of Independence. After the war, he was elected to a short term as governor of the state.

**Attucks, Crispus** *(c.1723-70)*
Little is known about the man who died in the so-called Boston Massacre. Some believe he was a sailor off a whaling ship, as were many in the mob he led toward the old State House that day, March 5, 1770. A small contingent of British soldiers was there. After what was either intense provocation or unwarranted violence, depending on the source, the soldiers fired. Attucks and two others died on the spot, and two others were mortally wounded. History cannot even identify his race with assurance, although he became a hero to generations of African-Americans. Some sources claim he was a Natick Indian, others that he was of mixed blood.

**Bell, Alexander Graham** *(1847-1922)*
One of that remarkable band of inventors that emerged in Europe and North America in the last half of the 19thC, Bell was first involved in the development of methods of communication for the deaf. He worked with his father and teachers of those with impaired hearing, first in Scotland, where he was born, then in Canada and Boston, where he lectured at Boston University and continued his work on technological solutions to the isolation of deaf people. Only a few years after his arrival in America, he delivered his famous message to his assistant over a device that came to be called the telephone: "Watson, come here, I want you." Many of his subsequent inventions continued to focus on solutions to the problems of the deaf, along the way aiding in the development of the phonograph (gramophone). In later years, his interests shifted to aviation and hydrofoil vessels.

**Bird, Larry** *(born 1956)*
For well over a decade, Bird was the embodiment of Boston's favorite professional team, the basketball Celtics. Despite occasional grumbling that he would not have received as much adulation had he not been a white man in a sport dominated by African-Americans, Bird proved his superb athleticism again and again with his steady play and last-second heroics. Plagued by injury, he retired after the 1991–92 season and an appearance with the "Dream Team" at the Barcelona Olympics. Although he made clear more than once that his first loyalty was to his tiny hometown of French Lick, Indiana, he remains a Beantown institution.

**Brooke, Edward William** *(born 1919)*
A brief but highly lauded career as state attorney general propelled Brooke into the US Senate in 1967. The first African-American elected to that body since the Reconstruction period following the Civil War, he was a Republican of moderate ideological views. He was defeated in a re-election bid in 1978 after examination of his financial history by the Senate Ethics Committee. Too late, he was cleared of any impropriety.

**Bulfinch, Charles** *(1763-1844)*
By far the most influential architect of his time, Bulfinch's commissions are still encountered in every corner of old Boston, even though the

majority of his buildings have been lost. The landmark State House and the original Massachusetts General Hospital stand out, but much of Beacon Hill also is credited to him, as are University Hall at Harvard and several Massachusetts courthouses. He designed many churches, but the only one still extant in Boston is St Stephen's, on Hanover Street. Despite all this activity, the energetic Bulfinch also held the office of first selectman, a post approximating that of mayor, for 19 years.

**Copley, John Singleton** *(1738-1815)*
Colonial America had little time for the arts, so Copley had scant competition for his acknowledged role as its leading painter. His portraits of important figures, including Samuel Adams and Paul Revere, made his reputation and, eventually, his fortune. Born in Boston, he moved often between his hometown, New York, and Philadelphia until he gained the attention of the painter Benjamin West, who urged him to come to London. Copley followed the advice, arriving there in 1775 and thus missing the Revolution by months. In England, he moved on to the larger canvases with historical themes for which he became known there.

**Curley, James Michael** *(1874-1958)*
The quintessential Irish-American politician, Curley held office at municipal, state and federal levels. It is as mayor of Boston, however, that he is remembered — scornfully by some, with affection by most. He was elected to that position four times between 1911 and 1945, with time out for the governorship and stints as a US congressman. His popularity was partly due to his effusive personality and ready wit, partly to his carefully cultivated "man of the people" persona. It didn't hurt that he took obvious delight in tweaking the sensibilities of the Brahmin Establishment. His famous slogan, uttered only partly in jest, was "Vote often and vote early for James Michael Curley." Convicted of mail fraud in 1946, he attended to his mayoral duties from a jail cell for five months before President Harry S. Truman commuted his sentence. That conviction was the end of his public career. Curley was surely the inspiration for the central character of the bestselling novel and subsequent movie, *The Last Hurrah.*

**Eddy, Mary Baker** *(1821-1910)*
It is no coincidence that the founder of the Christian Science movement was often in poor health in her early years. Moving about New England most of her life and through three marriages, Eddy eventually alighted in Boston for seven years and then settled in the suburb of Chestnut Hill. She was pastoral leader of the Mother Church she initiated in Boston and founded the *Christian Science Monitor* two years before her death. The chapel and basilica built during her lifetime form the nucleus of the monumental Christian Science World Headquarters.

**Emerson, Ralph Waldo** *(1803-82)*
One of the towering figures of 19thC literature due to his poetry and numerous essays, Emerson was a major proponent of the transcenden-

talism advocated by Kant, Coleridge and Wordsworth. The emphasis made by that philosophy on independent thought and distrust of conventional authority proved highly appealing to Henry David Thoreau (see page 33), who became Emerson's close friend and disciple. Emerson's widely expressed views on the exquisite balances of nature and on the inherent evils of slavery brought him more adherents than opponents, at least in the North.

### Fuller, R. Buckminster *(1895-1983)*

The futurist engineer, author and architect was born in Milton, on the fringe of Greater Boston. His self-chosen role as an iconoclast was established early on, when he was twice expelled from Harvard. Widely known for his geodesic domes (tetrahedrons, which were put to a variety of exhibition and industrial uses), he enjoyed considerable acceptance in the last decades of his long life. The principle that underlay all his designs was *Dymaxion,* the intent of which was to utilize minimal energy and materials for maximum output. That eco-philosophy was put to work on houses and on a car that took years to make the jump from drawing board to reality in the 1930s. Fuller was rediscovered by the apostles of the environmental and alternative lifestyle movements of the 1960s.

### Garrison, William Lloyd *(1805-79)*

Slavery was the defining issue of the mid-19thC, affecting debate on virtually every issue from the admission of new states to international trade. Garrison made it his life's cause, attacking the institution with relentless vigor and a purity of outrage that made him enemies not only in the South, but around the corner in Boston. His moral fixation was given voice in his newspaper *The Liberator,* which he wrote, edited and published from 1831 until almost three years after President Lincoln issued the Emancipation Proclamation in 1863.

### Hancock, John *(1737-93)*

His name appears first on the Declaration of Independence in a large looping sprawl, and it came to refer colloquially to any signature. An important merchant in Boston, he came into frequent conflict with representatives of the British Crown. After one of his ships was confiscated and burned following the accusation that it was used for smuggling, he was elected to the colonial legislature by a sympathetic populace. Allied with the fiery Sam Adams, he later escaped arrest for sedition and went on to become president of the Continental Congress. He was elected twice as governor of Massachusetts, both during and after the Revolution.

### Harvard, John *(1607-38)*

Arriving in Charles Towne only a year before his death, teacher and preacher Harvard stipulated that his library of 320 books and half of his small estate be used to benefit the first college in England's American colonies. The college was given his name.

### Hawthorne, Nathaniel *(1804-64)*
By all accounts a glum and pessimistic man, Hawthorne inexplicably married an adherent of the essentially euphoric philosophy of transcendentalism. It must have helped, for after many impecunious years as a writer and editor, he wrote the novel for which he will always be known: *The Scarlet Letter* (1850). That was followed immediately by the nearly as successful *The House of Seven Gables*. Later novels were never finished or received scant attention. Among his friends were Herman Melville and President Franklin Pierce, about whom he penned a biography.

### Homer, Winslow *(1836-1910)*
First acclaimed for his work as an illustrator-correspondent of the Civil War, Boston-born Homer abandoned that profession in 1876 and went on to even greater success as a painter of realistic seafaring and genre scenes. He worked in oils and watercolors; typical of the results are the haunting *Breaking Storm* and *Gulf Stream*.

### Holmes, Oliver Wendell, Jr. *(1841-1935)*
The future jurist grew up in the shadow of a celebrated author-physician father. Holmes Sr. was dean of the Harvard Medical School, a popular poet and essayist, and a lecturer much in demand beyond the campus. Holmes Jr. wasn't intimidated. After Harvard Law School, he spent 20 years on the Massachusetts Supreme Court, and in 1902 was appointed Associate Justice of the US Supreme Court by Theodore Roosevelt. Phrases from his many written opinions have become part of general, as well as legal, language. A devoted protector of the First Amendment, he insisted that no abridgement of freedom of speech or assembly could be allowed unless there was a "clear and present danger" in specific utterances. He was often at odds with other members of the largely conservative court, who routinely ruled against such basic notions of social legislation as minimum wage laws. That circumstance resulted in his sobriquet, "The Great Dissenter."

### James, Henry Jr. *(1843-1916)*
New York City was the author's birthplace, and Beacon Hill and Harvard the fruitful arenas of his young adulthood. Possessed of the sturdy ego essential to those intent upon literary esteem, he was in his mid-30s when he wrote to his brother William: "I rather think I shall become a sufficiently great man." This was no hollow boast. Only a few months later, his novel *Daisy Miller* was published to considerable acclaim in England, where he had lived since 1876. James' reputation flourished, leading some to proclaim him the father of the modern novel. Not surprisingly, the principal characters in his books often were expatriate Americans, usually of the monied classes or at least moving in their company. They were, as frequently, both highly spirited and innocent of European ways. Among his honored works was *The Bostonians,* published in the US over a decade after he took residence in England. He became a naturalized British subject in the year before his death.

**James, William** *(1842-1910)*
His novelist brother Henry may be more widely known, but William made deep marks on his chosen fields of inquiry. In the admirable manner of 19thC intellectuals, he wove together discoveries and teachings in physiology, psychology and philosophy. He dubbed his embracing theories "Pragmatism," delineated in a book of the same name. His musings and conclusions are dense and intricate, hardly accessible to the casual reader, but no less important for that to the philosophical canon. James lectured at Harvard from 1872 to 1907.

**Kennedy, Edward M.** *(born 1932)*
Despite many personal tragedies and a public career dogged by the notorious Chappaquiddick scandal, "Ted" Kennedy has forged a reputation as the most effective voice for liberal causes in the US Senate. He is the only living son of Joseph Patrick Kennedy, a millionaire businessman who was, briefly, US Ambassador to Great Britain. Ted's oldest brother Joseph died in World War II, and John and Robert were victims of assassins. His aspiration to the Presidency is a dying ember, but given his popularity in Massachusetts and the travails he has already survived, few are willing to wager that he won't remain in office as long as he chooses.

**Lodge, Henry Cabot** *(1850-1924)*
One of the most accomplished members of a prominent Brahmin family, Lodge is less remembered for his authorship of several biographies than for his political career. He was a congressman from 1887–93, when he moved to the Senate and stayed until his death. Firmly conservative on domestic economic policy and increasingly isolationist in foreign affairs, he was a constant thorn in the side of Woodrow Wilson (president from 1913–21). Wilson fought hard for US participation in the League of Nations, but Lodge rallied the opposition and ratification was denied. A grandson, Henry Cabot Lodge Jr., also became a senator and was Richard Nixon's vice-presidential candidate in their losing campaign against John F. Kennedy and Lyndon B. Johnson in 1960.

**Longfellow, Henry Wadsworth** *(1807-82)*
Easily the most popular narrative poet of his time, 20thC revisionists have sneered at what they regard as his sentimentality and ungainly meters. Far removed from the murky self-indulgence of recent poetry, Longfellow told romantic stories of heroes and tragedies and great feats. His considerable success was built upon such longer works as *The Song of Hiawatha* (1855) and *The Courtship of Miles Standish* (1858) and buttressed by shorter pieces that included *The Village Blacksmith* and *The Wreck of the Hesperus.* He even rewrote history and made it stick, as in *Paul Revere's Ride* (1861). Revere was only one of three men to ride out that fateful night, and he was captured before completing his mission. But generations of Americans grew up to "Listen, my children, and you shall hear/Of the midnight ride of Paul Revere," and the names of William Dawes and Samuel Prescott have been all

but forgotten. Longfellow lived in a house on Brattle St. in Cambridge from 1837–82. It is now designated a national historic site and can be visited (see page 120).

**Mather, Cotton** *(1663-1728)*
The deeply conservative theologian was a Congregationalist minister in Boston, where he was born. He was ordained after graduation from Harvard in 1681. From then until his death, he wrote an astonishing number of books and pamphlets, estimated at over 400 by some sources. He was accused of actively supporting the Salem witchcraft trials; at the least, he wrote about them without condemning the responsible theocracy. His father Increase (1639–1723) served as president of Harvard and insisted on the right of colonial self-governance, but was silent on the moral issues of the Salem trials.

**Morison, Samuel Eliot** *(1887-1976)*
Born in Boston, Morison was a professor at Harvard for 40 years, with time out for three years at Oxford and service in World War II. His writings include Pulitzer Prize-winning biographies of Christopher Columbus and Revolutionary naval hero John Paul Jones. Included in his prodigious output was a 15-volume history of US naval operations from 1941–45. At the end of that conflict, he was a rear admiral. After retiring from Harvard in 1955, he continued to write, notably *The Oxford History of the American People* and the two-volume *The European Discovery of America*.

**Olmsted, Frederick Law** *(1822-1903)*
A travel writer who specialized in observations about the slaveholding society of the South, Olmsted simultaneously forged a glowing reputation as a landscape architect in the US and Canada. He designed Central Park and Prospect Park in New York City and the park on Mount Royal in Montréal. In 1869, Boston authorities began consultations with him about an overall scheme for their city. This led to commissions for the Arnold Arboretum and the Fens. Their success encouraged him to pursue a dream that had been frustrated in New York: a green belt of grandly landscaped spaces that stretched across the entire city, now called the Emerald Necklace. Pleased with the welcome his ideas received in Boston, he moved his firm there from New York.

**Parker, Robert Brown** *(born 1932)*
Upon graduation from Colby College, Parker tried his hand at advertising and other businesses in New York and Boston. Awarded a master's degree from Boston University in 1957, he chose to enter academia as a literature professor, working at several colleges, but most of the time at Boston's Northeastern University. His early books after receiving his Ph.D. in 1971 had such weighty themes as *The Personal Response to Literature* and *Order And Diversity*. He is known to his loyal readership not for these, however, but for his series of over 20 crime novels featuring the one-name private investigator, Spenser, and his mysterious

sidekick Hawk. In 1990, Parker had occasion to complete an unfinished manuscript by Raymond Chandler, *A Year at the Races*. To his fans and many literary critics, that effort secured his substantial reputation in the pantheon of writers of detective fiction.

### Poe, Edgar Allen *(1809-49)*

Born in Boston but raised in Virginia by foster parents, Poe was one of the very few accomplished authors of the first half of the 19thC. His academic careers at West Point and the University of Virginia were brief, due to his habitual flouting of their rules. Impoverished for most of his adult life, these failures, and the alcoholism and gambling that provoked them, alienated his wealthy foster father. In 1837, Poe moved to New York with his 13-year-old bride. He eventually achieved recognition for his poetry with *The Raven,* which led to fame for such mystery stories as *The Gold Bug* and *The Murders in the Rue Morgue.* It was too late. He drank himself to death.

### Revere, Paul *(1735-1818)*

In the manner of many generalist early Americans, Revere was a gold- and silversmith, a dentist, a printer, and a soldier in the French and Indian War (1754–63). After that conflict, he and many other colonials began to see themselves less as Englishmen and more as citizens of a new nation. Revere was an early member of the secretive Sons of Liberty, agitators against British rule. He and Sam Adams participated in the Boston Tea Party. But the action that consolidated his near-legendary role as patriot was the April night in 1775 when he galloped into the countryside to warn of the British expeditionary force that was setting out in what proved to be the opening thrust of the Revolution. Forgotten is the fact that he never reached Concord, for he was captured by the British. But a famous poem by Henry Wadsworth Longfellow romanticizing the ride shaped the history learned by every American schoolchild.

### Thoreau, Henry David *(1817-62)*

The individualistic author's views on *Civil Disobedience,* the title of his 1849 essay, had influence on crusades as diverse as those of Gandhi, Martin Luther King and the British Labour movement. Known also as a transcendentalist philosopher and devoted naturalist, his writings have resonance with present-day environmentalists, especially through his cherished book, *Walden.* Born in Concord and educated at Harvard, he drew early intellectual sustenance from Ralph Waldo Emerson, who later became a close friend.

### Updike, John Hoyer *(born 1932)*

After graduation from Harvard, Updike worked for *The New Yorker* magazine. His first novel, *The Poorhouse Fair,* was published while he was still in his twenties. With occasional exceptions, his subsequent fiction has dealt with the challenges and disappointments of middle-class life, often with a New England background. Two of them, *Rabbitt is Rich* (1982) and *Rabbitt at Rest* (1990) won the Pulitzer Prize. He has also turned his elegantly precise style to short stories, criticism, essays and poetry. He now lives in a small town near Boston.

### White, Kevin Hagan *(born 1929)*

In 1960, White won the office of Secretary of State over Republican Edward Brooke, who later became a US senator. Bored with that ceremonial post, White ran for mayor of Boston in 1967. While less colorful than many of his predecessors, White managed to keep enough people content to hold the office until 1984. His tenure coincided with the long, combustible controversy over the busing of school-children to achieve racial balance. Despite severe unrest and some violent episodes, the city survived that wrenching experience, not least because of White's calming presence. Along the way, he twice defeated Louise Day Hicks, the leader of the anti-busing forces. He is also credited by preservationists with putting a stop to the mass razing of buildings and unchecked development that masqueraded as urban renewal in the 1950s and '60s. His administration passed and enforced codes that contained the scale of new buildings and encouraged the salvation of as many older structures as possible.

### Williams, Theodore Samuel *(born 1918)*

Few observers have claimed that baseball's Ted Williams was a team leader, a more than mediocre outfielder, or that he was possessed of a lovable personality. But he was one of the most prolific sluggers in the history of America's favorite game. Statistically, he was second only to the mythic Babe Ruth, posting a ·344 lifetime batting average and hitting 521 home runs. He remains the only player since 1930 to exceed a single year average above ·400. Apart from military service in World War II and Korea, he spent his entire playing career, from 1939–60, with the Boston Red Sox.

### Winthrop, John *(1588-1649)*

Scion of English gentry, Winthrop became a lawyer after study at Cambridge. He was a member of the Massachusetts Bay Company, created to establish a colony on the Charles River. A committed Puritan religionist, he led a group of like-minded settlers to America in 1630. Despite the fact that the Puritans were fleeing religious persecution in Europe, they proved no more tolerant than their erstwhile tormentors. Winthrop, as governor of the colony, insisted on a theocratic form of governance and participated in the banishment of former friends he adjudged to be heretics. His was a profound influence, for both good and ill, on the early history of Massachusetts. His son John became founder and governor of several settlements in Connecticut, and his grandson Fitz-John occupied the same post in the colonies unified by his father.

# The arts in Boston

Boston has supported the arts enthusiastically since the early days of the republic. A music society was formed in 1774, the first in the country. The **Boston Athenaeum** was founded as a private library in 1807, and its early interest in the collecting of fine art and antiques led directly to the creation of the **Museum of Fine Arts**. The city enjoys an enduring literary and publishing tradition, and a roster of authors and poets who are among the most important in America's history, including **Ralph Waldo Emerson**, **Nathaniel Hawthorne** and **Walt Whitman**. A theater dating back to 1852 still stands in the active district that has been home to opera, ballet and plays since before the Revolution. And the city had its own symphony orchestra (the **Boston Symphony Orchestra**) by 1881.

But although it displays, studies, appraises and generally appreciates art to the fullest in its many colleges, universities and museums, Boston has not enjoyed the presence of significant numbers of practicing visual artists. Europe summoned them throughout the last century and the first half of this one, and New York has been the undisputed center of the art world since 1945.

Those artists who draw nourishment from associations with others on similar quests insist upon being where the galleries and museums and markets are, while those requiring solitude are unlikely to seek it in a city. This has long been true. **James Abbott McNeill Whistler**, for example, was born in nearby Lowell, but spent most of his creative life in Paris and London. Realist painter **Winslow Homer** was born in the city, but spent much of his creative life in Paris and England before settling in Maine, a virtual recluse.

This is not to assert that Boston has no art scene. It has many galleries and a half-dozen museums concerned primarily with painting, sculpture and the visual arts, containing work that although chiefly of regional significance is in no way lacking in value or interest. A neighborhood of recycled warehouses called the **Leather District**, near Fort Point Channel, is sometimes compared, not very accurately, to New York's SoHo, and galleries and art schools stage frequent exhibitions.

So, while Boston art-lovers are hardly likely to witness the launching of the next great artistic "ism," they can revel in the wealth of choices offered by such institutions as the three Harvard University Arts Museums (the **Fogg Art Museum**, **Arthur M. Sackler Museum** and **Busch-Reisinger Museum**), and the delightful **Isabella Stewart Gardner Museum**, in addition to the illustrious **Museum of Fine Arts**.

# The architectural heritage

By both fortuitous accident and specific intent, Boston, Cambridge and the surrounding towns preserve an architectural heritage that enjoys examples of every period since the earliest colonial days. One by-product of these troves of protected historic structures is that blocks and entire neighborhoods retain a scale long since lost to many larger American cities.

### EARLY COLONIAL *(17th century)*
The earliest houses have an almost medieval aspect, with center chimneys, steeply pitched roofs, small casement windows with leaded panes, and second-story overhangs. But instead of mortar or masonry, wood from the dense forests were the building materials of choice. Shingles were used instead of the tiles remembered from England. The usual interior arrangement was four rooms equally divided on either side of a center hall leading to the cooking area at the rear. When the roof was

The Job Lane House, a **colonial saltbox house** in Bedford, Massachusetts.

extended to cover the kitchen, the style was known as a saltbox, reproduced repeatedly up to this day throughout New England. Characteristic of the early Colonial period are the 1677 **Paul Revere House** and the oldest surviving structure in Cambridge, the **Cooper-Frost-Austin-Hitchings House** (1691). Examples are more abundant in the nearby suburbs, as in Beverly (the 1636 **Balch House**) at the northeastern extreme beyond Salem, and in the small colonial coastal town of Ipswich (the 1640 **Whipple House**).

A variation on this is the Cape Cod style, just as simple but more compact, designed to stand up to the often fierce weather of its eponymous original location. One of its virtues was expandability, allowing growth room by room as required by additional children and increasing prosperity. There are many examples along the Cape, of course, and inland, and the resulting connecting structures not infrequently comprise units erected over three or four centuries. One example among many is the **Sheldon-Hawks House** (1743) in Deerfield, Massachusetts.

### GEORGIAN *(late 17th to mid-18th century)*
Boston was one of the first American settlements to exploit the Georgian vogue, as was called the prevailing architectural fashion in England under the three monarchs named George. It was first seen toward the end of the 17thC and ended with a sudden lurch, it will come as no surprise, in 1776. Distinguished examples in Boston include the **Old South Meeting House** (1729) and **Old North Church**, also known as **Christ Church** (1723).

Georgian was imitative, in part, of the Italian Renaissance, as interpreted by such important English architects as Christopher Wren and Inigo Jones. Formal, symmetrical facades featured more elaborate entrances than seen previously, sometimes bracketed by pilasters and surmounted by triangular pediments. Facing materials could be lapped boards, fieldstone or occasionally brick, often determined by the eagerness of the owners to impress their neighbors. Inside, the center hall layout was retained, but rooms more often featured wood paneling, and more rooms had fireplaces.

### FEDERALIST *(late 18th to early 19th century)*
Revolutionary fervor would not tolerate the continuation of an architectural conceit known as Georgian. What more logical new direction could there be than Federalist? True, even a patriot might have conceded that it was an evolutionary baby step away from its immediate predecessor. The Federalist style employed the careful balance of Georgian and the boxy center-hall configuration. It was, however, a touch less kingly in most of its manifestations than its British antecedent.

Fanlight windows rather than pediments usually topped the main entrances, and shuttered sash windows on the top floor were nearly always half the height of those on the floor below. While wood was often the siding material, brick was ever more the preferred material. Interiors, in contrast, were often grander in scale and more conspicuously decorated than in Georgian designs. Round or oval rooms were incorporated, often with urns and floral motifs carved around lintels and mantels.

Examples can be seen on **Beacon Hill**, where there are many homes designed by Charles Bulfinch (1763–1844). One of the most important American architects of his time, he applied Federalist principals to residences, a hospital, warehouses and churches all over Boston. At least 40 of his commissions survive, the most prominent being the gold-domed **State House** (1797), which dominates the Boston Common. Bulfinch was also responsible for all three houses of **Harrison Gray Otis** (1796, 1802, 1806) and entire blocks, such as the **Swan Houses** (1805) on Chestnut St.

"Adam" was a rarely used alternative label for Federalist, for it referred to two English brothers rather than two American presidents.

### GREEK AND GOTHIC REVIVAL
*(mid-19th century)*
Both Georgian and Federalist styles drew on Classical Greco-Roman details, but once the young country settled into nationhood, the second quarter of the 19thC saw a heightened enthusiasm for outright Greek and Gothic Revival. The former employed four or more columns to support a pediment that thrust over the porch. Public buildings that used this scheme were often constructed from

**Quincy Market**

granite, a material that was available in generous abundance in the Boston Bay area.

These overlapping modes dominated from 1820–60, as displayed by the Athenian "temple" that is **Quincy Market** (1826 — illustrated on page 37), and in the Neo-Gothic pointed arches and steeples of the **Church of the Covenant**, designed by the son of the architect of New York's similar homage to medieval workmanship, Trinity Church. Young Alexander Parris established his reputation with Greek Revival, as realized in his several granite warehouses and in his Cathedral **Church of St Paul** (1820). His influence is also seen in the **Ether Dome** of Massachusetts General Hospital (1823). It was Charles Bulfinch's last commission in Boston, a deviation from his previous work perhaps brought about because Alexander Parris executed the working plans.

In the increasingly popular attached town houses of **Beacon Hill** and **Back Bay**, Greek Revival was largely confined to decorative facades.

## VICTORIAN *(late 19th century)*
In the Victorian era after the Civil War, an unabashed enthusiasm for virtually all European styles took hold. Motifs ranged from Venetian Renaissance to French Second Empire to Tudor to Romanesque, not infrequently all on the same building — a result often called Kitchen Sink.

More disciplined architects of the period, however, produced many handsome structures. The **Old City Hall** (1865) is a paragon of the French Second Empire style, which employed mansard roofs, stacked columned tiers, considerable ornamentation, and, in this case, rows of high arched windows and a large crowning tower. Equally impressive is the **Ames-Webster Mansion** (1872), especially in its richly detailed interiors of carved woodwork, stained glass and large murals.

The most influential architect of the time, H.H. Richardson, resurrected Romanesque with such adroitness that many name the result after him. Richardson Romanesque is as readily loathed as it is admired, with its

rounded arches and squat, massive proportions. It did not adapt readily to residential use, but Richardson was at his best with **Trinity Church** (1877). Conical turrets in front visually heighten the impact of the central tower grouping, which marks the intersection below of the Greek-cross floor plan. The exterior walls are of rusticated polychromatic stone blocks, with many rounded arches over deeply recessed doors and windows. **Sever Hall** (1880) on the Harvard campus is less monumental but presents a more harmonious facade. Both have been designated National Historic Landmarks, and cannot be razed or altered without permission.

H.H. Richardson's **Trinity Church**

In the last two decades of the 19thC and into the first of the 20thC, Beaux Arts had impact. It borrowed most obviously from the French Renaissance, with dignified if somewhat florid exterior decoration, lighter and less labored than Richardson. In other cities, it is most apparent in large public buildings, but in Boston's **Back Bay**, it is also evident on attached four- and five-story mansions, as at **128 and 130 Commonwealth Avenue** (1882).

**EARLY 20TH CENTURY**
In the new century, technology prompted fresh looks at old design assumptions. Architects were now able to design much taller buildings with steel and reinforced concrete, no longer restricted to masonry, and the hydraulic elevator was invented. The versatility of the new metal-frame skeleton was tested early on with the **Berkeley Building** (1905), the exterior of which suggests a battle between Gothic Revival and Beaux Arts.

Skyscrapers had now become a reality, as was increasingly seen in New York and Chicago, where buildings of 20 floors or more were routine by 1900. Alarmed by this potential threat to Boston's human scale, municipal authorities imposed a height limit of 125 feet.

City restrictions did not apply to federally-owned properties, however, and when more space was needed for downtown's 1847 **Custom House**, a 500-foot, 30-story tower was added in 1915. It is a curious exercise, a vaguely Renaissance campanile with elephantiasis, rising from what was now a dwarfed Greek Revival base. Yet it became a treasured landmark. Shorter, but employing a mock-Classical overlay of 20thC technology, is the **Boston School Committee Building** (1914).

Similarly, mid-rise luxury apartment hotels were making their appearance, sturdy and dignified to lure the middle and upper classes from their detached houses. The **Hotel Cambridge** (1898) and **Charlesgate Hotel** (1901) are early examples.

Innovation slowed during the decade of World War I, picking up again in the prosperous 1920s. Significant stylistic change came with the introduction of what is now called Art Deco. In effect, it was a simplification of the Classical Revival motifs, updated with optimistic references to emerging technologies and powerful industries: radio, aviation, shipping, film, hydro-electricity, automobiles. In Boston, the **Batterymarch Building** (1928) is emblematic, its height visually extended by the narrow street it stands on and by brickwork that shades from dark in tone at the bottom to light at the top.

By the end of the 1930s, Deco was already fading, worn thin by its faddish nature and submerged under the radical but increasingly attractive notions of the German Bauhaus School. These were promulgated by Walter Gropius and his adherents, who had started to immigrate to the New World as war clouds gathered in the Old. Among them were Marcel Breuer, Mies van der Rohe and Lazlo Moholy-Nagy. Their mentor's 1937 house in outlying Lincoln must have been startling at the time of its completion, with its expanses of glass, flat roof, boxy shape and utter lack of superficial adornment.

## MID- TO LATE 20TH CENTURY

Further developments were delayed until peacetime economic recovery in the late 1940s. A technique was developed in which walls of glass without a weight-bearing function were literally hung on the sides of steel skeletons. One of the first and most enduring realizations of this so-called International Style is the **Harkness Commons** (1950) at Harvard, designed by Gropius after he became head of the design faculty. Acceptance of his form of Modernism made others acceptable. The Massachusetts Institute of Technology commissioned Eero Saarinen to create its **Kresge Auditorium** (1955), an arresting structure that billows in a low dome, echoing his TWA terminal in New York.

Modernism has taken other directions since then, far from the too-often sterile glass slabs that only pretend to serve any cause other than profit. (Many critics place the 1959 **Prudential Center** in that company.) Arguably the most significant architect on the Boston cityscape of the last two decades is I.M. Pei. It might be assumed that the city, with its staid image, would not be hospitable to esthetic leaps of faith. Wrong. While the unfortunate Prudential Center complex was in its first stages, Pei and

**Boston City Hall,**
heart of the Government Center

his firm were devising a master plan for a new Government Center in a blighted downtown area. At its heart is the **Boston City Hall** (1968), startling at first, magnetic soon after. Formed of raw cement, it gets wider as it goes up, integrating majestic rectilinear protrusions and a bricked plaza that flows through its center, inviting access. The architects Kallmann, McKinnell & Knowles later produced the distinguished **Boston Five Cents Savings Bank** (1972).

Pei had more direct responsibility for several specific buildings. His contributions (1968–73) transformed the **Christian Science World Headquarters** into one of the most compelling open spaces in the city, and his **John F. Kennedy Library** (1979) in nearby Dorchester is a masterful joining of stark geometric shapes. After these and many other contributions, Pei has been forgiven the engineering problems that afflicted his **John Hancock Tower** (1975).

The Post-Modernist trend of the 1980s was a revival in decorative interest and borrowings from eras before the Bauhaus invasion, as in the somewhat gaudy **75 State Street** (1988) by the redoubtable Skidmore, Owings & Merrill firm. A more successful product of this enthusiasm is **116 Huntington Avenue**, with a rounded corner and an exterior of variegated materials that recalls Art Deco. Probably the Post-Modernist affectation will not last much longer, but its successor has yet to make itself apparent.

# We say tomato

"Two great nations divided by a common language," intoned George Bernard Shaw. Despite the alleged homogenizing effect of shared movies, satellite television and international travel, the languages spoken in the United Kingdom and the United States bear less resemblance to each other than ever. British readers might therefore find the brief glossary offered on the following pages to be of assistance when deplaning on this side of the Pond.

People arriving in Boston expecting to be greeted in the accents of The Kennedys are disappointed. For reasons no one has satisfactorily explained, Teddy, Bobby, Jack and the rest of their numerous brood speak or spoke in distinctive cadences and pronunciations all their own. Unlike some Southerners and many inhabitants of the New York metropolitan area, Bostonians are understandable to just about anyone with even a tenuous grasp on the mother tongue.

That is, with one significant exception: the native-born have a near-universal inability to formulate the letter "r," and, under many circumstances, "o." Wherever "r" appears, it sounds like "ah," or sometimes "uh." The classic illustration is "Park your car in Harvard Yard," which comes out, approximately, as "Pahk yuh cah in Hahvahd Yahd." Similarly, "Boston Harbor water" issues forth as "Bahston hahbah wahtah." And if your nickname happens to be "Norm," as was that of a character on the popular *Cheers* situation comedy, respond to "Nahm." Even separate letters or acronyms suffer this fate. A video cassette recorder, for example, is known by its initials: "Vee-cee-ah."

Otherwise, expect no significant impediments to communication, except in encounters with those recent immigrants who constitute a substantial portion of the population, many of whom drive taxis. It will also be noted, from time to time, that a few third-generation Irish-American citizens have contrived to retain the lilting tongue of a land they've never seen.

Some Britishisms will simply draw blank stares, as when the newly knighted Andrew Lloyd Webber said he had been "sent up rotten" by his friends. This means absolutely nothing to an American, nor do such formulations as "cocking a snook" or "winkle him out." Other phrases make sense, but not in the way intended. "He wouldn't wear that" will be taken literally, rather than that the man in question wouldn't tolerate something.

It can get worse. The British man who has just met an attractive American woman and hopes to see her the next day will want to avoid declaring, "I'll knock you up tomorrow," as he conceivably might on his home turf, since that would mean he intended to get her pregnant. He will further want to avoid suggesting to a disappointed friend that he "keep his pecker up," or referring to a messy situation as a "cockup."

Why? Just think about it a minute.

# British English–American English

## TRAVELING AND VACATIONS

bonnet   *hood*
boot   *trunk*
bumper   *fender*
bureau de change   *foreign exchange*
campsite   *campground*
car park   *parking lot*
caravan   *trailer*
coach   *bus*
crossroads   *intersection*
district   *precinct*
dual carriageway   *four-lane highway*
footpath   *sidewalk*
give way   *yield*
hire (noun)   *rental*
holidaymaker   *vacationer*
lorry   *truck*
motoring association   *automobile club*

overtake   *pass*
package holiday   *vacation package*
petrol   *gasoline, gas*
post box   *mailbox*
poste restante   *general delivery*
puncture (noun)   *flat tire*
queue   *line*
rank (taxi)   *taxi stand*
return (ticket)   *round trip*
ring road   *beltway*
roundabout   *traffic circle*
saloon car   *sedan*
single (ticket)   *one-way*
subway   *underpass*
underground, tube   *subway*
windscreen   *windshield*

## LEISURE

bathing   *swimming*
cinema   *movie theater*
football   *soccer*

horse-riding   *horseback-riding*
paddle   *wade*
rowing boat   *rowboat*
sailing boat   *sailboat*

## SHOPPING

banknote, note   *bill*
braces   *suspenders*
chemist   *drugstore, pharmacy*
cotton wool   *absorbent cotton, cotton balls*
crisps   *chips*
dummy   *pacifier*
handbag   *purse, pocket book*
jacket   *coat*
knickers, underpants   *panties*
mackintosh   *raincoat*
nail varnish   *nail polish*

nappy   *diaper*
newsagent   *newsstand*
precinct   *mall*
pullover   *sweater*
sanitary towel   *sanitary napkin*
sticking plaster   *Band-aid*
suspenders   *garter belt*
sweet   *candy*
trousers   *pants*
vest   *undershirt*
waistcoat   *vest*

## DINING

aubergine   *eggplant*
barman   *bartender*
bill   *check*
biscuits   *crackers*
book/booking   *reserve/reservation*
chips   *fries*
Cos lettuce   *Romaine lettuce*

cockles   *clams*
courgette   *zucchini*
draught   *draft*
endive   *chicory*
lager   *beer*
lavatory   *bathroom*
lay the table   *set the table*
off-license   *liquor store*

plate    *silverware, flatware*
pudding    *dessert*
serviette    *napkin*
spend a penny    *go to the
  bathroom*

spirits    *liquor*
takeaway    *takeout,
  to go*
whisky    *Scotch*
wholemeal    *wholewheat*

## LODGING
3-pin (plug)    *3-prong*
bed-sitter    *studio, efficiency
  apartment*
call box    *telephone
  booth*
council housing    *housing
  projects*
dear    *expensive*
dustbin    *garbage can*
flat    *apartment*

homely    *homey*
lift    *elevator*
self-catering (apartment,
  cottage)    *housekeeping*
terraced house    *rowhouse,
  brownstone (the term used
  in New York)*
torch    *flashlight*
(telephone) trunk call    *long
  distance*

And they keep on comin', as in the following hodge-podge (hotch-potch) of examples. Americans say zee (zed) and zero (nought). They drive counterclockwise (anti-clockwise) around their traffic circles (round-abouts). To an American, a comfortable hotel might seem like a home-away-from-home (home-from-home). After some arduous adventure, he or she might be pleased to be home free (home and dry). And indigent Americans may find themselves on welfare (on the dole). . . . So it goes.

# Practical information

This chapter is organized into six sections:
* **BEFORE YOU GO**, below
* **GETTING THERE**, page 47
* **GETTING AROUND**, page 48
* **ON-THE-SPOT INFORMATION**, page 53
* **USEFUL ADDRESSES**, page 56
* **EMERGENCY INFORMATION**, page 58

Each section is organized thematically rather than alphabetically. Summaries of subject headings are printed in CAPITALS at the top of most pages.

## Before you go

**TOURIST OFFICES OVERSEAS**
American visitors should make contact with the **Greater Boston Convention and Visitors Bureau** *(P.O. Box 490, Boston, MA 02199* ☎ *536-4100)*. Visitors from the UK can obtain much useful information from the **US Travel and Tourism Administration** *(P.O. Box 1EN, London W1A 1EN* ☎ *(071) 495-4466* Fx *(071) 495-4377)*.

**DOCUMENTS REQUIRED**
British citizens and citizens of New Zealand, Japan and all Western European countries except Ireland, Portugal and Greece do not need a visa to visit the US, provided that their stay will last for 90 days or less and is for vacation or business purposes. If arriving by air or sea, the visitor must be traveling with an approved carrier (most are) and must have an **onward or return ticket**. (Open or standby tickets are acceptable.) If entering overland from Canada or Mexico, no visa is required. An unexpired **passport** is also essential.

A British citizen needs a **visa** for a stay in the US longer than 90 days for whatever reason, or if he/she has a criminal record, has suffered from tuberculosis, is suffering from AIDS, is HIV-positive or has previously been refused a visa. The US Embassy in London has a useful recorded message for all general visa inquiries *(* ☎ *(0898) 200290)*. If you need a visa, it is wise to allow plenty of time.

To rent a car, a valid **driver's license** is required; non-US citizens will also need a passport. If arriving by private car from other states or Canada, bring the **car registration** and **certificate of insurance**. Consider taking out short-term extra coverage for theft and/or collision.

**Senior citizens** are eligible for discounts in many hotels but may be asked to show **identification** in order to claim them.

## TRAVEL AND MEDICAL INSURANCE
Medical care in the US is good to excellent, but costly. Theft, unfortunately, is common. Extra medical and baggage insurance is therefore strongly recommended. If you are a member of an automobile club, this can be arranged through them; American Express also offers baggage insurance to cardholders. Larger hotels have doctors on call, but visits are expensive.

## MONEY
It is wise to carry cash in small amounts only, keeping the remainder in travelers checks. **Travelers checks** issued by American Express, Bank of America, Barclays, Citibank and Thomas Cook are widely recognized, as are those sold by MasterCard and Visa. Make sure you read the instructions included with your travelers checks. **It is important to note separately the serial numbers of the checks and the telephone number to call in case of loss.** Specialist travelers check companies such as American Express provide extensive local refund facilities through their own offices or agents. Many shops accept dollar travelers checks, but often require one or two kinds of identification.

**Charge and credit cards** are welcomed by nearly all hotels, airlines and car rental agencies, most restaurants and garages, and many stores. American Express, Diners Club, MasterCard and Visa are the major cards in common use. While **personal checks** drawn on out-of-town banks are not normally accepted, many hotels will cash small amounts in conjunction with a credit card.

A worldwide instant money-transfer system introduced by American Express is the **MoneyGram**® service, available from any American Express Travel Office *(for details of locations ☎ 800-543-4080 in US or Canada)*. It is open to all customers, whether or not they hold an American Express Card.

The recent proliferation of automatic teller machines has made it easier for travelers to obtain **cash**. Almost any ATM will permit cash advances against two or three of the major credit cards. In addition, if your hometown bank is a member of a nationwide network — PLUS and CIRRUS have the broadest coverage — it is possible to withdraw cash from your checking account. A four-digit Personal Identification Number (PIN) is required; obtain one before leaving on a trip. At the same time, ask the amount of any service charge for each withdrawal. The reported range is from zero to $6 and even more, which might affect the frequency with which withdrawals are made, and the amounts.

## CUSTOMS ALLOWANCES
Visitors and US citizens may take in 200 cigarettes, 50 cigars or three pounds of tobacco, one US quart of alcohol and up to $100-worth of

duty-free gifts. Importing narcotics is absolutely forbidden, nor are you permitted to bring in meat products, seeds, plants or fruits. There are no US restrictions on what you take out, although obviously any regulations imposed by the country to which you are traveling onward are another matter.

## TIME ZONE
Boston is in the US **Eastern Time Zone**, one hour ahead of the Central Time Zone, two hours ahead of the Mountain Time Zone and three hours ahead of the Pacific Time Zone. All zones on Daylight Saving Time put their clocks forward one hour from April to October to benefit from extra daylight.

The US Eastern Time Zone is five hours behind Greenwich Mean Time (GMT) in winter, or four hours behind GMT from the last Sunday in April to the last Sunday in October during Daylight Saving Time.

## CLIMATE
May, June, September and October are the most agreeable months, incorporating the best days of the short and unpredictable spring and fall seasons. Extended periods of oppressive humidity and temperatures of 90˚F (32˚C) and more are common in July and August, when every Bostonian able to do so heads for the northern hills or the coastal resorts. The colorful fall foliage season usually occurs during the middle two weeks in October in the areas around Boston.

December through February feature frequent cold rains and snowstorms, and readings at or below freezing point. Even in deepest winter, however, the music and theatrical seasons are in full swing, and the snow-clad streets of Beacon Hill and Back Bay take on a beguiling Dickensian appearance.

## WHAT TO WEAR
From October to April, the winds that accompany rain often turn umbrellas inside-out. So a raincoat with a warm zip-out lining is a good investment, as are collapsible rubber boots and a waterproof hat. Americans are inclined toward high settings of interior heating and air conditioning, and visitors are advised to practice the art of layering clothes: be prepared to add or peel off a layer at need.

In recent years Bostonians have grown less formal in what they wear. Men feel most comfortable with a jacket at medium-priced and luxury restaurants, but nowadays a tie is mandatory at only a few establishments. Otherwise, in a city whose nightlife is dominated by tens of thousands of university students, denimed informality reigns.

## GENERAL DELIVERY
A letter marked "General Delivery," addressed to a specific post office, will be held there until collected. Identification is usually required when collecting mail, and a fee may be charged. Some commercial firms also provide this service for their customers. Those listed on the opposite page are centrally located:

- **American Express Travel Service**   1 Court St., Boston, MA 02108. Map **12**E10.
- **Central Post Office**   25 Dorchester Ave., Boston, MA 02210. Map **12**G11.
- **Thomas Cook**   245 Summer St., Boston, MA 02143. Map **12**F10.

# Getting there

### BY AIR
**Logan International Airport**, linked to downtown Boston by two tunnels under the harbor, receives flights by more than 50 foreign and domestic airlines. Daily shuttle flights to New York and on to Washington, DC are operated by **USAir** and **Delta**. Small feeder and commuter airlines link the city with other New England cities and beach resorts on Cape Cod and the Maine coast.

### BY TRAIN
Long-distance **Amtrak trains** arrive and depart refurbished **South Station** *(Atlantic Ave. and Summer St., map **12**F11 ☎ 345-7451)*, connecting with New York, Philadelphia, Washington, Chicago, and points w and s. Commuter trains use **North Station** *(Causeway and Friend Sts., map **12**D10 ☎ 722-3200)*.

### BY BUS
**Greyhound-Trailways buses** have their own downtown terminal *(10 St James Ave., map **11**G9 ☎ 423-5810)*. Connections can be made with every large city and most smaller ones across the continent. Regional New England routes are serviced by **Peter Pan Trailways** *(555 Atlantic Ave., map **12**F11 ☎ 426-7838)*.

### BY CAR
From upstate New York to the w, **Interstate I-90** (a toll highway also known as the Massachusetts Turnpike) ends in downtown Boston; from New York City in the s, **I-84** and **I-95** provide a choice of approaches into the greater Boston metropolitan area. **I-95** continues n to the Maine coast, **I-93** heads toward the ski resorts of New Hampshire and Vermont and thereafter on into Canada, and **State Route 3** runs s to Cape Cod.

Bridges across the Charles River between Boston and Cambridge are free, but a toll is charged for the use of the Sumner and Callahan tunnels between downtown Boston and Logan Airport. Automobile clubs will suggest the best route from your point of departure.

# Getting around

## FROM THE AIRPORT TO THE CITY

**Taxis** are plentiful at Logan Airport, which is only three underwater miles from downtown, closer to the center city that it serves than almost any comparable airport in the nation. The problem is the almost continuous traffic jam afflicting the two tunnels, which diminishes the convenience. Depending on road conditions and destination, the taxi fare is about $10–$15, plus tip.

A scenic and cheaper method is the **Airport Water Shuttle**, which makes the trip to Rowe's Wharf *(map 12E12)* in seven minutes. It operates all year, every 15 minutes Monday to Friday 6am–8pm and every 30 minutes Sunday noon–8pm (no service Saturday or major holidays). The one-way fare is $8, and of course other transport must be used to and from Rowe's Wharf. At the other end of the route, a free bus carries passengers from the dock to the terminals. Total travel time from Rowe's Wharf to the most distant terminal is about 25 minutes.

Passengers with light luggage find that the MBTA **subway** from the airport is the fastest and least expensive way to downtown and Back Bay hotels. Free buses shuttle between the airline terminals and the subway station. Travelers with heavy or numerous bags are apt to have difficulty, however, for porters aren't available. A **minibus** service is provided between the airport and several of the larger hotels; inquire when making room reservations.

**Private limousines** are clean and comfortable, but cost at least twice as much as taxis. If two or more passengers share the limo, however, the outlay is lighter. It is best to arrange in advance to have a limo waiting (see OTHER TRANSPORTATION, page 52). **Cars** can be rented at all airport terminals (see RENTING A CAR, page 50).

A word to the wise when the time comes to leave Boston: despite the nearness of downtown to the airport, heavy traffic, bad weather, accidents and road repairs can cause serious delays. To be safe when returning by car or bus to the airport after a visit, leave at least 30 minutes earlier than you might otherwise expect.

• For further information on transport from and to the airport
☎800-235-6426.

## PUBLIC TRANSPORTATION

**Subways, streetcars and buses** are operated by the municipal transportation agency, the **MBTA**, known simply as the **T**. The system, which is one of the oldest in the country, grew somewhat haphazardly into the present combination of buses, streetcars (trams), often referred to as trolleys, and trains, operating at street level, underground and on elevated segments.

A single fare covers journeys of most lengths within the city; it is cheaper than most systems in the country. Peak rush hours, to be avoided if at all possible, are 8–9am and 5–7pm.

• For information on subways and buses ☎722-3200 or
800-392-6100.

## SUBWAYS

Four lines radiate outward from downtown Boston, reaching into Cambridge and suburbs to the s, w and n. Designated by colors — Red, Blue, Orange and Green — they cross at six transfer points. Principal intersections are at the **State** station *(map 12E10)* for the Blue and Orange lines, and the **Park Street** station *(map 12E10)* for the Red and Green lines.

The latter two lines have extra branches, or spurs, so be sure that the correct train or trolley is being boarded. Signs indicate the final destination. Make sure it is *beyond* the desired station. The platform designations "Inbound" and "Outbound" refer to trains/streetcars heading toward or away from downtown, where all four lines come together.

The basic fare is under $1, paid by token or exact change, but there are supplemental charges for distant stations, mostly outside the city limits. Free transfers are allowed at the several points in downtown Boston where lines intersect or come close together. Senior citizens and disabled persons are eligible for sharply discounted fares ( ☎ 722-5438). Children aged 5–11 pay lower fares, too, and those under 5 ride for free.

An "MBTA Passport," good for unlimited travel on bus and subway for one, three or seven days, can be purchased at the Visitors Bureau information booth at 147 Tremont St. on Boston Common *(map 12 F10)*. For other sites ☎722-3200. If you plan to use the **T** four or more times a day, the Passport provides modest savings.

- Trains and streetcars operate Monday to Saturday 5am–12.30am, Sunday 6am–12.30am.
- See the color map of the **T** rapid transit system, at the back of this book.

## BUSES

For most tourists and other visitors, MBTA buses are seen primarily as supplements to the train and streetcar routes. They fill in gaps in the subway system and connect **T** stations with distant points and suburbs. Fares are even cheaper than the subways, albeit usually for shorter distances. Exact change is required for fares. More than 200 buses are air conditioned, and an increasing number of them are equipped with the platforms that allow the boarding of persons in wheelchairs.

- For general information ☎722-3200 or ☎722-5050 (recording).

## TAXIS

Licensed, metered taxis in Boston are of no particular color and there is no reliable way to determine whether one is free or not. Most have roof lights, but those have no useful purpose other than identifying cars as taxicabs. Taxis can be hailed anywhere, although they might well be occupied or on radio call. Wherever possible, use the taxi stands found outside major hotels and at important intersections or visitor attractions.

Boston has 1,525 licensed taxis, which display a metal medallion: an insufficient number when demand is high, as in bad weather or during rush hours. It may be necessary to ask the hotel concierge or restaurant headwaiter to call a taxi.

Taxi drivers are required to take passengers to any destination in the city. This doesn't necessarily mean they actually will do so, particularly if a prospective passenger looks as if he or she might want to go to a dangerous or out-of-the-way neighborhood. It is best to get in the cab before announcing where you wish to go. Once inside, don't expect comfort. The security barrier between the driver and his passengers often forces taller people to sit sideways. Given all this, it would be pleasant at least to report that fares are low. They aren't.

Many taxi drivers are recent immigrants to the city, often from countries where English is not the primary language. For that reason, it is wise to know the full address of your destination and the nearest cross street. Simply asking for a particular hotel or restaurant, no matter how well-known, may draw a blank stare from the driver. And even then, he (and it is usually a "he") will expect a tip that is 20 percent of the total fare. Taxis have electronic meters that can print out receipts.

Passengers with complaints about service should note the taxi number and ☎536-8294 (TAXI). The experience of other unhappy passengers suggests, it must be said, that satisfaction is unlikely. However, **Checker Cabs** ( ☎ 536-7000) have proven to be roomier and cleaner than most others, although no guarantee should be assumed.

Other taxi companies that operate 24 hours include:
* **Cambridge**    ☎876-5000
* **Green Cab**    ☎628-0600
* **I.O.T.A.**    ☎426-8700
* **Red Cab**    ☎734-5000
* **Town Taxi**    ☎536-5000

## DRIVING
The best advice is, *don't!* Using a car in Boston borders on irrationality, at least for visitors unfamiliar with its winding, often narrow streets and the confusing patterns of one-way streets. Native drivers are prone to risky, unpredictable maneuvers. Street parking is all but nonexistent in downtown districts, and outdoor lots and garage parking are expensive. If you must bring a car to Boston, at least try to confine its use to evenings after 9pm and on weekends, to visit any of the several interesting suburbs or colleges, or for touring the countryside and more distant parts of the city.
* For further details and information, contact the **American Automobile Association**, or seek advice from your own automobile club.

## RENTING A CAR
Car rental agencies are located at airline terminals and at offices throughout the city. See also Yellow Pages under *Automobile Renting* and *Leasing*. Most vehicles are equipped with radios, automatic transmission and air conditioning at no extra charge. A credit card can be presented in lieu of a deposit, in which case the driver is allowed to be as young as 18. Otherwise, a cash deposit is required, and the driver must be over 21. Rent-it-here-leave-it-there, weekend and unlimited-mileage packages are available.

## WALKING

One of the worst US cities in which to drive is one of the best for walking. Apart from Beacon Hill and a few slightly elevated areas, Boston's terrain is fairly flat and rarely taxing. The districts of greatest interest to tourists and business travelers are contiguous: Beacon Hill next to Government Center, the downtown shopping and financial districts merging with Back Bay. Only the old North End is somewhat isolated, cut off from the rest by the ganglia of surface and elevated highways known officially as the Central Artery, and not infrequently as the "Distressway," with its eternal bumper-to-bumper traffic and road construction.

Even though most of the streets seem to have been plotted by meandering cows, this proximity of neighborhoods is easy to master. Back Bay, in particular, follows a standard grid pattern in an eight-street-wide band extending along the s bank of the Charles River from the Public Garden to Massachusetts Ave.

Cambridge, N of the Charles, is an amiable sprawl, a collection of settlements that slowly started to merge into the larger city even while the British were still in charge. Directly opposite central Boston is the large campus of Massachusetts Institute of Technology. Harvard University is farther up the Charles, its dozens of buildings dominating Harvard Square and Cambridge Common and spilling over into Boston itself.

## RAIL SERVICES

Commuter rail service is provided from suburbs to the N and W, and from other towns and cities as far away as Providence, Rhode Island in the s, and Ipswich to the N. They arrive at **North Station** *(Causeway and Friend Sts., map 12 D10 ☎ 722-3200)* and **South Station** *(Atlantic Ave. and Summer St., map 12 F11 ☎ 345-7451)*, which is also the terminus for interstate Amtrak trains from Canada, New York, Chicago, Washington, Florida and intermediate points *( ☎ 736-4545 or 800-872-7245)*.

## DOMESTIC AIRLINES

Most major domestic airlines serve Boston's Logan Airport, including the USAir Shuttle and the Delta Shuttle to New York and on to Washington, DC. The two services have hourly flights during the day and early evening. The 800 numbers below are for reservations and information on North American airlines. Several airlines share office space in downtown Boston at 144 Federal St. *(map 12 F11)* and/or at 2 Center Plaza *(map 12 E10)*, in addition to those at the airport.

- **AeroMexico**   800-237-6639
- **Air Canada**   800-776-3000
- **American**   800-433-7300
- **Continental**   800-525-0280
- **Delta**   800-221-1212
- **Mexicana**   800-531-7921
- **Midway**   800-866-9000
- **Northwest**   800-225-2525

- **TWA**      800-221-2000
- **United**   800-241-6522
- **USAir**   800-428-4322

## FERRY SERVICES

A water shuttle runs all year between Logan Airport and Rowe's Wharf *(map 12 E12)* at the edge of downtown Boston. For hours of operation, see FROM THE AIRPORT TO THE CITY, page 48. Two companies offer commuter ferry service between Rowe's Wharf and Hewitt's Cove in Hingham *(off map 6 F6)*, on the South Shore: **Boston Harbor Commuter Service** ( ☎ *740-1253*) and **Mass Bay Lines** ( ☎ *542-8000)*. Schedules fluctuate with the seasons, so call ahead for times.

## OTHER TRANSPORTATION

Hourly rates for **private limousines** are high, but most offer special "night out" rates. Some companies have only one or two vehicles; others have fleets. Most of their garages are located in the suburbs, so their addresses are unnecessary. A few among the many reputable firms, all with toll-free 800 numbers:

- **Commonwealth**   ☎787-5575 or 800-558-5466
- **Excel**   ☎864-4801 or 800-894-3923
- **Lynette's**   ☎938-0014 or 800-698-0014
- **Pedersen**   ☎890-9004 or 800-696-9004; classic cars, including Rolls-Royce
- **Standard**   ☎569-3880 or 800-634-0045
- **W.B.T.**   ☎628-7577 or 800-402-0501; 6- to 12-passenger stretch limos.

  **Bicycles** can be rented from the following:

- **Back Bay Bikes**   333 Newbury St. (Boston). Map **10**G6 ☎247-2336
- **Community Bicycle Supply**   490 Tremont St. (Boston). ☎542-8623
- **Earth Bikes**   35 Huntington Ave. (Boston). Map **10**G8 ☎267-4733
- **Little Shop of Bicycles**   293A North St. (Boston). Map **12**E11 ☎720-4330
- **Surf 'n' Cycle**   1771 Massachusetts Ave. (Cambridge) ☎661-7659

  Rides in **horse-drawn carriages** begin from Quincy Market *(map 12 E11)* for most of the year, day and night, in decent weather. Establish the rate in advance.

# On-the-spot information

## PUBLIC HOLIDAYS

**January 1**. Martin Luther King Day, **third Monday in January**. President's Day, celebrated on a 3-day **weekend in mid-February**. Patriots Day, **third Monday in April**. Memorial Day, a 3-day **weekend at the end of May**. Independence Day, **July 4**. Labor Day, **first Monday in September**. Columbus Day, **second Monday in October**. Election Day, **first Tuesday in November**. Veterans Day, **November 11**. Thanksgiving, **last Thursday in November**. **December 25**.

- As in the rest of the country, schools, banks, post offices and most public services are usually closed on these days, although many of the larger stores stay open on the 3-day weekends.
- A number of other special days are observed with religious services, parades, gift-giving or other celebrations. These include:

Chinese New Year, **January/February**. St Patrick's Day, **March 17**. Easter and Passover, **April**. Mother's Day, **May**. Bunker Hill Day, **Sunday before June 17**. Rosh Hashanah, **September**. Halloween, **October 31**. Chanukah, **December**.

## BANKS

Customary banking hours are Monday to Friday 9am–4pm; some banks are open Saturday mornings. Travelers checks can be cashed at all banks.

Many banks have 24-hour automatic teller machines, allowing withdrawals from personal checking or savings accounts or cash advances against credit cards. If your hometown bank is a member of the CIRRUS or PLUS ATM networks, you should be able to find a participating local bank and machine. It is not a good idea to use the machines late at night, when they are obvious targets of criminals.

- See MONEY on page 45 for further details.

## SHOPPING, EATING, ENTERTAINMENT AND RUSH HOURS

**Shops**     Department stores, clothes and sports equipment stores usually open at 9 or 10am and close at 6 or 7pm. Late-night shopping is typically on Monday or Thursday, usually until 8.30 or 9pm. Many department and electronics stores, especially those in shopping malls, are open Sunday afternoon and have several late nights.

**Eating out**     Although fast-food stands, coffee shops and delicatessens open by 8am and don't close until 10pm or later, more formal restaurants more or less confine themselves to noon–3pm and 6–11pm.

**Nightlife**     Bars and discos stay open until 1 or 2am.

**Rush hours**     Driving, or using public transport between 8–9am and 5–6.30pm, should be avoided, if possible, and the situation is almost as bad for an hour before and after those times.

## MAIL AND TELEPHONE SERVICES

**Post offices** are usually open Monday to Friday 8am–5pm, Saturday 9am–noon, but there are individual variations. The **main post office**

at 25 Dorchester Ave. *(map 12 G11)* is open Monday to Friday 8am–8pm, Saturday 8am–5pm.

**Telephones** are everywhere. Try to use those in shops or public buildings: the ones installed on street corners are sometimes out of order. The **area code** for both Boston and Cambridge is **617**. **Local calls** need only their 7-digit number. When calling an **out-of-town number**, dial **1**, then the area code, and finally the 7-digit number.

**Direct dialing** to all US numbers and many foreign countries is available, but calls are best made from hotel rooms, bearing in mind the number of coins required for a pay phone. This convenience is offset by the fact that most hotels add surcharges. Cheaper rates apply after 5pm and on weekends. The **UK code** is **011 44**.

There are independent shops specializing in **fax**, **telex** and **postal services**; larger hotels also offer these services. **Money** can be wired from one Western Union office to another, and a mailgram might arrive sooner than a letter; see also the advice on **MoneyGram®** on page 45. **ITT** is the primary international cable service ( ☎ 797-3311).

## PUBLIC REST ROOMS (TOILETS)
Those in MBTA stations should be avoided. Rest rooms in museums and public buildings are usually satisfactory. *In extremis,* duck into the nearest hotel.

## SMOKING REGULATIONS
In the absence of stringent municipal regulations, many businesses are imposing their own rules on smoking tobacco. Increasing numbers of offices and some restaurants ban smoking entirely, and many of the remainder provide nonsmoking tables or sections. Hotels reserve as many as half of their rooms for nonsmokers.

Smoking isn't allowed on trains or streetcars, or on buses. It isn't permitted on subway platforms, either, but that rule is widely ignored. Many taxis post signs that forbid lighting up.

## SAFETY
Boston and Cambridge have lower crime rates than most US cities their size. Sad to say, that doesn't amount to a ringing endorsement. Prudence is still in order. Carrying cameras, passports, credit cards and fat wallets through Boston Common at midnight, for example, is not to be recommended. Deserted and dimly lit streets and parks are to be avoided by solo walkers after sundown. Parking a car overnight on city streets is a mistake, especially if any potentially salable objects are visible inside. That includes stereos and tape decks. What's more, Boston has one of the highest auto theft rates in the country.

In subway stations and at bus stops, stay close to other waiting passengers. At airports and railroad stations, carry your own luggage and don't surrender it to anyone but clearly identifiable hotel personnel. Use the strongboxes that are increasingly available in rooms, or ask if the hotel has secure safes. Leave expensive (and expensive-looking) jewelry at home, or wear it only when traveling exclusively by taxi or private car.

If the hotel uses plastic passcards instead of keys, don't write the room number on the cardkey — commit it to memory or carry it elsewhere. In the hotel room, use the peephole in the door to check the identity of callers. If uncertain, call the front desk.

When leaving a hotel, take only one or two credit cards and enough cash for the activities you plan for each excursion. Most important of all, be aware at all times of what is going on around you and your companions. If you feel threatened when walking along a street, don't be embarrassed to duck into a hotel or a well-lit store and ask for help.

All that said, don't jump at every sound, and don't think that reading this book on a street corner will brand you as a tourist. Chances are, the natives already *know* you're not from here.

## TIPPING

In **restaurants** tip the waiter at least 15 percent of the bill before tax; 20 percent is more usual in luxury establishments, or if the service warrants it. Meals are subject to a 5-percent tax, so tripling that amount equals the usual minimum tip. A few restaurants add a service charge, so don't tip twice.

**Bellmen** expect a dollar per bag. **Doormen** get 50¢–$1 for hailing a taxi; tip **chambermaids** a similar amount for each night of a stay. **Rest-room attendants** should be given 50¢, to be left on the conspicuously displayed plate. When there is a stated fee for checking **coats and parcels**, that is sufficient; otherwise, give $1 per item. **Tour guides** expect $2–5, depending upon the length of the tour.

Many **hotels** add a service charge to room-service meals and beverages; again, don't tip twice.

## DISABLED TRAVELERS

Access to most places has been improved by federal regulations. Many **rest rooms** provide special facilities for disabled people, and most **hotels** have at least a few specially designed rooms.

**Subways** offer steeply reduced fares for disabled passengers; for information about obtaining the necessary pass ☎722-5438. Getting down to the subway is a different matter. An increasing number of stations are wheelchair-accessible, but not all of them. Larger maps pinpoint the usable stations with a black-and-white wheelchair symbol (♿). Increasing numbers of **buses** are equipped with movable platforms that permit boarding of persons in wheelchairs. Seeing-eye dogs are permitted everywhere.

For assistance, contact **The Information Center for Individuals with Disabilities** *(27-43 Wormwood St., Boston 02210, off map 12 G12* ☎ *727-5540).*

## LOCAL PUBLICATIONS

Special arts and leisure sections and events calendars appear on Thursday and Sunday in the daily *Boston Globe* and on Friday in its tabloid competitor, the *Boston Herald*. They provide useful reviews and listings of current plays, concerts, movies, exhibitions, ballets and operas.

So does the youthful weekly newspaper *Boston Phoenix,* which emphasizes rock concerts and the more offbeat alternative arts and presentations. The monthly "lifestyle" magazine *Boston* gears itself to an older, more affluent audience.

# Useful addresses

**TOURIST INFORMATION**
**American Express Travel Service**　　1 Court St., Boston, map **12**E10 ☎723-8400, and 44 Brattle St., Cambridge, map **7**B2 ☎661-0005; they are valuable sources of information for any traveler in need of help, advice or emergency services.
**Greater Boston Convention and Visitors Bureau**　　P.O. Box 490, Boston, MA 02199, map **10**G7 ☎536-4100 for mail and telephone information, or the information kiosk at 14 Tremont St. on Boston Common for personal inquiries.

**TOUR OPERATORS**
As in most cities, the skills and personalities of the guides assigned to tour groups vary greatly. Too often, their spiels turn out to be tangled nests of opinion, half-digested facts and failed attempts at humor. Some imagine they are the main attraction of the trip. Since there is no way to predict in advance the ability of the guide you are landed with, prepare to enjoy the views, use the tour to get to know the lay of the land, and filter the guide's utterances through a fine net of skepticism.
- **Bay State Cruise Company**　☎723-7800. Cruises short and long, around the harbor and all the way to Provincetown on Cape Cod. Variations include lunch and sunset trips, as well as whale-watching excursions.
- **Beantown Trolleys**　☎966-6100. A mock streetcar makes a 90-minute circuit, with running commentary. It can be boarded and debarked at several points, all day.
- **The Blue Trolley**　☎876-5539 (TRO-LLEY). Buses made to look like streetcars make 16 stops, at which passengers are allowed to board and disembark at will throughout the day.
- **Boston By Foot**　☎367-2345. Walking tours, obviously. Call to reserve and to learn starting points, which vary. Most tours take 90 minutes.
- **Boston By Sail**　☎742-3313. Two sailboats on 90-minute cruises by moonlight and at sunset, as well as during the day.
- **Boston Sightseeing Tours**　☎899-1454. Various minibus tours.
- **Brush Hill Tours**　☎236-2148. Many different tours varying in length from 90 minutes to 8 hours, mostly of Boston and Cambridge, but with excursions to outlying towns and Cape Cod.
- **Charles River Boat Company**　☎742-4282. The 65-foot *Charles I* was built in traditional style to carry up to 100 passengers up the Charles; lunch, cocktail or dinner cruises.

- **Don Quijote Tours**   ☎328-9425. 3-hour tour of Boston and Cambridge, narrated in Spanish.
- **Gray Line**   ☎426-8800. Half- and full-day tours, some including Lexington and Concord.
- **Old Town Trolley Tours**   ☎269-7010. 100-minute riding tours of Boston in orange and green "streetcars," allowing passengers to debark and reboard at several stops along the route. It operates all year. Similar tours of Cambridge are available spring through summer; they take 75 minutes.

## MAIN POST OFFICE
**General Post Office**   25 Dorchester Ave., Boston, map **12G11** ☎654-5729 or 654-5083 (recording). Open daily, 24 hours, for self-service; open Monday to Friday 8.30am–5.30pm, Saturday 8.30am–5pm, for full service.

## TELEPHONE SERVICES
**Greater Boston Convention and Visitors Bureau**   ☎ 536-4100
**International calls**   Dial operator
**MBTA travel information**   ☎722-5050
**Telephone information**   ☎411 for local numbers; for towns/cities outside Boston ☎1, then the area code, then 555-1212
**Time**   ☎637-1234
**Traffic report** (during rush hours)   ☎ 976-2323
**Weather**   ☎936-1234

## PLACES OF WORSHIP
**Baptist**   The First Baptist Church, 110 Commonwealth Ave. Map **11F8**.
**Catholic**   St Stephen's Church, 401 Hanover St. Map **12D11**.
**Episcopal**   Christ Church, Zero Garden St. (Cambridge), map **7B2**; Emmanuel Church, 13 Newbury St., map **11F8**.
**Jewish**   Boston Synagogue, 55 Martha Rd. Map **11D9**.
**Lutheran**   First Lutheran Church, 299 Berkeley St. Map **11F8**.
**Methodist**   Old West Church, 131 Cambridge St. Map **12E10**.
**Presbyterian**   Church of the Covenant, 67 Newbury St. Map **11F8**.
**Unitarian**   First & Second Church of Boston, 66 Marlborough St. Map **11F8**.

## LIBRARIES
**Boston Athenaeum**   $10\frac{1}{2}$ Beacon St. Map **12E10** ☎227-0270.
**Boston Public Library**   Copley Sq. Map **10G8** ☎536-5400.
**Boston Public Library, North End**   25 Parmenter St. Map **12D11** ☎227-8135.
**Cambridge Public Library**   449 Broadway, Cambridge. Map **7B3** ☎349-4040.
**Widener Memorial Library**   At Harvard University. Map **7B2** ☎495-2413

# Emergency information

**EMERGENCY SERVICES**
For **Police**, **Ambulance** or **Fire** in Boston and Cambridge ☎**911**. No coin is required if using a phone booth.

**ILLNESS OR INJURY**
City ambulances telephoned on **911** carry the patient without charge to the nearest municipal hospital. If a private hospital is preferred, call one of the private ambulance services, for which a fee is charged:

*   **Chaulk Ambulance** ☎326-3277
*   **Fallon Ambulance** ☎482-8181
*   **Reardon Ambulance** ☎282-0100.

The vast and highly-regarded **Massachusetts General Hospital** *(55 Fruit St., map 11D9* ☎ *726-2000 for general calls* ☎ *726-2000 for emergencies)*, better known as "Mass General," is an obvious choice.

Other hospitals, with their general and emergency numbers:

*   **Beth Israel**    330 Brookline Ave., map **9I4** ☎735-2000 and 735-3337
*   **Boston City**    818 Harrison Ave. ☎ 534-5000 and 534-4075
*   **Boston University Hospital**    88 East Newton St., off map **10I8** ☎638-8000 and 638-6240
*   **Brigham & Women's**    75 Francis St. ☎ 732-5500 and 732-5636
*   **Cambridge**    1493 Cambridge St., map **8B4** ☎ 498-1000 and 498-1429
*   **Deaconess**    185 Pilgrim Rd., map **9I3** ☎ 732-7000 and 732-8761
*   **New England Medical Center**    750 Washington St., map **12G10** ☎956-5000 and 956-5566

**LATE-NIGHT DRUGSTORE (PHARMACY)**
**Phillips**    155 Charles St., Boston, map **11F9** ☎523-4372

**HELP LINES**
**Alcoholics Anonymous**    ☎426-9444
**Child abuse**    ☎800-792-5200
**Dental emergency**    ☎508-651-3521
**Drug and Alcohol Hotline**    ☎547-8100
**Personal Crisis**    ☎244-4350
**Poison**    ☎232-2120
**Rape help line**    ☎492-7273
**Suicide Prevention**    ☎247-0220
**Traveler's Aid Society**    ☎542-7286 or ☎542-9875

**AUTOMOBILE ACCIDENTS**
*   Call the police immediately
*   If the car is rented, telephone the number printed in the rental agreement
*   Do not admit liability or incriminate yourself
*   Ask witnesses to stay and give statements
*   Exchange names, addresses, car details, insurance companies and 3-digit insurance company codes
*   Remain to give your statement to the police

**CAR BREAKDOWNS**
Call one of the following from the nearest telephone:
*   The number indicated in the car rental agreement
*   The local office of the AAA (if you are a member)
*   The nearest garage or towing service.

**LOST TRAVELERS CHECKS**
Notify the local police immediately, then follow the instructions provided with your travelers checks, or contact the issuing company's nearest office.
*   Contact **American Express** ( ☎ *800-221-7282)* if you are stranded with no money.

# Planning your trip

## When to go to Boston

In summer, Boston is hot and humid for long stretches. Yet summer remains one of the most desirable times for a visit, for it is then that this great city for walking is at its informal best, with its sidewalk cafés, breezes coming off the bay, open-air concerts on the Esplanade, the swan boats cruising the lagoon in the Public Garden, and crews stroking their shells up and down the Charles.

While affluent Bostonians still flee to summer cottages by the sea or in the New England hills, there is never that impression of an abandoned city given by, say, Rome in August. Most restaurants remain open for business, as do the museums and landmark buildings. Concerted private and municipal efforts bring about a full schedule of cultural and popular events, as a glance at the BOSTON CALENDAR, on the following pages of this chapter, will reveal.

The best weather comes from late April to May and from September to mid-October. September, when tens of thousands of students return to study at the many colleges and universities in the area, has a busy, festive air. The prodigious theater and concert season kicks into high gear at that time, too. For all those reasons, hotels are heavily booked then. Demand slackens in December to March. It can't be denied that there are bone-chilling days and weeks, but winters are not unusually severe. Snowfalls of more than a few inches are infrequent, and one charming aspect of snow in Boston is the Dickensian air it lends to the historic streets of Back Bay and Beacon Hill.

Visitors who are intent on a shopping vacation will encounter large crowds and frayed tempers in the weeks between Thanksgiving and Christmas. The biggest sales are in January to February. In early fall, sports enthusiasts find that the seasons of the major professional and university teams overlap.

# When to go to New England

Northern New Englanders joke that there are three seasons: winter, mud, and July. It isn't quite that bad. Obviously, this Atlantic northeast corner of the US has its extremes, but they have been put to good use. Vermont, New Hampshire and western Massachusetts enjoy more top-flight ski resorts than any area east of the Mississippi River. To be sure, the peaks are not as high nor the runs as long as in the Rocky Mountains, but that doesn't deter the crowds of eager skiers who drive up from distant points to the east, south and west from late November through March.

Surely the most popular time of all is the fall foliage season, when the changing leaves spread blankets of color across the rolling mountains and billowing fields of rural New England. The phenomenon starts in late September in the most northerly parts, edging down into Massachusetts in mid-October, somewhere between the 10th and the 15th, then slightly later in Connecticut. Prior climatic conditions can alter the intensity of colors and the times that the change occurs, of course. In any event, every hotel, motel, inn, and bed and breakfast is booked up months ahead, and most of them charge more than their normal rates.

Similarly, even for one-night stops from June through August at the popular seaside resorts — the Maine coast, the North Shore above Boston, and Cape Cod, Martha's Vineyard and Nantucket to the south — arrangements should be made well in advance: really, the preceding January isn't too early. Those visitors who can do without sunbathing and water sports will find that the shoulder months of May and September are far less crowded and that accommodation is more readily obtained.

# The Boston calendar

See also SPORTS IN BOSTON (pages 193–96) and PUBLIC HOLIDAYS (page 53).

## JANUARY

Early January: **Budweiser World of Wheels** at Bayside Exposition Center, Dorchester. Lavish display, the largest in New England, of scores of custom cars. • Between mid-January and early February: **Chinese New Year**, in Chinatown. A day of fireworks and celebrations featuring traditional silk lions and a fearsome dragon that snakes and dances along Beach St. to frighten away evil spirits ( ☎ *426-8855 for details).*

## FEBRUARY

February is designated **Black History Month**: libraries, schools, universities, TV stations and neighborhood associations sponsor a wide range of events highlighting the contributions of African-Americans to American history and culture. Newspapers carry daily specifics of the scheduled films, concerts, tours and lectures ( ☎ *742-1854 for information).* • February 12–22: **Lincoln and Washington Birthday Sales**. On the days around these national holidays, stores mount large sales.

Mid-February: **Boston Festival**. Ten days of events showcasing Boston as a winter destination, including outdoor laser light concerts, parades, dance recitals, and ice-skating in the Public Gardens. • Late February for nine days: **New England Boat Show** at Bayside Exposition Center, Dorchester. Displays of pleasure craft, power and sail, and related aquatic sports ( ☎ *242-6092).*

## MARCH

March is **Women's History Month**: lectures, films and related events are listed in local publications. • Early March, for one week: **New England Spring Flower Show** at Bayside Exposition Center, Dorchester. The oldest horticultural show in the US, with 40 fully realized gardens on nearly four landscaped acres. • Sunday before March 17: **St Patrick's Day Parade** at East Broadway, South Boston. No one has to have ancestors from Galway or Cork to be Irish on this day ( ☎ *536-4100).*

## APRIL

Early April, for four weeks: **Big Apple Circus**. The one-ring extravaganza from New York comes to town. The location varies ( ☎ *426-6500 for details).* • Mid-April, harbingers of spring: the opening of the **baseball season** with Boston Red Sox at Fenway Park ( ☎ *267-8661)* and launching of the **Swan Boats** in the Public Garden. • Patriot's Day, third Monday in April: running of the **Boston Marathon**, the oldest (1897) in America; preceded by three days of festivities for both runners and spectators. Also, re-enactments of incidents that constituted the start of the American Revolution, including Paul Revere's ride and the battle at Lexington.

## MAY

First Sunday in May: **May Fair** in Harvard Square. Games, food, art exhibits, entertainments. • Early May: **Boston Pops** concert season begins at Symphony Hall, with its repertoire of favorite symphonies and Sousa marches ( ☎ *266-1492). • Mid-May: **Greater Boston Kite Festival** in Franklin Park. Biannual **art show** on Newbury Street ( ☎ 267-9473). • Late May: **Street Performers Festival** in Faneuil Hall Marketplace. Three days of musicians, mimes, jugglers and other buskers ( ☎ 523-1300).

Late May to early June: **Cambridge River Festival**, on the banks of the Charles River. Themed celebrations of summer and the arts, with music, crafts displays, dancing, street theater and parades ( ☎ 349-4380). Unofficial **start of spring** on Lilac Day at the Arnold Arboretum, Jamaica Plain ( ☎ 524-1719).

## JUNE

All month: **music and street fairs**, many of them free. There is dance, jazz, pop and early music by groups and companies performing outdoors and in concert halls, under various sponsorships.

First weekend in June: **Bay Village Street Fair** at Church St., between Tremont and Stuart Sts. Antiques, crafts, home-cooked goods for sale at scores of booths, with entertainment by clowns, mimes and musical performers ( ☎ 482-6173). **Victorian Promenade** in the Public Garden. The biennial event has walkabouts by celebrants in period dress playing Victorian lawn games ( ☎ 227-8955). **Festival of St Anthony**: the North End is lined with booths selling games of chance, sizzling sausages, *calzone,* pizza and flavored ices. Religious observances dominate during the day; secular entertainments take over after dusk. Go hungry, for the aromas are irresistible.

Early June: **Dairy Festival** on Boston Common. A colonial law insisted that cows must be allowed on the Common once a year. About a hundred of them spend the week there, an excuse for milking and butter-churning demonstrations and the sale of much ice cream. **Dragon Boat Festival**, on the Charles River. Chinese arts festival, with folk dances and martial arts demonstrations, and featuring a race between boats suitably decorated with dragon heads ( ☎ 635-3485).

Second Saturday in June: **Lesbian and Gay Pride Day**. Parade through Back Bay. • Sunday before June 17: **Bunker Hill Day** in Charlestown. The first important battle of the Revolution is commemorated with a re-enactment, followed by a foot race and parades with bands and floats.

Two days in late June: **Copley Square Book Festival** in Copley Square Park. More than a hundred book stalls, with readings, music and playlets. • Late June to early July: **Harborfest**. The six-day festival incorporates **Independence Day**, with a wraparound schedule of over a hundred events, including food tastings and jazz.

## JULY

Early July: **Harborfest** continues, with patriotic ceremonies, food, music and performers. • July 4: **Independence Day** all over town. The Declaration of Independence is read from the balcony of the Old State House. When it is not in dry dock, "Old Ironsides" — the USS *Constitution* — is towed out of the harbor, turned around, and returned to its Charlestown berth. The Boston Pops orchestra stirs the blood with patriotic tunes played under a night sky full of bursting rockets. • Weekends in July: **North End Italian Feasts.** Saints and The Madonna are celebrated in three-day block parties around the North End. Eating, music, games (☎ 523-2110). • Mid-July: **Boston Pops Esplanade Concerts**. The venerated orchestra moves outdoors for a week of free concerts by the bank of the Charles.

Mid- to late July: **Puerto Rican Festival**, at various locations. Several days of festivities, including a road race and a carnival, culminating in the Puerto Rican Day parade (☎ 635-4505). **Asian-American Festival** on the Esplanade. Family entertainment, Asian foods, craft demonstrations (☎ 439-7700). • Late July to early August: **US Pro Tennis Championships** at Longwood Cricket Club, Chestnut Hill. The country's oldest pro tennis championship lasts a little over a week (☎ 731-4500).

## AUGUST

Throughout August: **North End Italian Feasts**. More weekend festas with food and games of chance, as in July. • Wednesday evenings in August: **Citystage Concerts** at Government Center Plaza. Free outdoor concerts of varying kinds of music (☎ 725-4006).

Late August: **August Moon Festival** in Chinatown. Joyful celebration of the coming harvest season, with lion dance, music and appropriate foods. Date varies according to Chinese year (☎ 542-2574). • Third weekend in August: **Boston Seaport Festival** at Charlestown Navy Yard. Tall ships visit the harbor, and nautical skills are demonstrated (☎ 534-5832). **Caribbean Carnival** in Franklin Park. Steel bands and calypso rock the Roxbury neighborhood for eight days of hearty eating and dance, leading up to the crowning of a king and queen and an exuberant parade with extravagantly costumed participants. • August 26: **Faneuil Hall Marketplace Birthday Celebration**. Take a slice of the monster cake and walk among street performers and musical groups, from morning to late evening (☎ 523-1300).

## SEPTEMBER

Mid-September: **Opening of NFL season** at Foxboro Stadium. The professional New England Patriots football team kicks off. • Second Saturday in September: **Back Bay Street Dance** in Marlborough St., between Gloucester and Fairfield Sts. An evening with live Forties music for jitterbugging and foxtrotting; food and drink, too (☎ 247-3961). • Sunday afternoon in mid-September: **Art Newbury Street** in Newbury St., between Arlington and Hereford Sts. Pedestrian traffic only, the better to visit Newbury's art galleries and listen to musical groups ( ☎ *267-9473).*

## OCTOBER
Early October: **opening of NHL season** at Boston Garden. The Bruins, Boston's often beleaguered professional hockey team, begins its long season. • Sunday nearest October 12: **Columbus Day Parade** in North End or East Boston. Second only to the St Patrick's Day Parade in intensity and numbers. • Late October for one week: **Ellis Memorial Antiques Show**. On one day of the run, the public is invited to bring in objects for appraisal. Otherwise, a wide range of antiques and collectibles are on display. **Ringling Bros. and Barnum & Bailey Circus**: America's only surviving multi-ring circus makes a one-week stand at Boston Garden, announced by a small parade of its elephants and clowns.

Third Sunday in October: **Head of the Charles Regatta** on the Charles River. University crews from many countries propel about 1,000 shells over a three-mile downriver course from the starting line at Boston University Bridge. Much boisterous behavior on the river banks, abetted by prodigious beer-drinking.

## NOVEMBER
Early November: **Opening of NBA season** at Boston Garden. Frequent champions, the Boston Celtics professional basketball team, undertake a season that runs until the following spring. **New England Crafts Festival** at the World Trade Center. Three days of crafts demonstrations and displays. • November 11: **Veterans Day Parade** from Commonwealth Ave. to Columbus Ave. Marching bands, fife and drum corps, bagpipers. • Day after Thanksgiving: **Boston Ballet Season** at the Wang Center for the Performing Arts begins with the traditional Christmas performances of the *Nutcracker.*

## DECEMBER
All month: **Christmas Celebrations** on various sites. Tree-lighting ceremonies at the Prudential Center and on the Boston Common. Caroling on Louisburg Sq. on Beacon Hill. Christmas walks and house tours. "Revels" of folk tales and traditions at Harvard University's Sanders Theater. Holly Fair at the Cambridge Center for Adult Education, with jugglers, musicians and a crafts show. Gaudily or cunningly decorated store windows, especially at Jordan Marsh and Filene's. For general information about holiday events ☎536-4100.

Mid-December: **Boston Tea Party Re-enactment**, Boston Tea Party Ship & Museum. The early rebellious act against British "taxation without representation" is re-created with brio. • December 31: **New Year's Eve**, all over the city. Called "First Night," the celebrations comprise at least a hundred events, most of them indoors, and including film, dance, video and musical performances of diverse nature. At midnight, the New Year is ushered in with a spectacular fireworks extravaganza above Boston Harbor.

# Finding
# your way

## Boston and Cambridge: an overview

The easiest way to form a mental image of the layout of the city is to read the following text in conjunction with a decent map. You will find the map page-references given below useful if you are using our color maps, at the back of this book.

**Turn to maps 11 & 12:**
The oldest part of Boston occupies a knob of land that knuckles into Boston Harbor, defined on the north and west by an elbow bend in the Charles estuary and on the east by the inner harbor and Fort Point Channel. Much of what is most cherished by Bostonians is found in this compact area, slightly more than two miles across at its widest point. The partially elevated Fitzgerald Expressway slices off the tip, which is the mostly Italian **North End**, containing the famous Old North Church and Paul Revere House, the oldest in the city.

On the western side of the Expressway is the old **West End** and the **Government Center**, next to the immensely popular Faneuil Hall Marketplace. A portion of the rejuvenated waterfront, with its new hotels, ferry services and the New England Aquarium, is immediately east of the Marketplace.

Residential **Beacon Hill** rises to the west of these areas, and its gold-domed State House overlooks the Boston Common. Adjacent to the Common, on the east and south, is **downtown**, incorporating the **Financial District**, the small **Theater District** and **Chinatown**. Several of the city's major convention and luxury hotels are in this area, as are a number of churches and department stores. Long-distance Amtrak trains arrive at South Station, at the southern edge of the Financial District.

Below the Theater District, along Tremont St., is a gentrifying residential neighborhood known as the **South End** *(partly on map 10)*, notable primarily for the Boston Center for the Arts and a handful of striving bistros.

The Freedom Trail curls through parts of most of these districts and over the Charlestown Bridge to **Charlestown**, on the north bank of the Charles estuary. The Battle of Bunker Hill took place here, and USS *Constitution*, "Old Ironsides," is moored at the Charlestown Navy Yard.

To the northeast *(see map 6)*, two miles off the North End, is **East Boston**. Its principal importance to the visitor is the presence of Logan International Airport.

**Turn to maps 9 & 10:**
From old Boston, history and development flowed south and west, along the Charles. **Back Bay** was the name of a large fetid marsh at the edge of the river. Over three decades, it was filled in and a posh 19thC residential neighborhood grew along its regular grid of streets, following the main thoroughfare, broad Commonwealth Ave. At the landward side of Back Bay are central **Copley Square**, a crucial focus of Victorian Boston that shares Trinity Church, Old South Church, the Boston Public Library and the Copley Plaza Hotel. Adjoining the Square on the west is an unmissable example of 1960s urban renewal, the **Prudential Center**, with Boston's second-tallest skyscraper.

Gathered around the Square and Center are a number of good-to-excellent restaurants, many shops, and nine important deluxe and business hotels. South of the "Pru" is the monumental Christian Science Center. Continuing in the same direction, Huntington Ave. passes, in sequence, Symphony Hall, Northeastern University (just beyond Jordan Hall), the Museum of Fine Arts, Isabella Stewart Gardner Museum, a few streets to the w, and, eventually, Boston College.

**Turn to maps 5 & 6:**
Behind and to the N of the museums are **The Back Bay Fens** *(still on maps 9 & 10)*, parklands that are part of the Emerald Necklace greenway that curls lazily south, along the border of the prosperous suburb of **Brookline**. A curving belt of largely residential neighborhoods girdles these areas, of interest primarily to those who live in them.

Well below Downtown, east of the working-class neighborhood of Dorchester, is **South Boston**. It has a distinct Irish-American identity and composition. To its west, a good way below Back Bay, is **Roxbury**, populated mostly by African-Americans and other minorities.

**Turn to maps 7 & 8:**
**Cambridge**, on the north side of the Charles River, is an independent municipality. For most residents, it is a co-equal extension of Boston, and is treated accordingly in this book. Two of the nation's most prestigious educational institutions grace the city, Harvard University and the Massachusetts Institute of Technology (MIT). Harvard is the oldest in the country, with thousands of distinguished alumni who have served commerce and government since the first years of colonization. Its campus sprawls around Harvard Square, inland, and down to the Charles, a few miles upriver from downtown Boston. The orderly campus of MIT faces Back Bay, straddling Massachusetts Ave.

**Getting around**
Every likely tourist destination mentioned in this book is within reach of the extensive public transportation system — by subway, streetcar, bus, or a combination. Many out-of-town locations can be reached by rail or bus as well, although a car is often preferable.

# Exploring Boston

## Boston on foot

Few American cities reward the enthusiastic walker in as many ways. Despite the office towers that have sprouted over the last three decades, Boston retains companionable proportions. At every turning, its parks, distinctive neighborhoods, abundant historical associations, waterside belvederes, and four centuries of striking architecture occupy the mind and fill the eye.

In the following pages, the five suggested walks, one of them in Cambridge, are representative but hardly exhaustive.

A number of the places mentioned along these walks are discussed at greater length in SIGHTSEEING. Places printed in **BOLD SMALL CAPITALS** have a full entry of their own in that chapter.

### WALK 1: THE FREEDOM TRAIL

*Allow 1 hour for walk plus 2 more hours to visit sites along the route. See color map 12F10–D11 and WALK 1 map, page 73. T Park Street (Red and Green Lines).*

Much of the civil unrest and agitation that escalated into the American Revolution occurred in and around Boston. The city was home to patriots and presidents whose names still resonate in history books: Adams, Revere, Franklin, Hancock. This route through old Boston passes many of the sites where they lived and plotted against English rule. It should be noted, in passing, that British visitors may need to get a close grip on their capacity for indignation. Plaques and descriptive brochures usually present the American view of events, and the language of victorious revolutionaries is rarely even-handed regarding the actions of their perceived oppressors.

To reach the starting point, walk s from the Park Street T station along Tremont St. and the edge of the **BOSTON COMMON** to the Boston Tourist Information booth. Attendants there answer questions and provide maps and other materials about the Freedom Trail and the city. A red line painted on the sidewalk leads the way. Over the winter and between maintenance jobs the line fades and sometimes disappears altogether, and in other places is replaced by bricks or stones embedded in the sidewalk. That being the case, the following description proceeds as if the line were not there. Refer to the map on page 73.

From the information booth, retrace a few steps n and turn left on the first path into the Common. This 44 acres of parkland was just that — a "common" ground kept for the benefit, or punishment, of citizens. Cattle and sheep grazed there, soldiers trained, and miscreants, witches and occasional Quakers were pilloried or executed beneath its trees.

The path leads uphill past the **Brewer Fountain** (1867) toward the MASSACHUSETTS STATE HOUSE, its presence rendered even more august by its gleaming gold dome. The building was designed by Charles Bulfinch, Boston's leading architect during the post-Revolutionary period. It replaced the original State House, seen later on this walk, in 1795 and became a model for similar structures throughout the former colonies, including the Capitol in Washington, DC. Only the brick facade is by Bulfinch, the rest of the building having been added over the last century. The copper-clad dome was forged at Paul Revere's foundry. It wasn't painted gold until after the Civil War, and was temporarily returned to its original gray color during World War II, so as not to provide a target for German warplanes or ships.

At the top of the stairs opposite the State House, turn right. Standing there, facing the State House, is an unusual war monument by one of the most important sculptors of the late 19thC, Augustus Saint-Gaudens. It commemorates a profoundly important episode of the Civil War. Many free Northern blacks wished to volunteer to fight for the Union against the slave states of the Confederacy, but were at first denied the opportunity. When the War Department decided to change that policy, it stipulated that any units of African-Americans that were formed had to be led by white officers. Saint-Gaudens' sculpture depicts men of the 54th Massachusetts Regiment marching off to war, their young colonel, Robert Gould Shaw, on horseback. He and 32 of his men were killed in an attack on a fort near Charleston, South Carolina. Their story formed the basis of Edward Zwick's 1991 film, *Glory.*

After the monument, turn right again, down the steps and heading toward the **Park Street Congregational Church** at the corner of Tremont. Built in 1809, it was the site 20 years later of abolitionist William Lloyd Garrison's first public demand for an end to slavery. Immediately beyond the church is the **Old Granary Burying Ground**, named after the storage barn that once stood at the corner. Begun in 1660, it contains the remains of Paul Revere, Samuel Adams, John Hancock and merchant Peter Faneuil, as well as five victims of the Boston Massacre.

At the next corner is the OMNI PARKER HOUSE hotel (see the hotel entry on page 146), which likes to claim that it is the oldest hotel in continuous operation in America. In fact, the building itself dates only from 1927, and there are several older functioning hotels in this city. Ho Chi Minh and the black militant Malcolm X worked at the Parker House as young men.

Opposite the hotel is **King's Chapel**. The wooden original was erected in 1687 on the orders of King James II, and was the first Anglican church in America. Since the Puritan settlers had fled England to get away from what they saw as Anglican heresy, the church was not welcomed. To avoid interrupting services, the present granite building, designed by Peter Harrison, was erected around the earlier structure in 1749. When it was completed, the wooden church inside was dismantled and the pieces thrown out the windows. The exterior is ungainly, with a square tower squatting atop a portico of wooden columns treated to look like stone. The money was never found to build a planned steeple. After the Revolution, King's Chapel became America's first Unitarian church.

Continue past the entrance for a look at Boston's first cemetery, which was committed to that purpose in 1630. John Winthrop, the first governor of the colony, is interred under the table stone over to the left (N). Incidentally, gravestone rubbings are not permitted in this or any other historic burial ground in the city.

Return to the corner of Tremont St. and turn left, down what at this point is called School St. Behind King's Chapel is the 1865 **Old City Hall**. A modest example of French Second Empire design, it served its governmental function until it was replaced in 1968. It now contains offices and one of the city's often heralded restaurants, **Maison Robert**. Two statues stand in the courtyard. The one on the left is of Benjamin Franklin. Statesman, politician, inventor and publisher, Franklin is associated with Philadelphia, but he was born in Boston, and his parents are buried in the Old Granary Burying Ground. Josiah Quincy, subject of the other statue, was Boston's second mayor and the builder of Quincy Market, soon to be seen on this walk.

At the end of School St., on the left, is the **Old Corner Book Store**. Built as an apothecary shop around 1718, it was destined to become a literary landmark of uncommon importance. After the publishers Ticknor and Fields occupied it in 1833, it became the frequent meeting place of many of that firm's most renowned authors. That shining roster included Ralph Waldo Emerson, James Russell Lowell, Nathaniel Hawthorne, Henry David Thoreau, Henry Wadsworth Longfellow, John Whittier, Alfred Tennyson, Robert Browning and Harriet Beecher Stowe. Even Charles Dickens dropped by. The *Boston Globe* now owns the restored building, using the upper floors for offices but retaining the ground floor as the **Globe Corner Bookstore** (see page 186 in SHOPPING). Maps and prints of the city are among its bestselling items.

Diagonally across Washington St. is the **Old South Meeting House**. The simple but handsome brick church (illustrated opposite) with its wooden steeple is the second oldest in the city, dating from 1730. British visitors and architecture buffs may note a resemblance to some of the churches of Christopher Wren. "Old South" became a principal meeting place for agitated Bostonians during the tempestuous years before the Revolution. Much of the populace gathered here after the Boston Massacre to protest the presence of British troops, and four years later, the Boston Tea Party was launched from behind these doors. No longer a church, it now serves as a museum.

Turn right (N) on Washington St. upon leaving Old South, repassing The Globe Corner Bookstore. Spring Lane, an alley on the right, ran to the "Great Spring" that supplied water to the city for more than two hundred years.

Continue on Washington, soon reaching, on the right, the OLD STATE HOUSE, a fierce gold eagle roosting above its doorway. Built in 1713, it served as meeting place for the governor and other court-appointed officers, as well as for the popularly elected colonial assembly. That

The **Old South Meeting House** (1730), built of brick with a wooden steeple

proximity was the cause of frequent confrontations. One such followed the Boston Massacre, when Sam Adams demanded that Governor Hutchinson remove the two regiments of British soldiers garrisoned in the city. In 1776, the new Declaration of Independence was first read from the balcony at the harbor end of the building. A brick pedestrian passageway separates the Old State House from the **National Park Service Visitor Center** *(15 State St., map 12E10)*. Inside are exhibits, park rangers who answer questions and pass out brochures, and that sought-after rarity, clean public rest rooms.

On the traffic island on State St. near the balcony at the far end of the Old State House, the circle of paving stones constitutes the **BOSTON MASSACRE MONUMENT**. For that tragic incident, in which a squad of far outnumbered and probably frightened young British soldiers fired upon an unruly mob of taunting colonials, killing five citizens, both sides share the ample blame. Interestingly, the rebel patriots John Adams and Josiah Quincy defended the soldiers in court and all but two were acquitted.

Cross State St. The **Bank of New England**, at that corner, is not a particularly distinguished building, but inside is a mural by Larry Rivers, titled *Boston Massacre*. After a look, cross Congress St. Looking back at the Old State House, notice the silver unicorn and golden lion at the roof line. They are 19thC replicas of originals that were torn down and burned during the Revolution as symbols of the hated monarchy.

Proceed N on Congress. Ahead on the left is now seen the back of the striking **Boston City Hall**, completed in 1968, which form the heart of the GOVERNMENT CENTER. Save it for a later visit, for in less than a block, a plaza opens up on the right.

In its middle is **Faneuil Hall**, a gift to the city by the prominent merchant Peter Faneuil. The core of the Georgian market and meeting place was erected in 1740, rebuilt after a fire in 1762, expanded by Charles Bulfinch in 1806, and restored in 1992–93. The statue in front is of Samuel Adams. The hall continues to serve as a space for a variety of lectures, exhibits, concerts and other events, as well as focal point for Boston's number-one tourist attraction, FANEUIL HALL MARKETPLACE.

To glimpse what that is all about, walk ahead, keeping to the right of the Hall. Behind Faneuil Hall is **Quincy Market**, a long Classical Revival building of granite with columned porticos at both ends. Named after Josiah Quincy, the mayor at the time, it was erected in 1826 as an expansion of the market that operated on the ground floor of Faneuil Hall, as were the similar shed-like structures on either side of Quincy Market, the **North and South Markets**. The three were refurbished and, in part, re-created in 1976 as part of a restoration project by the Rouse Company, which later took on similar efforts in cities all along the Eastern Seaboard. Restaurants, food stalls and a variety of shops now occupy the three buildings.

Cut in front of Quincy Market, turn left on North St., then right on Union St. Over to the left is the new BOSTON CITY HALL, and adjacent to Union is a narrow park. The two statues there are of James Michael Curley, the Irish politician extraordinaire who served four terms as mayor in the period from the start of World War I to four years after World War II. His last campaign was conducted from a jail cell, and he was never known for his unshakable ethics, but he remains one of the city's beloved public figures.

There are several pubs of considerable age along this block, the oldest (1826) and best-known, **Ye Olde Union Oyster House**, at #41. Its raw bar is visible through the front window, a likely spot for a break over a few fresh raw oysters and a Boston brew.

Bear right, down narrow Marshall St., then right again on Hanover St. Continue across what will be for years to come a messy construction site attendant to work on the Central Artery/Fitzgerald Expressway. Walk under the elevated highway. In warm weather, this area is often taken up by a greenmarket. Other times, it can be the least appetizing portion of this walk, with its litter and refuse and population of inebriates and street people.

But it is over quickly, as the Trail now enters the **North End**. The first settled precinct of Boston, it was home to many of its famous early citizens, including Paul Revere, whose house is open to the public. It has long borne an Italian identity, as soon becomes obvious from the products and meals offered in its many small shops and restaurants. On the other side of busy Cross St. (take care), bear right to pick up Hanover St. In one block, turn right on Richmond St., then left into the triangular intersection known as North Square.

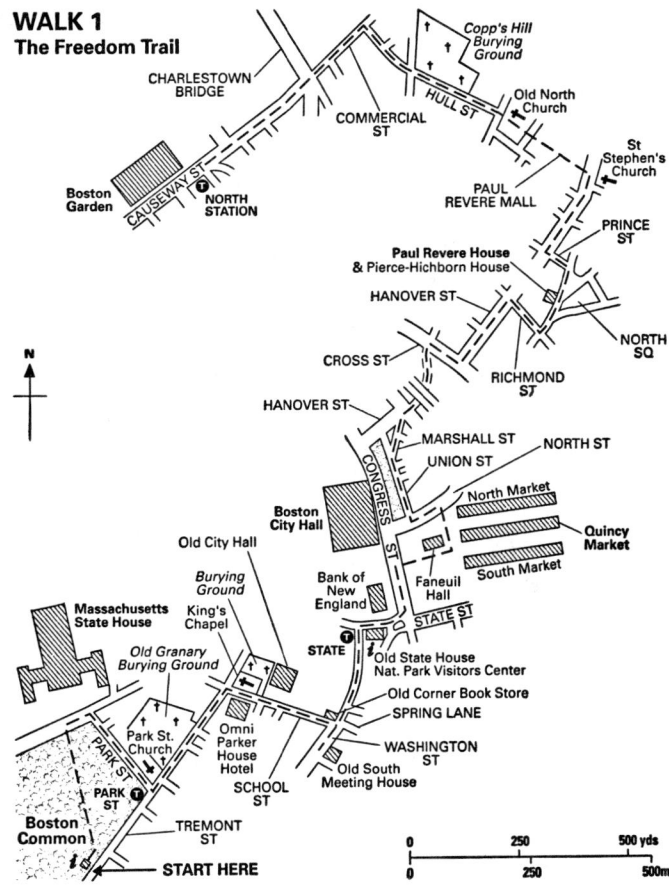

# WALK 1
## The Freedom Trail

    This neighborhood was a red-light district in the early 19thC, notorious for dangerous taverns, roistering sailors and staggering numbers of homicides. No longer afflicted by those problems, the square is easily identified by the building on the left, a small clapboard house of medieval aspect, with its overhanging upper story: the **PAUL REVERE HOUSE**. Although probably considered rather grand in its time and place, it is now difficult to imagine how Paul Revere managed to raise *sixteen* children here, even though they weren't all there at the same time. Dating from about 1680, it is the oldest surviving 17thC structure in Boston. This was the waterfront in his time, all of the land on the other side of the square being created later by landfill.

Next door to the Revere House is the **Pierce-Hichborn House**, built in 1711 and purchased in 1781 by Revere's cousin, Nathaniel Hichborn. Both houses may be visited.

Continue to Prince St., at the end of North Sq., and turn left. Back on Hanover St., turn right. This is the main business street of the North End, and the gathering place for the several *festas* that mark the summer calendar.

In two blocks, on the right, is ST STEPHEN'S CHURCH (1804). Charles Bulfinch designed five churches in Boston; this is the only one that survives. Commissioned for a Unitarian congregation, the changing character of the neighborhood over the next half-century eventually led to its purchase by the newly influential Catholic diocese.

Opposite the church is the Paul Revere Mall, an open space that connects St Stephen's with the OLD NORTH CHURCH. In warm weather, it bustles with children and watchful mothers, and old men playing cards while their wives gossip. The equestrian statue, as you might expect, is of Paul Revere.

The mall narrows as it approaches the back of Old North, also known as Christ Church. Built in 1723, the oldest church extant in Boston, it is constructed of brick with a three-tiered wooden steeple, reminiscent of Christopher Wren. It was in that steeple that the signal lanterns were displayed on the night of April 18, 1775, setting Revere off on his "midnight ride" to warn the rebel militia of the route of the advancing British force. If the gate to the courtyard at the back of Old North is open, go through and into the church; if it is locked, turn left, right, and right again to reach the front of the church. After a visit (■), walk up Hull St., opposite the entrance.

At the top of the hill is COPP'S HILL BURYING GROUND, first put to that use in 1659. Unlike the King's Chapel and Old Granary cemeteries, this has no famous historical figures in residence. It is the highest vantage point in the North End, though, and was used to bombard Charlestown, across the harbor, prior to the battle of Bunker Hill. Opposite the cemetery gate is a small gray clapboard house with white trim (**#44**). Said to be the narrowest house in Boston, it is only a little over ten feet wide at the front, with one window on each floor — four, counting the dormer at top. Proceed down Hull St. on the other side of the hill. This ends at Commercial St. Turn left.

In two blocks, the red line of the Freedom Trail turns right, up and over the Charlestown Bridge. Its objective is the shipyard where the USS *Constitution* ("Old Ironsides") is berthed. While that is a worthy destination, the walk from here to there is over a mile and not especially interesting. We suggest, then, that a separate visit, using subway or taxi, be made to Charlestown at another time.

For now, continue straight ahead, as Commercial becomes Causeway St. Shortly, the large building on the right is BOSTON GARDEN, home of the professional Celtics basketball team and the Bruins hockey team. A cherished institution with a rich history in sports, it is nevertheless dated and dilapidated, and is scheduled to be razed. Opposite is the North Station **T** stop for the ride back to the hotel.

## WALK 2: HARBORWALK

*Allow 1 hour for the walk, up to 2 hours more to visit sites along the route. See color map **12**E10–F12 and* WALK 2 *map overleaf.* **T** *State (Orange or Blue Line).*

With a maritime heritage begun by the first landfall of the Europeans and diminished only by the arrival of large cargo and passenger planes, Boston has much to reveal of its dependence upon — and exploitation of — the sea. This route starts at the Old State House and follows the water's edge, passing the Aquarium, two museums, and a replica of one of the ships involved in the Boston Tea Party. It is a walk best taken in warmer weather, for winds off the water can make it chilly from October to March, even when it is comfortable a few blocks inland.

Begin at the **National Park Service Visitor Center** in the pedestrian walkway opposite the **OLD STATE HOUSE**. A map and short brochure for this walk are available from the rangers inside. There is supposed to be a blue line painted on the sidewalk to show the way, but it has been worn away in the past, so its presence cannot be assumed. Exiting the Visitor Center, turn right and walk E on State St.

Rearing up on the right is the tower of the **Custom House**. It is a curious exercise in bureaucratic esthetics, one repeated in kind in other cities. The original Custom House was built in 1847, at the cusp of the ocean, as a reasonably harmonious Greek Revival "temple." By the start of the 20thC, more office space was deemed to be needed. So the authorities decided to erect a campanile-like skyscraper, the first in Boston. It sprouts from the overwhelmed temple, simultaneously awkward and grandiose.

Over to the left, glimpsed down the side street called Merchants Row, is the **FANEUIL HALL MARKETPLACE**. Cross to the N side of State St., entering the marketplace. On the immediate right is the South Market; ahead is the Greek Revival **QUINCY MARKET** (1824). Turn right (E) between the two long buildings, with their outdoor cafés and shops. The passageway ahead, under the peaked steel and glass roof, is **Marketplace Center**, intended both to house offices and shops and to point walkers under the elevated expressway to the waterfront. Go through and cross carefully to the other side of the very busy road. On the left is **Christopher Columbus Waterfront Park**; on the right is **LONG WHARF**, its principal occupant a Marriott hotel. Walk between the two, along the left (N) side of the hotel. At the end of the wharf is a pleasant surprise, a small park with benches and telescopes to observe the traffic in the harbor. A ferry leaves from here for Charlestown.

When ready, continue around the hotel, passing the front entrance, then bearing left. **Central Wharf** is next, host to the **NEW ENGLAND AQUARIUM**, opened in 1969. In the inlet between these wharves are a number of boats offering harbor cruises and whale-watching trips. The moving sculpture out in front is the creation of a Japanese sculptor, intended, so it is alleged, to suggest two whales swimming side by side. Over to the left of the Aquarium entrance is an open tank of harbor seals, which were rescued as orphan pups. To the right is a barge containing a sea lion pavilion.

Leaving Central Wharf, turn left (S) toward the twin Harbor Towers

# WALK 2
**Harborwalk**

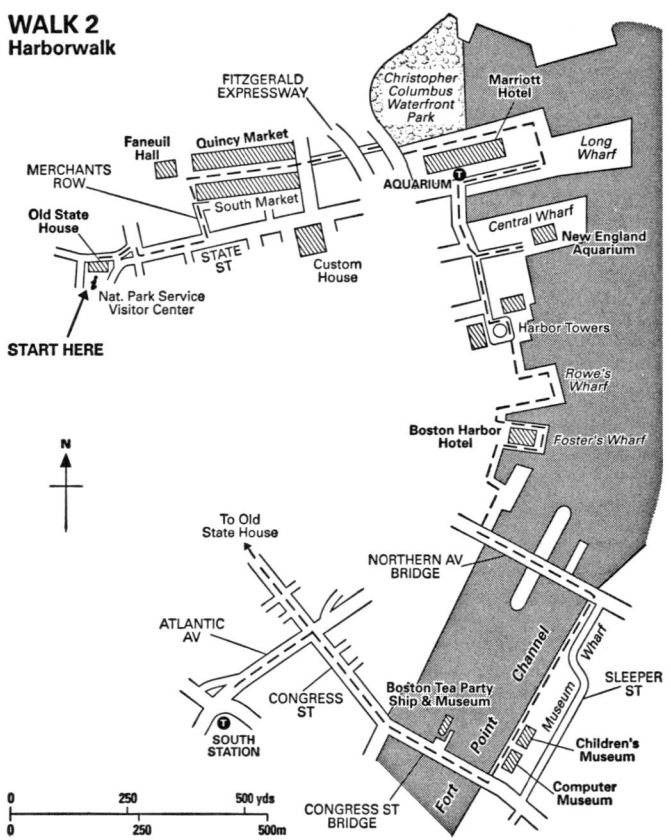

apartment buildings. Walk between them and around the end of **ROWE'S WHARF**, the first version of which was built in the 1760s. Continue to follow the edge of the wharf. Rounding the corner, a new (1987) complex of offices and residences of Post-Modernist bent comes into view, the block pierced by a handsome rotunda and high open archway. Enlightened building restrictions imposed by the city stipulated that the new structures must not cut off views and that public access to the water must be retained. Both conditions were satisfied with aplomb: the marinas are well used, and this is the departure point for the airport water shuttle. A fine new luxury hotel, the **BOSTON HARBOR** (see the hotel entry on page 140), takes full advantage of this setting.

Proceed s along the shoreline to the stairs that go up onto the Northern Avenue Bridge. Turn left on the bridge, which crosses Fort Point Channel and operates on a turntable to allow ships to pass. On the far side, cross over to the red fish-market/restaurant and walk past it, staying close to the channel. (If lengthy ongoing construction is still underway, it may be necessary to detour around it via parallel Sleeper St., returning to the edge of the channel by a right turn through the parking lot or on Congress St.) This is **MUSEUM WHARF**, named after the **CHILDREN'S MUSEUM** and the **COMPUTER MUSEUM**. Both are located in renovated warehouses, which are connected. They're easy to spot: a 1934 roadside booth in the shape of a giant old-fashioned milk bottle stands there, dispensing ice cream and sandwiches. Either museum can command the attention of youngsters for an hour or more, so it might be decided to return to them later.

To complete this walk, proceed across the Congress St. Bridge. Halfway across, on the right, is the **BOSTON TEA PARTY SHIP AND MUSEUM.** Featured is a full-scale replica of the *Beaver II,* one of the three ships boarded and stripped of its valuable cargo in December 1773 by angry colonials dressed as Indians. A cup of tea and an opportunity to throw a bale of tea overboard are benefits of admission.

Continuing over the bridge, turn left on Atlantic Ave. and walk one long block to reach the **T** at South Station. Or stay on Congress St. to return to the Old State House, where the walk began.

## WALK 3: BEACON HILL
*Allow 1 hour. See color map **11E9–12E10** and WALK 3 map on page 79.*
***T** Government Center (Blue or Green Line).*
• *See also entry on BEACON HILL on page 94.*

The gaslit streets of Federalist rowhouses and mansions of this upper-crust enclave constitute some of the most desirable real estate in the city. Given that reputation, its racy and ethnically diverse past may come as a surprise. The north slope of "The Hill" was the first gathering place of free blacks from the West Indies in the 17thC, not long after the colony was founded, and prestigious Mt. Vernon St. was once called "Mt. Whoredom." Eventually, however, Brahmin Boston established itself and flourished here, evidenced by the elite Boston Athenaeum and the State House built and controlled (at first) by the wealthy descendants of Puritan merchants and shipowners.

Begin this walk at the intersection of Tremont and Beacon Sts., where **King's Chapel** and the **Omni Parker House Hotel** are located (E of Tremont, Beacon becomes School St.). Go w up Beacon St., keeping to the s side of the road.

Shortly, at #10½, is the Greek Revival **BOSTON ATHENAEUM**, founded in 1807. The National Historic Landmark building opened in 1847, the final home of a society devoted to the pursuit of cultural and scientific knowledge. Known primarily as a library, its art collection eventually formed the core of the Museum of Fine Arts. Although private, parts of the Athenaeum are open on a restricted basis to the public.

Continuing, the 1808 Federal building at **#16** is the headquarters of the local bar association, and at the corner with Park St. is the **Amory-Ticknor House**, designed by the ubiquitous Charles Bulfinch in 1804 but altered frequently and substantially in later decades. Down to the left spreads **BOSTON COMMON**, and up to the right is the gold-domed **MASSA-CHUSETTS STATE HOUSE**. Cross Beacon and walk up the steps past the equestrian statue of General Joseph Hooker, who enjoyed high honors in the Mexican War but suffered ignominious defeat in the Civil War. The doors ahead are usually open, even when the State House proper is closed. Continue through the next set of doors and out onto Mt. Vernon St. Turn left, into the archway that pierces the rear extension of the State House.

Mt. Vernon is the noblest of The Hill's byways, many of its brick houses having front gardens, a few with curving driveways. Restrained and harmonious, it is decidedly lacking in flamboyance and jarring intrusions. Much of the pleasure it bestows lies in details: cobblestones, gas lamps, boot-scrapers, black iron fences, flowering trees, even the Christmas wreaths that stay on doors until spring.

Soon, on the right, is the 1804 **Nichols House Museum** *(55 Mt. Vernon St., map 11 E9 ☎ 227-6993 ✗ obligatory: open Mar-May and Sept-Nov Mon, Wed, Sat noon-5pm; June-Aug Tues-Sat noon-5pm; Dec-Feb Sat only noon-5pm)*. One of the many Beacon Hill houses attributed to Bulfinch, it is the only one that can be visited, which may be a good reason to schedule this walk to accommodate its limited hours. (Call ahead to make sure they haven't been changed.) The half-hour guided tour amply illustrates the many years the house was occupied by Rose Nichols, a writer and landscape architect who died in 1960 and left it intact to the city. Within are antique furnishings of the last five centuries, accumulated by Ms. Nichols and her father.

Bankers John and Nathaniel Thayer commissioned the out-of-scale attached houses at **#70** and **#72** in 1847. Considered ostentatious then — they still are, come to think of it — they were saved from the wrecker's ball in the 1960s. A little farther, at **#85**, is the second of three houses designed by Bulfinch for Harrison Gray Otis. Completed in 1802, it is now on the National Register of Historic Places. Otis intended to establish a pattern of large detached mansions such as this for The Hill, with gracious proportions and grand entrances. Among many distinctive details of this building are the octagonal cupola surrounded by the roofline balustrade.

Continuing downhill, the next corner is on **Louisburg Square**, the heart of the south slope. The long, tilted green space in the center, with its tended bushes and statues of Christopher Columbus and Aristides "The Just," is surrounded by a wrought-iron fence and cobblestoned streets. Only householders bordering the square have access to the park. While their houses follow no single plan, they are variously pleasing to the eye, the sun striking sparks from their bowed front windows. At Christmastime, the square is the site of carolers and bell ringers, traditions begun by Beacon Hill residents.

Turn right and circle the park counterclockwise. Jenny Lind, the singer billed as the "Swedish Nightingale" by the unquenchable promoter P.T. Barnum, was married at **#20**. Author Louisa May Alcott purchased **#10** after her success with *Little Women*, published shortly after the Civil War. She died there in 1888, two days after her father, Bronson, passed away in the same house.

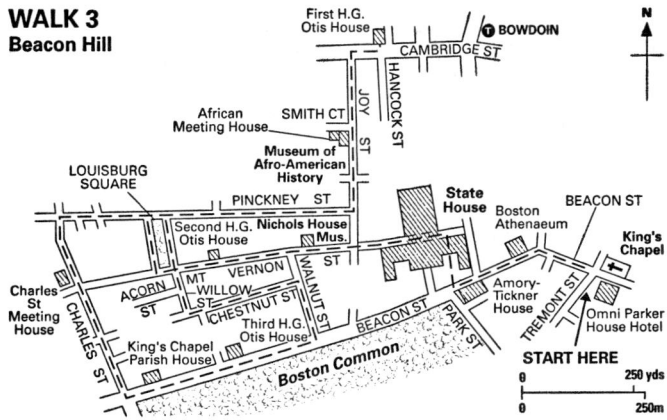

After circuiting the square, walk back E up Mt. Vernon a few steps and down narrow Willow St., on the opposite side. Have a camera ready, for the next corner on the right is **Acorn St.**, a constricted lane that is one of the most charmingly compact and unspoiled blocks in the city. Its scaled-down houses face garden walls of their larger Mt. Vernon neighbors; they were once home to craftspeople and tradesmen whose services were required by wealthier clients on the bigger streets. Turn left, uphill, on Chestnut St.

In a few steps, notice the purple glass in the windows at **#29a**: Bulfinch again. This is the oldest building on this side of The Hill. Those violet panes, the result of excess manganese used during their manufacture in England, were at first deplored but then became fashionable. Homeowners began to specify the tinted glass — as will be seen elsewhere on this walk. Edwin Booth lived here for a while. The greatest actor of his era, he is more often remembered as the older brother of John Wilkes Booth, assassin of Abraham Lincoln.

At the top of Chestnut St., on the right, is a Quaker meetinghouse. Turn right on Walnut St., right again on Beacon, overlooking The Common once again. Be alert to the daredevil rollerbladers who like to sail down this slope. At **#45** is the third of the three houses designed by Bulfinch for Harrison Gray Otis. At #63–64 are two more bow-front buildings with panes of that prestigious purple glass, the **King's Chapel Parish House** and **Rectory**.

At the bottom of the hill, turn right on **Charles St.**, a commercial thoroughfare that in other cities might by now have succumbed to the tackier manifestations of tourism: T-shirt shops, fast-food stands and the rest of it. Here, so far at any rate, they are conspicuously absent. Instead, the merchants of Charles St. continue to serve neighborhood residents, with a pleasing collection of bookstores, greengrocers, bakeries, antique emporia, a friendly tavern or two, and moderately priced restaurants.

Time for a snack or a meal? A likely candidate coming up on the right is **Rebecca's** *(21 Charles St., map 11 E9* ☎ *742-9747)*, the most favored unit of a local chain. Open daily for lunch and dinner, it is especially popular for Saturday and Sunday brunch.

On the w side, at the corner of Mt. Vernon, is the **Charles Street Meeting House**, a former church by Asher Benjamin, a contemporary of Bulfinch. In 1804, when it was built, the Charles River nearly lapped at its foundation. Among those who mounted its pulpit were William Lloyd Garrison and his fellow abolitionists Sojourner Truth and Harriet Tubman. It has been converted into shops and offices. At the next corner, turn right (E) up Pinckney St.

That familiar quote from American history books, "Millions for defense, but not one cent for tribute," was penned by the revolutionary politician Charles E. Pinckney in 1797, when French officials refused to meet his peace delegation without first receiving bribes. Although he had no Boston connection, Pinckney was regarded as an admirable statesman, and the new street was named in his honor. It climbs steeply past the N end of Louisburg Sq. At **#24** is an unusual house renovated in 1884 by William Ralph Emerson, nephew of the poet Ralph Waldo. The differing sizes and placement of the windows and doors anticipated 20thC architectural motifs by decades. Farther on, at **#5** and **#7** are two of the few surviving wooden houses, dating from c.1790.

Turn left (N) on **Joy St.** Named after a landowning apothecary, this street was central to the early African-American community of the North Slope. Today, the neighborhood retains a Bohemian image, in stark contrast to the patrician gentility of the South Slope traveled earlier in this walk. The buildings of Joy St. are far less homogeneous in aspect, and gentrification is only starting to claim them from the mix of college students and blue-collar workers who have long crowded into them.

By far the most important block in local African-American history is **Smith Court**, two blocks down Joy St. On what amounts to a short mews are seven buildings of profound significance.

On the near corner is the **Abiel Smith School** *(46 Joy St.)*, the first formal school for black students in Boston, opened in 1835; before then, they had been taught in private homes and in the church next door to the school. When the state legislature outlawed school segregation in 1855, the Abiel Smith School was closed. Today it is the **Museum of Afro-American History**.

Next door, at 8 Smith Court, is the 1806 **African Meeting House** *(for ⚑ ☎ 742-1854)*, the oldest surviving black church edifice in the US, which also served as a classroom until the opening of the adjacent Abiel Smith School. In 1832, the New England Anti-Slavery Society was founded here, at the urging of William Lloyd Garrison.

Opposite the school and meeting house are five residences, built of clapboard or brick and characteristic of those available to black citizens in the early 19thC. The oldest is **#3**, built in 1799. By the time tenements such as the one at the w end of Smith Court were being built to house the immigrants of the 1880s and '90s, blacks on the North Slope had started moving to the communities of Roxbury and the South End.

Continue down Joy St., emerging on busy Cambridge St. Turn right. At Hancock St., cross Cambridge — carefully! — to the free-standing Federal house opposite, the **HARRISON GRAY OTIS HOUSE** ( 𝙓 *obligatory, on the hour, Tues-Fri noon–5pm, Sat 10am–5pm*). It is the first of three houses designed by Bulfinch for Harrison Gray Otis, in 1796, and the only one of the Otis houses open to the public.

Taxis are fairly easy to obtain on Cambridge. The nearest **T** station is Bowdoin, two blocks to the E. **GOVERNMENT CENTER** and **FANEUIL HALL MARKETPLACE** are about ten minutes' farther on, walking in the same direction.

## WALK 4: BACK BAY

*Allow 1½ hours. See color map **10**G7–**11**F9 and WALK 4 map, page 83.*
**T** *Arlington (Green Line).*
• *See also entry on BACK BAY on page 92.*

At the time of the Revolution, the entire Back Bay district was a marshy bulge in the Charles River, good only as a hunting ground for ducks and other game birds. A dam was built in 1814, roughly parallel to Beacon St., to harness tidal power for factories and mills. The expected benefits from the dammed land did not materialize, so from 1852 the land was reclaimed, over a period of 30 years, moving W from the edge of the Boston Common. House-building began almost as soon as the earth settled. Fortunately, a master plan was already in place, stipulating a grid plan with broad central boulevards and sharply restricting the presence of industry and commerce.

Back Bay is a large neighborhood, and this walk provides only a taste. Further explorations W and N of this route can be rewarding as long as you bear in mind that most of the district is residential and of interest primarily to admirers of late 19thC architecture. Many distinguished architects of the time made contributions to the area, notably the New York firm of McKim, Mead & White, and Boston's own H.H. Richardson. Lending order to the neighborhood are the north–south streets, which ascend from Arlington, bordering the Public Garden, through Berkeley, Clarendon, Dartmouth, Exeter, and on to Hereford.

Starting at the Arlington **T** station, on the corner with Boylston St., walk W on Boylston St. past the **Arlington Street Church**. Looking up ahead and to the left, notice how the mirrored **JOHN HANCOCK TOWER**, the city's most distinguished skyscraper, dominates the scene. In front of it, much lower, but still higher than most around it, is the original **JOHN HANCOCK BUILDING**, with its stepped pyramidal cap and spire. (Both buildings have observation decks, if you wish to detour when you reach them.)

At Berkeley St., the next intersection, the building on the SE corner is the 1905 **Berkeley Building**, an early exploration of the possibilities of steel-frame construction, the turn-of-the-century technique that supplanted the practice of weight-bearing masonry walls. This one is decked out in Beaux-Arts style, with a pronounced Neo-Gothic flair. Across the street is the **F.A.O. Schwartz toy store**, with its big bronze statue of a teddy bear playing with alphabet blocks. And diagonally opposite the

Berkeley, on the NW corner, stands a building now called **Louis** after the upmarket men's clothier currently in occupation there. Three stories high, with brick pilasters bracketing horseshoe-arched windows and supporting the roofline pediment, it was constructed in 1862 for the Society of Natural History. It is surrounded by an unusual amount of open space.

At the next corner, Clarendon St., pause to look down one of the most photographed streets in Boston. Directly ahead is the massive redstone Romanesque TRINITY CHURCH of Henry Hobson Richardson, considered to be his ultimate creation. From this angle it is reflected in the JOHN HANCOCK TOWER, providing a prominent example of the way old and new architecture cohabits, successfully, for the most part, in Boston. Another angle will be presented later.

For the moment, turn right (N) on Clarendon. In one block is a turreted Teutonic pile of the sort favored by wealthy citizens of the late Victorian period. Turn left on Newbury St., one of the glossiest of Boston's shopping streets. The first and second floors are given over to boutiques and art and antiques galleries, interspersed with cafés that set out tables on fine days. If you are an enthusiastic shopper you may wish to return here on a separate occasion.

Turn left (S) on Dartmouth St. In one block is another photo opportunity combining John Hancock Tower, Trinity Church and COPLEY SQUARE. With those two imposing structures, plus the 1912 **Copley Plaza Hotel** on the S side and the 1895 BOSTON PUBLIC LIBRARY closing the W end, Copley Square is among the noblest examples of contained urban expanses found in North America. As an extra fillip, there is the 1875 **New Old South Church** on the nearby corner of Boylston and Dartmouth. Its delightfully excessive Victorian Gothic presence is accentuated by the pointed windows, spires and campanile, as well as the striking Italianate lantern above the crossing of the nave and transept.

Retrace your steps to Newbury St., cross to the far side and turn left. At the edge of the parking lot there, the side of a building supports a three-story *trompe l'oeil* mural that pretends to be the front of a Back Bay mansion. The balconies, veranda and windows of the "mansion" are populated by famous people, not all of them Bostonians. On the left side of the porch are familiar politicians, including John F. Kennedy and John Adams. In a window up above, for no obvious reason, is Rembrandt, and in another, Raul Revere. Bette Davis, Sammy Davis, Jr., and Ray Bolger in his Scarecrow "Oz" disguise are on view, as are baseball great Babe Ruth, conductor Leonard Bernstein and Ben Franklin. There are dozens more, providing a name-that-celeb game that can last a half-hour. When you've finished playing, proceed W on Newbury.

At the intersection with Exeter, on the left, is the Harvard Bookstore Cafe *(map 10 G7* ☎ *536-0095, open Mon-Thurs 8am-11pm, Fri and Sat 8am-midnight, Sun noon-11pm).* Its name is an accurate description, apart from the fact it has no affiliation whatever with the university across the river. Browse, then choose a sandwich, settle in at an outside table and make up histories for passersby. Opposite is a Romanesque Revival building that used to be the Exeter Theater, dating from 1885. On its ground floor now is a bar-restaurant; above it is a bookstore.

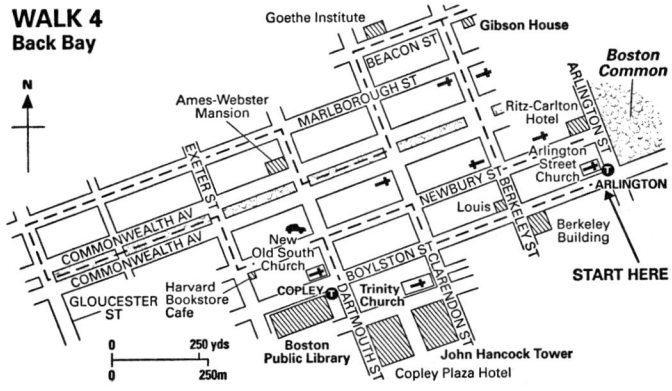

Turn right (N) on Exeter. The next avenue, not counting the service alley that runs behind the length of Newbury, is Commonwealth Ave., the spine of Back Bay. The green strip down the center promenade, planted with trees, is part of Frederick Law Olmsted's **Emerald Necklace** greenway. Cross over to it and turn left, walking down the middle of the greenway. This linear park is used in part as a commemorative concourse, with statues of persons thought deserving of the honor by some group or other. A few actually are, such as the one first encountered. This one depicts a man in a cap and slicker sitting atop a prow of rock. He is Samuel Eliot Morison, a Harvard professor and historian celebrated for his Pulitzer Prize-winning books on naval warfare and exploration.

Near the center of the same block, at **#217** on the N side, is a Renaissance Revival building, larger than the adjacent mansions and faced with a different material. A double porch with Ionic columns catches the eye at the center of the facade, as does the deeply carved decorative frieze above the fourth floor. The building was designed by Stanford White, a New York architect much in demand until his murder by a jealous husband in 1906.

The Classical Revival mode also informs the outsized six-story building at **#270**, one block farther, on the s side. Once a hotel and now a student dormitory, it employs Greco-Roman motifs, notably for the entrance, which resembles a triumphal gate suitable at least for Caesar's brother-in-law. Most of the windows have triangular or eyebrow pediments, and the meticulously worked cornice is particularly attractive.

At Gloucester St., cross over and walk N. Turn right (E) on Marlborough. This is the prettiest, most residential and least spoiled of Back Bay streets. Illuminated by gaslamps and lined with magnolia and aged conifers spreading over the wavy brick sidewalks, it retains a large measure of its late 19thC ambience. The streetlights here and on Beacon Hill have been left on 24 hours a day since it was found to be cheaper than hiring people to light them every night and douse them each morning.

Leaving Marlborough's tranquility, turn right at Dartmouth. At the corner (**#164**) is what must be the most banal of H.H. Richardson's many commissions, built in 1870. The huge **Ames-Webster Mansion** at the next corner was built in 1872 for a congressman and expanded to its present size a decade later for a subsequent owner. Reputed to possess a domed skylight by John La Farge and a spectacular grand staircase and ballroom, it is now used for offices and is regrettably not open to the public. Cross to the central strip of Commonwealth and turn left (E).

A house on the N side, **#121**, deviates markedly from the Back Bay norm. In what is known as Ruskin Gothic, it employs several different facing materials and considerably more decorative detail, especially as the eye moves up to the pointed dormers jutting from the mansard roof. Turn left (N) on Clarendon and right on Beacon. On the opposite side, at #170, is the **Goethe Institute**, a German cultural center offering films, lectures and concerts to the public ( ☎ 262-6050). If the ensuing blocks seem to have a livelier, casual air, attribute that to the presence of students of **Emerson College**, which commands several buildings in this area. The college is noted for its courses in film and television, and budding movie-makers are nearly always in evidence, training their cameras on fellow-students they have induced to perform.

In the middle of the S side of the street, after Berkeley, is one of the oldest homes in Back Bay and the only one regularly open to the public. **Gibson House** *(137 Beacon St., map 11 F8 ☎ 267-6338; mandatory* **✗** *at 1, 2 and 3pm May 1-Oct 31 Wed-Sun, Nov 1-Apr 30 Sat and Sun only.)* Built for the Gibson family in 1860, they occupied it for nearly a century, until 1956, when it became a museum. The interiors and furnishings are authentic to their 19thC origins.

Finally, retrace your steps to Berkeley and turn left (S). In three blocks, turn left on Newbury, coming soon to the august **Ritz-Carlton Hotel**. If you are properly attired and it is late afternoon, the famous Ritz high tea of finger sandwiches, scones, pastries and properly brewed and warmed pots of tea is the perfect treat to top this stroll through Victorian Boston. Otherwise, turn right to reach the Arlington **T** station.

## WALK 5: HARVARD AND OLD CAMBRIDGE

*Allow 1½ hours. See color map **7**B1–B3 and* WALK 5 *map opposite.* **T** *Harvard (Red Line).*

Cambridge, which was initially called New Towne, was designated capital of the Massachusetts Bay Colony in 1630, the same year as the founding of Boston. It assumed its present name, in honor of the English university town, after John Harvard's bequest of his small library to the existing divinity school. While the present city sprawls along the Charles and incorporates large residential and industrial districts, its core retains many historical structures conveniently near to Harvard Square. That is where this walk begins.

HARVARD SQUARE is, in fact, only the intersection of Massachusetts Ave. and three other streets. An island at its heart contains the **T** station, plus a newsstand selling newspapers and other publications from around the

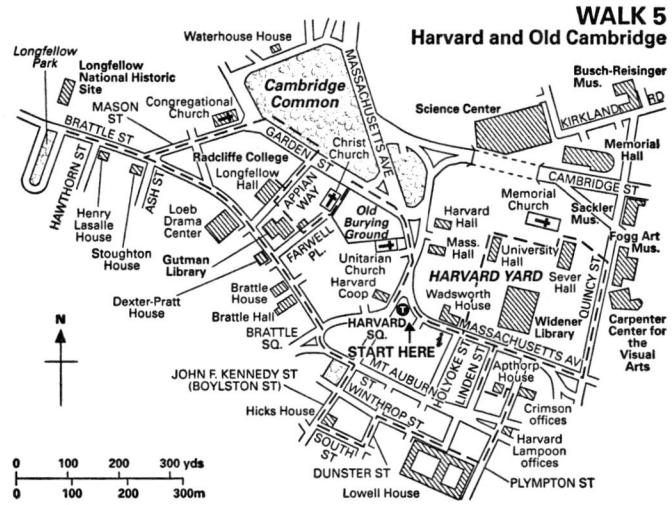

**WALK 5**
**Harvard and Old Cambridge**

country and the world. Even in deepest, dankest winter, the square bustles. But at the first hint of spring, it explodes with activity. A recent renovation provided a small brick arena, taken up most of the year with street musicians and performers of every stripe and level of aptitude. Nearby is a tourist information booth manned by volunteers who hand out maps and brochures and answer questions. This is also the stop for sightseeing trolley tours.

Cross to the other side, where the **Harvard Coop** is located. What started as a store for textbooks and classroom materials has grown into a small department store that attracts at least as many tourists as students. (It also has, on the second floor, two of the very few public rest rooms available around the square.) Walk right (N) in front of the Coop on Massachusetts Ave. Across the way is the oldest part of the Harvard campus, to which this route will return. Soon, on the left, is a tan-colored wooden **Unitarian church** built in subdued Gothic style in 1833, the fifth on this site. Beyond it is the **Old Burying Ground**, a.k.a. "God's Acre." It contains a numbers of colonists and early Harvard presidents, as well as white and black soldiers of the Continental Army, some of them killed at the battle for Breed's Hill.

Bear left around the cemetery. At the end of the iron fence is **Christ Church**, designed by Peter Harrison, who was also responsible for King's Chapel in Boston (see WALK 1, page 69). Future President Teddy Roosevelt taught Sunday School classes here while attending Harvard. Completed in 1761, it was the first non-Puritan church in Cambridge and is one of only two surviving pre-Revolutionary buildings facing **Cambridge Common**, the large green now seen over to the right.

Turn left along the path between the burial ground and the church. This empties into Farwell Place, behind the church, a short block of mostly clapboard houses. Down on the right, the gray house with white trim and green shutters is the 1827 **Nichols House**. The titular occupant was a battlefield surgeon during the Civil War. Just beyond it, turn right on the brick path that leads past its front door into a small grassy area. The modern concrete building on the left is the **Gutman Library**, a unit of the largest university library in North America. The small wooden house over to the right dates from 1772.

Appian Way is the next street; turn right a few steps, then cross over and enter the brick-pillared gateway to the right of **Longfellow Hall**. In back of the hall is the quadrangle of RADCLIFFE COLLEGE, which was founded in 1879 with the intent of providing young women with an education of the same rigor and high standards as Harvard. The two institutions merged in 1965, but Radcliffe graduates still receive diplomas from both. Return to Appian Way and turn left. Straight ahead is Cambridge Common.

Cross over Garden St. onto the s side of the Common, toward the Civil War monument with a statue of Lincoln, turning left to approach a set of three British cannon captured in 1775. Beside them is a tablet alleging that Washington first took command of the Continental Army under the nearby elm. Even if this tree had been a mere sapling on July 3, 1775, it would now be towering over the Common. It doesn't, so it is obviously a 20thC replacement. Continue past the cannon. Glance N toward the far end of the park. The small gray house over there, **Waterhouse House** (sic), is the only residence erected beside the Common before the Revolution: Dr. Benjamin Waterhouse, who lived there during the Revolution, introduced smallpox vaccination to the US in 1800.

Cross the street at the next corner, where a stone **Congregational church** stands. Although relatively young (dating only from 1870), the weathervane on its steeple has been dated to 1721. Walk down Mason St., left of the church. It soon merges with **Brattle St.**, known as "Tory Row" in the 18thC when it was lined with dwellings occupied by Loyalists to the British Crown. Today it is still a street of the privileged, although most of the grand houses now on view date from the last century.

Bear right. At #105 is the 1759 LONGFELLOW NATIONAL HISTORIC SITE, used by Washington as his headquarters for several months from mid-1775 to early 1776. However, the mansion is named after the poet, who first lived there as a boarder in 1837. Longfellow purchased the house in 1843 and lived there until his death in 1882. The yellow building with white trim and black shutters (illustrated opposite) is as well maintained as it looks, largely because Longfellow's descendants lived there until 1974 and had the funds to maintain it. Across the road is **Longfellow Park**, which runs down to what was, in the poet's time, the edge of the Charles River. In his will, Longfellow stipulated that the grassy mall be kept open and undeveloped.

There are many further attractive houses to be seen along Brattle St. Energetic walkers may wish to continue about half a mile farther w as far the 1688 **Hopper-Lee-Nichols House** *(open Tues and Thurs 2-5pm)*. In

The Georgian
**Longfellow National
Historic Site**

any event, return on the opposite side of Brattle toward Harvard Sq. After
one block, at the corner of Hawthorn St., is the 1746 **Henry Lasalle
House**. Often hanging at the front of the house is a flag that incorporates
the Union Jack and the familiar red-and-white stripes of the eventual
American banner. This was the standard that the Continental Army carried
well into the Revolution.

At the next corner, Ash St., is the shingled **Stoughton House** (1883),
by H.H. Richardson, the late 19thC architect of TRINITY CHURCH in Boston
who briefly abandoned his brick Romanesque style for this commission
for an important local family.

Note that most of the street signs in this area also give the names of
the streets in the 17thC. Brattle St., for example, was Watertown Lane in
1634. Continuing, the contemporary concrete edifice on the right is the
**Loeb Drama Center**, which shelters a respected repertory theater mount-
ing classical and modern plays.

In the next block is the **Dexter-Pratt House** (1808), once the home
of the blacksmith made famous by Longfellow ("Under the spreading
chestnut tree, the village smitty stands . . . "). It is now a bakery and a café
with outdoor tables in good weather, and marks the edge of the shopping
district around Brattle Sq. Soon, on the right, is **Brattle House**, the home
of the eponymous lawyer and preacher, who was also an officer in the
militia until his loyalist convictions forced him to leave the area in 1774.
At #40 is **Brattle Hall**, a dining-and-entertainment center containing an
art/revival cinema, bars and restaurants. Continue straight ahead, crossing Brattle Sq. to Mt. Auburn St., opposite. In one block, turn right on
what is known both as John F. Kennedy and Boylston St. The small park
there was once New Towne Market, identified as such by an architectural
fragment in the center.

In two blocks, cross over into South St., marked by the white frame
**Hicks House** (1762), named after a former owner who was said to have
been a participant in the Boston Tea Party. He was killed by British troops
in 1775. In one block, turn left (N) on Dunster St., then right (E) on
Winthrop. The Georgian-Revival **Lowell House** at the next corner is one
of Harvard's dormitories. Walk along its N side, through the iron gate,
down the stairs out to Plympton St. and turn left.

The mock château squatting in lone splendor at the next intersection, diagonally across Mt. Auburn, is home to the *Harvard Lampoon,* the university's satirical magazine, which has witnessed the beginning of many literary careers. Note the stork weathervane atop the w end of the "castle." Continuing up Plympton, halfway up the block on the right is the office of the more solemn Harvard publication, the *Crimson,* a daily newspaper.

Opposite is an anonymous brick building masking a large white wooden structure, the 1760 **Apthorp House**. British General Burgoyne and his officers were confined here in 1777 after their defeat at Saratoga, in New York. Enter the garden to the left of the stone marker providing this information, bearing left, then right, around the front of the house. It may feel like trespassing, but it isn't — these are university buildings. Exiting into Linden St., turn right. At Massachusetts Ave., turn left.

The next corner is Holyoke St. The old yellow house on the opposite side of Mass Ave., at #1341, is **Wadsworth House**, residence of the Harvard presidents from 1726 until 1849. Cross over at the light. Bear right of Wadsworth House to enter the HARVARD UNIVERSITY gate, which displays the head of a wild boar centered in the arch. This leads into hallowed **Harvard Yard**, probably the most famous campus quadrangle in America. Most buildings around the quad are 19thC, but if you walk straight ahead, the two brick buildings on the left, bordering another entrance, are much earlier. The nearest one is **Massachusetts Hall**, dating from 1720, and the one parallel, to the N, is **Harvard Hall**, from 1766.

Now look right. Standing out from the other buildings is the pale granite **University Hall**, designed by Charles Bulfinch in 1815. In front of it is a seated statue purporting to depict John Harvard, who bequeathed his library to an existing divinity school. The legend on the pedestal reads *Founder 1638.* The monument is widely known as the "statue of three lies." Lie #1: sculptor Daniel Chester French had no idea what Harvard looked like, so he used a student of the 1880s as a model. Lie #2: Harvard wasn't a founder; he was a benefactor. And lie #3: the institution was founded two years earlier, in 1636.

Walk past University Hall and bear right around the N end. A large **memorial church** from 1931 dominates the N side of the next quadrangle. Down to the right is the **Widener Library**, and directly ahead is massive **Sever Hall**, by H.H. Richardson (1880). Veer left around Sever and look left. In the gap between Memorial Church and another building is seen the massive **Memorial Hall**, an overwrought Victorian Gothic monument (1876) to Harvard men who died in the Civil War. Now bear right across the diagonal path to the gate on Quincy St.

Opposite is the **Fogg Art Museum**, the most prominent of seven Harvard art and science museums open to the public, comprising the HARVARD UNIVERSITY ART MUSEUMS and HARVARD UNIVERSITY NATURAL HISTORY MUSEUMS. Turn right. s of the Fogg is the CARPENTER CENTER FOR THE VISUAL ARTS (1963). Little though it does to enhance the reputation of the revered French architect Le Corbusier, it is the only design of his ever to be completed in the United States, two years before his death.

Quincy leads back s to the intersection of Harvard St. and Mass Ave. Turn right to return to the **T** station at Harvard Square.

# Sightseeing

## Boston's rich patrimony

With a population far below one million, Boston is not a big city, even counting the annual influx of 250,000 college and university students. But because it was one of the first settlements in North America, it has had more than 360 years to accumulate the cultural traditions and material resources that bring in their wake the monuments, parks, theaters, museums and educational institutions of a far larger metropolis.

In North America, only New York can fairly be said to surpass Boston in depth and breadth of patrimony. Combined with its sister city Cambridge, it can preen over more than a dozen museums of art, history and science — too much to be possibly absorbed in a week of the most diligent marching through galleries. In the North End, on Beacon Hill and along Brattle St. in Cambridge are churches and dwellings rife with remembrances of historical figures and ordinary people who helped build a nation from wilderness.

By all means, then, experience the star attractions, but make time also to wander without any rigid plan, contemplating the details and sudden pleasures encountered along the way.

**USEFUL TO KNOW**

**Opening and closing times**    Most museums are closed on Monday, which can be the best day to schedule a visit to the NEW ENGLAND AQUARIUM or to some of the more distant sights, such as the JOHN F. KENNEDY LIBRARY AND MUSEUM, the FRANKLIN PARK ZOO or the ARNOLD ARBORETUM. Museums and historic houses often close rooms for repair or new installations. During the winter, opening hours are usually shorter, and buildings may be closed entirely on some weekdays or even for a month or two. To avoid disappointment, call ahead before making a special journey.

**Ticket prices**    Most of the museums and historic buildings are run by nonprofit organizations, which is not to imply that admission prices are inexpensive. However, ticket prices are nearly always lower for senior citizens, children and students, and several museums have free hours on Friday evening or Saturday morning.

**Getting there**    Boston's largely praiseworthy public transportation system — the MBTA — reaches within a few blocks of at least 90 percent of the sights listed on these pages. In the entries that follow, the nearest subway or streetcar station is indicated by a **T**, as the rapid transit network

# Boston's sights, classified by type

Every item in these lists can be found in this SIGHTSEEING chapter, either via the alphabetical headings or through the INDEX.

Two symbols are used, for easy reference: the ★ symbol, meaning "Recommended sight" (for the most important sights), and the ⑪ symbol, meaning "Building of architectural interest."

Two lists worth pointing out are VIEWPOINTS (for outstanding views of the city) and YOUNG INTEREST (places of special interest for children). Many places (for example, the Faneuil Hall Marketplace) appear in more than one list.

## DISTRICTS, SQUARES AND STREETS
Back Bay ★ ⑪
Bay Village
Beacon Hill ★ ⑪
Charlestown
Chinatown
Combat Zone
Copley Square ★ ⑪
Downtown Crossing
The Embankment ★
Financial District
Government Center ⑪
Harvard Square ★
Kenmore Square
Louisburg Square ★ ⑪
North End ★
Post Office Square
South End

## PARKS, GARDENS AND OPEN SPACES
Arnold Arboretum
Back Bay Fens
Boston Common ★
Cambridge Common
Castle Island Park
Christopher Columbus
   Waterfront Park
Franklin Park and Zoo
Georges Island
Harbor Islands State
   Park
Mount Auburn Cemetery
Post Office Square
Public Garden ★

## CHURCHES
Christian Science Center ⑪
King's Chapel
Old North Church ⑪
Old South Church
Park Street Congregational Church
St Stephen's Church ⑪
Trinity Church ★ ⑪

## FAMOUS HOMES
Isabella Stewart Gardner
   Museum ★ ⑪
Longfellow National Historic
   Site ★ ⑪
Harrison Gray Otis House ⑪
Pierce-Richborn House
Paul Revere House

## HISTORIC BUILDINGS
Boston Public Library ⑪
Bulfinch Pavilion / Ether Dome
Custom House
Faneuil Hall ★ ⑪
Old City Hall
Old Corner Book Store
Old State House ★ ⑪
State House ★ ⑪
Symphony Hall ⑪

## MUSEUMS AND GALLERIES
Bell History Center
Boston Athenaeum
Boston Center for the Arts
Boston Public Library ⑪
Charlestown Navy Yard
Children's Museum

Computer Museum
Isabella Stewart Gardner
    Museum ★ 🏛
Hart Nautical Museum
Harvard University Art Museums
Harvard University Natural History
    Museums
Institute of Contemporary Art
John F. Kennedy Library and
    Museum 🏛
List Visual Art Center
MIT Museum
Museum of Fine Arts ★
Old State House ★ 🏛
USS Constitution Museum

### SCIENCE AND TECHNOLOGY
Bell History Center
Children's Museum
Christian Science Center 🏛
Computer Museum
Charles Hayden Planetarium
MIT Museum
Museum of Science

### MODERN (20thC) BUILDINGS
Boston Architectural Center
Boston City Hall 🏛
Carpenter Center for the Visual
    Arts
Christian Science Center 🏛
Faneuil Hall Marketplace ★ 🏛
Government Center 🏛
John Hancock Building
John Hancock Tower ★ 🏛
John F. Kennedy Library and
    Museum 🏛
Prudential Center

### MONUMENTS AND CEMETERIES
Boston Massacre Monument
Bunker Hill Monument
Central Burying Ground
Copp's Hill Burying Ground
Mount Auburn Cemetery
Old Granary Burying Ground

### GENERAL AND/OR HISTORIC INTEREST
"Cheers" (Bull & Finch Pub)
Boston Garden arena

Boston Tea Party Ship & Museum
Boston University
Bunker Hill Pavilion
Charlestown Navy Yard
Faneuil Hall Marketplace ★ 🏛
Fenway Park stadium
The Freedom Trail ★
Harvard University ★ 🏛
Massachusetts Institute of
    Technology
New England Aquarium ★
Radcliffe College
USS Constitution

### LANDMARKS
Callahan and Sumner Tunnels
Charles River
Harvard Bridge
Hatch Memorial Hall
Long Wharf
Longfellow Bridge
North Station
Rowe's Wharf

### VIEWPOINTS ⇜
Bunker Hill Monument
Copp's Hill Burying Ground
Georges Island
John Hancock Building
John Hancock Tower
John F. Kennedy Library and
    Museum
Longfellow Bridge
Prudential Center

### YOUNG INTEREST ⚶
Boston Tea Party Ship & Museum
Children's Museum
Computer Museum
Faneuil Hall Marketplace
Franklin Park and Zoo
Georges Island
Harbor Islands State Park
John Hancock Building
    observation deck
John Hancock Tower observatory
Charles Hayden Planetarium
Mapparium
Museum of Science
New England Aquarium
Prudential Center observation deck

is familiarly known, followed in parentheses by the line or lines that serve that station. In a few clearly indicated cases, it is necessary to take a bus, or a walk of perhaps more than five or six blocks.

#### HOW TO USE THIS A TO Z SECTION
- The entries are arranged in alphabetical order. Titles that include a person's name are alphabetized by family name (surname), ignoring first names: thus, look for ISABELLA STEWART GARDNER MUSEUM under G for Gardner (not I for Isabella).
- Cross-references to other entries or to other sections of the book are printed in SMALL CAPITALS, often with page references.
- If you cannot find a particular entry in the following A to Z, try the INDEX. Some lesser sights do not have their own entries but are included within other entries: you can find them via the INDEX.
- Look for the ★ symbol next to the most important sights and 🏛 for buildings of architectural interest. Good views (◀€) and places of interest for children (❀) are also indicated.
- The availability of guided tours is shown by 𝒓, followed by any useful details.
- **For a full explanation of all the symbols used in this book, see page 7.**

# Sights A to Z

## ARNOLD ARBORETUM
*The Arborway and Centre St., Jamaica Plain. Map 5E2* ☎524-1717 ▣ 𝒓 *on Sun in May–June and Sept–Oct. Open daily sunrise to sunset.* **T** *Forest Hills (Orange Line), then a short walk on The Arborway.*
Part of Frederick Law Olmsted's "Emerald Greenway," this 265-acre park and botanical garden is owned and administered by Harvard University. About 7,000 species of plants, shrubs and trees crowd the rolling property, including a bonsai collection.

Obviously, the months to make the longish **T** ride are from April to early October. A day in late May is designated "Lilac Day," the unofficial start of Boston's spring. Before setting out, call the number above to find out which flowers are in bloom.

## BACK BAY ★ 🏛
*S of the Charles River, map* **9–10**; *see also* WALK 4 *map on page 83.* **T** *Arlington, Copley or Hynes Convention Center/ICA (Green Line).*
Until the middle of the last century, Back Bay was just that — a bulge in the Charles River that nearly cut off peninsular Boston from the mainland. Experiments in harnessing the tidal power of the estuary had proved disappointing, and the malodorous mud flats and marshes did little otherwise to enhance the urban experience.

A dam had already been built across the bay in 1821, in effect an extension of Beacon St., to what is now Kenmore Sq., and railroad beds cut across the enclosed water by 1835, so partial control of the tidal flow was already in place. It was decided to fill the entire expanse, a total of more than 600 acres. Emerging technologies of the Industrial Revolution were of considerable benefit, including the railroads and early versions of earth-moving machinery propelled by steam. Work on this vast project began in 1852.

Fortunately, a master plan of parallel streets with a central grand promenade was soon in place, for houses and churches started going up almost as soon as the landfill settled. Between 1860 and 1890, 32 schools and churches were erected, and the newly fashionable streets were lined with the Victorian mansions of the wealthy and well-to-do.

- See WALK 4: BACK BAY for a short (approximately $1\frac{1}{2}$-hour) walk around the district.

## THE BACK BAY FENS
*Map 9I5–10G6.*

In 1880, as the development of Back Bay was nearing completion, Frederick Law Olmsted came to town on a mission. His towering reputation as a landscape architect was already established, with the success of his designs for Central and Prospect Parks in New York City, soon to be followed by other projects in Buffalo, Montréal and Chicago. His task here was to transform the sluggish, polluted Muddy River into parkland.

He did better than that, creating his famed "Emerald Necklace" of connected green spaces. It wound from the Boston Common all the way to the ARNOLD ARBORETUM and FRANKLIN PARK, over nine meandering miles to the s. Swamps were drained, and dozens of species of trees and decorative marsh grasses were planted to overhang riffled ponds and the drifting stream.

It was an irresistible setting for many of the city's foremost cultural institutions. The MUSEUM OF FINE ARTS and ISABELLA STEWART GARDNER MUSEUM stand at the water's edge, as do a number of schools and colleges, and the large complex of hospitals that have clustered around Harvard Medical School.

Sadly, The Fens also curl through neighborhoods that are best not traversed on foot, especially after dark, and much of it has been too long neglected.

## BAY VILLAGE
*Map 11G9.* **T** *Arlington (Green Line).*

An unexpected enclave of compact rowhouses stands at the edge of the Theater District, about six square blocks E of Arlington St., W of Charles St., S of Stuart St. and N of Tremont St. Built in the early 19thC, it looks like a pocket-sized version of Beacon Hill, complete with brick sidewalks and gas street lamps. Author Edgar Allen Poe lived here for a time. The slow decline of the neighborhood was arrested in the 1950s, when individuals interested in historical preservation began to restore the houses as homes and offices. Bay Village deserves a short detour if you are in the area.

# BEACON HILL ★ ▥

*Map 11E9; see also* WALK 3 *map on page 79.* **T** *Park Street (Green Line) or Charles/MGH (Red Line).*
From 1625, when William Blackstone became the first European to live on the Shawmut Peninsula, until the late 18thC, there was at this site a knobby elevation with three summits called the Trimountain. The highest crest held a beacon meant to sound the alarm when there was threat of an attack; that is the source of the present name. Even when work began on the STATE HOUSE in 1795, there were only a handful of houses on what was destined to become the most desirable residential neighborhood in Boston. In the ensuing development of the next two decades, the three hills were scraped and molded into one, losing an estimated 110 feet in elevation. The resulting tons of earth were used as landfill in the Charles River, pushing the waterline well beyond Charles St., on the W, and removing the Mill Pond that stood between the North End and the Old West End.

The acclaim that attended the completion of Charles Bulfinch's gold-domed State House led to his many commissions for private homes on Beacon Hill. With some exceptions, other architects imitated his Federalist style, and the Hill remains enchantingly harmonious in aspect, with its gaslights, shade trees, cobblestoned streets and brick rowhouses with flourishing gardens front and back. Charles Dickens, who detested most of what he encountered in America, loved Beacon Hill, perhaps because it reminded him of parts of London. While the neighborhood is often associated with the wealthy Brahmin class, it was also home and frequent meeting place of the intellectual and artistic elite of the middle decades of the 19thC. Henry James, Louisa May Alcott, William Dean Howells, Edwin Booth, Jenny Lind and Francis Parkman were all residents for various periods.

Quite different demographic patterns pertained on the S, or State House, slope of the Hill and the opposite side. At the same time that the Brahmins were having their grand residences built, the N slope was becoming humbler home to many of Boston's African-American citizens. In time, they moved to outlying areas, and university students, blue-collar families, and persons who favored bohemian lifestyles took their places. Elements of all these influences persist, although signs of gentrification of the N slope are increasing.

- See WALK 3: BEACON HILL for a short (approximately one-hour) walk around the district.

# BELL HISTORY CENTER
*New England Telephone Building, 185 Franklin St. (Pearl and Congress Sts.), Boston. Map 12F11* ☎743-0795 🖭 *Open Mon–Fri 8.30am–5pm. Closed Sat; Sun.* **T** *State or Downtown Crossing (Orange Line)*
The New England Telephone Building, on the S side of POST OFFICE SQUARE, preserves a scrap of 19thC technological history. Inside the front doors on Franklin St. and immediately to the right is the attic room in which Alexander Graham Bell transmitted the first sounds of speech over an electrical wire, on June 3, 1875.

The room reassembled here was originally on the fifth floor of a building at 109 Court St. Before that building was demolished in the late 1920s, Bell's assistant Thomas Watson supervised the dismantling of the room, including the workbench, floor, ceiling — even the window. Each piece was numbered so it could be put back together when a suitable location was found. On the bench are several of the devices used by the inventor, and in one wall is a trophy case containing, among other items, the first switchboard and replicas of early telephones.

## BOSTON ARCHITECTURAL CENTER
*320 Newbury St. (Hereford St.), Boston. Map 10G7* ☎*536-3170* ▣ *Open Mon–Thurs 9am–10pm; Fri 9am–8pm; Sat 9am–5pm; Sun noon–5pm. T Hynes Convention Center/ICA (Green Line).*

The neighbors can't have been pleased with this intruder. While the 1967 cast concrete building is hardly a blot on the short history of modern architecture, it sticks out like a throbbing thumb in its immediate neighborhood of brick and granite rowhouses and shops. The *trompe l'oeil* mural on the w wall is some compensation.

## BOSTON ATHENAEUM
*10½ Beacon St. (Bowdoin St.), Boston. Map 12E10* ☎*227-0270* ▣ ✗ *on Tues and Thurs, by appointment. Open Mon–Fri 9am–4pm; Sat (Oct–May only) 9am–4pm. Closed Sun; major holidays. T Park Street (Green or Red Line).*

A Greek Revival building near the STATE HOUSE on BEACON HILL contains a library begun in 1807 by the Anthology Society, a group committed to advancing culture and higher learning. This building — the fifth one the society moved into, in 1847, after outgrowing five others — housed the society's expanding accumulations of books and artworks, among them the American and European paintings that eventually formed the core collection of the MUSEUM OF FINE ARTS.

Works by Gilbert Stuart, John Singer Sargent and other artists remain in the Athenaeum's possession and are displayed throughout the building. In the vestibule is a statue of George Washington and a large painting of Daniel Webster, the prominent 19thC political leader famed for his oratory. Portions of the personal libraries of the first president are included among the 700,000 volumes contained on the five floors. Prints, architectural plans, drawings, posters, photographs and maps, most of them from the 19thC, are among the related items stored here.

• While most of the first floor and parts of the second are open to the public, this is a private organization and access to other sections is limited. The best way to see more is by guided tour.

## BOSTON CENTER FOR THE ARTS
*539 Tremont St. (Berkeley St.), Boston. Off map 11G8* ☎*426-5000* ▣ *Open Mon–Fri 9am–5pm. Closed Sat; Sun. T Back Bay/South End (Orange Line).*

Five buildings in the gentrifying South End constitute the Center, incorporating art studios, four performance spaces that range in seating capacity from 40 to 876, an after-school program for children from homeless shelters, and visual arts exhibitions in the Mills Gallery. The primary component is the domed **Cyclorama**, which was originally built to house a 400-by-50-foot circular 1884 painting of the Battle of Gettysburg during the Civil War. For several decades after the painting was removed from this building, the Cyclorama was put to other uses, which included spells as a velodrome and a flower market. Now it is a venue for concerts and other performances, as well as for occasional exhibitions.

## BOSTON CITY HALL  🏛

*Map 12E10.* **T** *Government Center (Blue Line).*
See GOVERNMENT CENTER.

## BOSTON COMMON  ★

*Map 11F9.* **T** *Park Street (Green Line).*
The large park beneath BEACON HILL is usually described in benign terms — how it was preserved for the good of the citizens of the new settlement, with cattle grazing and soldiers drilling, etc. etc. But there was a darker side.

The Puritans were an intolerant lot, and persons judged to have transgressed the community's stiff standards of conduct were punished here, as well. In the early decades, there were pillories, stocks, ducking stools, a gallows, cages and whipping posts used to correct the behavior of scolds, drunks, Sabbath breakers and petty criminals. It is said that the first occupant of some newly built stocks was the carpenter, his bill for his work having been deemed too costly. Hangings of heretics were not infrequent. Mary Dyer, who espoused liberal religious convictions, was one of the first to be executed. There is a statue of her on the lawn of the STATE HOUSE.

Bounded by Charles, Boylston, Tremont, Park and Beacon Sts., the land was sold to the new settlers by William Blackstone (a.k.a. Blaxton), the recluse who lived there for five years before inviting the colonists across the river in Charles Towne to join him. The first European to live in what the local Indians called Shawmut, he soon regretted his action and departed for what was to become Rhode Island, where he was, once again, the first white settler.

The Common today is the site of picnics and frequent municipal celebrations, which often center on the bandstand in Parkman Plaza. Within its 48 acres are a baseball field and tennis courts, the Frog Pond and Brewer Fountain. On the southern edge, near Charles St., is the CENTRAL BURYING GROUND, added to the Common in 1756. Its most famous resident is painter Gilbert Stuart.

Unhappily, the fate of all too many American center-city parks has befallen the Common. Escalating criminal incidents prompted the imposition of a nightly curfew. Judicious visitors will avoid entering the park after dark.

- The Freedom Trail (the formal route for a one- to two-hour historical walk: see WALK 1: THE FREEDOM TRAIL on page 68) starts at the information booth on Tremont St., near the Park Street **T** station.

## BOSTON GARDEN

*150 Causeway St. (Canal St.), Boston. Map **12D10** ☎227-3200 or 227-3206 (for general info.); 720-3434 (for tickets) ▨ ✗ available. Open for scheduled events. T North Station (Orange or Green Line).*

This is the secular house of worship for sports-addicted Bostonians. The creaky old arena is home to the local professional basketball team and hockey squad, to traveling circuses, pop stars and rock groups, and to occasional prizefights. The undisputed resident heroes are the Celtics of the National Basketball Association, winners of 16 championships. The Bruins (typically pronounced "Broons") have been less successful, taking the Stanley Cup five times.

Approaching its 70th birthday, the Garden has no air conditioning and few amenities of modern sports arenas. So, beloved though it is, discussions are underway either to refurbish it or raze it and build a new one.

Behind and below the arena is **North Station**, terminal for trains to the northern suburbs.

## BOSTON MASSACRE MONUMENT

*Map **12E11**; see also WALK 1 map on page 73. T State (Orange or Blue Line).*

A simple circle of paving stones set into a traffic island E of the Old State House marks the spot where British soldiers fired upon an angry mob of colonials, killing five. See WALK 1: THE FREEDOM TRAIL, page 71.

## BOSTON PUBLIC LIBRARY ☷

*666 Boylston St. (Copley Sq.), Boston. Map **10G8** ☎536-5400 ▣ ✗ available. Open Mon–Thurs 9am–9pm; Fri, Sat 9am–5pm. Closed Sun. T Copley (Green Line).*

Taking up the w flank of Copley Sq. and offering a gracefully restrained counterbalance to H.H. Richardson's massive Romanesque Revival TRINITY CHURCH, the library was designed by a Richardson apprentice, Charles Follen McKim. He went on to head the most famous architectural firm of the late 19th and early 20thC, McKim, Mead & White.

The library was founded in 1848, but this building dates from 1895. It is in the Italian Renaissance style popularized by the McKim firm, as in the Villard Houses in Manhattan. But while most of the New York commissions were of dark sandstone, the library used the more readily available granite.

To undergird the *palazzo* character, McKim drew well-known artists of the time into his scheme. Daniel Chester French, sculptor of the statue of Lincoln in his Memorial in Washington, DC, was responsible for the bronze doors of the main entrance; John Singer Sargent painted the murals depicting *Judaism and Christianity* on the third floor. Most impressive, perhaps, is the barrel-vaulted second-floor reading room, **Bates Hall**. It is nearly 220 feet long and 50 feet high, the coffered ceiling richly carved. At the w end of the building is a modern addition (1972) by Philip Johnson. While it doesn't add much esthetically, neither does it unduly detract.

Full programs of films, lectures and exhibitions continue during a phased renovation expected to consume several more years before completion.

## BOSTON TEA PARTY SHIP & MUSEUM

*Congress St. Bridge (Harborwalk), Boston. Map 12F11* ☎ *338-1773* ▨ ✱
*Open daily 9am–6pm in summer; until 5pm in spring and fall. Closed Thanksgiving; Christmas; New Year's Day.* **T** *South Station (Red Line).*

This isn't the actual ship and it isn't moored where the three original merchant ships were berthed that December in 1773, all of which subtracts little from the gleeful participation in a sanitized simulation of an event that hurried the onset of full rebellion. Kids get to put on "Indian" headdresses and heave bales of "tea" over the side of the replicated brig *Beaver II* (which are promptly hauled back aboard by their tethers).

Costumed guides tell the tale of the night that a band of about 50 infuriated tax-resisters, whipped into a lather by speakers at a meeting in Old South Church and led by the fiery Sam Adams, crept along dark streets to the waterfront. They boarded three merchant ships of the British East India Company and proceeded to dump the contents of 343 tea chests into the harbor. The Crown's response was the enactment of the punitive "Intolerable Acts," which, among other things, closed the port to all trade, dispatched 4,000 troops to Boston, and authorized them to demand lodging in private homes.

Among the objects on view on the *Beaver II* is a tea chest "believed" to have been on board that night. The ship is 110 feet long, with 10,200 feet of rigging. A galley, the crew's quarters and the cargo hold are part of the tour. On a day in mid-December, an elaborate re-enactment of the symbolic event is staged.

* A visit to the Tea Party ship, which is moored beside the Congress St. Bridge across Fort Point Channel, can be combined easily with stops at the nearby CHILDREN'S MUSEUM and COMPUTER MUSEUM.

## BOSTON UNIVERSITY

*Map 9G3-4.* **T** *Kenmore (Green Line).*

Founded in 1839, B.U. is one of the region's largest private universities, with more than 28,000 students. Under the controversial leadership of

John R. Silber, who became the university's president in 1971, it has increased its endowment fund from under $19 million to over $370 million and markedly improved its faculty and physical plant. Buildings of the urban campus sprawl between Commonwealth Ave. and Storrow Drive, w of Kenmore Sq.

Dr Martin Luther King, Jr. was a student at the university, and among the holdings of its **Mugar Memorial Library** is a collection of his writings and other papers.

## BULFINCH PAVILION / ETHER DOME
*Massachusetts General Hospital, Fruit and Grove Sts., Boston. Map 11D9.*
*Open Mon–Fri 9am–4pm, unless meetings are in session. Closed Sat; Sun.*
*T Charles/MGH (Red Line)*
Massachusetts General Hospital — "Mass General" — has built its enviable reputation over two centuries. Now a very large complex of several buildings covering several city blocks, it first attracted international notice in 1846, when ether was successfully used for the first time on a patient undergoing surgery. That event took place in the domed amphitheater of this 1823 Greek Revival structure, now dwarfed by the buildings surrounding it.

Charles Bulfinch is credited with the amphitheater's design, although it looks not at all like those in the Federalist style for which he is known. Substantial subsequent alterations and additions are partly to blame. It was his last commission in Boston and is still a working part of the hospital. There are displays of 19thC medical instruments and devices. Find it by walking N on Grove St. from Cambridge St.

## THE BULL & FINCH PUB    See "CHEERS."

## BUNKER HILL MONUMENT
*Monument Sq., Breed's Hill, Charlestown. Off map 12B10* ☎ *242-5641* 📷 ◀€
*Open daily 9am–5pm. Closed Thanksgiving; Christmas; New Year's Day.*
*T Community College (Orange Line), then a moderately long walk.*
The first major battle of the Revolutionary War took place in the hills N of Charlestown, two months after the skirmishes at Lexington and Concord in 1775. On June 16, British General Gage, headquartered in Boston, was informed that a force of 3,500 American militiamen were fortifying Breed's and Bunker Hills.

Gage decided on a frontal attack after a bombardment of Charles Towne from his batteries on Copp's Hill in what is now the North End. He committed only 2,200 men to the effort. Resplendent in their full dress uniforms of crimson and white, they marched up three sides of Breed's Hill toward the rebel trenches. It was hot that day. The uniforms were made of wool and each soldier carried 125 pounds of musket, ammunition and rations. They marched in even ranks up the slope, anticipating the first withering fusillade.

For long minutes, nothing happened. Low on ammunition, Colonel William Prescott had commanded his colonials, "Don't fire until you see the whites of their eyes!" The British continued up the hill, maintaining formation despite stone walls and other obstacles. Now the Americans fired. Hundreds of Redcoats fell in the first volleys. They regrouped and attacked again. And failed. By the time they reached the crest on the third try, the Americans were out of powder and ball. The British had won, but it was a hollow victory. Almost half of them, 1,054 men, had been killed or wounded. Only 441 Americans had fallen. General Gage was recalled to England in disgrace. The cannon his troops captured on Breed's Hill are on display in the Tower of London.

The **monument** commemorating the battle is a 220-foot obelisk of Massachusetts granite, visible from many parts of Boston and Cambridge. Its cornerstone was laid in 1825 by the Marquis de Lafayette, the French officer who played such an important role in the American Revolution, but the monument wasn't completed until 1843. An observatory at the top yields excellent views, after climbing 294 steps. Hourly talks are given by rangers, who use four dioramas to illustrate the progress of the battle. Call ahead to be certain they are on duty during the colder months. Each year on June 17, there is a re-enactment of the battle.

## BUNKER HILL PAVILION
*55 Constitution Rd. (formerly Water St., near Charlestown Navy Yard), Charlestown. Map 12C10* ☎*241-7575* 🖃 ➝ *✗ available* 🖳 *Open June–Nov daily 9.30am–5pm (Sept–Nov until 4pm). Closed Dec 1–May 31.* **T** *Haymarket (Orange Line), then City Square bus.*
A 30-minute multimedia presentation utilizes 14 screens and surround sound to describe the Battle of Bunker Hill. It is a skillful blend of sound and fury, with simulated explosions and cannon fire, and narration by an actor playing Paul Revere.

- City versus State confusion reigns about the address of the Bunker Hill Pavilion. *They* say they're on the recently renamed Constitution Rd.; so do the State authorities; but the City authorities still insist it's Water St. Our advice: look out for both!

## BUSCH-REISINGER MUSEUM    See HARVARD UNIVERSITY ART MUSEUMS.

## CALLAHAN AND SUMNER TUNNELS
*Map 12C12–D12.*
These parallel toll tubes under Boston Harbor connect downtown Boston with East Boston and, more important, Logan International Airport. In theory, they make possible a 15-minute trip between hotel and terminal. Coming or going during the ever-expanding rush hours can more than double that time. A third tunnel, as yet unnamed, is to be completed by the end of the century.

## CAMBRIDGE
*Map 7&8, 9&10, 11.*
Boston's sister city, an independent municipality, sprawls along the N bank of the Charles River and well inland. It has a much lower skyline, with extensive residential neighborhoods and low-lying industrial districts.

HARVARD UNIVERSITY, the nation's oldest, and MASSACHUSETTS INSTITUTE OF TECHNOLOGY dominate the city's consciousness, not surprising considering that nearly one quarter of the 95,000 residents of the city are students. And that doesn't count the faculty, administrators and support personnel employed by the two prestigious institutions. All those university people give the city a liberal tinge, prompting the appellation "People's Republic of Cambridge."

Much of the nightlife and many of the restaurants touted by Boston guidebooks and tourist materials are actually located in Cambridge. Residents are called "Cantabrigians," by the way.

## CAMBRIDGE COMMON
*Map 7B2. T Harvard (Red Line).*
See WALK 5: HARVARD AND OLD CAMBRIDGE, pages 85–86.

## CARPENTER CENTER FOR THE VISUAL ARTS
*Quincy St., Cambridge. Map 7B3 ☎495-4700 ▭ Open Mon–Sat 9am–5pm. Closed Sun. T Harvard (Red Line).*
HARVARD UNIVERSITY has the only Le Corbusier building in the US, on the main campus next to the FOGG ART MUSEUM. Reinforced concrete, a material the architect championed, was used to create the sculptural quality for which he is celebrated. But truth to tell, it isn't a structure to make anyone forget the French architect's many other outstanding projects, such as La Tourette convent or the Villa Savoye in Poissy.

## CASTLE ISLAND PARK
*E end of William J. Day Blvd. Map 6D4 ▭ ✗ of the fort available ( ☎727-5218 for info. and reservations). T Broadway (Red Line), then the #9 or #11 bus, then a short walk.*
While it was still an island, the star-shaped **Fort Independence** was built there, in 1801. The fort survives, but landfill long ago made the island the tip of a peninsula that also contains South Boston. They command the nearly enclosed Pleasure Bay. In 1827, during his brief and troubled military career, Edgar Allen Poe was stationed at the fort with an artillery unit.

The pleasant walk around the bay should be saved for warm days. **Castle Island Beach** has picnic tables and public toilets, but swimming in Boston Harbor cannot be encouraged.

## CENTRAL BURYING GROUND
*Map 11F9. T Boylston (Green Line).*
The 1756 cemetery on the S side of Boston Common contains the grave of artist Gilbert Stuart. See BOSTON COMMON.

## CHARLES RIVER
*Map 7–11.*
Named after King Charles I (1600–49) at the time of the earliest English explorations of the New England coast, the river forms the boundary between Boston and Cambridge and, where it meets the Mystic River,

creates Boston Harbor. It has suffered a good deal of prodding and narrowing and abuse since John Winthrop arrived with his colonists. But on the first warm day of spring, when sailboats dance and skip on the expanse beside the LONGFELLOW BRIDGE, sculls slice across its surface, and flowering trees are clouds of pink and white hovering on its banks, there is no more splendid course of water to be found in urban America.

It used to be wider, wilder. Until the 19thC, all of Back Bay was a swollen belly of the river, and its water once lapped over Charles St. at the base of Beacon Hill. But those filled-in flats were, by most accounts, salt marshes and muck that were no great loss to the city. The final collar tightened around the neck of the estuary was the dam that choked off its tidal flow in 1910. It's tame now, placid. And Boston and Cambridge are unimaginable without it.

## CHARLESTOWN
*Map 11B9–12B12.* **T** *Community College (Orange Line).*
John Winthrop landed his band of Puritans in 1629 in what they called Charles Towne and was known to the Indians as *Mishawum.* It was not a pleasant year. The water was brackish, unfit to drink, and in summer the mosquitoes assaulted them without mercy. When offered the opportunity to move across the bay to the pure springs of the Shawmut Peninsula, the colonists did so with alacrity.

In time, though, new settlers confronted Charlestown's problems, and the town grew. By the time of the Revolution, it had hundreds of houses, wharves and commercial buildings. Angered by snipers firing on his troops in Boston, British General Howe bombarded the town with his cannon on Copp's Hill. Nearly 400 buildings burned to the ground, an outrage that was not soon forgotten. The Battle of Bunker Hill (see page 99) took place on the heights N of the devastated town shortly thereafter.

Charlestown was rebuilt, with the aid of a grant from the new Continental Congress. In 1786, the first Charles River bridge was opened, made of wood and, at 1,503 feet, the longest bridge in the world. That, and the establishment in 1801 of the CHARLESTOWN NAVY YARD, greatly stimulated growth, and by the mid-19thC, it could claim to be a full-fledged city. But then Charlestown allowed itself to be annexed by Boston.

Now Charlestown is again in transition, with extensive public works underway around City Sq., and pockets of gentrification as well as areas of blight.

## CHARLESTOWN NAVY YARD
*Water St. (Chelsea St.), Charlestown. Map 12B11* ☎ *242-0543* 🖾 *Open daily 10am–6pm (summer), 10am–4pm (winter).* **T** *Haymarket (Green and Orange Lines), then #93 bus. Or water shuttle from* **T** *Aquarium (Blue Line).*
Inhabited by Europeans since 1625 and situated at the confluence of the Mystic and Charles Rivers, CHARLESTOWN was a logical choice for a shipbuilding and maintenance center. It was on this shore too that British troops landed in 1775 for the assault on Breed's and Bunker Hill. (The obelisk monument to those battles can be seen from the

navy yard grounds.) In 1800, the federal government purchased this land to build a naval yard, which served through the several wars of expansionist America until it was closed by President Nixon in 1974, with a devastating loss of revenues and jobs. Many suspected this to be Nixon's revenge against Massachusetts, for being the only state to vote against his re-election two years earlier.

Today, much of the yard is being converted to office and residential use, partly by rehabilitating the existing buildings. The western part, however, is now a stop on the extended FREEDOM TRAIL and embraces a national park with a World War II destroyer, an engaging nautical museum and the USS *Constitution* — "Old Ironsides."

Entering from the main gate, the visitor information center is over to the right. Docked a few yards beyond is the destroyer USS *Cassin Young*. Although she was built elsewhere, more than a dozen others much like her were constructed here during World War II. The *Cassin Young* served in the Pacific and saw action at Iwo Jima and Okinawa. She can be boarded, and tours are led by park rangers.

Normally, the USS *Constitution* is moored nearby. Until about 1995, however, she is in the dry dock 100 yards away from her customary berth, in preparation for her 200th birthday in 1997. The dry dock, straight ahead from the entrance, dates from 1833. The *Constitution* can be visited while the work proceeds. A crew of active-duty sailors dressed in period uniforms act as guides.

The frigate boasts a proud record, especially during the war of 1812. Her nickname, "Old Ironsides," is said to derive from the awestruck shout of a British sailor aboard the HMS *Gerriere*. Seeing his ship's cannonballs bounce off the rock-hard live oak hull of *Constitution*, he yelled, "Her sides are made of iron!" *Gerriere* burned and sunk in less than an hour after engaging the *Constitution*, a fate that later befell the *Java*, *Cyane* and *Levant*. Popular outcries have saved "Old Ironsides" from being scrapped several times in ensuing years. Relatively little of the present ship is in fact original, for the masts and timbers have had to be replaced several times over.

Near the ship is the **USS Constitution Museum** ( ▨ ☎ *426-1812, open daily in summer 9am-6pm, in winter 9am-4pm, in spring and fall 9am-5pm).* Definitely worth a detour, it concerns itself primarily with the ship, but there are also intriguing exhibits that deal generally with naval history. Inside the door is a large, intricately detailed model of "Old Ironsides" in full sail. Throughout the two floors are exhibits that entice the active participation of visitors. One of the most commanding is a computer game that allows the player to devise an escape from enemy ships, seen through the eyes of various crew members. One costumed artisan shows how to make model ships; another demonstrates knot-tying. Plans are afoot to expand the museum into two adjacent buildings in time for the 1997 bicentennial.

## "CHEERS" (The Bull & Finch pub)
*84 Beacon St. (Brimmer St.), Boston. Map 11F9* ☎*227-9605* ▣ *Open daily 11am-1.30am.* **T** *Arlington (Green Line).*

The second most-visited single attraction in Boston (after Faneuil Hall Marketplace), this basement tavern was a partial inspiration for the popular TV situation comedy, *Cheers*. The series ended in 1993, after an 11-year run. An estimated $7 million is reputed to be spent annually in the city as a direct result of enthusiasm for the show, including sales of *Cheers*-related souvenirs and business for the pub. Fans who stop in for a look may be disappointed, though. An exterior shot of the tavern opened each episode, but the inside bears no resemblance to the set for the show, which was shot on a Hollywood sound stage.

Visitors from Great Britain, where *Cheers* has been seen in syndication for years, will be interested to know that their own *Fawlty Towers* partially inspired the producers during the early stages of creation.

(See also NIGHTLIFE, page 177.)

## CHILDREN'S MUSEUM
*300 Congress St. (Sleeper St.), Boston. Map 12F11 ☎426-8855 ▨ (but ▨ Fri 5–9pm) ▣ ♣ Open Tues–Sun 10am–5pm (Fri until 9pm). Closed Mon (except school vacations). T South Station (Red Line), then walk across Congress St. Bridge.*
A 40-foot wooden milk bottle, which was once a 1930s roadside dairy bar, marks the entrance to the rehabilitated warehouse on MUSEUM WHARF. (Next door is the COMPUTER MUSEUM.) Members of the under-13 set can spend fruitful hours here, for while the museum has an educational mission, it doesn't slather learning with a trowel over the children. There are lots of hands-on exhibits, with sculptures to climb, computers to manipulate, and clothes to try on in **Grandmother's Attic.** Small animals can be held and touched at the **Living Things** exhibit. Slightly older youngsters enjoy the musical artifacts of olden times — the 1950s and '60s — in **The Clubhouse.** Crafts and drama groups are among many other possibilities.

## CHINATOWN
*Map 12F10–G10. T Chinatown (Orange Line).*
Variously described as the third or fifth largest community of Chinese-Americans in the US, this Chinatown is said to have 3,000 residents. It seems like many more on weekends, when families return from their homes throughout the metropolitan area to shop, eat and visit friends. Hemmed in by the Fitzgerald Expressway, Harrison Ave. and Kneeland and Essex Sts., the neighborhood contains dozens of restaurants, food markets and souvenir stores. At its eastern edge is a ceremonial gate funded by the people of Taiwan.

## CHRISTIAN SCIENCE CENTER 🏛
*Massachusetts and Huntington Aves., Boston. Map 10H7 ☎450-2000 ▨ ✗ available. Church open Tues–Sat 10am–4pm, Sun 11.15am–2pm; closed Mon, some holidays. Mapparium open Tues–Sat 9.30am–4pm; closed Sun, Mon. T Prudential or Symphony (Green Line).*
Mary Baker Eddy, founder of the Church of Christ, Scientist, commissioned the original "Mother Church" of this complex, which was built in 1894 in the Romanesque Revival style, with rusticated granite exte-

rior. It was all but enclosed by the larger, more polished Renaissance addition completed in 1904. Beneath its mammoth dome is an organ with no less than 13,595 pipes.

To the E of the church is a **plaza** with a 670-foot rectangular reflecting pool with administration buildings at either end, a 1973 project of the ubiquitous I.M. Pei firm. The continuously circulating water in the pool is used to run the air conditioning system in the new buildings. To the W is the older Christian Science Publishing Society building. Inside it is the popular **Mapparium (✷)**, a sphere of colored glass 30 feet in diameter with a geographically correct projection of Earth as it would appear from the inside. A pedestrian bridge bisects the globe, allowing visitors to examine it from within. The political boundaries represented are unchanged from the time of its completion in 1935. Share no secrets while on the bridge, for even mere whispers are magnified for all to hear.

## CHRISTOPHER COLUMBUS WATERFRONT PARK
*Map 12E11.* ***T*** *Aquarium (Blue Line).*
A patch of green along the revitalized harborfront, this park between LONG WHARF and Commercial Wharf provides a respite for tourists from FANEUIL HALL MARKETPLACE and lunch breaks for office workers from the FINANCIAL DISTRICT. It faces an inlet filled with fishing boats and pleasure craft. The park is dedicated to Christopher Columbus, in recognition of its proximity to the Italian NORTH END.

## COMBAT ZONE
*Map 12F10.* ***T*** *Downtown Crossing (Red Line or Orange Line).*
This was an attempt made in the 1970s to confine pornographic bookstores and cinemas, bars with nude dancers, and related "adult" activities to a controllable area. On the whole, it was successful. But now this already constricted two blocks of Washington St. is being squeezed by Chinatown from the S and the Lafayette Place shopping development from the N. Whether it will squirt out into other nearby blocks is uncertain. Those interested in taking a look may be wise to confine their stroll to daylight hours.

## COMPUTER MUSEUM
*300 Congress St. (Museum Wharf), Boston. Map 12F11* ☎*423-6758* ▨ ✷
*Open daily mid-June to Labor Day 10am–6pm (Fri until 9pm); Labor Day to mid-June Tues–Sun 10am–5pm. Closed Mon (except school vacations) from Labor Day to mid-June.* ***T*** *South Station (Red Line).*
Winking, blinking screens and hands-on displays instantly engage the interest of the computer generation, leaving most of their guardians nonplussed, if not entirely in the dark. Nearly 100 exhibits invite participants to compose music or make pictures or fly simulated planes. Robots are the featured attractions of the **Smart Machines Gallery**, and the central show-stopper is a two-story, walk-through model of a desktop computer. Special exhibits track new advances in technology.

Next door is the CHILDREN'S MUSEUM. Both are on MUSEUM WHARF, in renovated and connected warehouses.

## COPLEY SQUARE ★ ⅲ
*Map 10G8. T Copley (Green Line).*
Every city with aspirations to grandeur needs a monumental heart, a space that explains it to the world and reminds its citizens what it is and has been. Copley Square isn't quite the Piazza San Marco or Trafalgar Square, but it does its job better than any other in America.

At the time of the Civil war, this was the fetid marshland of Back Bay, slowly being transformed by a hugely ambitious landfill project. The first building of note to be erected was H.H. Richardson's **TRINITY CHURCH**, on the E side. Given the sponginess of the new earth, 4,500 wooden pilings were needed to provide the sturdy underpinning to support the massive structure. The church, completed in 1877, still holds pride of place, but has shared some of its light with the Renaissance Revival **BOSTON PUBLIC LIBRARY** (1888), on the W side, and, for a while, the first home of the Museum of Fine Arts, which was on the S.

This last position has been taken up since 1912 by the **COPLEY PLAZA** hotel (see page 142), still the grande dame in its guise of Italian *palazzo*. Its architect was Henry Hardenbergh, known for his more flamboyant Plaza Hotel in New York. At the NW corner is the **Old South Church**, Italianate also, but airier and decked out in lacy frippery.

The "New" Boston of the late 19thC made room for the New Boston of the mid-20thC. Thrusting diagonally into the gap between Trinity Church and the hotel is I.M. Pei's **JOHN HANCOCK TOWER**. At 60 stories, it might seem to ignore its neighbors, but its mirrored sides reflect the sky and clouds and serve to amplify the dignity of both church and hotel.

In winter, the open plain these buildings face can seem heartlessly desolate, and it is then that the random collection of indifferent commercial buildings on the N side of the square seems particularly unfortunate. However, all comes to right in spring and summer, when flowerbeds burst into life, shoppers sit and throw their heads back to catch the sun, office workers chat and eat their bagged lunches, and skateboarders and rollerbladers weave among the walkers. Then the square and the city it epitomizes join hands in pride.

In passing, it is interesting to note that in this hotbed of Revolutionary rage, the square is named after the painter John Singleton Copley, a Tory to the bone, who left Boston when it became obvious that war was inevitable and lived in England for the rest of his life. Obviously, all is forgiven, John.

### COPP'S HILL BURYING GROUND
*Hull and Snowhill Sts., Boston. Map 12C11 ◁≶ T North Station (Orange Line).*
Boston's second oldest cemetery started accepting internments in 1659, yet one of its markers carries the date 1625, before the founding of Boston. In all likelihood, the woman it commemorates died at Plymouth and her remains were moved here by her husband. The most celebrated occupants are members of the Mather family, but the burial ground is also the final resting place of many of the colony's earliest African-American citizens. Before the Battle of Bunker Hill, the British set up a battery of cannon here, with which they set Charles Towne afire.

When it is not in dry dock, the rigging of "Old Ironsides" can be seen at CHARLESTOWN NAVY YARD, across the harbor. Across the street from the cemetery gate, at #44, is a 200-year-old house, only $9\frac{1}{2}$ feet wide, and probably the narrowest in Boston.

- See also WALK 1: THE FREEDOM TRAIL, page 74.

## CUSTOM HOUSE
*State and India Sts. (McKinley Sq.), Boston. Map 12E11. T Aquarium (Blue Line).*
When completed in 1847, the US Custom House was a graceful Greek Revival "temple," standing at the edge of the harbor. Landfill placed it a few blocks from the water. By the turn of the century, believing the Custom House to be no longer sufficient to its task, the federal government, in its wisdom, decided to expand it — upward. Ignoring municipal height restrictions, a 30-story tower in the shape of a Venetian campanile was added, reducing the temple to mere footstool. According to some definitions, the tower was the city's first true skyscraper.

Eventually, however, revenues from maritime trade declined, and in 1986 the building was closed. Purchased by the city the following year, it has since remained empty, awaiting firm plans for its use and reopening. One much-touted proposal is to link the tower with an adjoining building to create a hotel. If that happens, perhaps the former 25th-floor observatory will be reopened.

## CYCLORAMA   See BOSTON CENTER FOR THE ARTS.

## DOWNTOWN CROSSING
*Winter and Washington Sts. Map 12F10. T Downtown Crossing (Red or Orange Line).*
Two blocks E of the Boston Common, Winter St. crosses Washington St. and magically becomes Summer St. Staring at each other across the intersection are the city's largest department stores, **Filene's** and **Jordan Marsh** (see page 187 for both). For one block in each direction, road traffic is restricted to facilitate shopping at a variety of mid-range and discount stores, offering books, cakes and breads, cutlery, photographic equipment, jeans, jewelry and the inevitable T-shirts. Street musicians often take up sidewalk space. The presence of unsavory elements, especially toward dark, can be unsettling, but the crowds and vigilant police keep actual problems to a minimum.

## THE EMBANKMENT ★
*Map 10F6–11E8. T Charles/MGH (Red Line)*
Essential to the green belt that follows the Boston shore of the Charles from the dam well past the last buildings of Harvard University, the Embankment is a linear park that lies between LONGFELLOW BRIDGE and the length of Back Bay. Breakwaters and docks provide anchorage for the fleets of pleasure boats that sail this widest expanse of the river. Storrow Lagoon is reserved for model boats.

The **Hatch Memorial Shell** (much referred to in the ENTERTAINMENTS chapter later in this book) is here, just past the end of Mount Vernon St.

as it descends from Beacon Hill. The Boston Pops Orchestra has performed there in a series of free summer concerts for decades. Playgrounds, picnic tables, cycling (and rollerblading) paths and ample room simply to lie about add to the attractions for people of all ages. A few hours here beneath the sun or the stars might well be the memory of Boston that lingers longest.

## FANEUIL HALL ★ ⏛
*Dock Sq. (Congress St.), Boston. Map 12E11 ☎720-0085 ▨ Open daily 9am–5pm. Closed Thanksgiving; Christmas; New Year's Day. T State (Blue or Orange Line).*
Wealthy merchant Peter Faneuil financed the construction of the brick hall as a gift to the people of Boston, who in 1742 numbered about 10,000. At that time, public buildings typically served more than one function. Faneuil intended the ground floor to be a farmers' market and the upstairs to be for town gatherings. In those twin roles, the hall became so central to civic activities that it was trebled in size over the next 65 years, including reconstruction after a fire in 1761. By then, anger over taxes imposed by the British Crown fueled many of the debates in the hall led by Sam Adams, James Otis and others. The last major modifications were carried out to designs by Charles Bulfinch, and intermittent renovations since then have not significantly altered that final appearance.

Exhibitions and other activities currently occupy the ground floor, although it has been used recently for food stalls. On the second floor is the **Great Hall**, which is still used for lectures and convocations. A large painting at the back depicts Daniel Webster holding forth in the same room before an audience that includes George Washington, who was at that time a colonel. When the traditional town-meeting form of governance was ended in 1822, the hall became a forum for debating such emotional issues as the abolition of slavery and women's suffrage. A National Park ranger gives regular talks about this history.

Up on the fourth floor is the headquarters of the Ancient and Honorable Artillery Company, another meeting room, which is ringed with portraits of officers and paintings of conflicts in which the Company participated. Visitors can spare themselves that steep climb without fear that they've missed anything of significance.

A statue of Sam Adams stands in front of the main (w) facade. The weather vane atop the steeple is in the shape of a grasshopper, installed when the hall went up in 1742. No one is certain why that symbol was chosen, but probably it was inspired by similar weather vanes on the Royal Exchange Building in London.

Several versions of the proper pronunciation of "Faneuil" have been suggested, including "Funnel" and "Fan'l." The one most widely used today rhymes with "Daniel."

## FANEUIL HALL MARKETPLACE ★ ⏛
*Commercial Ave., Clinton, Congress and Chatham Sts. Map 12E11 ☎523-3886 (for general information) ✤ Shops open Mon–Sat 10am–9pm; Sun noon–6pm.*

**T** *State (Orange or Blue Line), Government Center (Green or Blue Line), or Aquarium (Blue Line).*

Faneuil Hall was the centerpiece of an ambitious effort which, taken in concert with the adjacent GOVERNMENT CENTER (completed in the 1960s), constitutes an imaginative and highly successful urban renewal project, imitated but not yet matched by cities all along the East Coast. An estimated 14 million people visit the Marketplace annually, making it by far Boston's most popular attraction. It is equally favored by natives, who meet and eat in its scores of food stalls, outdoor cafés, bars, restaurants and shops — more than 125 of them. Appetizing cooking aromas permeate the entire area.

Immediately E of Faneuil Hall is QUINCY MARKET (illustrated on page 37), a shed-like granite structure with Greek Revival columned porticos at both ends. Tree-shaded promenades separate it from the parallel **North** and **South Market** buildings, which are constructed mostly of brick. Each of the three markets is 535 feet in length. At the E end of the complex is the recently completed **Marketplace Center**, bordering Commercial St. and screening off the elevated Fitzgerald Expressway. It contains still more shops and eating places.

Every day, tens of thousands of pedestrians stroll past the Marketplace's outdoor vendors and street performers, which include musicians, jugglers, clowns, acrobats and exhibitionist mimes. Special events are carefully spaced throughout the year, including concerts by 500 bell-ringers at Christmastime, a February ice-carving festival, food fairs and fashion shows.

The food stalls in Quincy Market open earlier than the retail stores, and the restaurants and bars in all four buildings generally stay open until 11pm or later.

## FINANCIAL DISTRICT
*Map 12F10–E11.*
The concentration of high-rise office towers s of the FANEUIL HALL MARKETPLACE and w of the Fitzgerald Expressway looks and behaves like similar districts in New York, San Francisco and other major North American cities. That is, it bustles throughout the day with the urgent errands of bankers and brokers, then falls eerily silent at dusk, when the skyscrapers form empty windswept canyons. There are a few hotels, notably LE MERIDIEN and the SWISSÔTEL LAFAYETTE (see pages 145 and 148), and many prominent sights are located around the perimeter, including the OLD STATE HOUSE, the NEW ENGLAND AQUARIUM, CHINATOWN and the Theater District.

## FOGG ART MUSEUM
*32 Quincy St., Cambridge. Map 7B3. **T** Harvard (Red Line).*
See HARVARD UNIVERSITY ART MUSEUMS.

## FRANKLIN PARK AND ZOO
*Blue Hill Ave. and Seaver St., Dorchester. Map 5D3–E3 ☎442-2002 or 442-0991 (recording) ▨ ✿ Open Apr–Oct Mon–Fri 9am–4pm, Sat, Sun 10am–5pm; Nov–Mar daily 9am–3.30pm. Closed Christmas; New Year's Day.*
***T** Forest Hills (Orange Line), then the #16 bus.*
Frederick Law Olmsted designed Franklin Park, which contains a public golf course, cycling and jogging paths, riding stables, playing fields, cross-country skiing trails, fishing ponds, picnic areas, greenhouses and, at its eastern corner, a relatively modest zoo.

This is one case in which a car can be useful. The zoo is at the outer edge of the city, in an area that can grow dangerous as dusk approaches. By train and bus, it can take well over an hour from downtown, especially on weekends, when there are longer gaps between buses. In truth, it is likely to be of interest primarily to parents with children to amuse, for it can't fairly be compared with such major zoological parks as those in San Diego, Toronto or New York. Adults with limited time lose little by excluding it from their sightseeing plans.

The exhibits are laid out thoughtfully, with four principal groupings in a logical oval plan. Following the route in a counterclockwise direction, the first compounds are labeled **Hooves & Horns**, with pens of Barbary sheep, Sika deer, antelopes, zebras, wallabies, llamas, gnus and, proving this isn't an iron-clad category, an ostrich. Next, at some distance is the **African Tropical Forest.** Featured within the none-too-persuasive jungle setting are recently acquired gorillas and wart hogs. Also amid the plantings and pools are dwarf crocodiles and a pygmy hippo, as well as a panther and antelopes.

Next is **A Bird's World**, with a walk-through outdoor aviary containing ducks and a few brilliantly hued Chinese pheasants. Inside the nearby pagoda-like building is a subtropical habitat with egrets, ibis, roseate spoonbills and other wading birds. The final pavilion, which is back near the zoo entrance, is the **Children's Zoo**, with cuddly animals for viewing and petting.

## THE FREEDOM TRAIL ★
*See WALK 1 map on page 73.*

One of the city's premier visitor attractions is the marked route through old Boston, passing many of the sites closely associated with the American Revolution. It forms the subject of WALK 1: THE FREEDOM TRAIL, which starts on page 68.

## ISABELLA STEWART GARDNER MUSEUM ★ ⬛
*280 The Fenway (Palace Rd.), Boston. Map 9I5 ☎566-1401 or 734-1359 (for concert information) ⬛ ✗ on Thurs ⬛ Open Tues–Sun 11am–5pm. Closed Mon; some holidays. T Museum or Brigham Circle (Green Line, Arborway Branch).*

A woman of privilege and substance with the taste to exploit those resources, Isabella Stewart was born in New York in 1840 but came to Boston in 1860 as the wife of John L. Gardner. Her collecting began with rare books and manuscripts but soon expanded to take in painting, sculpture and decorative arts.

Eccentric and headstrong and with not the slightest interest in maintaining a facade of discreet gentility, she enthusiastically spent her fortune on herself and her passions. She became friends with many of the artists she supported, notably John Singer Sargent and Anders Zorn, and indulged her love for things Italian in this Venetian *palazzo* she built for herself in 1902.

The museum was opened to the public a year later, but continued to serve as her home until her death in 1924. Reportedly, everything — medieval tapestries and chests, Renaissance paintings, first editions — is exactly where it was when she was alive. If so, that helps explain why an estimated $200-million-worth of artworks were stolen with such ease in 1990, a crime that remains unsolved. Much of the remaining collection looks as vulnerable as it would be in anyone's living room.

Nothing about the uninspired exterior hints at the bounty within. Enter through the door at the left. Hold on to the admission receipt, which is required for access to the upper floors. Opposite the ticket counter is the **Yellow Room**, named after the damask wallcovering in that color. Closely hung paintings include a portrait by Sargent, an early seascape by Whistler, and up near the ceiling, treated almost negligently, a Matisse canvas of a St-Tropez terrace.

Exiting, turn left. Over to the right is the unquestioned focal point of the museum, the central **Court**. It intentionally reminds viewers of ancient, faintly decayed palaces off Venetian side canals, as if unoccupied for long periods of time. Colonnaded cloisters enclose it on three sides, while the fourth wall is pierced by long windows with pointed tripartite tops and balustrades along the bottom. A double staircase rises from the garden to the second floor, and the space is made an atrium by the glass roof four stories up. In the middle of the court is a large Roman mosaic, and statuary and ornamental columns stand among flowerbeds and orange and palm trees. The plants and flowers are supplied by the museum's own greenhouse.

To the left of the court is the **Spanish Cloister.** The antique tiles on the wall are from a 17thC Mexican church. In the middle of the right wall is a 12thC stone portal from Bordeaux. At the end is one of the undisputed treasures of the museum, a large canvas by Sargent, *El Jaleo* (1882). Painted when he was only 26, it ranks as one of his masterpieces. In the foreground, a gypsy dancer performs in front of a line of singers and guitarists. His light source is from below, casting deep shadows on the wall. Gardner or her advisors were wise enough to place their lamps down in front, enhancing the effect.

Return to the other end of the cloister and turn left into the **North Cloister**, then left again into the **West Cloister**. That juncture is marked by a 3rdC Roman sarcophagus decorated with reliefs of dancers sporting themselves in honor of Dionysus, god of the grape. Toward the end of the West Cloister is a staircase to the second floor.

At the top is the **Early Italian Room**, consisting mostly of late Medieval and pre-Renaissance altarpieces and religious paintings. One, in five sections, is by Simone Martini, a contemporary of the very influential Giotto. A door on the right leads into the **Raphael Room**, with crimson damask walls, 18thC Venetian chairs and a massive fireplace. Raphael is represented by two paintings over in the left-hand corner — one, a small *pietà* displayed atop a table, the other, a large portrait of the poet and scholar Count Tommaso Inghirami. To the right of the doorway to the next room is a Botticelli, *The Tragedy of Lucretia,* which looks not at all like his famous Venus on a clam shell. This is laid out as a kind of play, the action taking place amid towering colonnades that nearly overwhelm the actors.

Next, in the **Short Gallery**, is Anders Zorn's full-length portrait of Ms. Gardner whirling into the frame from a balcony overlooking the pageantry of Venice's Grand Canal; the technique of luminous light tones and warm darks is reminiscent of Sargent. In the same room are cases containing drawings by widely diverse artists, from Michelangelo to Degas. Then comes the **Little Salon**, decorated with florid Louis XV furnishings.

Bear right to enter the long, high **Tapestry Room,** hung with a few minor paintings and ten large Belgian tapestries of the mid-16thC. The museum's endowment and the benefactor's firmly worded bequest bring Saturday and Sunday concerts to this hall weekly, from September to May.

At the end, turn right through a small anteroom with Japanese screens into the **Dutch Room**. Rubens, Vermeer and Rembrandt, monumental figures of the High Renaissance, are all represented. But so are Hans Holbein (either side of the door just entered), Albrecht Dürer (over on the right) and the Spanish master, Zurbarán. Exit at the far corner and go up the stairs to the third floor.

Catching the eye immediately in the **Veronese Room** are the tooled leather wall panels. The painting in the ceiling was attributed to Veronese, a claim apparently now in doubt. Another of Ms. Gardner's many interests are seen in the selected items from her collection of lacework.

Pass into the **Titian Room,** dominated by his famous epic canvas, *The Rape of Europa.* Painted about 1560 for Felipe II of Spain, it shows the princess Europa being borne into the sea by a muscular bull, the form taken by Zeus, the god who loved her. The painting is all the more remarkable for the fact that Titian was in his 80s when he completed it. Over to the right of the exit is Velázquez's full-length portrait of Felipe IV of Spain.

Entering the aptly named **Long Gallery**, to the left there is another Botticelli, *The Madonna of the Eucharist.* Visible around The Madonna's head are slight alterations the artist made in the course of painting. The rest of the gallery is filled with cases of rare books, manuscripts, and photos and letters received by Ms. Gardner from friends and artists, covered by cloth to protect them from the light. Religious sculptures and portions of church fixtures are also on view.

Another antechamber empties into the last gallery, the **Gothic Room.** It contains a small Giotto, but pride of place is given to Sargent's large portrait of Ms. Gardner, in a long black dress with pearls around her waist. The artist used this room as a studio during the winter before the museum was opened to the public.

A staircase beyond the far door descends to the ground floor, where, at the back, are the small but popular museum shop and café. Circling around through the Spanish Cloister and into the exit hall off the North Cloister, one last gallery is encountered, on the right: the **Blue Room,** which contains late 19thC and early 20thC paintings, among them works by Gustave Courbet, Whistler, Sargent, Degas and Monet.

- While the museum can be visited comfortably in an hour, its decidedly personal and idiosyncratic character is best grasped at leisure, especially in tandem with one of the mood-setting musicales.

## GEORGES ISLAND

*Map* **6D6** ☎ *727-5290 for information about cruises, sports and activities etc.*
◀€ ✱

Boston Harbor and Massachusetts Bay have many islands, over a score of which form the **Harbor Islands State Park**. Used for a variety of purposes over the years, notably for military installations, prison and hospitals, most have reverted to a wild state, with vines and undergrowth creeping over the ruins.

Georges Island is the favorite destination of harbor cruises from LONG WHARF and ROWE'S WHARF, largely because of its romantically ramshackle Civil War-era **Fort Warren**. It is reputed to have ghosts, perhaps of the Confederate soldiers who were imprisoned here. Fishing, swimming, picnicking and scrambling over ruins are the principal activities, here and on nearby islands reached by free shuttle boats from Georges Island: **Gallups Island**, **Lovells Island**, **Peddocks Island**, **Grape Island** and **Bumpkin Island**.

## GOVERNMENT CENTER 🏛

*Map 12E10.* **T** *Government Center (Green or Blue Line).*

Boston's first exercise in large-scale urban renewal managed to avoid the sterility of efforts undertaken elsewhere in the 1950s and '60s. The I.M. Pei architectural firm, which shaped so much of what came to be known as the "New Boston," was given its first major commission here. Set for obliteration was the seedy neighborhood around Scollay Square, home of the Old Howard, a theater that had degenerated from presentations of opera through vaudeville and burlesque to strip shows. Known to generations of college boys in search of risqué diversion, Scollay Square was a cinder in the eye of proper Bostonians. Its near-total demolition provided a 56-acre site for new municipal and state office buildings.

At the heart of the development is the **Boston City Hall** (see THE ARCHITECTURAL HERITAGE, page 40). While Pei drew up the master plan for the Center, this innovative building, the most visually arresting of the new structures, was the result of the teamwork of two other firms (Kallmann, McKinnell & Knowles, and Campbell, Aldrich & Nulty). It is remarkable that a committee could arrive at such an individualistic solution. While public reaction to the final result didn't inspire the disdain, indeed loathing, accorded the Prudential Center, which was completed during the same decade, neither was the new City Hall universally accepted. All the same, it set a new and different standard for municipal architecture, one that has been imitated elsewhere.

The City Hall's decidedly sculptural quality is underscored by the use of raw cast concrete that bears the impression of the wood forms that contained it. The shape (see the illustration on page 40) is nearly an inverted pyramid, decidedly top-heavy, with asymmetrical cubicles and recesses and supporting piers. Passages and large portals positively invite entrance, a quality much to be praised in a seat of government.

The Hall rises from a sweeping, stepped, brick plaza, as if it had erupted from below the surface. Chill and windswept during the cold months, from spring to fall it often bubbles with civic celebrations, musical events and political rallies. On the N side of the plaza are the dual towers of the **John F. Kennedy Federal Office Building**, designed by the father of the Bauhaus movement, Walter Gropius. Given time, perhaps they will assume a less banal appearance. Fashions do change.

On the S side is the 1816 **Sears Crescent**, the only old building within the development to survive the wreckers' ball. Hanging from its W end is a large steaming teakettle that once advertised the presence of a store selling that very product. Across adjacent Cambridge St., the new, larger **Center Plaza** building has a curving facade intended to echo that of the Sears Crescent.

Finally, the tallest building at the perimeter of the plaza, at the E end of the Sears Crescent, is the 41-story **Bank of New England** *(28 State St.),* erected in 1968. Cloaked in rose granite to harmonize with the brick of the older buildings in the vicinity, its chief distinction is a large mural by Larry Rivers rather fancifully illustrating the Boston Massacre that took place across the street, outside the OLD STATE HOUSE.

## JOHN HANCOCK BUILDING

*175 Berkeley St. (St James Ave.), Boston. Map 11G8* ⇐ *T Arlington (Green Line).*
Opened in 1947, this faintly Art Moderne building is now overshadowed by its successor, the JOHN HANCOCK TOWER. It continues to stand out, however, with its stepped pyramidal cap. An illuminated beacon up there signals public information, its message encapsulated in verse: Clear blue, clear view; Flashing blue, clouds due; Steady red, rain ahead; Flashing red, snow ahead. In summer, the flashing red signal refers to something of far greater import: it means the Red Sox baseball game has been canceled. Also up there is an **observation deck**.

## JOHN HANCOCK TOWER ★ 🏛

*Hancock Place (Copley Sq.), Boston. Map 11G8* ☎247-1977 ▦ ⇐ ✳ *Open Mon–Sat 9am–11pm; Sun (May–Oct) 10am–11pm, (Nov–Apr) noon–11pm. Closed Thanksgiving; Christmas. T Copley (Green Line).*

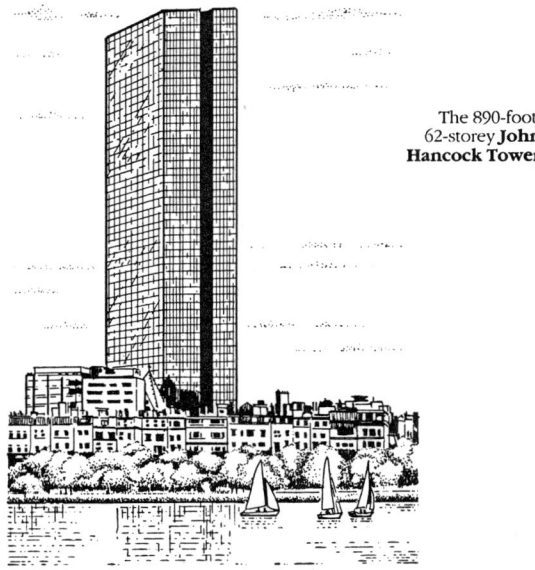

The 890-foot, 62-storey **John Hancock Tower**

New England's tallest skyscraper once seemed doomed to be its most conspicuous catastrophe. As it neared completion in 1975, giant panes of glass began to whip off the curtain walls, to shatter on the streets below. Nearly 400 panes were replaced by sheets of plywood while engineers attempted to uncover the problem. Multiple lawsuits loomed and the inevitable jokes emerged — it was the only skyscraper with termite problems, they said, the world's highest monument to plywood. When the puzzle was finally solved, all 10,000 panes had to be replaced.

Now that they are secured, with an early-warning system to anticipate potential difficulties, the early mishaps seem to have done little to tarnish the lustrous reputation of its designer, I.M. Pei. Under the right conditions, the reflecting walls seem almost to disappear into clouds and blue sky, and they serve to emphasize, rather than diminish, neighboring TRINITY CHURCH. The wedge shape dominates the skyline, a stylish rebuke to the very ordinary Prudential Tower, a few blocks to the w.

On the 60th floor is an **observatory**, refurbished in 1993. A recorded chat by an architectural historian with obvious affection for his city provides an amusing, faintly professorial commentary on individual structures seen far below. A darkened chamber on the same floor gives an effective dissertation on the seminal events of 1775, using sound and lights on a scale model of the city as it was then.

## HARBOR ISLANDS STATE PARK    See GEORGES ISLAND.

## HARVARD BRIDGE
*Map 10E6–F6.*
Boys will be boys, especially if they are as bright and frisky as the students at MASSACHUSETTS INSTITUTE OF TECHNOLOGY. That prestigious institution is located at the Cambridge end of this bridge carrying Mass Ave. into BACK BAY in Boston.

In 1958 it struck a group of MIT undergraduates that the bridge should be properly measured. Meters and yards and feet and centimeters were boring, so they elected to use the Smoot. Fellow classmate Oliver Reed Smoot, that is. He was 5'7" at the time, and diligence and precise surveying techniques subsequently determined that Harvard Bridge was exactly 364.4 Smoots and one ear long. Markings on the sidewalks of the bridge duly recorded Smoot intervals. When the bridge was rebuilt some years later, the Smoot marks were reproduced. There was discussion about measuring with a new Smoot, for by then son Stephen had matriculated. Fortunately for tradition, it was decided that there was "no Smoot like an old Smoot."

## HARVARD SQUARE  ★
*Intersection of Massachusetts Ave. and Cambridge St. Map 7B2.*
Even in dankest, darkest winter, the square is lively, with its important MBTA station, famous out-of-town newspaper-and-ticket stand, stores including the university's **Coop** (see WALK 5, page 85), and cafés and other enterprises catering to students and faculty. But at the first faint breath of spring, HARVARD UNIVERSITY men and women and professors, citizens, street people, artists and assorted bohemians are out in force.

When the **T** station was refurbished recently, a small performance area was provided, and it is fully utilized by dancers and musicians of wildly varying levels of talent. All around them are the certifiably brainy young people lucky enough to be students at one of the country's finest universities. They do what comes naturally — debate, backpack, roller-blade, rap, ogle, challenge, idle, skateboard, daydream, snuggle. Sightseeing "trolley" buses stop at the sizable newsstand, where you can purchase tickets for plays, concerts and other events. A small booth staffed by Chamber of Commerce volunteers hands out tourist information, and a large outdoor café nearby provides opportunity for lingering examination of the unprogrammed pageant.

## HARVARD UNIVERSITY ★ ⊞

*Map 7A2–B2* ▣ *𝒳 available.* **T** *Harvard (Red Line).*

Arguably the most influential university in the world, Harvard has trained not only American business leaders, scientists, physicians and statesmen, but children of the privileged from every nation on the globe. Six US presidents were graduates, including both Adamses, both Roosevelts and John F. Kennedy. Often as not, their advisors and opponents were also alumni. Degrees in law or medicine from Harvard are virtual guarantors of professional success, and the faculty has produced 33 Nobel Laureates and 31 Pulitzer Prize winners. Harvard's library, the oldest in the country and the largest of any university anywhere, has nine million volumes, and the endowment is well over $4 billion.

While the main campus is in Cambridge, four of its ten graduate and professional schools are located in Boston. The university is the largest landowner and taxpayer in Cambridge, with more than 360 acres of land and about 460 buildings in the metropolitan area. Its off-campus facilities include the 265-acre ARNOLD ARBORETUM in Jamaica Plain, a villa in Florence, Italy, and the Dumbarton Oaks estate in Washington, DC.

Several university museums devoted to the arts and sciences are open to the public (see the next two entries), as are many events in the crowded cultural calendar ( ☎ *495-1718 for info.)*

- 𝒳 Tours of the campus (▣) leave from the **Harvard University Information Center** on Harvard Square *(1350 Massachusetts Ave.* ☎ *495-1573)* Monday to Friday at 10am and 2pm, and Saturday at 2pm.
- See also WALK 5: HARVARD AND OLD CAMBRIDGE for a short (approximately 1½-hour) walk around the district.

## HARVARD UNIVERSITY ART MUSEUMS

*Broadway and Quincy St., Cambridge. Map 7B3* ☎*495-9400* ▣ *(but* ▣ *on Sat morning): single ticket valid for all three museums. Open Tues–Sun 10am–5pm. Closed Mon; major holidays.* **T** *Harvard (Red Line).*

Harvard shares its wealth, not least in the seven art and natural history museums it makes available to the public. Oldest and most important of the three devoted to art is the **Fogg Art Museum** *(32 Quincy St.),* which was founded in 1891. The interior centers on a two-story atrium modeled on a 16thC Italian courtyard, appropriate to a collection especially notable for its late Medieval and Renaissance sculpture and paintings.

On the ground floor are Dutch and Flemish landscapes, Italian and Spanish portraits and religious themes, all from the 17th and 18thC. Most visitors will find few individual canvases that are familiar, but there are works by Juan de Ribera, Botticelli, Rubens and Fra Angelico, and one of the eight galleries contains paintings and sketches by early American artists John Singleton Copley and Benjamin West.

On the second floor are 19thC European and American paintings, with prominent works by Gainsborough, George Romney and Ingres. These lead naturally to the Impressionists and Post-Impressionists, who are usually deemed to mark the beginning of modern art. One of Degas' sculptures of a ballet dancer, with a tutu of real cloth, is here, as are sketches by Cézanne and Renoir and seascapes by Monet. They are joined by the so-called American Impressionists Winslow Homer, Thomas Eakins, George Inness, James McNeill Whistler and Boston's own John Singer Sargent. Gallery IV contains a collection of decorative arts of England and of the American colonial and post-Revolution periods.

At the back of the second floor is the entrance to the **Busch-Reisinger Museum**, specializing in art and design from Central and Northern Europe since 1880. A large gallery to the right of the entrance has special exhibitions, often devoted to such major figures as Paul Klee. In the seven remaining rooms are paintings, prints and sculptures by Expressionists Max Beckmann, Vasily Kandinsky and Edvard Munch.

The **Arthur M. Sackler Museum** *(corner of Quincy St. and Broadway)*, third of this group, is a few steps N. The 1985 Sackler is noted for its collections of Asian and Middle Eastern ceramics, prints, calligraphy, ivories, jades, sculptures and miniature bronzes. Pieces from China dominate, but Greek vases and Korean and Japanese scrolls are also among the permanent collection. The ground-floor galleries are reserved for temporary exhibitions.

# HARVARD UNIVERSITY NATURAL HISTORY MUSEUMS
*24 Oxford St. (entrance also from Divinity Ave.), Cambridge. Map **7**A2*
☎495-1910 ▨ *(but* ☒ *on Sat morning): single ticket valid for all four museums. Open Mon–Sat 9am–4.30pm; Sun 1–4.30pm. Closed major holidays.*
**T** *Harvard (Red Line).*

Four discrete museums of natural history are contained in this single building. Many of the exhibits are somewhat specialized for a general audience, but there are highlights that make it worth finding time for at least a short visit.

The **Botanical Museum** has by far the biggest attraction: the **Ware Collection** (★) of glass flowers. Over 3,000 individual blooms were created by the German artists and glassblowers, Leopold Blaschka and his son Rudolph. It took them from 1887 to 1937 to complete — not so long considering they reproduced every petal and pistil in exquisite detail. Their "garden" is a delight and probably unique.

Fossils of mastodons and dinosaurs and a pair of stuffed Chinese pheasants owned by George Washington are only a few of the exhibits in the **Museum of Comparative Zoology**. Begun during the mid-Victorian era of eager scientific inquiry, the collection retains that combined sense of scholarship and wonder.

Oldest of any of the university repositories, the **Mineralogical and Geological Museum** will probably prove of scant interest to most visitors, although many of the gems and minerals on display are visually attractive.

Featured in the **Peabody Museum of Archeology and Ethnology** is a hall devoted to Native American cultures. Recently overhauled, it employs various interactive devices to illuminate the history of cultural contacts between Europeans and the people they called Indians. Hundreds of artifacts, from vessels and basketry to clothing and tools, are intelligently presented.

## CHARLES HAYDEN PLANETARIUM    See MUSEUM OF SCIENCE.

## INSTITUTE OF CONTEMPORARY ART
*955 Boylston St. (Hereford St.), Boston. Map 10G7  ☎266-5152  ▨ Open Wed 11am–5pm; Thurs–Sat 11am–8pm; Sun 11am–5pm. Closed Mon; Tues; major holidays. T Hynes Convention Center/ICA (Green Line).*

In 1886, the adjoining buildings at this corner were police and fire stations. The firehouse is still operational, but the former police quarters now contain exhibits that would probably have been illegal in puritanical 19thC Boston. One recent example was an exploration of cross-dressing as an art form; another was a showing of the highly controversial homoerotic photographs of Robert Mapplethorpe. Not all its exhibitions are so off-kilter, but even those showcasing slightly more conventional paintings and sculptures tend to be irreverent.

Without a permanent collection, the Institute, in existence since 1936, is free to mount such shows as it wishes, and supplement them with films, lectures, video programs and performances that operate at various levels of comprehension. There is a homemade quality to much of this, as in the invitation to a rumination on fashion that was intended to be "challenging to the mind and ngaging the spirit." Venturesome museum-goers interested in having their spirits ngaged should call ahead, for the hours noted above are not always strictly observed.

## KENMORE SQUARE
*Map 9G5. T Kenmore (Green Line).*

The intersection of Commonwealth Ave., Beacon and other streets at the western edge of Back Bay has a disorderly air, comparable to that of a dormitory room occupied by four university students. That's apt, for it is only a block away from the campus of BOSTON UNIVERSITY, and the businesses in and around the square cater primarily to the interests of young adults. That means hip-to-hip bars, alternative rock clubs, discos, a large bookstore owned by the university, and fast-food restaurants. **Fenway Park**, the home stadium of the Red Sox baseball team, is two blocks s.

With all that, the task of identifying the square is made still easier by the presence of a huge neon sign advertising Citgo gasoline, so long on the Kenmore scene it has taken on the status of icon. Threats to remove it have been thwarted by neighborhood residents and preservationists.

## JOHN F. KENNEDY LIBRARY AND MUSEUM  🏛
*Columbia Point, Dorchester. Map 6D4  ☎929-4523  ▨ ◄€ Open daily 9am–5pm. Closed major holidays. T JFK/U.Mass (Red Line), then the free shuttle bus.*

It is now a tradition that US presidents create libraries in which to store papers and mementoes of their administrations. The 35th President only had a thousand days in which to build a record, but he was a literate, witty, highly articulate man who exposed his ideas frequently to examination by the international media. This monument to his tragically shortened term in office is one of I.M. Pei's more dramatic commissions.

I.M Pei's **John F. Kennedy Library and Museum**

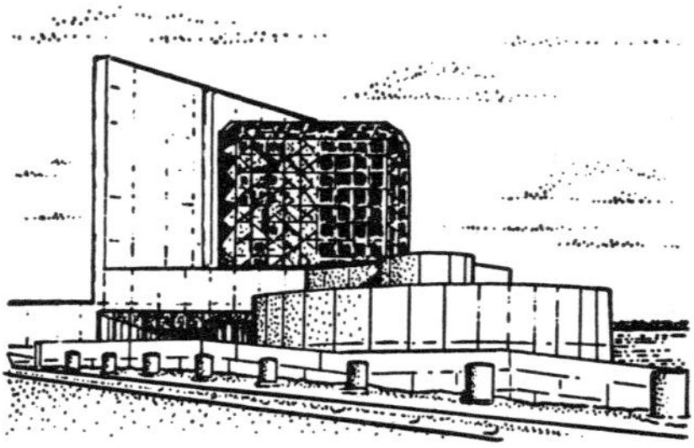

Opened in 1979, the nine-story pyramidal tower and adjoining pavilion make their statement with sharply geometric shapes and white walls that are starkly etched against the nearby bay. Despite the relative youth of the building, several additions and renovations have been made, the latest in 1993, when interiors were extensively altered to accommodate several new and reorganized exhibits of memorabilia. On view as well is the President's sailboat, *Victura*. A 30-minute film on the life and times of JFK is a brisk, if somewhat shallow, introduction.

- The bus leaves the library ten minutes past the hour from 8am to 5.50pm, stopping in both directions at the nearby University of Massachusetts campus. An important warning is that there are no eating places in or near the library-museum.

## KING'S CHAPEL

*Tremont St. (School St.), Boston. Map **12**E10.* ***T** Park Street (Green or Red Line).*
See WALK 1: THE FREEDOM TRAIL, pages 69–70.

## LONGFELLOW BRIDGE

*Map **11**E8* ⋞ ***T** Charles/MGH or Kendall/MIT (Red Line).*
Riders of the subway are treated to fine views of Boston and the Charles River when Red Line trains emerge from underground tunnels to cross the 1907 Longfellow Bridge. Four decorative towers at the center span are thought to resemble dining table utensils; hence the nickname "Salt and Pepper Bridge."

## LONGFELLOW NATIONAL HISTORIC SITE ★ 🏛

*105 Brattle St. (Hawthorn St.), Cambridge. Map **7**B1* ☎*876-4491*
*Open daily 10am–4.30pm. Closed Thanksgiving; Christmas; New Year's Day.*
***T** Harvard (Red Line).*
Brattle St. is the most elegant in Cambridge, once favored by wealthy merchants and shipping magnates. The yellow Georgian mansion with white trim at #105 (illustrated on page 87) had existed 78 years before

the poet after which it is now named even saw it. John Vassall was the builder, a Loyalist who found it prudent to flee Cambridge at the outbreak of the Revolution. During the siege of Boston, one of Washington's infrequent early victories over the British, the future Father of his Country made his headquarters here.

The second owner, physician Andrew Craigie, enlarged the house and reportedly entertained often and extravagantly. But when he died, he left his widow deeply in debt. She found it necessary to take in boarders, one of whom, in 1837, was Henry Wadsworth Longfellow. Poets, much as now, didn't make much money in those days, but Longfellow married well, and his new father-in-law bought the house and gave it to the couple in 1843. His wife, Fanny Appleton, died there later in a freakish fire. Longfellow stayed until his death in 1882.

The mansion was in the possession of his children and their descendants until they gave it to the National Park Service in the 1970s. That fact helps account for the excellent condition of the building and the presence of many of Longfellow's books and furnishings. Among these is a chair made from the tree mentioned in his poem about his friend the blacksmith: "Under the spreading chestnut tree the village smitty stands . . . "

- See also WALK 5: HARVARD AND OLD CAMBRIDGE, page 86.

## LONG WHARF
*Map 12E11–12.* **T** *Aquarium (Blue Line).*
Back in 1710, when the Atlantic Ocean nearly reached the foundation of the Old State House, a wharf was extended from the end of State Street (or King Street, as it was called in those days) 1,700 feet out into the harbor. It doesn't seem that long now, because landfill pushed the waterline out. Today, most of what remains of the wharf is occupied by the MARRIOTT LONG WHARF hotel (see page 145). Cruises to GEORGES ISLAND depart from the wharf.

## LOUISBURG SQUARE ★ ≡
*Map 11E9.* **T** *Charles/MGH (Red Line).*
See WALK 3: BEACON HILL, page 78.

## MASSACHUSETTS GENERAL HOSPITAL ("Mass General")
*Fruit and Grove Sts., Boston. Map 11D9.*
See BULFINCH PAVILION / ETHER DOME.

## MASSACHUSETTS INSTITUTE OF TECHNOLOGY (MIT)
*Map 9E5–10E6* ▣ **𝄞** *available* **T** *Kendall (Red Line).*
Massachusetts Institute of Technology first opened its doors in 1861, and occupied various sites around Copley Sq. before moving across the river to Cambridge in 1916. One of the two most important institutions of its kind in the US (its only clear rival being the California Institute of Technology at Pasadena), MIT now spreads over 128 acres along the shore opposite Back Bay. The achievements of its faculty and graduates are impressive, just one measure being the fact that two dozen of them have won the Nobel Prize. With the international recognition that

kind of record brings, its enrollment of about 9,800 includes students from over 90 foreign countries.

MIT's comparative youth and the sobriety of its largely Neoclassical buildings do not bestow the brick-and-ivy majesty of neighboring Harvard. However, there are attractions for the casual visitor on campus. Among these are outdoor sculptures by Picasso, Louise Nevelson, Henry Moore and Alexander Calder, and two striking buildings designed by Eero Saarinen, the **Kresge Chapel** and **Auditorium**.

Belying its stereotype as a collection of drudges and computer nerds, MIT has several museums devoted more to the arts than the sciences. Admirers of ship models shouldn't miss the **Hart Nautical Museum** *(55 Massachusetts Ave.* ☎ *253-5942* ◨ *open daily 9am-8pm).* The **List Visual Art Center** *(20 Ames St.* ☎ *253-4680* ◨ *open Mon-Fri noon-6pm, Sat-Sun 1-5pm)* has a permanent collection of hundreds of paintings and sculptures as well as frequent temporary exhibits. And the more general **MIT Museum** *(265 Massachusetts Ave.* ☎ *253-444* ◨ *open Tues-Fri 9am-5pm, Sat-Sun 1-5pm, closed Mon)* displays scientific devices and mementoes relating to the history of MIT, in addition to its collection of paintings.

- ✗  Tours of MIT (◨) are offered by the **Information Office** *(77 Massachusetts Ave.* ☎ *253-4795, open Mon-Fri 9am-5pm).*

## MASSACHUSETTS STATE HOUSE    See STATE HOUSE.

## MOUNT AUBURN CEMETERY
*580 Mt. Auburn St. (Brattle St.), Cambridge. Map **5**C2 ☎547-7105. Open daily 8am–7pm (summer), 8am–5pm (winter).* **T** *Harvard (Red Line), then either the #71 or #73 bus.*

It may seem that the Boston/Cambridge area has an unusually large number of burial grounds on its list of sightseeing musts. This one, opened in 1831, is different in that it is at least as important as park and botanical garden. Recognizing this, the office has one map showing the location of graves of famous people, another pointing out the horticultural highlights. They might consider a third: an identification booklet for birdwatchers. Hundreds of species have been identified here during the migration seasons, which are also the times when the flower beds and other plantings have their lushest colors.

Among the prominent Bostonians and Cantabrigians interred here are the founder of Christian Science, Mary Baker Eddy, architect Charles Bulfinch, author and physician Oliver Wendell Holmes, poet Henry Wadsworth Longfellow and painter Winslow Homer. An **observatory** provides an overview of the 174 acres.

## MUSEUM OF FINE ARTS ★
*465 Huntington Ave. (Forsyth Way and Museum Rd.), Boston. Map **9**I5 ☎ 267-9377 or 267-9300 (recording)* ◨ *(but* ◨ *on Wed 4–9.45pm)* ⬤ ✗ *available* ═ ⬛ **Entire museum** *open Tues–Sun 10am–4.45pm (Wed until 9.45pm).* **West wing** *only also open Thurs and Fri 5–9.45pm. Closed Mon; major holidays.* **T** *Museum (Green Line, Arborway Branch).*

Many cities far larger than Boston would be delighted to have a repository of this scope and quality. A quick skim of the extensive collections simply isn't possible. To do it even scant justice, at least two visits are necessary, and then only after deciding upon the galleries of greatest personal interest.

That isn't easy, considering the amount of space given to European and American painting of the 17th–20thC, an exceptional gathering of Asian arts and artifacts, and the almost numbing quantities of Greek and Etruscan ceramics. Time should also be made for a look at the rooms given to the enchanting assemblies of musical instruments, ship models and early American furnishings and decorative arts.

The founding nucleus of the museum was provided by the BOSTON ATHENAEUM, a cultural center that housed the first paintings in its Beacon St. headquarters from 1870–76. A home of its own was then opened on Copley Sq., on the site of the present Copley Plaza Hotel. The museum moved on to its present Huntington Ave. quarters in 1909.

The original building is in spare Classical Revival temple style, with expansions in 1915 and 1928. Entrance is now through the West Wing, an admirably forthright modern addition (1981) by the influential I.M. Pei.

- For an overview of the collections, pay admission at the booth inside the door and go straight ahead to the information booth to pick up a copy of the floor plan and calendar of events. (They are available in several languages.)
- Incidentally, it will soon be noticed that the museum doesn't provide much fixed seating in its galleries. To compensate, portable seats are available at the front door.

From the information booth, take the escalator to the second floor. Bear right, past the painting of Washington crossing the Delaware and through the doors labeled **Asian Art**. After an entry room of Tibetan bronzes and drawings on cotton, turn right down a long hall of Chinese pottery. Amid the many pots and vases of the 6th–13thC, note the ceramic pillows, certain to have created work for the royal acupuncturist.

At the end of the hall, circle the room of Japanese Buddhist sculptures, painted screens and Edo stoneware and go into the two **Bernat Galleries**. The first of these has many items of different categories, including teapots and altar sets, porcelain and earthenware figurines, scroll paintings and a cup carved from rhinoceros horn; the second displays such larger pieces as multipaneled screens, furnishings and vases of considerable scale. Over on the right are intricately carved wooden bowls and lacquered trays. Bear right into a narrow room with a splendid glazed earthenware horse about two feet high at center stage and a stylized camel bearing musical instruments. At the upper rotunda, make a 180° turn through exhibits of Buddhist and Taoist sculptures and out the door first entered. Bear right, down the hall with the arched skylight.

On the left is the **Gund Gallery**, usually given to traveling shows and other special exhibitions; on the right, the main museum restaurant. At the end of the hall, turn right into the **Evans Wing of European Paintings**. An entire visit could be profitably spent in this wing alone, with galleries on both sides of the central hall.

First encountered are French and Italian painters of the Baroque period. After them, turn right into the Renaissance, then right again into 14th and 15thC and Gothic depictions of Madonnas and martyrdoms in tempera on wood with gilt frames. Proceeding down the hallway, rooms on the left are given to Spanish artists, the Dutch and Flemish, more Italians and 18thC miscellany. Don't miss the 19thC landscapes by Turner in the gallery on the left at the far end. His *Fall of the Rhine at Schaffhausen* (1806) and *Slave Ship* (1840) tellingly illustrate his evolution from realist to precursor of Impressionism.

Across the hall is a small room of Post-Impressionists, with several Van Goghs, the most familiar a portrait of Madame Roulin. Nearby is Cézanne's *Self-Portrait with a Beret*. The last, largest room of this wing is devoted to Impressionists. At one end is a bronze sculpture of a dancer with a skirt of real tulle, a surprise to viewers who think of Degas exclusively as a painter. Opposite is Gauguin's rumination on mortality, *Where Do We Come From?*, a large canvas from his Tahitian period and one of his most famous.

Following this, through the glass door, are a series of European period rooms and decorative arts of the 16th through 19thC. Medieval art, mostly altarpieces and religious carvings, make a buffer before a hall of Roman mosaics, ceramics and other artifacts, including a case of delicately hand-blown glass. Circle clockwise through the following spaces filled with Hellenic sculptures and impressively proportioned amphorae and other vessels decorated in traditional tones of sepia and dark brown.

This collection is among the most important MFA holdings, deserving of careful attention. Eventually, though, continue around to the right, entering the Egyptian galleries. Stay alert for the cases of smaller objects that include an ivory and ebony box, a thumbnail-sized scarab from 1800BC, and what looks like an ancient cribbage board. Monumental icons and panels of glyphs follow, then ceramics, carvings and housewares. These end in the **Upper Rotunda**, glimpsed previously. Take the stairs down to the ground floor.

To tour the **first floor**, walk past the information booth and turn right through the doors labeled "Asian Art." This long gallery hall has ceramics from Iran and Syria of the 10th–14thC; the third case down has some especially attractive pieces, including a 12thC earthenware elephant. At the end, turn right into rooms of sculptures and architectural fragments from Cambodia and other parts of Southeast Asia.

Bear left, through displays of Japanese prints of considerable complexity of detail, with tangled forests, fierce samurai and ferocious gods. Next to these are intricately designed porcelains which demonstrate that the arts of 5th–8thC Korea were as highly developed as those of contemporaneous Japan and China. Continuing in a counterclockwise direction, the next room reveals sets of fearsome samurai armor and weaponry, as well as richly embroidered robes.

Back in the hallway originally entered, turn right into a hall of Indian prints and watercolors. Off to the right is a collection of Hindu temple sculptures depicting Vishnu, the preserver, voluptuous Shiva, the destroyer, and less prominent deities, most of them blessed with multiple limbs. On the opposite side of the corridor is the **Torf Gallery,** used for special exhibitions. Continue in the same direction, into the vestibule of the original Huntington Ave. entrance, nowadays closed. On the other side is the Nubia section, objects from the African kingdoms of the upper Nile reaches that include the alabaster funeral figures over on the right.

Bear right through the next gallery of artifacts from Babylon and Persia into rooms of even more Greek and Etruscan vases and amphorae to complement those on the floor directly above. Also on view are helmets, figurines and such relatively utilitarian pieces as bronze mirrors and braziers. Circle around and out through the Near Eastern section, along a short hall of Egyptian relics dating to two millennia BC.

This empties, rather joltingly, into a room of American silverwork. Across it, slightly to the left, is a chamber of mummies and sarcophagi. Leaving it, turn left, through the room of silverware that serves as introduction to several galleries of 17th–19thC American and European decorative arts and furnishings. At the far end of this section, a staircase descends to rooms of American crafts, the not-to-be-missed highlight being a gallery of large ship models, complete down to belaying pins and links in anchor chain. One of the smaller models is made of ivory, bone, silk and brass. Most are of the 19th and early 20thC.

Back on the **first floor,** a section of furniture in the American Federal style that emerged after the Revolution leads logically into a room of paintings by John Singleton Copley (1738–1815) and his contemporaries, among them Benjamin West and Gilbert Stuart, famous for his portraits of George Washington. Copley's best-known work is probably the portrait of Paul Revere, leaning on his right elbow, jaw in hand.

Following these is a room of folk and primitive canvases, including the familiar *Peaceable Kingdom* (1840) by Edward Hicks. More remarkable, perhaps, is the large portrait of the Reverend John Atwood and his family, painted in 1845 by a self-taught 17-year-old, Henry F. Derby. A doorway leads into 19thC American landscapists and genre painters, where efforts of several Hudson River School artists — Church, Cole, Bierstadt — are seen to good advantage.

Next door, an open-sided gallery is devoted to afternoon tea; chamber music is on offer there Tuesday to Friday from 2.30–4pm. Next on are "American Masters": the late 19thC realists Thomas Eakins, Albert Pinkham Ryder and George Inness, among others. Following them are what many historians call the American Impressionists, although these works bear little resemblance to those of Monet and his fellows in France. John Singer Sargent is most prominent, with four pictures. (For Boston's most impressive canvas by this highly accomplished artist, be sure to visit the ISABELLA STEWART GARDNER MUSEUM, where his memorable *El Jaleo* is hung.)

The galleries on this floor finish with a flourish, in a large space devoted to large post-World War II American and European works. Considering what has immediately preceded, the canvases by such luminaries as Jackson Pollock and Robert Motherwell are as startling as cold water flung in the face. They are joined by Joan Miró, the young Picasso and Juan Gris. Finally, there is the **Foster Gallery,** reserved for special exhibitions and recent acquisitions.

Bearing right, go past the airy museum café on the left, with its refreshing splashes of live greenery. The **Remis Auditorium** is on the right, where solo instrumentalists and small chamber groups are typical concert fare. Lectures and films are also scheduled. Along the way are sculptures by Aristide Maillol and David Smith.

Beyond the café is the **Museum Shop**, with an excellent selection of gifts, reproductions, needlepoint kits, calendars, books, and such absolute essentials as the Mummy Tin Box with 12 Hieroglyphic Pencils.

## MUSEUM OF SCIENCE
*Science Park (on the Charles River Dam), Boston. Map 11C8–D9* ☎*723-2500* ▨ *(but* ▣ *on Wed afternoon)* ▣ ✿ *Open daily May–Aug 9am–5pm (Fri until 9pm); Sept–Apr Tues–Sun. Closed Mon from Sept–Apr, except on Mon holidays.* **T** *Science Park (Green Line).*

A dam built in 1910 across the Charles from Boston's Old West End to East Cambridge serves several useful purposes: controlling the tidal flow of the river, adding another connection between the two cities, and providing a site for the Hayden Planetarium and this museum. Hanging in the lobby is the human-powered Daedalus plane created at the Massachusetts Institute of Technology. Hands-on exhibits and graphic demonstrations of scientific principles help to make understandable the mysteries of astronomy, earth sciences, computers and zoology, to name a few of the fields covered. New chicks in their hatchery and a device that creates actual bolts of lighting before wide eyes are understandable favorites with children.

The attached **Omni Theater** has a giant screen 76 feet in diameter used to show films on subjects ranging from mountain gorillas to Antarctica to the vanishing rainforest.

At the Boston end of the complex is the **Charles Hayden Planetarium** ( ☎ *523-6664).* Daily shows of the New England night skies are changed by the season, and highly sophisticated laser productions are on offer Friday to Sunday.

• Separate entrance fees are charged for the museum, Omni Theater and planetarium, but there are discounts if purchasing more than one ticket.

## MUSEUM WHARF
*Map 12F12* ✿ **T** *South Station (Red Line).*

The BOSTON TEA PARTY SHIP & MUSEUM, the CHILDREN'S MUSEUM and the COMPUTER MUSEUM are within a few steps of one another on the s side of Fort Point Channel. They are the reason for the name of the wharf between the Northern Ave. Bridge and Congress St. Bridge.

## NEW ENGLAND AQUARIUM ★
*Central Wharf (Milk St.), Boston. Map 12E12* ☎*973-5200* ▨ ✿ *Open July 1– Labor Day Mon–Fri 9am–6pm (Wed, Thurs until 8pm), Sat, Sun, most holidays 9am–7pm; Sept–June 30 Mon–Fri 9am–5pm (Thurs until 8pm), Sat, Sun, most holidays 9am–6pm. Closed Thanksgiving; Christmas.* **T** *Aquarium (Blue Line).*

Boston had no aquarium after 1956, when the old one on Castle Island closed. That was an unacceptable deficiency for a seaport with a major fishing industry, so this project was undertaken as part of the waterfront redevelopment. It opened in 1969, introducing some notable innovations. Today, it contains more than 2,000 specimens.

To the left of the entrance is an open tank of seals rescued as orphan pups from nearby waters. Several boats in the adjacent inlet offer harbor and whale-watching cruises.

- Obtain a schedule of events when purchasing tickets for the aquarium to know the times of the dolphin and sea lion shows in the adjacent floating amphitheater (**Discovery**), and for dives in the main tank.

Inside, the first exhibit encountered is the **penguin rookery**, an open pool with rocks which contains more than a score of two kinds of the playful birds, called Jackass and Rockhopper. The second name is self-explanatory, while the first refers to its characteristic bray. The second tank is used for special exhibits, which have in the past included frogs and toads, ornamental carp, turtles and a gathering of small, stinger-less, cownose rays, which visitors were encouraged to touch.

From there, a ramp leads up to the **Thinking Gallery**, tanks with various themes intended to provoke deeper curiosity about aquatic life. Large groupers and spiny lobsters share one. The next holds fish that haven't evolved significantly from their prehistoric ancestors, including long-nosed gar and the South American lungfish. Others illustrate various habitats, such as salt marshes and mangrove swamps, the practical reasons why fish swim in schools, and how species adapt to deep-sea abysses and various other extreme conditions.

Continuing clockwise, look for the **Rivers of the Americas Gallery**, dealing with marine life in the Amazon Basin and along the coastlines of the Northern Hemisphere. One of these has an anaconda that seems not to have an end; another has a school of piranha. Following these are a re-creation of a New England tidepool with sea urchins, periwinkles and horseshoe crabs, and tanks devoted to creatures of the waters off New England and Canada, including salmon, lobsters and octopi. Along the way are computer games and interactive devices, such as one that allows viewers to change water currents to see how the fish react.

Clearly, this is not just another commercial operation. The aquarium takes its educational mission seriously, as is demonstrated by its graphic representation of the sorry state of Boston Harbor and a discussion of plans to reverse the effects of pollution.

Proceeding from exhibit to exhibit via ramps that circle the **giant central tank**, visitors now find themselves near the top of the building. Here is access to the ramp that spirals around the cylindrical tank down to the ground floor. This, the aquarium's main attraction, simulates a Caribbean coral reef. It is 23 feet deep and 40 feet across and has over 800 specimens, from sharks and Moray eels to sea turtles and blowfish. Being inches away from them is almost more excitement than some children can stand, especially when divers enter the tank to minister to their finny charges.

At the bottom, continuing around to the right, is the **Tropical Gallery**, easily the most colorful of the exhibits. Flashing, shimmering, glinting, glowing, these beautiful fishes look as if a child's kaleidoscope had broken and scattered its crystals over the ocean floor. They are a decided highlight, but there is more to come. Exiting the building and bearing left, visitors enter a floating amphitheater, titled **Discovery**, where sea lions and the ever-popular bottlenose dolphins perform (when they are not spending the winter in Florida).

- Announcements of upcoming shows, which take place at least four times a day, are made over the aquarium speaker system. Arrive for them on time, as the doors are closed when each show begins.

## NORTH END ★
*Map 12C11–D11.* **T** *Haymarket (Orange or Green Line).*
Known for over a century for its dense concentration of immigrants from Sicily and Abruzzi and their descendants, the North End is the oldest part of Boston, where John Winthrop moved his colonists in 1630. Here is the PAUL REVERE HOUSE, the OLD NORTH CHURCH from which he received the signal to begin his famous ride, and the COPP'S HILL BURYING GROUND, where the British set up their cannon to bombard Charlestown before the Battle of Bunker Hill.

With its narrow streets echoing with the shouts of mothers summoning their children, the old men playing cards, and their wives gossiping in shops or on park benches, it can easily be taken as a neighborhood of a seaside village in southern Italy. The chief preoccupation and vocation of the populace might well be the providing of food and the eating of same. There are at least 65 restaurants and nearly as many butchers, greengrocers, bakeries, fishmongers, pizzerias and dark *caffès* redolent with tobacco smoke and espresso. The main street is Hanover, site of pushcart markets and the many summer weekend *festas* and saints' days.

- See also WALK 1: THE FREEDOM TRAIL, pages 72–75.

## OLD CITY HALL
*School St., Boston. Map 12E10.* **T** *State (Blue or Orange Line).*
See WALK 1: THE FREEDOM TRAIL, page 70.

## OLD CORNER BOOK STORE
*Washington St. (School St.), Boston. Map 12E10.* **T** *State (Blue or Orange Line).*
See WALK 1: THE FREEDOM TRAIL, page 70.

## OLD GRANARY BURYING GROUND
*Tremont St., Boston. Map 12E10.* **T** *Park Street (Red or Green Line).*
See WALK 1: THE FREEDOM TRAIL, page 69.

## OLD NORTH CHURCH (Christ Church) 🏛
*193 Salem St. (Hull St.), Boston. Map 12D11* ☎523-6676 🖃 *but donations are encouraged* **Ƴ** *available. Open daily 9am–5pm. Closed Thanksgiving; Christmas.* **T** *Haymarket (Green or Orange Line).*
This National Historic Landmark, dating from 1723, is the oldest church in Boston. Those familiar with the designs of Christopher Wren in England will see resemblances here, especially in the single brick tow-

er, the stepped wooden cap and slender spire painted white. This steeple is a 1954 replacement, erected when the old one was blown down in a hurricane, but the weather vane at the top dates from 1740.

The interior contains boxy pews with high sides intended to help keep in the heat of hot bricks brought in by the occupants. It was here, on April 18, 1775, that sexton Robert Newman was called upon to hang the two signal lanterns alerting Paul Revere and William Dawes that the British were advancing by sea on Concord.

- See also WALK 1: THE FREEDOM TRAIL, page 74.

## OLD STATE HOUSE ★ 🏛

*206 Washington St. (State St.), Boston. Map **12**E10 ☎720-3290 Open daily 9.30am–5pm. Closed Thanksgiving; Christmas; New Year's Day. **T** State (Blue or Orange Line).*

In 1711, when the population was only about 9,000, more than a hundred buildings in the present downtown area were destroyed in a disastrous fire. Among them was the original Town House, which had served as meeting hall and center of local government. This was its replacement, opened in 1713. It was known as the Town House until the Revolution, when it was renamed.

During that initial period, it contained both the offices of the Royal Governor and the elected Massachusetts Assembly, a juxtaposition that grew more and more volatile. The Boston Massacre took place outside in 1770. Six years later, the Declaration of Independence was read from the balcony at the eastern end. In the resulting fire of rebellion, those symbols of the Monarchy, the golden lion and silver unicorn that rested upon the cornice, were torn down. The lion and unicorn now seen in the same position are replicas put in place during a later restoration.

Charles Bulfinch's "New" STATE HOUSE on Beacon Hill acquired the functions of the Old State House in 1798. After a short period as the city hall in the 1830s, the Old State House declined into shoddy commercial uses, and many inept deletions and additions were made to its structure. By the 1870s, there was talk of razing the building entirely. But when the City of Chicago offered to buy the building and ship it to the shore of Lake Michigan, the insult to Boston pride stirred a campaign to save it, which accomplished its aims by 1882.

Presently the Old State House is a museum. An introductory film strives to present a balanced view of the events leading up to the Revolution, and leads into the permanent collection of maps and artifacts of the period on the main floor. The second floor has temporary exhibits, usually concerned with contemporary, usually civic, issues.

- See also WALK 1: THE FREEDOM TRAIL, pages 70–71.

## HARRISON GRAY OTIS HOUSE 🏛

*141 Cambridge St. (Lynde St.), Boston. Map **11**E9 ☎227-3956 compulsory, on the hour. Open Tues–Fri noon–5pm; Sat 10am–5pm. Closed Sun; Mon. **T** Bowdoin (Blue Line).*

Harrison Gray Otis was a wealthy socialite and politician. He is remembered especially as the third mayor of Boston, as an astute investor, and as the developer of the Beacon Hill district. This is the first (1796) of three houses he had built to designs by Charles Bulfinch. All three survive, but this is the only one open to the public.

Otis' vision of Beacon Hill saw it evolving as a community of freestanding mansions, much like this building and the two others at 85 Mount Vernon St. and 45 Beacon St. Alas, it didn't happen, for land costs and tax regulations encouraged builders to abut the houses on either side of their lots. This Federalist dwelling now stands on busy Cambridge St., which leads from GOVERNMENT CENTER to the LONGFELLOW BRIDGE into Cambridge. Over the decades, it was moved back 40 feet, the spacious lawn and drives were reduced, and it served purposes that seemed not to auger well for its preservation, including stints as a Turkish bath and boarding house.

Fortunately, it is now owned and maintained by an historical society. The interior has been restored to the period when it was occupied by the Otis family, and the exterior has the rather severe but pleasingly formal elements of the Bulfinch style.

- See also WALK 3: BEACON HILL, page 81.

## PARK STREET CONGREGATIONAL CHURCH
*Park St. (Tremont St.), Boston. Map 12E10. T Park Street (Red or Green Line).*
See WALK 1: THE FREEDOM TRAIL, page 69.

## POST OFFICE SQUARE
*Map 12E11–F11. T State (Blue or Orange Line).*
A neglected space in the Financial District was transformed in 1991 into an award-winning pocket park, bringing light and color into an area that sorely needed both. After the unkempt parking garage that had blighted the block was razed and new parking levels were constructed below ground level, the roof became a garden of flowering fruit and magnolia trees shading teak benches and flowerbeds. It has a small café in a whimsy of a glassed Victorian gazebo, and in spring and summer there are lunch-hour entertainments at least two days a week.

The square is named after the **Post Office** at the N end; on the E is **LE MERIDIEN** hotel (see page 145), in a stately former bank; on the S, the **New England Telephone and Telegraph Company Building**, which contains the workshop in which Alexander Graham Bell invented the telephone (the BELL HISTORY CENTER). Try to ignore the **Bank of Boston**, which muscles its way into the SW corner, a Darth Vader of a building with an intimidating overhang that bulges out over the sidewalk.

## PRUDENTIAL CENTER
*800 Boylston St. (Huntington Ave.), Boston. Map 10G7 ☎236-3318 ▣ ◄€*
**Observatory** *open Mon–Sat 10am–10pm; Sun noon–10pm. T Prudential (Green Line).*
One of the earliest urban renewal projects, this complex and its central tower permanently altered the city skyline and its human scale. Scorn and downright dislike were its fate from the time the plans were first announced, and time has proven those complaints were largely justi-

fied. Its low base of wind-whipped shopping malls and offices stands above street level, unnecessarily segregating it from the neighborhood with which it uneasily coexists. The 52-story skyscraper at its heart is as ungainly as such structures can get to be, looming far above tree-lined streets lined with three- and four-story shops and residences, smugly making a virtue out of its own mediocrity.

One genuine virtue is the **"Skywalk" observatory (✿)** on the 50th floor of the Prudential Center, over 700 feet up, which affords 80-mile views in all directions. Only the new John Hancock Tower surpasses it in height, and that otherwise commendable building doesn't provide these magnificent 360° vistas.

## PUBLIC GARDEN ★
*Map 11F9* ✿ *T Arlington (Green Line).*
Boston's first large land reclamation project stands to the w of the BOSTON COMMON. The two parks are separated by Charles St., which at one time marked the edge of the city. By 1839, landfill to the w made the new botanical garden possible. In this harmonious blend of the formal French style of layout and the informal English manner, weeping willows, giant elms and dogwoods shade the pathways, and the spring blossoms of the Japanese pagoda trees are spectacular.

An amoeba-shaped pond with a Victorian suspension bridge across its narrow midsection provides the focal point. The famous swan boats *(■ ☎ 725-4505)* have plied its waters since 1877. They are propelled by pedal power applied by the operator from his or her station between the wings of the large swans, at the stern.

As in the Common, there are many fountains and monuments, not least among them the sculpture of a mother duck and her eight ducklings near the NE corner of the Garden, inspired by the popular children's book by Robert McCloskey. The Public Garden figured prominently in his *Make Way for Ducklings,* and this 1987 sculpture provides a coveted spot for photographs of children. Prominent among the other statues is that of a triumphant George Washington on horseback facing the E end of Commonwealth Ave.

## QUINCY MARKET
*Map 12E11. T Aquarium (Blue Line) or State (Orange or Blue Line).*
See FANEUIL HALL MARKETPLACE.

## RADCLIFFE COLLEGE
*Map 7B1–2. T Harvard (Red Line).*
Founded in 1879 as an independent institution for women, Radcliffe became coeducational in 1965 after affiliation with HARVARD UNIVERSITY. Always a highly selective college that enrolled only the most qualified students, it retains its own identity despite being under that famous umbrella. An unusually comprehensive resource is its **Arthur and Elizabeth Schlesinger Library**, devoted to the history of women in America. Graduates receive diplomas from both Harvard and Radcliffe.

• See also WALK 5: HARVARD AND OLD CAMBRIDGE, page 86.

# PAUL REVERE HOUSE

*19 North Sq. (Moon St.), Boston. Map* **12***D11* ☎*523-1676* 📟 *Open daily 9.30am–5.15pm (Nov 1–Apr 14 until 4.15pm), except Mon Jan–Mar. Also closed Thanksgiving; Christmas; New Year's Day.* **T** *Haymarket (Green or Orange Line).*
Revere's military exploits were far less distinguished than his career as a silversmith and businessman. He served in the ranks without earning particular distinction in the Revolution, and didn't even finish his much-recounted ride to alert the Minutemen, being captured by the British before he reached Concord. Yet he is remembered as a patriot to be ranked with Washington and Adams because of Longfellow's romanticized account of his action on April 18, 1775: "Listen, my children, and you shall hear/Of the midnight ride of Paul Revere . . . "

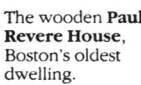

The wooden **Paul Revere House**, Boston's oldest dwelling.

This house, the oldest wood dwelling in Boston, was built c.1677, almost 60 years before Revere was born and nearly a century before he bought it. Its overhanging second story gives it the Medieval aspect the colonists remembered from Europe. Revere fathered 16 children by two wives and raised them here, albeit not all at the same time. Given its compact dimensions, it's difficult to imagine even half that number finding room under the same roof. Some of the existing furnishings were his, and the rest are of the same period.

Next door, sharing a common garden court area, is the brick **Pierce-Hichborn House** *(29 North Sq., same* ☎ *and hours as Revere House).* Moses Pierce built the house in 1711, and it was purchased by Revere's cousin, Nathaniel Hichborn, in 1781. Only four rooms are open while restoration continues.

• Combination tickets allow entrance to both houses.

## ROWE'S WHARF
*Map 12E11–12.* **T** *Aquarium (Blue Line).*
A showpiece of the ongoing waterfront renaissance, Rowe's Wharf supports a striking Post-Modern office-residential development. Its central architectural feature is a high coffered archway that pierces the building to allow a view of the water from Atlantic Ave. The complex also contains the luxurious BOSTON HARBOR hotel (see page 140).

• Water shuttles make frequent trips between here and Logan Airport, and cruise boats debark for excursions to the Harbor Islands, in particular to GEORGES ISLAND.

## ARTHUR M. SACKLER MUSEUM
*Corner of Quincy St. and Broadway, Cambridge. Map 7B3.* **T** *Harvard (Red Line).*
See HARVARD UNIVERSITY ART MUSEUMS.

## ST STEPHEN'S CHURCH 血
*401 Hanover St. (Clark St.), Boston. Map 12D11* ☎*523-1230* ◙ *Open Sun–Fri 8am–4pm; Sat 10am–6pm.* **T** *Haymarket (Orange Line).*
Charles Bulfinch designed 12 churches in Boston. Only this one, finished in 1804, survives, facing w along the Paul Revere Mall to the back of OLD NORTH CHURCH. It first served a Unitarian congregation, but then waves of Irish, and later Italian, immigration transformed the character of the North End. It became a Roman Catholic church in 1862 and remains so today. It is on the Freedom Trail (see WALK 1, page 74).

## SOUTH END
*Partly shown on map 10I7–H8.* **T** *Back Bay/South End (Orange Line).*
Until the early 19thC, Washington St., which runs in a northeasterly direction through this neighborhood, was the narrow causeway that provided Boston's only connection to the mainland. Squeezed between BACK BAY and South Bay (when they were both still water), this strip of land was the "South End." Expansion of the district followed landfill operations in the middle decades of the 19thC, about the same time as the development of Back Bay.

The South End wasn't given the same grand plan of linear parks and boulevards, so it became a more modest working-class district, housing an increasingly polyglot population of Eastern Europeans, Italians, Greeks and Middle Easterners from the waves of immigration that crashed ashore between 1880 and 1925. Gentrification is lately evident in a number of tony restaurants and increasing rehabilitation of the Victorian rowhouses.

## STATE HOUSE (Massachusetts State House) ★ 血
*Beacon St. and Park St., Boston. Map 12E10* ☎*727-3676* ◙ *Open Mon–Fri 9am–5pm. Closed Sat; Sun.* **T** *Park Street (Green or Red Line).*
Charles Bulfinch made his considerable reputation with this, the "new" State House, built in 1797 to replace the OLD STATE HOUSE on State St. Two centuries later it remains the most familiar architectural symbol of the city, its gold dome hovering above the trees of BOSTON COMMON. Bulfinch's contribution was the red-brick core structure beneath the dome.

The s portico has a loggia of seven archways at the top of the front staircase. They are surmounted by a porch of Corinthian columns, and that, in turn, by the pediment supporting the dome. Patriot Sam Adams laid the cornerstone in 1795, and the copper sheeting for the dome was made and installed by Paul Revere's firm. The copper was painted dark gray and stayed that way until 1861, when it was gilded. Except for World War II, when the copper was painted gray again in the fear of aiding German bombers and ships, it has been gold ever since.

Over the years, the building's continuing role as the seat of state government has inevitably required expansion. A long annex, inexplicably made of *yellow* brick, was extended from the back in 1895, increasing office and council space sixfold. As eccentric a solution as could be imagined, it was fortunately masked from general view two decades later. New L-shaped wings, of equal proportion and faced in marble, were added to either side of the original building in 1917. The red brick was painted white to match the marble, and then was stripped back to the original brick ten years later. So it stands today.

Observers from the air have commented that the State House and its extensions resemble a giant bird, assembled by a pixilated creator. There is the plumed yellow tail, the flapping white wings, the squat red body and the noble golden head.

Of the many statues set around the State House, only two are of women. The fates these two met are dismaying, especially among all the military men and politicians with whom they keep company. One statue is of Anne Hutchinson, mother of 14 children, who was banished from the colony in 1637 for her liberal religious views. She and her family moved to frontier New York, where all but one of them were slaughtered by Indians in 1643. The other is of Mary Dyer, judged a heretic and hanged from a tree on the Boston Common in 1648. There are many who feel that it is high time to honour a woman of accomplishment who met a *natural* end.

## SYMPHONY HALL 🏛

*301 Massachusetts Ave. (Huntington Ave.), Boston. Map 10H7 ☎266-1492. Open according to concert schedules of the Boston Symphony Orchestra and the Boston Pops. T Symphony (Green Line).*

Charles McKim, apprentice and friend of H.H. Richardson and partner in the celebrated New York architectural firm, McKim, Mead & White, completed a number of commissions in Boston. The best known is the BOSTON PUBLIC LIBRARY on Copley Sq., which like this building is in the Renaissance Revival style for which the firm is remembered.

In effect, McKim was creating here a suitable box to demonstrate the acoustical theories of a Harvard physics professor, Wallace C. Sabine. Both men were up to the task. The **Boston Symphony Orchestra** and the **Boston Pops** perform here, as do many visiting bands.

## TRINITY CHURCH ★ 🏛

*206 Clarendon St. (Copley Sq.), Boston. Map 11G8 ☎536-0944 ▣ ✗ by appointment. Open Mon–Sat 8am–6pm; Sun 8am–7.30pm. T Copley (Green Line).*

Few major churches dominate the squares they command as H.H. Richardson's finest work does COPLEY SQUARE. The adjacent JOHN HANCOCK TOWER is many hundreds of feet taller, but its mirrored skin reflects the church and sky, almost seeming to disappear.

Richardson worked in the revivalist style of the late 19thC, so closely associated with him that it is often spoken of as "Richardson Romanesque." With its massive central tower, six pointed turrets and hulking rounded arches on clustered columns, the building reminds some observers of the fortress churches of 11thC northern Spain, when such edifices did double duty, elevating the spirit and protecting the person.

Trinity Church rests on the landfill of Back Bay, not the firmest foundation for a structure of such heft: the central tower alone weighs over 9,500 tons. The engineering plan therefore called for 4,500 pilings to be driven down through the surface earth and clay and water table to firmer footing. The polychromed facing is of several earth-toned materials — bricks, tiles, stones — in patterns that start out relatively simple at the base and grow more intricate as the eye moves upward.

Noted artists of the time contributed to the richly finished interior, so different from the unadorned spaces of early Protestant meeting houses. John La Farge, muralist and stained glass artisan, was one of them; William Morris, later associated with the Arts and Crafts movement, was another.

## USS CONSTITUTION ("Old Ironsides")
See CHARLESTOWN NAVY YARD.

# Where to stay

## Boston and Cambridge: making your choice

The 1980s saw a surge in hotel construction that nearly doubled Boston's capacity to house visitors. Economic uncertainty has slowed that trend for the time being, but obtaining suitable accommodation should prove no problem, especially during the colder months. And in the warm months, even from May past Labor Day in September, booking rooms a week or two in advance is usually time enough to avoid disappointment. If the purpose of visiting Boston is a major convention or trade exposition, however, bear in mind that hotels near meeting sites fill up much earlier.

With the renovation and expansion of the **Hynes Convention Center**, adjacent to the PRUDENTIAL CENTER, the large commercial hotels in the immediate vicinity are increasingly in demand. Families and leisure travelers may wish to consider hotels and motels at the edges of the **downtown** district, which contains many of the principal tourist attractions, including FANEUIL HALL MARKETPLACE and THE FREEDOM TRAIL, or in CAMBRIDGE. The efficient public transportation system brings even the suburbs within reach of all that Boston has to offer.

### WHAT TO EXPECT

While standards of service infrequently match those of the renowned deluxe European and Asian hostelries, creature comforts are equal or superior to those found abroad, especially in mid-range and less expensive hotels and motels. Twin beds with sagging mattresses, as can still be found in some of Europe's luxury hotels, are unacceptable to American travelers. Accordingly, rooms are invariably equipped with either one king- or queen-sized bed or two double beds, and the mattresses are firm, even hard. Since remote-controlled color television sets with large selections of cable channels are the rule in American homes, they are also present in all but the meanest bare-bones hotels.

Those are minimal attributes. In the relentless competition for paying customers, managements have piled on the flourishes and enticements to the point — at the luxury level, at least — where there seems little else they *can* provide. Responding to increasing demand, most hotels now have nonsmoking rooms or floors. In deference to the New England weather, swimming pools at an unusually large number of hotels are indoors, often next to fitness centers with weight-lifting machines, exercycles, whirlpool baths and saunas. Rooms in first-class and deluxe quarters are equipped with all manner of gadgets and amenities: hairdryers, scales, terry robes, baskets of toiletries, direct-dial and bathroom telephones, minibars . . . . Newspapers are placed at doors each morning. Same-day dry cleaning and laundry are available Monday to Saturday, and even Sunday in some places. Around-the-clock room service, once in danger of extinction by the lords of cost-accounting, can again be taken for granted at the better (as in "more expensive") hotels.

Rampant technology keeps raising the ante. Telephones often have jacks for modems. Personal computers, printers and fax machines are available for rent. Now seen on some room televisions are on-demand showings of movies still in first-run theatrical release, as well as channels that provide information about restaurants and public transport, and updates on the current status of room charges. Even small hotels will have one or two conference rooms, and most can supply audiovisual and related equipment.

Another commendable trend is the upgrading of hotel restaurant operations, with several dining rooms appearing on local-consensus "best" and "top twenty" lists, including **Aujourd'hui** at the FOUR SEASONS, **Julien** at LE MERIDIEN, **Seasons** at THE BOSTONIAN, and the unnamed room at the RITZ-CARLTON.

Laws regarding ease of access for people using wheelchairs have required hotels to provide rooms with wider doors and modified bathrooms. Some hotels have embraced that need with enthusiasm; others have done only what is minimally expected. Inquire when reserving.

Most — not all — visitors will be relieved to know that dogs and other pets are usually prohibited or at least discouraged.

## BUDGET ACCOMMODATION

Obviously, there is a connection between price and convenience, and Boston's overall cost of living is as high as any city in the country. So while European visitors are apt to consider it inexpensive, if not exactly a bargain paradise, the first reaction of many North Americans when quoted Boston room rates is a sharp intake of breath.

There remain strategies to avoid the deeper bites. Although the metropolitan area can easily occupy a week or more of vacation time, most people stay only three or four days. If they schedule that visit over a weekend, they can take advantage of the discount packages offered by almost every hotel. Savings over weekday tariffs can amount to 40 percent per night and sometimes more, and usually apply Friday and Saturday. Extra inducements may include free parking, complimentary breakfasts, even theater tickets or sightseeing tours. Parents will want to inquire whether children accompanying them can stay in their room at lower or no charge and what is the age limit for this benefit. Additionally, discounts are routinely given to persons over 62 or 65 and to guests who can claim even a tenuous connection with a recognizable corporation.

In any event, never accept the published "rack rate" initially quoted by reservations clerks. Simply asking for something less expensive often results in a comparable room at 10 or 15 percent less.

Increasingly popular as a way to save money and meet local people are bed-and-breakfast arrangements in private homes. This movement hasn't caught fire to the degree it has in other East Coast cities, but there are some possibilities. See the listing of agencies near the end of this chapter (in BED AND BREAKFAST, pages 148–49), which concludes with addresses of agencies that rent rooms and flats for stays of as little as one week (SHORT-TERM RENTALS, page 149).

A state occupancy tax of 9.7 percent is added to room bills.

## LOCATION

About a dozen large convention and business hotels cluster around Copley Square and the adjacent Prudential Center. Two super-deluxe hotels, the RITZ-CARLTON and the FOUR SEASONS, face the Public Garden, two blocks apart; their nearest rivals, LE MERIDIEN and the BOSTON HARBOR, are in the Financial District. Most of the others are scattered through downtown.

Over in Cambridge, four worthy choices are the CHARLES and THE INN AT HARVARD, near Harvard Square, and the HYATT REGENCY and ROYAL SONESTA beside the Charles River, with unimpeded vistas of the Boston skyline.

## CARS

Planning to drive into the city? Conventional advice urges that you park the car in a garage and leave it there until you are ready to leave or to make day trips into the surrounding countryside. Most of the hotels we recommend have garages or parking lots on the premises or nearby, some of them free to guests.

## TIPPING

Tipping is expected, need it be said, but is not especially complicated. Give the **bellman** about $1 per bag, and something extra if the bags are heavy or he must take them a long way. A **doorman** expects something for merely opening a car door, and about $1 if he devotes some time to hailing a taxi or summoning a car from the garage. **Chambermaids** are accustomed to receiving about $1 per night for routine cleaning of an average room, and a little more for suites. Most of the hotels mentioned here add a service charge of 15 to 18 percent to room service bills, in which case, no further gratuity is required.

## RESERVATIONS

In the following pages, toll-free "800" numbers are for reservations only. Don't expect the 800 operator to be able to answer very specific questions, since he or she may not even be in the same state, let alone at the hotel.

If you experience difficulty in obtaining lodging, help might be available from **Citywide Reservation Services** ( ☎ *267-7424 or 800-468-3593)*, which claims linkage with over 100 hotels, inns and bed-and-breakfasts. Or try **Meegan Hotel Reservation Service** ( ☎ *569-3800 or 800-332-3026)*, which has an office in Terminal C at Logan Airport.

## HOW TO USE OUR HOTEL LISTINGS

**Location:** With each street address, to help you pinpoint the location, we give the nearest important cross street. The nearest **T** station to the hotel is also indicated.

**Contact details:** Telephone and fax numbers are given, and the address includes the zip code.

☎ The telephone area code for Boston and Cambridge is **617**.

**Symbols:** A hotel noted for its luxurious standards is indicated by a 🏨 symbol following its name. Look for 🖥 if you need a hotel with a business center. Other symbols show price categories and credit cards, and give a résumé of the available facilities. **See page 7 for the full list of symbols.**

**Other facilities:** Unless otherwise stated below, all hotels have room TV and telephones, private baths, elevators, air conditioning, and accept two or more major credit cards.

**Prices:** The costs corresponding to our price symbols are based on **average charges for a double room with bathroom**. Although actual prices will inevitably increase after publication, our relative price categories are likely to remain the same.

| Symbol | Category | Current price |
|---|---|---|
| ▥ | very expensive | over $220 |
| ▤ | expensive | $180–220 |
| ▥ | moderate | $140–180 |
| ▯ | inexpensive | $90–140 |
| ▭ | cheap | under $90 |

# Boston and Cambridge hotels A to Z

## OUR RECOMMENDATIONS, CLASSIFIED BY PRICE

**VERY EXPENSIVE** ▥
Boston Harbor ▥
The Charles ▥
The Colonnade ▥
Copley Plaza ▥
Four Seasons ▥
Le Meridien ▥
Ritz-Carlton ▥
The Westin Copley Place
**EXPENSIVE** ▥
Back Bay Hilton
The Bostonian ▥
Guest Quarters
Marriott Long Wharf
Omni Parker House

Royal Sonesta
Sheraton Boston Hotel & Towers
Swissôtel Lafayette
**MODERATE TO EXPENSIVE** ▥ to ▥
Boston Park Plaza Hotel & Towers
Eliot
Hyatt Regency Cambridge
Lenox
Logan Airport Hilton
**MODERATELY PRICED** ▥
Holiday Inn Government Center
Howard Johnson 57 Park Plaza
The Inn at Harvard
**INEXPENSIVE** ▥
Copley Square

---

### BACK BAY HILTON
*40 Dalton St. (Belvedere St.), Boston 02115. Map 10G7 ☎236-1100 🖷267-8893 ▥ 335 rms ⬤ 🖳 ☐ &
Indoor ≈ ♆ ☎ ⊇ ♈ T Hynes Convention Center/ICA (Green Line).*
*Location: In Back Bay, near Prudential Center.* The relatively small, visually cluttered lobby doesn't present a particularly positive image, nor is it helped by the litter of handwritten notes taped to various pieces of front desk equipment. But businesspeople involved in trade shows appreciate that the Hynes Convention Center is across the street, and their children and spouses enjoy the all-year pool and Newbury St. shopping. The slender high-rise has only 16 rooms per floor, which eliminates those endless echoing corridors found in too many Hiltons. **Boodles**, the in-house restaurant, gets decent marks for grilled beef and fish. Off-season and weekend discounts are attractive.

### BOSTON HARBOR ▥
*70 Rowe's Wharf (near Atlantic Ave.), Boston 02110. Map 12E11 ☎439-7000 or 800-752-7077 🖷330-9450 ▥ 230 rms ⬤ & ◁ from most rooms ≈ ♆ ☎ ⊇ ♈ ♩ 🖳 ⬛ T Aquarium (Blue Line).*
*Location: On the waterfront, near the*

*Financial District and Faneuil Hall Marketplace.* As the latest paragon of contemporary luxe, this Post-Modern caravanserai can be fairly compared to the FOUR SEASONS and LE MERIDIEN. That is neither a minor compliment nor faint company. Every aspect of comfort and service has been considered, with particular attention to the corporate traveler blessed with a generous expense account. One unique advantage is the airport shuttle boat that docks steps away from the back door. It neatly circumvents the nearly inevitable traffic jams most other visitors have to suffer by going the tunnel route.

The fully-equipped business center operates Monday to Friday 7am–8pm and Saturday 9am–5pm, offering rental pagers and cellular phones, fax machines and computers, express mail, collating and binding of reports, and translation and secretarial services . . . and that's only a partial list. A glimpse of the interactive future is on hand in each room. Something they call the "Concierge Network" allows guests to call up late-release films on demand, or locator maps of restaurants and ATMs, or the current status of their accounts, among many features.

The health club has a 60-foot lap

pool and every device a fitness fanatic might reasonably demand. Meals at **Rowe's Wharf** receive more than their share of valentines from contented diners. (Don't miss the Sunday brunch.) There are even marina slips for those who choose to arrive by private yacht.

## THE BOSTONIAN 🏨

*Faneuil Hall Marketplace (Clinton St.), Boston 02109. Map 12E11* ☎*523-3600, or 800-343-0922 (outside Massachusetts)* 📠*523-2454* 🎫 *152 rms* 🚗 🖻 ᕑ ⊒ ♈ ♪ 🔳 *T Haymarket (Green Line).*

*Location: Downtown, across the street from Faneuil Hall Marketplace.* Most of the building is relatively new (1982), but faced with brick to harmonize with the elderly buildings of old Boston that surround it. The Bostonian enjoys a burnished reputation as the city's top small hotel. A member of the fussy Preferred Hotels group, it must adhere to strict requirements of service and facilities. All rooms have VCRs, many have private balconies, a few have whirlpool baths or the rare luxury of woodburning fireplaces. To enjoy the last, request lodging in the restored 19thC Harkness Wing. **Seasons**, the glamorous rooftop restaurant, is among the most honored in the city, having nurtured a number of celebrity chefs who have ventured out to their own successful enterprises. They have included Lydia Shire of BIBA and Jasper White of JASPER'S (refer to pages 155 and 162).

Much of what draws visitors to Boston is a few minutes from the front door. The FREEDOM TRAIL is just outside, QUINCY MARKET a few paces more, and GOVERN-MENT CENTER, the old NORTH END, and the Financial and Theater Districts are all within walking distance. After a busy day, followed by dinner and a play, the **Atrium** piano lounge is an inviting stop for a brandy before bed. A nearby health club is available to guests. Weekend discount packages are bargains, given the good value on offer.

## BOSTON PARK PLAZA HOTEL & TOWERS

*64 Arlington St. (Park Plaza), Boston 02117. Map 11G9* ☎*426-2000 or*
800-225-2008 📠*426-5545* 🎫 *to* 🎫 *977 rms* 🚗 🖻 ᕑ ⊲∈ *from high rooms* ≋ *available* ♈ ⊒ ♈ ♪ 🔳 *in some rooms.* *T Arlington (Green Line).*

*Location: Between Back Bay and downtown, near the Public Garden.* If possible, reserve in the luxury-level **Towers** section, with its more spacious guestrooms and more extensive appointments and services. But standard rooms aren't too much of a come-down, equipped with the usual gadgets, including cable TV with pay-per-view movies. Several floors are reserved for nonsmokers. At street level, taking up almost an entire city block, is the eternally popular LEGAL SEA FOODS restaurant (see page 162), where there is a takeout section for those who prefer to skip the often long waits for tables. Location is as good as it gets, with Newbury St. shopping, the Theater District, BOSTON COMMON and the start of the FREEDOM TRAIL all within easy striking distance. Several airlines have ticket offices off the lobby, and a free airport shuttle is available. In the evenings, there is piano music in the bar, while the **Terrace Room** stages musical revues.

## THE CHARLES 🏨

*One Bennet St. (Eliot St.), Cambridge 02138. Map 7C1* ☎*864-1200 or 800-882-1818* 📠*864-5715* 🎫 *296 rms* 🖻 ᕑ ⊲∈ *from some rooms* ≋ ♈ ⊒ ♈ ♪ ⟿ 🔳 *T Harvard (Red Line).*

*Location: Overlooking JFK Memorial Park and near Harvard Square.* The banal exterior isn't promising, resembling as it does just another brick apartment house, but be not dismayed. Cambridge's top luxury hotel houses excellent restaurants, a fetching jazz bar and a state-of-the-art health club and spa. The last facility provides extensive hair and beauty treatments in addition to the weight machines, indoor pool, steam room and whirlpool. Guestroom furnishings, deviating from the rather stark contemporary decor of the public rooms, include such reproduced Americana as pine wardrobes and pencil-post beds with quilted down comforters. Some rooms have computer and modem

141

ports. Nonsmoking floors are available.

On the higher-priced **Club** level, complimentary breakfasts and afternoon snacks and drinks are served in the private lounge. **Rarities** is the formal restaurant, rivaling the best hotel dining rooms of the Boston area. The **Bennett St. Cafe** serves all meals and is prized for its Sunday brunch. Room service is available at any hour.

### THE COLONNADE 🏨
*120 Huntington Ave. (Newton St.), Boston 02116. Map **10**H7 ☎424-7000 or 800-962-3030 ☒424-1717 ▥ 288 rms* ⬟ ⇝ 🍷 ⇋ ⛾ 🍴 ▤ 🛄 🛢 *T Prudential (Green Line).*

*Location: Opposite the Prudential Center.* Not every hotel has a rubber duck in every tub. This one does. In most other respects, it falls somewhere between first-class and luxury status, largely because of its laudable efforts to be the perfect business stopover. In addition to its full-service "Corporate Class Office," a number of bedrooms are equipped with computers, modems, laser printers, fax machines, cellular phones and coffee-makers. *USA Today* awaits outside the door each morning. Room 523 has been converted to a compact fitness center, with rowing machine, exercycle, treadmill, Universal weights, and stair-climber. The rooftop pool is open from June to August. SYMPHONY HALL and the Hynes Convention Center are a few blocks away. **Zachary's Bar**, on the ground floor, is a prime showcase for jazz, Wednesday to Saturday. Wines are offered by the glass. Live entertainment is often scheduled for the **Café Promenade**, as well, and outdoor dining is offered in warm weather.

### COPLEY PLAZA 🏨
*138 St James Ave. (Copley Sq.), Boston 02116. Map **10**G8 ☎267-5300 or 800-826-7539 ☒267-7668 ▥ 370 rms* ▤ ⛾ 🍷 ⇋ ⛾ 🍴 *T Copley (Green Line).*

*Location: On Copley Square, near Prudential Center and John Hancock Tower.* The hotel's graceful facade helps make Copley Square the grandest urban space in New England. Dating from 1912, the Copley Plaza gained new owners in 1989. They slathered gilt paint and gold leaf with abandon on the marvelously overwrought lobby and hallways. Grand scale is retained in both public and private sectors, including wide hallways and what may be the largest bedchambers in the city. The **Plaza Bar**, for example, soars two stories to its coffered ceiling, with high arched windows draped in velvet and shut off by ranks of shutters: quite a setting for the singer-piano player who holds forth Tuesday to Saturday. The **Plaza Dining Room** is as splendidly proportioned and bedecked, and afternoon tea in the lobby **Tea Court** is as gracious as the surroundings demand. Bathrooms still bear a between-the-wars stamp, but now with new marble and fixtures. Two floors are reserved for nonsmokers. A small fitness center has been installed, with Lifecycles, stairclimbers, treadmills and weight machine.

Good weekend rates and packages include passes on the Boston **T**. All-you-can-eat Friday dinner and Sunday brunch buffets make weekends even more affordable.

### COPLEY SQUARE
*47 Huntington Ave. (Exeter St.), Boston 02116. Map **10**G8 ☎536-9000 or 800-225-7062 ☒236-0351 ▥ 143 rms* ▤ ⇋ 🍷 *T Copley (Green Line).*

*Location: In Back Bay, near Symphony Hall.* More than 100 years old, the Copley Square retains much of the charm and some of the deficiencies of the time of its construction. Most obvious are the widely divergent sizes and configurations of its rooms. Guests should be prepared to request changes after they have seen their assigned rooms, for preferable accommodations at the same rate are more likely to be available than in younger hotels. Furnishings also differ substantially, with some old, some new. Windows here can actually be opened. Otherwise, most present-day conveniences can be anticipated, with cable color TV and closed-circuit movies, as well as room safes and coffee makers. Voice mail is available.

On the ground floor are the venerable **Cafe Budapest**, a Hungarian restaurant which remains a sentimental favorite with many Bostonians, and the popular **Original Sports Saloon**, with its TV sets tuned to the sports events of the moment, and photos of local heroes. There are nonsmoking floors. Considering the central location and reasonable tariffs, this is one of the city's lodging bargains.

**ELIOT**

*370 Commonwealth Ave. (Massachusetts Ave.), Boston 02215. Map 10G6* ☎*267-1607 or 800-443-5468* ☒*536-9114* 🎫 *to* 🎫 *94 rms* 🛏 🖼 ☕ 🖭 *in most rms.* **T** *Kenmore (Green Line).*
*Location: In the heart of Back Bay.* An inviting boutique hotel that would not be out of place in London's Belgravia, the polished Eliot is still largely undiscovered, even by natives. This, even though it abuts the august Harvard Club and is named after a former president of that distinguished university. Built originally as a residential hotel to serve Harvard Club members, nearly all its units are one- and two-bedroom suites. All have sitting rooms, desks and wet bars, with French doors closing off the bedrooms. Many also contain serving pantries with basic crockery and flatware, coffee-makers, microwave ovens and stocked refrigerators. Despite its corner location on two busy avenues, traffic noise is acceptably low. Phones have modem connections. Both the *Boston Globe* and *USA Today* are delivered to the rooms in the morning. Breakfast is taken in a cheery nook downstairs, where a cook conjures up omelets to order. That is the only meal served, but there are many acceptable restaurants nearby. Book ahead, for the Eliot enjoys unusually high occupancy rates.

**FOUR SEASONS** 🏨

*200 Boylston St. (Charles St.), Boston 02116. Map 11F9* ☎*338-4400* ☒*423-0154* 🎫 *288 rms. Valet* 🛏 🖼 ♿ *Indoor* 🏊 ♨ 🍽 ⚏ ☕ ♪ 🖭 **T** *Arlington (Green Line).*
*Location: Facing the Public Garden.*

Taste and discernment inform every aspect of the Canadian-owned Four Seasons chain, which boasts several of the continent's clearly exceptional hotels. Staff members are meticulously trained in providing the kind of attention that makes all guests feel like potentates, or at least highly influential officeholders. Many among them are blessed with the knack of recalling names after only one hearing. A multimillion-dollar upgrading completed in 1993 has made the public areas even more inviting, their lovely furnishings and antiques already enhanced by huge displays of exotic blooms. The large lounge, with windows facing the Public Garden, has live piano Monday to Thursday evenings and a jazz trio Friday and Saturday. The fireplace gives off its comforting warmth and crackle throughout the winter; light meals and afternoon tea are served. On the top floor are a fitness center and an indoor pool with windows overlooking the city.

Conceding that it has more competition than might be expected in a city this size, the management piles on extras. One that might be especially appreciated by business travelers on hectic schedules is same-day laundry and dry cleaning every day of the week. A week-round complimentary limousine shuttles guests to downtown locations. The histories and quirks of frequent guests are kept on computer, so that their allergy-free pillows or favorite wine will be waiting. Stay a total of 25 nights and the terry robes will bear your monogram. And, the AUJOURD'HUI restaurant is superior to all but a few in the metropolitan area. One quibble? The bedrooms are visually chilly, but just a bit. Anyway, the cable TV has over 50 channels, so who notices?

**GUEST QUARTERS**

*400 Soldiers Field Rd. (Cambridge St.), Boston 02134. Map 7E2* ☎*783-0090 or 800-424-2900* ☒*783-0897* 🎫 🛏 🖼 ♿ ⧉ *Indoor* 🏊 ♨ ☕ ♪ 🖭 **T** *Central (Red Line).*
*Location: On the Charles River, beside the River St. Bridge.* When hotels offer

suites in the same price range as others charge for their standard rooms, compromise is often implicit. If this unit of an expanding national chain has any such liability, it could be its relative distance from downtown Boston. The management can counter, on the other hand, that HARVARD SQUARE is only a mile away and that complimentary van service is provided to major destinations in both Boston and Cambridge. It is also convenient to an interchange of the Massachusetts Turnpike. At minimum, the suites have two rooms, wet bar, and bath; a few have balconies. Children under 12 can stay in the suite for free. Since the sitting-room sofa converts to a bed, parents are permitted a measure of privacy. **Sculler's** is a jazz showcase, which attracts patrons from all over the metropolitan area.

### HOLIDAY INN GOVERNMENT CENTER

*5 Blossom St. (Cambridge St.), Boston 02114. Map 11E9* ☎*742-7630* ☒*742-4192* ▥ ▰ ▣ ⅙ ◂€ *from higher floors* ⇌ ⛱ ⇶ ♈ *T Charles/MGH (Red Line) or Bowdoin (Blue Line).*

*Location: At N base of Beacon Hill, near the Charles River.* No surprises and no serious disappointments at this unit of the international chain. It's convenient to MASSACHUSETTS GENERAL HOSPITAL and within walking distance of the FANEUIL HALL MARKETPLACE. A connected garage and easy-on, easy-off proximity to highways make it a good choice for families on driving vacations who want to be downtown and still avoid most of Boston's notorious traffic. An outdoor pool helps keep children occupied, and an exercise room with a choice of workout machines is available.

### HOWARD JOHNSON 57 PARK PLAZA

*200 Stuart St. (Charles St.), Boston 02116. Map 11G9* ☎*482-1800* ☒*451-2750* ▥ ▰ ▣ *Indoor* ⇌ ⇴ ⇶ ♈ ♫ *T Arlington (Green Line).*

*Location: Between downtown and Back Bay, s of Boston Common.* Moderate prices and the Theater District setting are the principal draws for this large, slab-sided representative of the

national chain. Parking is free, and so are children under 18 who share their parents' rooms. Guests have access to a downtown tennis club.

### HYATT REGENCY CAMBRIDGE

*575 Memorial Drive (near River St.), Cambridge 02139. Map 7E2* ☎*492-1234 or 800-233-1234* ☒*491-6906* ▥ *to* ▥ *469 rms* ▰ ▣ ⅙ *Indoor* ⇌ ⇴ ⇶ ♈ *T Central (Red Line).*

*Location: On the Charles River.* Cliché though it has become, the Hyatt formula still doesn't permit boredom. Inside the pyramidal building is the trademark atrium rising to the roof, with balconies and tiers and glass-bubble elevators zipping up and down the 16 floors like water bugs. There is the splashing pool below, a piano player with his own thrusting aerie, several levels of nooks and lounges. Up top is the requisite rotating bar-restaurant, and above the parking garage is what must be the largest hotel health club in the metropolitan area.

Available in the **Hyattrain** are an indoor lap pool, Universal weight machine, treadmills, Stairmasters, Lifecycles, whirlpool and steam room. A free shuttle bus makes the circuit of major Cambridge and Boston sites for up to 12 hours a day. Nonsmoking rooms are available. On-command pay movies can be ordered on the room TV. And, relentlessly cheery staff members keep asking if you need your parking ticket validated.

### THE INN AT HARVARD

*1201 Massachusetts Ave. (Harvard St.), Cambridge 02138. Map 7C3* ☎*491-2222 or 800-528-0444* ☒*496-5020* ▥ *113 rms* ▰ ▣ ⇶ ⚌ *T Harvard (Red Line).*

*Location: On Harvard Square.* HARVARD UNIVERSITY owns this new off-campus hotel, opened in 1990. Its focal point is a four-story atrium that contains a small restaurant and a lounge with wing chairs and sofas. Two large copies of Baroque garden statues are an odd counterpoint to the vaguely Georgian-Colonial fixtures and architecture, but no matter. The front desk crew is uncommonly cordial and helpful, and housekeeping standards are high. Room telephones have voice mail — in effect, personal answering machines — and armoires hide the cable TV sets. Nightly turn-down service and terry robes are touches usually found in more expensive hotels. The atmosphere of an urban (and urbane) inn is enhanced by the efforts of the kitchen, which goes well beyond such American (or New England) conventionalities as roast turkey and Indian pudding.

### LENOX
*710 Boylston St. (Exeter St.), Boston 02116. Map 10G7 ☎536-5300 or 800-225-7676 ⓕ267-1237 ▥ to▥ 220 rms. Valet ⬤ 🖻 ☕ ⬛ ⬛ Ⅺ ♪*
**T** *Copley (Green Line).*
*Location: In Prudential Center.* Recent renovations have undeniably improved what had been an increasingly dowdy hotel, built in 1900. Prices have gone up accordingly. Rates are negotiable, though, and discounts are substantial on weekends. The Lenox is operated by the Saunders family corporation, which also owns the even older COPLEY SQUARE HOTEL, and there is a similar Continental flavor. Some corner rooms have working fireplaces, a rare treat in the depths of a Boston winter. There's a larger fireplace in the lobby. Several sorts of decorative treatments are used, from Colonial American to French Provincial to Oriental.

On the ground floor, the **Lenox Pub & Grill** is more coffee shop than pub; **Diamond Jim's Piano Bar** is a pleasant retreat for a drink or two. Front rooms are at a premium on the occasion of the Boston Marathon: the finish line is nearby. A shuttle service to the airport is available.

### LOGAN AIRPORT HILTON
*75 Service Rd. (Logan International Airport), East Boston 02128. Map 6C4 ☎569-9300 or 800-445-8667 ▥ to▥ 542 rms. Free ⬤ ☕ ⬛ 'Ⅴ' ⬛ Ⅺ ▣*
**T** *Airport (Blue Line).*
*Location: In Logan Airport.* Routine in every other respect, this Hilton does

enjoy the distinction of being the only hotel within the airport boundaries. Similarly situated hotels elsewhere are primarily for workaholics and people with very early or late flights. But Logan is only minutes away from downtown, and it has its own subway stop. A free shuttle bus travels a circuit of the several terminals and the **T** station every 10–15 minutes, around the clock. Soundproofing is effective: even though rooms overlook the runways, a departing Jumbo jet sounds no louder than muffled rolling thunder. A channel on the room TV provides updates on flight times and status. On-demand pay movies are available. Room service is often slow, and they could probably do with more staff.

### MARRIOTT LONG WHARF
*296 State St. (near Atlantic Ave.), Boston 02109. Map 12E11 ☎227-0800 ⓕ236-5885 ▥ 400 rms ⬤ ☕ ◀€ from most rooms. Indoor ⮀ 'Ⅴ' ⬍ ⬛ Ⅺ ♪ Ⅴⅰ ⬛* **T** *Aquarium (Blue Line).*
*Location: On the harbor, near Faneuil Hall Marketplace.* At last look, the ubiquitous Marriott chain had four hotels in the immediate metropolitan area. This is the most visible — newer, and prominently occupying LONG WHARF in the rejuvenated downtown waterfront district. The building is long and only five stories tall, with a stepped configuration that makes it appear that all rooms have balconies (which they don't). Bedrooms are placed around a central atrium, with executive-class rooms on the top floor. Extras up there include free breakfasts and cocktails. In addition to FANEUIL HALL and GOVERNMENT CENTER, the NEW ENGLAND AQUARIUM is next door, and the colorful NORTH END is in the immediate vicinity. **Rachael's** nightclub provides music for dancing; the renovated **Harbor Terrace** restaurant has views of harbor activity. Children under 18 can stay in their parents' room free. Weekend packages are steeply discounted.

### LE MERIDIEN ▦
*250 Franklin St. (Congress St.), Boston 02110. Map 12F11 ☎451-1900 or*

800-543-4300 ✉423-2844 ▥ 326 rms.
Valet ⬅ 🖭 ♿ Indoor ♨ ♀ ☎ ≕ ☯ ♪
🖭 ⚏ T *Downtown Crossing (Red Line).*
*Location: Downtown, in the Financial
District, not far from the Faneuil Hall
Marketplace.* An exercise in enlightened
entrepreneurship, the Boston entry of
the French luxury chain uses the rehabilitated former headquarters of the
Federal Reserve Bank. Erected in 1922,
the neo-Renaissance palazzo has been
restored to its original grandeur, especially in the spaces housing the **Julien**
and **Cafe Fleuri** restaurants and the
**Julien Bar** (see page 162 for our entry
on JULIEN.) Sunday brunch in the café is
remarkable, with sushi, spa cuisine,
eggs cooked to any order, smoked seafoods, and tables full of guilty pleasures. The bar was once the meeting
room of the bank's board of governors,
and they felt no compulsion to restrain
themselves, not on the evidence of its
gilding and carvings and coffered ceilings, and two murals by N.C. Wyeth,
father of Andrew. That tradition has
been carried through with important
modern artworks in public areas, including a Jacques Lipshitz sculpture.

Three floors were added to the six-
story building, and a pyramidal glass
structure up top. The sloping walls provide views of the towers of the Financial
Center, especially dramatic at night.
Their only deficiency is their tendency
to absorb solar heat, which can make
the rooms uncomfortably warm during
brief seasonal transition periods, as between winter and spring. Compensa-
tions include voice mail and express
laundry and dry cleaning. Four floors
are reserved for nonsmokers. Fax, secretarial services and interpreters are
available in the business center. A warm-
weather café overlooks the renovated
POST OFFICE SQUARE.

## OMNI PARKER HOUSE
*60 School St. (Tremont St.), Boston 02108.
Map* **12**E10 ☎227-8600 ✉742-5729
▥ 541 rms ♿ 🖭 ♀ available ≕ ☯ ♪
♥♪ T *Park Street (Red Line).*
*Location: Downtown, near Boston
Common.* The Parker House has sev-

eral claims to fame. First, foremost and
shakiest is its boast that it is the "oldest
continuously operating hotel in the US."
This, despite the fact that the present
building dates from 1927, decades
younger than the COPLEY SQUARE, LENOX
and COPLEY PLAZA. More intriguing are
the alleged employments of Viet-
namese revolutionary Ho Chi Minh and
the American black militant, Malcolm X.
And readers of a certain age might remember the baked products known as
Parker House Rolls.

The location is the bonus, directly on
the FREEDOM TRAIL, at the base of BEACON
HILL and near GOVERNMENT CENTER and
FANEUIL HALL MARKETPLACE. On weekends,
big band music of the 1930s and '40s is
played for dancing. Bedrooms are un-
remarkable, some only with showers,
some with refrigerators.

## RITZ-CARLTON 🏨
*15 Arlington St. (Newbury St.), Boston
02117. Map* **11**F9 ☎536-5700 or
800-241-3333 ✉536-1335 ▥ 278 rms.
Valet ⬅ 🖭 ♿ ◁≡ from upper floors ♨
available ♀ ☎ ≕ ☯ ♥ 🖭 T *Arlington
(Green Line).*
*Location: In Back Bay, looking E over
the Public Garden.* In a city blessed
with several fine hotels of the highest
order, the Ritz-Carlton is challenged but
slips not an inch from its position at the
pinnacle. With about two employees
for every guest, there is an atmosphere
of caring and concern from doorman to
concierge to chambermaid. The human
touch is sustained by the elevator operators, surely among the few people still
so employed. Some compare it to a
return to family, which it may be, with
the stipulation that this family dresses
for dinner. Even a 5pm drink in the
reassuringly proper bar requires the
wearing of a jacket, and boors in shorts
and "I'm with Stupid" T-shirts are suffered not at all, let alone gladly.

Bedrooms are spacious, with an
English manor atmosphere, and have
remote-control cable TV, VCR, hair-
dryer, terry robes and clock radios. Accurate bathroom scales tell the awful
truth about a few meals in the dining

room, which is unnamed according to Ritz tradition, but one of the city's most honored restaurants. Help in shedding those extra pounds is available in the penthouse fitness center, small, but equipped with Universal weight machine, treadmills, Nordic Track, stairclimber, Lifecycles, and a unisex sauna (take a bathing suit).

For still more cosseting, select a room on the **Club** level. Benefits largely involve an exclusive lounge, complete with a working fireplace. Breakfast and light lunches are served there, followed by tea, cocktails and hors d'oeuvres, and later, cordials and chocolates. A library of video tapes is available. At the door each weekday morning is a copy of the *Wall Street Journal*. The rapid expansion of the Ritz-Carlton chain may be diluting its reputation, as some critics grouse, but just here, all's right with the world.

### ROYAL SONESTA

5 Cambridge Parkway (Edwin Land Blvd.), Cambridge 02142. Map **11**C8
☎491-3600 ⊠661-5956 ▥ 400 rms
🛏 ▣ ♿ ◁€ from many rooms. Indoor ☼
♨ ⇆ ♈ ☂ ▣ **T** Lechmere (Green Line).
*Location: On the Charles River, near the Museum of Science.* One distinguishing characteristic of this Cambridge high-rise is its collection of contemporary art. Unusually daring for a hotel, the mostly abstract sculptures, paintings and drawings are on display in both public and private areas. Another feature is unobstructed views of Boston all the way from the NORTH END to BACK BAY. Otherwise, this is a fairly conventional first-class hotel popular for business meetings and weddings.

The original tower, now called the **East Wing**, was joined not long ago by a larger **West Wing**. Both of them have bars and restaurants, one of which, **Davio's**, is a decided improvement over the standard in this category. The health club, on the ground floor of the East Wing, is fully equipped, with fixed and free weights, rowing machine, exercycle and stair-climbers. Next to it is a pool with both lap lanes and a play

area under a glass atrium. A "day of beauty" program in the spa offers facial, massage, manicure and pedicure. Bedrooms are done in pastels that would be more at home in Florida, but are large enough, and have cable TV with pay-per-view movies. Across the street is the large Cambridgeside shopping mall, and the hotel provides a free shuttle service to various points in Boston and Cambridge.

### SHERATON BOSTON HOTEL & TOWERS

39 Dalton St. (near Boylston St.), Boston 02199. Map **10**G7 ☎236-2000 or 800-325-3535 ⊠236-1702 ▥ 1,252 rms. Valet 🛏 ▣ ♿ ◁€ from many rooms. Indoor ☼ ♨ ⇆ ☂ ♈ ♈ ⇆ ♨
**T** Prudential (Green Line).
*Location: In Prudential Center.* There is a low rumble here, all the time, as if it were not a hotel but a giant spaceship on a journey to other galaxies. That soon passes out of your consciousness, though, submerged by the efficiency and breadth of services of this "hospitality machine." While it can't claim a warm and fuzzy personality, not with over 1,200 guest rooms, it has just about every facility and gadget that travel in the late 20thC demands. The health club on the fifth floor has a large pool with a retractable roof along with a sufficiency of exercycles and weight equipment. Every room has two phones and a coffee maker; an iron and ironing board are stored in the closet.

Keeping in mind its primary market, the management has opened a new executive center to assist in arranging meeting space and audiovisual equipment, as well as work areas with voice mail and modems for keeping in touch with the office and clients. There is direct connection with the Hynes Convention Center. Executive floors in the tower section provides a lounge with views of Back Bay and Cambridge in which to take breakfast or pre-prandial drinks and hors d'oeuvres. *USA Today* is delivered each morning.

The restaurants in the hotel are adequate. Weekend discounts are as much as 60 percent off weekday rates.

## SWISSÔTEL LAFAYETTE

*1 Ave. de Lafayette (Lafayette Pl., between Washington and Chauncy Sts.), Boston 02111. Map 12F10* ☎*451-2600 or 800-621-9200* ⊠*451-0054* ▥ *500 rms* ▬ ▣ ᴖ ≋ ᵞ ⊒ ᵞ ♪ ▣ **T** *Downtown Crossing (Red Line).*

*Location: At the edge of the Financial District.* Presumably the canny Swissôtel chain will bring this comfortable but rather lackluster acquisition up to the high level of its other holdings. In the meantime, there are good reasons to choose it as a base of operations. A large adjacent parking garage is one, allowing visitors to follow good advice to avoid driving in the city, while having their cars available for day trips to the historic suburbs or the North Shore. The Theater and Financial Districts are in walking distance, as are CHINATOWN and the resurgent waterfront.

The lobby lounge meets gustatory needs throughout the day, with a menu of snacks and light meals from 11am to 11pm, free "happy hour" hors d'oeuvres, and a Friday and Saturday night dessert buffet. Piano music accompanies those choices. The sixth-floor health club is open daily, with a 20-yard lap pool and saunas. The *New York Times* or *Wall Street Journal* are delivered in the morning. Weekend packages include discount shopping coupons and free parking. The third-floor lobby provides a reassuring extra measure of security, considering the COMBAT ZONE and declining DOWNTOWN CROSSING shopping district are nearby.

## THE WESTIN COPLEY PLACE

*10 Huntington Ave. (Dartmouth St.), Boston 02116. Map 10G8* ☎*262-9600* ⊠*424-7483* ▥ *848 rms. Valet* ▬ ▣ ᴖ ◄€ *from most rooms. Indoor* ≋ ᵞ ⇔ ⊒ ᵞ ♪ ▣ *in many rooms.* **T** *Copley (Green Line).*

*Location: At the sw corner of Copley Square, near Prudential Center.* An escalator whisks visitors up past double waterfalls to the sweeping second-floor lobby, full of shops and lounges and eating areas. Guestrooms start on the eighth floor, and the building tops out at the 36th. An enclosed "skybridge" connects with the Copley Place shopping mall, which includes a Neiman-Marcus department store and a cinema. An indoor pool is the focus of the health club, which also has a sauna, whirlpool and weight machines. Massages can be arranged. Rooms are large and attractively furnished, most with vistas of Back Bay and the Charles River. Of the several restaurants and lounges, **Turner Fisheries** is favored by both visitors and natives, known especially for its rendition of clam chowder. Discounted room rates dip into the inexpensive range on winter weekends.

# Bed and breakfast

The impersonality and often stunning expense of a stay in Boston have inspired the beginnings of a bed-and-breakfast movement. While it hasn't grown as dramatically as in some other American and Canadian cities, there are agencies that maintain lists totaling perhaps 300 possibilities. (Some member homes are listed with more than one agency.)

Unlike the British model, these are rooms in private homes whose hosts provide breakfast, usually of the minimalist continental variety. They are not conventional inns with dining rooms and signs out front, as are found in villages all over New England. Accommodations range from utilitarian rooms with a bath down the hall to charmingly furnished suites with most hotel comforts and gadgets. And even the most expensive among them rarely nudge into our moderate price band (▥).

A modest sense of adventure is required, if only because match-ups between guests and hosts are made by telephone or mail. Parties on both sides of the arrangement have distinct quirks and needs, and these must be clearly stated before money is exchanged. Among the considerations are rules about smoking, curfews, children and pets. A potential guest who regards a private bathroom or television as essential must say so, for these are available, but cannot be assumed. Ask too about the distance to the nearest public transport, the availability of parking and restaurants, and whether the hosts will be available to provide assistance or will simply leave keys and breakfast fixings in some prearranged place.

An advance deposit is inevitably required, and refunds are paid only under strict conditions. Most of the reservation agencies listed below accept one or two credit cards. While they describe their participating homes as fully as possible, they don't reveal names and addresses until the deposits have been received and cleared. They claim to set rigorous standards and conduct regular inspections, but this is a volatile business, with participants dropping out unexpectedly. No guarantees can be made about the quality of accommodation, nor even about the continued existence of the referral services listed below:

- **Bed & Breakfast Agency of Boston**  47 Commercial Wharf, Boston, MA 02110 ☎720-3540 or 800-248-9262.
- **Bed & Breakfast Associates Bay Colony, Ltd.**  P.O. Box 57166, Babson Park Branch, Boston, MA 02157 ☎449-5302 or 800-347-5088.
- **Bed and Breakfast Cambridge and Greater Boston**  P.O. Box 665, Cambridge, MA 02140 ☎576-1492 or 800-888-0178.
- **Host Homes of Boston**  P.O. Box 117, Waban Branch, Boston, MA 02168 ☎244-1308.
- **New England Bed and Breakfast**  1045 Centre St., Newton, MA 02159 ☎244-2112.

# Short-term rentals

Still another possibility is a short-term rental. Unhosted rooms and flats are available at rates well below comparable hotel costs, but usually only for periods of a week or more. You can save still further by cooking some or all of your own meals. Another virtue is the opportunity to live among local residents, rather than in the isolation of hotels. Agencies that advertise this service include:

- **AGH Rentals**  P.O. Box 517, Cambridge, MA 02140 ☎354-3500.
- **Boston Short-Term Rentals**  301 Newbury St., Boston, MA 02115 ☎262-3100.
- **Corcoran Management Company**  100 Grandview Rd., Suite 205, Braintree, MA 02184 ☎508-927-2116 or 800-287-2500.

# Eating and drinking

## Dining out in Boston and Cambridge

Boston was a little late in joining the food revolution that swept North America in the last decade, but it has now joined the ranks of the dedicated. Ever since a new generation of serious chefs started unfurling their knife-carriers a few years back, local periodicals have been eagerly charting their moves and strategies. Legions of loyalists follow their culinary heroes from tavern to trattoria to haute bistro. This doesn't mean that Bostonians are afflicted with the near-pathological gastromania of San Francisco or New Orleans or New York. But travelers who have been away from the city for a while will be pleased to discover that choices have expanded far beyond the prime ribs, chowders, and spaghetti with clam sauce they remember.

Allegiances to narrow ethnic specializations are relatively rare, or at least not often worth the notice. Despite the presence of large immigrant groups from every continent, Asian, Latin American and Eastern European cuisines barely figure in the roster of commendable restaurants. Not counting Italian dining places, too commonplace to be regarded as exotic, barely a handful of ethnics can be gathered, with only a couple of recommendable Chinese places, one Mexican, an Indian, and a Greek or two. Forget Cuban or Hungarian or Brazilian.

Most restauranteurs have simply leapfrogged the intermediate steps and gone down the multicultural route. As will be seen in the following pages, the majority of the most popular eateries practice galloping eclecticism. Sometimes this means the partial discipline of confining a menu to a limited supranational region, such as the Mediterranean basin. That leaves considerable latitude, of course, the possibilities bouncing from couscous to souvlaki to zarzuela to gnocchi.

At least as often, the chefs who prosper traffic in transglobal pastiches. Translated, that means bits and pieces of just about anything: lemon grass and okra tossed with chilpote peppers stirred with New Zealand clams dusted with *cilantro* ladled over rotini. That's only the merest exaggeration of what might be found on a single plate. What is agreeably surprising is how often such concoctions actually work, with enough novelty to pique the palate and sufficient substance to satisfy. These trained and experienced young chefs also absorbed the lessons of artistic presentation handed down by the disappearing *nouvelle* vogue, while recognizing that the puny portions characteristic of that creed don't do much to promote customer loyalty.

This prompts a warning to visitors from other countries who may be accustomed to meals consisting of several small courses. American restaurant-goers often make a dinner of just two appetizers, or an appetizer and dessert, or only a single main dish, but they expect whatever portion they order to be copious. Hence the existence of the "doggie bag." To the uninitiated European, this is the accepted American practice of packaging leftovers from restaurant meals to take home. Largely a charade playing out the thoughtful act of sharing dinner with the family pet, doggie bags more often provide for second human meals in front of the television a day later.

## WHAT TO EXPECT

Very few restaurants now preserve the traditionally rigid strata of staff. Sommeliers (wine stewards) are gone, for all practical purposes, and captains, who oversee waiters in specific sections of dining rooms, are fast disappearing. Hosts (a.k.a. *maître d'hotel*) check reservations and guide patrons to their tables. In smaller establishments, they may also take orders or pour wine. Waiters or waitresses have increasingly absorbed the captain and wine steward duties, describing dishes and bottles as well as serving the meals. They often function in teams, pooling their tips at the end of the day. Busboys (often recent immigrants) are the lowest paid. Distinguished by their different uniforms, they clear tables, refill water glasses and bring baskets of bread, but are neither prepared nor instructed to take food orders.

Service may be rushed, cordial, amateurish or distracted, depending upon circumstance and personnel. Only in the most luxurious restaurants do servers match the professionalism of waiters at upper-bracket European establishments. To most, waiting tables is a job, not a career, especially in a city where many people in the employment pool are university students.

Affectations and foolish or irritating practices persist, it must be said. Heading the second list is the no-reservations policy of many of the most popular restaurants, which results in long lines stretching from the bar all the way outside and down the street. Since this often means standing unprotected for up to an hour in severe Boston weather, dining out can prove to be an exercise in masochism.

The problem is compounded by those chefs who insist upon serving just dinner, and only five nights a week. That is their right, of course. But it smacks of self-indulgence and even contempt for the dining public. Since there are usually good reasons for such popularity — food or ambience, or simply what's fashionable — we advise that such restaurants be avoided like plague houses Thursday-to-Saturday evenings.

There are a number of alternatives, every bit as accomplished, that for some unknown reason have yet to enjoy the feverish favor accorded to BIBA, OLIVES and MICHELA'S. Try the under-appreciated ICARUS, CORNUCOPIA and DAKOTA'S, all of which are likely to have tables available on short notice. No sacrifice is made by choosing any one of them, unless you *prefer* to stand in the snow in order to dine shoulder-to-shoulder with other supplicants, for large chunks of disposable income.

Active fishing fleets still put in to ports within the metropolitan area, and seafood remains a staple, as it always has been in Boston. While the clawed Maine lobster is no longer a bargain, it can be had here at prices well below those of southern or inland cities. Average weights of individual specimens are in the $1\frac{1}{2}$-to-3-pound range, but monsters of 10 pounds or more are not unusual. Clams, oysters, mussels, cod and the related scrod are basic ingredients on many menus. It would be a shame not to sample them while in town.

## EATING ON A BUDGET

Be not concerned if cost is a limiting factor. It is entirely possible to eat well, or at least adequately, on a budget. There are in this city, after all, over a quarter-million largely impecunious university students, who guarantee that there will always be cheap places in which to eat. They make the streets around **Kenmore Square** in Boston and **Harvard Square** in Cambridge fruitful districts for quick, inexpensive meals. The food stalls and cafés of **Faneuil Hall Marketplace** trade fancy fixtures for moderate prices and considerable variety, from enchiladas to pasta primavera to lobster rolls to burgers to sushi.

Several local chains do as well or better, and are encountered all over Boston, Cambridge and the "streetcar suburbs." **Au Bon Pain** made its name with croissants and cappuccino, but quickly expanded into soups, sandwiches and light meals. **Boston Chicken**, whose namesake product is spit-roasted, not fried, has at least 15 outlets. Pizza, it will come as no surprise, is everywhere, but the many parlors of **Bertucci's Brick Oven Pizzeria** are not only ubiquitous, but set the standard against which others are often judged.

Even the elevated prices of meals at the acclaimed restaurants can be sidestepped. Lunch is nearly always less expensive than dinner, often by as much as 25 percent or even more. Same food, same cooks — just shorter menus. Some have early-bird or pre-theater meals at similarly trimmed prices. If you take your main meal in the middle of the day, dinner can be composed of two or more small dishes offered in the bars of full-service restaurants, as at MARAIS or DALÍ.

- See also the BARS WITH GOOD EATS suggestions in the NIGHTLIFE chapter (page 178).

## WHAT TO DRINK

When you are bellying up to that bar, keep in mind the local brews, which are infrequently found outside New England. **Sam Adams** bottles several lagers and ales, and is often available on draft. Other possibilities are **Harpoon** and **Yuengling**.

Although there are thriving taverns in every part of the city, the fact is that liquor consumption, especially of such darker spirits as Scotch and Bourbon, has been in sharp decline for many years. Concerns about health and drunken driving are obvious factors in that trend.

Wine, wine mixed with club soda ("spritzer"), and nonalcoholic drinks such as carbonated water with a twist of lime are replacing the three cocktails of the once common variety of business lunch. Red wine has enjoyed a slight resurgence in popularity due to reports that it contributes to health if taken in moderation.

Espresso and cappuccino are widely available, in both regular and decaffeinated versions.

## PLAN AHEAD

*Always* call ahead before making a special trip to a restaurant. At some of the most popular places, you may need to make reservations days ahead of time, especially on weekends. The clerk might ask for your telephone number, or request that you call by a certain time to confirm your intentions. Some have begun to demand a credit card number, an unacceptable practice that deserves to be squelched, but there it is. And even if reservations are not accepted, at least an estimate might be extracted on how long you could expect to wait for a table.

Another reason to call is that restaurants change their policies often, and sometimes seasonally. One that has been open only five nights a week may have expanded to seven. Or added lunch. Or now offers Sunday brunch, but only in summer. And, inevitably, some of the restaurants recommended in these pages or in other sources will go out of business, without warning.

## TIPPING

A 5-percent tax is added to bills. An average tip is 15 percent of the pre-tax total, and up to 20 percent in luxury restaurants or if the service has been exemplary. While waiters shouldn't be penalized for the sins of the kitchen, it is often difficult to determine who is responsible for perceived deficiencies. In such cases, fairness suggests that you give the waiter the benefit of the doubt.

## HOW TO USE OUR RESTAURANT LISTINGS

**Location:** Each address includes both the nearest important cross street and the neighborhood in which the restaurant is located. The nearest **T** station to the hotel is also indicated.

**Symbols:** The ⌒ symbol following a restaurant's name identifies it as a luxury establishment, and the ♣ symbol indicates that in the author's opinion it provides good value for money, in its class. Other symbols show the price category and any accepted credit cards. **See page 7 for the full list of symbols.**

**Prices:** The costs corresponding to our price symbols are based on **average charges for a meal for one person, including tax, tip and house wine.** Although actual prices will inevitably increase after publication, our relative price categories are likely to remain the same.

| Symbol | Category | Current price |
|---|---|---|
| ▥ | very expensive | over $100 |
| ▥ | expensive | $60–100 |
| ▥ | moderate | $35–60 |
| ▯ | inexpensive | $20–35 |
| ▭ | cheap | under $20 |

# Boston and Cambridge restaurants A to Z

## OUR RECOMMENDATIONS, GROUPED BY NEIGHBORHOOD

**BACK BAY**
Biba ▨
Blue Wave ▨ to ▨ ♣
Cactus Club ▨ ♣
Cottonwood ▨
Cottonwood Café ▨
Grill 23 ▨ ⌂
Harvard Bookstore Cafe
　▨ ♣
Legal Sea Foods (at Columbus Ave.)
　▨ to ▨ ♣
Legal Sea Foods (at Huntington Ave.)
　▨ to ▨ ♣
Mister Leung's ▨ to ▨
Parish Café ▨ ♣
**BEACON HILL**
Another Season ▨
Toscano ▨ to ▨
**CAMBRIDGE: CENTRAL SQ.**
Green Street Grill
　▨ ♣
**CAMBRIDGE: HARVARD SQ.**
Upstairs at the Pudding
　▨
Wursthaus ▨ to ▨
**CAMBRIDGE: INMAN SQ.**
East Coast Grill ▨
**CAMBRIDGE: KENDALL SQ.**
The Blue Room ▨ ♣
Legal Sea Foods (at Kendall Sq.)
　▨ to ▨ ♣
Michela's ▨
**CHARLESTOWN**
Olives ▨
Figs ▨ to ▨

**DOWNTOWN: CHINATOWN/
THEATER DISTRICT**
Blue Diner ▨ ♣
Cecil's ▨ to ▨ ♣
David's ▨
Imperial Teahouse ▨ to ▨ ♣
Marais ▨ ♣
Montien ▨ to ▨
Rocco's ▨
**DOWNTOWN: FINANCIAL DISTRICT**
Dakota's ▨ to ▨
Julien ▨ to ▨ ⌂
Sultan's Kitchen ▨ ♣
**DOWNTOWN CROSSING**
Locke-Ober ▨ ⌂
**FANEUIL HALL/GOVERNMENT CENTER**
Bay Tower Room ▨ ⌂
Durgin Park ▨
Gyosai ▨ ♣
Union Oyster House ▨ to ▨
Zuma's ▨ ♣
**NORTH END**
Cornucopia ▨ ♣
Jasper's ▨
**SOMERVILLE**
Dalí ▨ ♣
Redbones ▨ ♣
**SOUTH BOSTON**
Anthony's Pier 4 ▨
Jimmy's Harborside ▨
Jimbo's Fish Shanty ▨ to ▨
**SOUTH END**
Hammersley's Bistro ▨ to ▨
Icarus ▨ to ▨
St Cloud ▨

**ANOTHER SEASON** *Continental*
*97 Mt. Vernon St. (near Charles St.),*
*Beacon Hill. Map* **11E9** ☎*367-0880* ▨
▣ ▣ ▨ *Closed Sat lunch; Sun.*
**T** *Charles/MGH (Red Line).*
Chef-owner Odette Berry is possessed
of a restless creative instinct. None of
those menus permanently laminated in
plastic for her. Monday to Thursday, she
offers an inexpensive fixed-price dinner that changes every few days and
explores cuisines of many lands, as well

as a changing menu every month, with
nightly specials. She approaches these
from a solid knowledge of classic techniques, evidenced in utterly fresh products she tampers with as little as
necessary. Smoked sturgeon comes
with lightly dressed greens and a dollop
of whipped cream and American caviar
on the side; salmon and lamb are
cooked to moist perfection. If she has a
failing, it is a tendency to under-dress-
ing and sometimes wan flavorings. Ser-

vice, too, can be a little tentative, sometimes resulting in auctioning ("Who has the chicken?"). But those are nitpicks.

Her soothing setting is the basement of a Beacon Hill townhouse with custom murals of Edwardian-era Paris on the walls. She has only a beer and wine license, but the list is carefully chosen. Take a taxi or the **T**, for parking is very difficult in the immediate area.

### ANTHONY'S PIER 4  *Seafood*
*140 Northern Ave. (Pier 4 and B St.), South Boston. Off map 12F12* ☎*423-6363* ▥ ▤ ▣ ▨ ▨ *Open daily for lunch and dinner.*

Few natives admit to making the trek to Pier 4, at least without aunts or out-of-towners in tow. Nonetheless, huge numbers of eaters (this isn't exactly dining) are processed through this monster food factory, and they can't all be tourists and conventioneers. They are summoned to table by loudspeaker, which is also the means of advising the throngs about the arrival and departure of ships steaming past the big picture windows. In the hallways are displays of scrimshaw and related nautical items. Go for the views and fellowship, stick to the simplest varieties of seafood, and all will be well.

### BAY TOWER ROOM ⌂ *Eclectic*
*60 State St. (Congress St.), Faneuil Hall/Government Center. Map 12E11* ☎*723-1666* ▥ ▤ ▣ ▨ ▨ *Open nightly Mon–Sat for dinner only.* **T** *State (Orange or Blue line).*

Experience suggests that food quality deteriorates and prices escalate in direct proportion to their distance above terra firma. But since there are few more agreeable ways to pass a cocktail hour than by watching night fall over a great city, the sacrifice is often deemed small enough. Here, though, you give up nothing. This bi-level bar-restaurant atop a 33-story office building defies the dictum, or at least part of it. A great many ground-level restaurants would be overjoyed to be able to serve meals this good. They admittedly sound a little precious in writing — "pan-fried foie gras with goat cheese brioche and raspberry champagne sauce" — but presentations are attractive and tastes nearly always meld happily on the tongue.

The prices are among the highest in town, to be sure, but so is the venue. The main bank of windows opens onto the FINANCIAL DISTRICT and harbor, with FANEUIL HALL MARKETPLACE down below and the CUSTOM HOUSE tower directly in front. Those who wish to keep costs down can go for just a drink in the spacious lounge, perhaps adding one of the appetizers or light meals that are on offer there. Early Tuesday evening, there is live jazz; Friday and Saturday, a quartet plays for dancing. The rest of the time, an electronically programed piano tinkles in the background. A private club takes over at lunchtime. Men are expected to wear jackets and shirts with collars.

### BIBA  *Eclectic*
*272 Boylston St. (Arlington St.), Back Bay. Map 11F9* ☎*426-7878* ▥ ▣ ▣ ▨ *Closed Sat lunch.* **T** *Arlington (Green Line).*

Multiculturalism is evident at every turn of head and menu. On the ceiling of the main upstairs room are segmented paintings that might have had Southwestern, Asian Indian or even Afghan inspirations. Set about on shelves and walls are African weavings, Central American molas and primitive toys. If that doesn't set the theme, the menu does. Conventional headings are eschewed in favor of "Fish," "Meat," "Starch," "Legumina" and "Offal." Each category contains both appetizers and main courses, so diners are encouraged to mix and match.

If this comes across as more than a smidgen too clever, it is. And people who haven't dined here, but have been exposed to the superheated praise Biba has enjoyed since its opening, may be in for at least slight disappointment. Two of Boston's most honored chefs are at the controls, and their efforts to be all-embracing in their fabrications sometimes fall short. Various components are pushed together prettily in the center of the plate, where they either become (a) supernal marriages of flavors, or (b) something dangerously approaching mush. However, hits are far more frequent than misses, and most of these patrons appear deep-pocketed and sophisticated enough to bear up to any shortcomings of the kitchen. The chefs' enthusiasm for organ meats, while curious in a cholesterol-conscious age, proves that liver and kidneys and brains needn't always taste exactly as you suppose they will.

Noise levels here are high. The ground-floor bar is one of Boston's most chic night scenes, with wine by the glass and such tantalizing snacks as lamb *quesadillas* and marrow on toast. That might be the best way to sample Biba.

**BLUE DINER** ♣ *American*
*178 Kneeland St. (South St.), downtown.*
*Map 12G10* ☎*338-4639* ▥ *Open*
*Tues–Sun 24hrs; Mon 7am–midnight.*
*T South Station (Red Line).*
A classic 1940s diner has been taken over by people who love food and hate pretension (unless flowers count as pretense). For the full effect, sit at the Formica counter, inches away from the hash slingers, those deft practitioners of short-order cookery who waste not a single motion as they flip burgers by the hundred and plunge potatoes into bubbling vats of oil. Apart from the occasional chic digression — goat cheese salad, for one — they specialize in such damn-the-cholesterol fabrications as three-egg omelettes wrapped around corned-beef hash and ladled over with cheese sauce. A typical lunch menu might include meatloaf, turkey pot pie, chop suey, and fish and chips. Thick milkshakes and ice cream sodas go with this delectable lowbrow chow, but they are licensed to sell wine and beer, too. At peak hours, notably Sunday brunch, the owner has to resort to a waiting list.

**THE BLUE ROOM** ♣ *Eclectic*
*1 Kendall Sq. (a cluster of buildings on Hampshire St. and Cardinal Medeiros Ave., 1½ miles w of Kendall Sq. proper), Cambridge. Map 8D6* ☎*494-9034* ▥
▣ ▦ *Open nightly for dinner; Sun brunch.*

*T Kendall (Red Line), but then a fairly long walk: see above.*
Exposed brick walls, rough wood ceilings, bare tables and mismatched colors are meant to stand up to the casual abuse of a clientele comprised in large part of university students and their younger, untenured faculty. They are a self-absorbed lot, in their black tights and jeans and baggy sweatshirts, arranging their chairs and spreading their books about as if only they and their immediate friends were in the room. They often seem unaware of how tasty the food is, engrossed as they are in imminently assuming their rightful lofty places in the world. Those in attendance to eat, however, usually revel in the lack of cute clichés.

One special was a platter of "Mexican tastes," with rice and beans, two salsas, chilies, avocado salad, onions, pickled cabbage and tortillas, all to support a main choice of fish, sausage, pork or turkey. Another was wok-seared salmon with sweet soy sesame noodles, watercress and ginger. There's no denying that the kitchen bounces around the world for inspiration, but at least it endeavors to confine itself to one continent per plate. Asia and Latin America dominate. For this taste and quality, prices are more than fair, especially at the Sunday brunch buffet, with its resident jazz trio.

The restaurant is one of several in a cluster of recycled industrial buildings; it has patio dining in good weather. Just stay out of range when the future Kissinger or Kant at the next table revs up to an insight. The owners of The Blue Room also run the commendable **East Coast Grill** *(1271 Cambridge St., map 8B5* ☎*491-6568).*

**BLUE WAVE** ♣ *Eclectic*
*142 Berkeley St. (Stuart St.), Back Bay.*
*Map 11G8* ☎*424-6711* ▥ *to* ▥ ▣ ▣
▣ ▦ *Closed Sat lunch. T Arlington (Green Line).*
Perhaps the owners passed through New York's TriBeCa on their way from California's Venice to Boston's Back Bay. This recycled industrial workspace

might have been inspired by both areas, with its high ceiling crowded with exposed plumbing and ducts and bright splashes of color on the white walls. *Under* the glass tabletops are sandboxes with faux-naïf vignettes featuring little plastic orcas, marbles, lizards and other pretend flotsam. *On* the glass are shakers of sea salt and flavored olive oil and, eventually, grilled (not baked) pizzas and assorted pastas, of the sort that has been called "Cal-Ital." Given the kitchen's clear inclinations, the eats are best for those who really, *really* like olive oil and garlic. Service is subject to whim and distraction, and getting the bill poses the greatest challenge.

### CACTUS CLUB ♣ *Tex-Mex*
*939 Boylston St. (Hereford St.), Back Bay. Map* **10**G7 ☎236-0200 ▭ AE ⊡ ⊡ ▨ *Open daily for lunch and dinner.* **T** *Hynes Convention Center/ICA (Green Line).*
Purists beware. The kitchen observes no national or culinary boundaries, plucking a paella from Spain via Jalisco, *fajitas* by way of San Antonio. If lemon grass or kielbasa could even remotely be wedged under the chosen Tex-Mex umbrella, they'd probably do it. And there are the rooms: over the bar is an entire stuffed bison. In the dining room, an elk head. And saddles. Cowboy boots. A five-foot Mexican Day of the Dead skeleton in a dress. A jackalope, which is a jackrabbit with horns. Folksy Santa Fe wood coyotes and snakes. A ceiling made of doors. A row of potted cacti. Assorted Indian and Mexican gimcracks. It's fun, and that's all it's meant to be, although the menu makes a few lurches at claiming this to be healthy food. The post-collegiate Generation X crowd willingly stands in line waiting for tables or wiggle-room in the bar Thursday-to-Saturday evenings, doing no damage to Cactus Club's reputation as the best pickup spot in Boston.

To avoid that, and save money, arrive for lunch or between 4 and 6pm Monday-to-Thursday, when prices are lower. Expect the expectable, including *burritos, tacos, enchiladas, fajitas* and *empanadas,* most of it bountiful and tasty. Daily specials provide most of the surprises. Not-too-finicky vegetarians have a number of options, and even meat and fowl dishes use flesh primarily as a flavoring.

### CECIL'S ♣ *Eclectic*
*129 South St. (near Beach St.), downtown. Map* **12**G10 ☎542-5108 ▭ to ▭ ⊡ ⊡ ▨ *Closed Sat lunch.* **T** *South Station (Red Line).*
This welcome entry in the bleak Leather District near South Station does all it can to fill the needs of area workers. Caribbean/Spanish/Mexican only begins to corral the variegated tastes on hand, from the blistering Jamaican jerk pork to the bountiful "operetta" of seafood known as *zarzuela.* Lunch has pizzas and burgers, natch, but *enchiladas, pasta primavera* and Cuban *ropa vieja,* too. Service is casual and friendly. One of the managers is a musician, so there are folk singers Saturday night and an "open mike" session on Tuesday.

### CORNUCOPIA ♣ *Eclectic*
*100 Atlantic Ave. (Richmond St.), North End. Map* **12**D11 ☎367-0300 ▭ AE ⊡ ⊡ ▨ *Open daily for lunch and dinner.* **T** *Aquarium (Blue Line).*
The owners may have left a loyal clientele behind after the 1993 move from an old Financial District building for this waterfront site previously occupied by the unlamented Cherrystones. The lunch crowd was markedly thinner at first, presumably because the old crowd had yet to discover the new location. That must be the reason, because what comes out of the kitchen is as flavorful and eye-appealing as ever. The tangy black bean soup is a standard against which others should be measured, they do all kinds of wondrous things with the humble native scrod, and the bouillabaisse is a saffron broth choked with just-right mussels, clams, scallops and chunks of lobster, and whatever else emerged from the nets that day. Seafood can be found at these very reasonable prices elsewhere in the city, but rarely of higher quality. They even suggest an appropriate wine for each offer-

ing. With all this *and* views of the close-up marina and distant harbor traffic, Cornucopia can be forgiven the occasionally distracted service and the disjointed decor, half of it left over from the previous occupant.

### COTTONWOOD  Southwestern
*222 Berkeley St. (St James Ave.), Back Bay. Map 11G8* ☎247-2225 ▥ ▣ ▣ ▣ ▥ *Open daily.* **T** *Arlington (Green Line).*
Santa Fe danced with desert chic into Cambridge a few years back at the original **Cottonwood Café** location *(1815 Massachusetts Ave.* ☎661-7440). Now it pops and crackles like *jalapeño* seeds in a hot iron skittle at this slick Back Bay replica. The "*Nouvelle* Southwestern" cooking label caused its share of chortles when it journeyed east across the Mississippi. But to the degree that it established the existence of a creative, more thoughtful use of products and techniques of the region than the down-and-dirty "Tex-Mex," it had its value. The chicken diablo here might sound like just another store-bought packaged assemblage, but it delights the mouth with tender ribbons of the fowl sautéed with sweet red and green bell pepper, fresh rosemary and *chipolte* (a smoked chile) in a sherry butter sauce, with rice-and-raisins and plump black beans on the side. The menu-writers had a few attacks of the cutes, listing "snakebites," "Painted Desert salad" and "cowboy potstickers" among their offerings. Ignore the names, enjoy the results. If there is a deficiency, it lies in the often tame flavorings of dishes labeled "spicy."

Frozen margaritas are *the* drinks, their permutations including, but not limited to, peach, raspberry and strawberry. They are for that segment of the clientele not far removed from after-school cookies and ice cream. They surge into the bar-café, which has cheaper eats and louder patrons than the somewhat more subdued main rooms, occupied by people with mortgages and pre-schoolers. A jolly time is had by all, at least after the sometimes long wait in line.

### DAKOTA'S  Eclectic
*34 Summer St. (Otis St.), Financial District. Map 12F10* ☎737-1777 ▥ *to* ▥ ▣ ▣ ▥ *Closed Sat lunch; Sun.* **T** *Downtown Crossing (Orange or Red Line).*
Here's a dinner solution to all those no-reservations, trendoid eateries that measure success by how far their queues stretch down the street. Due to its nonresidential Financial District location, this Texas import serves 300 to 400 meals at lunch, but is nearly empty at night. That's especially true Friday and Saturday, when Biba, Michela's and their ilk are packed to the walls.

This is not at all a reflection on the highly skilled, conservatively creative kitchen at Dakota's. Fragrance and appearance are made to enhance the taste of dishes, not distract from them. Plump, juicy veal chops are joined with earthy mushrooms and sweet onions; smoked rainbow trout comes with roasted peppers, fried capers and toasted brioche; fat sea scallops are tossed with fresh spinach, slivers of prosciutto, sage and pasta in a buttery tomato sauce. And the restaurant's Southwestern credentials are attested by fried alligator chunks in a piquant salsa and venison sausage *quesadillas* with *jalapeños* and *cilantro*. This accomplished but under-appreciated restaurant deserves proper recognition.

### DALÍ  ♣ Spanish
*415 Washington St. (Beacon St.), Somerville. Map 8A4* ☎661-3254 ▥ ▣ ▣ ▥ *Open nightly for dinner only.* **T** *Harvard (Red Line), but then a long walk.*
According to the owner, most of his business is *tapas.* Should that sublime Spanish culinary invention manage to have escaped any reader's attention, the name refers to the tasty bar snacks whose origins are lost in centuries. Once upon a time, innkeepers placed a slice of bread over each glass of wine to keep flies out. (*Tapa* means "lid" or "cover.") When one of them decided to put a piece of cheese or chorizo on the bread, a new food category was born, evolving into something splendid. Now, the bars of Madrid and Seville are

lined with scores of platters of these gastronomic treasures.

Few restaurants on this side of the Atlantic duplicate this treat as successfully as this gaudy, cheerful tavern. Regular meals of *paella* and such are available, but go straight for selections from the long lists of hot and cold *tapas*. Make room for the *butifarra* (sausage) with figs, a sure winner, and for stuffed squid cooked in its own peppery ink. Stemmed caperberries are a pickled counter-note, and disks of baked goat cheese arrive in a basil-tomato sauce. *Sangría* or the good Rioja and Penedès wines are perfect beverages. (Beer is also available, but not liquor.) Between courses, the eye is treated to a gaudy collection of Dalí-esque decorative oddities. On the back wall is a painting of a voluptuous nude; hanging between bar and dining room is a clothesline draped with lingerie. Nothing quite goes with anything else . . . except more *tapas*.

### DAVID'S  *Mediterranean*
*123 Stuart St. (Charles St. South), Theater District. Map 11G9* ☎*367-8405* ▥ ▣ ▣ ▣ ▥ *Closed Sat lunch; Mon.*
**T** *Boylston (Green Line).*
Bnu, a well-regarded trattoria, occupied this space for years before abruptly shutting down in 1993. This new operation appears to have the necessary ingredients to beat the survival odds. It's within minutes of the major theaters and only a slightly longer walk from the Financial District. On the menu are *tapas* and appetizers, as well as main courses, which means diners in a rush or at leisure can tailor a meal to meet their needs. Recipes are drawn from the countries of the Mediterranean basin, always popular, and prices aren't intimidating. Pastas are best bets, usually tumbled with lots of vegetables and not too often with tomato sauce. The interior looks like a stage set for a production of *Kiss Me, Kate,* or an echo of Siena's Palio horse race, with pennants hanging from the ceiling and fleurs-de-lis stenciled around the door. David expects to have a liquor license by the

time these words are printed. From the outset, six wines were available by the glass.

### DURGIN PARK  *American*
*North Market Building, Faneuil Hall Marketplace. Map 12E11* ☎*227-2038* ▥ ▣ ▣ ▥ *Open daily for lunch and dinner.*
**T** *Aquarium (Blue Line) or State (Blue or Orange Line).*
Old Boston lives on in this only slightly gussied-up market restaurant dating back to when this neighborhood was populated by butchers and fishmongers, not singles on the make and tourists. Giant slabs of prime rib hang over the edges of the plates, preceded by copious bowls of clam chowder, accompanied by wallops of baked beans and followed by quite delicious clumps of Indian pudding. Lobsters, steaks and chops are also available, and most are good value. They are delivered to the communal tables by waitresses of legendary churlishness, alleged to be part of the fun. The trick is to arrive with your sense of humor intact and enough patience to wait an hour or more for your seats, since they don't accept reservations.

### GREEN STREET GRILL  ♣ *Eclectic*
*280 Green St. (Magazine St.), Central Sq., Cambridge. Map 8D4* ☎*876-1655* ▥ ▣ ▣ ▥ *Open nightly for dinner only.*
**T** *Central (Red Line).*
The restaurant sign outside resides under a larger one that reads **Charlie's Tap** — "tap" being Bostonese for a nononsense beer parlor. Inside, it looks like an Alabama roadhouse, with knotty pine paneling varnished almost orange, brash yellow ocher paint, and squares of imitation leather on the tables. Not very promising, especially after dealing with waitresses who act as if they'd rather be anywhere else. But they are at least adequate to their task, and they bring some of the most flavorful downhome grub to be found on the chilly side of the Mason-Dixon Line. The man rattling the skillets, co-owner John Levins, doesn't permit himself to be confined by the "soul food" label often

attached to his cooking. While his creations are unquestionably drawn from the Caribbean and the Sun Belt, mainly Creole, Cajun and Southwestern, he improvises with abandon.

There is, to quote one fairly typical selection from his frequently revised menu, "Beaten and boiled conch meat stewed in a red & green curry, grilled cactus leaf, green pea, scotch bonnet chile pepper, lime, thyme & Myer's rum sauce." Yes, it sounds desperate, but somehow it works, as does almost anything he puts together. That might include loin of rabbit with lobster, or sweet potato ravioli with grilled scallops, or a sausage that's made up of pineapple, red onion, sage and fiery *chipolte* peppers. Mr Levins works without a net but with a remarkably sure hand.

### GRILL 23 ♙ *Steakhouse*
*161 Berkeley St. (Stuart St.), Back Bay.*
*Map 11G8* ☎542-2255 ▨▨ ▣ ▣ ▣ ▨▨
Open daily for dinner only. *T Arlington (Green Line).*
Take a minute to walk a few steps E from the corner entrance to see the ornate bronze bas-relief portal that announced the **Salada Tea Building**. It helps set the tone for what is arguably Boston's top steakhouse. Grill 23 occupies much of the two-tiered ground floor, requisitely wood-paneled and marble-columned, the kind of setting demanded by middle-aged men who do torts, sell on margin and masticate slabs of red meat. They discuss these weighty matters while drinking goblets of foaming beer and inky clarets. While most choose among the several cuts of beef, the management is aware of such alternatives as fish and fowl. Portions are huge, as you might expect. The daintiest piece of meat is a 10-ounce filet mignon, and they roll right up into the two-pound range. One salad has center-cut disks of tomatoes and onions as big as hockey pucks; the round loaf of hash-browned potatoes is half a foot in diameter.

Those who enjoy this limited genre of cooking are unlikely to be disappointed, making it also just the place for those in temporary revolt over two decades of prissy presentations and nutritional nagging. At least 90 percent of the men wear suits and ties. Reservations are strongly recommended. Though only dinner is served, the Martinis start splashing in the clubby bar at 4.30pm.

### GYOSAI ♙ *Japanese*
*200 State St., Faneuil Hall Marketplace.*
*Map 12E11* ☎345-0942 ▨▨ ▣ ▣ ▣
▨▨ Open daily for lunch and dinner.
*T Aquarium (Blue Line).*
Sushi long since lost its novelty, leaving diners to wonder why raw fish had to be so expensive. It isn't, here, making this one of two or three places in Boston to recall what all the excitement was about when Americans discovered that the Japanese had a cuisine. Lunch is an especially good deal, with platters of assorted sushi and sashimi creations costing little more than routine burgers and fried potatoes. They come with pretty good soup and extraneous salad. On that plate might be *tekka maki* (tuna rolled in rice wrapped with sheets of seaweed), *kapp maki* (cucumber the same way), and pieces of *saba* (mackerel), *tako* (octopus) and *ebi* (shrimp) laid on firm fingers of sticky rice. These are straightforward presentations, the easiest to make and therefore cheaper than most. To sample higher reaches of the sushi maestro's art, order single pieces from the unusually long menu. For those who prefer their food cooked, there are a number of tempura dishes, as well as *tonkatsu* and *katsu*, pork or chicken breaded and deep-fried. Sapporo and Kirin beers are available. Wednesday to Saturday at 10.30pm, there is karaoke.

### HAMERSLEY'S BISTRO *Eclectic*
*553 Tremont St. (Clarendon St.), South End. Off map 11G8* ☎423-2700 ▨▨ to ▨▨ ▣ ▨▨ Open nightly for dinner only.
*T NE Medical Center (Orange Line).*
The eponymous owner is one of New England's most highly regarded chefs, and has been nominated for a James Beard award, billed as the "food world's

Oscars." His apprentices have gone on to considerable success, too, one of them heading the staff at MICHELA'S, in Cambridge. Gordon Hamersley chooses as his metier French bistro recipes — cassoulet, double-thick veal chops — from which he deviates often but with caution. This is honest, satisfying food. Even so deceptively simple an appetizer as the garlic flan explodes with flavor. Presentation, while nothing less than appealing, is not considered the crucial art. In spring, he moves on to lighter fare, such as salmon with a pecan crust and lobster butter, and soft polenta with wild mushrooms and *asiago* cheese.

### HARVARD BOOKSTORE CAFE ♣
*Eclectic*
*190 Newbury St. (Exeter St.), Back Bay. Map 10G7 ☎536-0095* ▢ ▣ ▣ ▣
*Open daily for breakfast, lunch and dinner.*
**T** *Copley Square (Green Line).*
The Harvard connection is spurious, but that august institution should have no objection to this use of its good name. It is a genuine bookstore, with clerks who care about the written word. Light meals and breakfasts are better than they need to be, given the attractive sidewalk café and engrossing opportunities for people-watching. Not surprisingly, intellectuals, artists and writers are a large part of the custom.

### ICARUS *Eclectic*
*3 Appleton St. (Arlington St.), South End. Off map 11G9 ☎426-1790* ▢ *to* ▢ ▣ ▣
▣ *Open nightly for dinner; Sun for brunch (part of the year).* **T** *Arlington (Green Line).*
With so many hot restaurants opening in the last few years, it isn't surprising that a few don't get the attention they deserve. The reservation phone should be ringing off the cradle at Icarus, but it still seems to be the semi-secret of loyal patrons. That situation is ripe for change. There is the setting, serene and not even slightly hip. The sturdy wood furniture might have done service at a private boys' school in New Hampshire. At one side is a statue of the son of Daedalus, who flew into the Sun on

wings of feathers and wax. The legend's relevance, here of all places, is unclear.
Certainly there is nothing ill-conceived about what the kitchen is doing, unless they might be judged guilty of large portions. Main courses are ample enough to skip appetizers, but everything is so promising that self-discipline isn't easy. Consider, from the seasonally adjusted card, such temptations as the pizzetta with goat cheese, caramelized onions and sun-dried tomatoes, or roasted buffalo mozzarella and yellow tomato *crostini* with basil. And those are just starters. Follow with medallions of veal with morels, chives and potato-and-leek gratin, perhaps, or with the fish of the day or the special pasta. Satisfaction is a virtual certainty. Jazz plays softly on the stereo, and Friday nights there is a live duo in the bar.

### IMPERIAL TEAHOUSE ♣ *Chinese*
*70 Beach St. (Hudson St.), Chinatown. Map 12F10 ☎426-8543* ▢ *to* ▢ ▣ ▣ ▣
▣ *Open daily for lunch and dinner.*
**T** *Chinatown (Orange Line).*
*Dim sum* is the reason to make time for this Chinatown institution. It stands near the ceremonial gate on Hudson St., at the edge of Chinatown. Downstairs is a recently refurbished dining room serving full meals. It isn't bad, but go here for lunch, which is when *dim sum* is available. As is usually the case at such places, walk up to the second floor and obtain a number from the plate next to the cashier. The host will not necessarily follow the logical sequence, since he is concerned not with equity but with filling tables. But eventually, everyone is called and seated. Once at table, diners pay rapt attention to the carts being rolled past, pointing at anything that looks good. The women pushing the carts aren't much help, so put aside food prejudices and keep ordering until full. Along the way there might be chicken feet and assorted compilations of offal, but try to save room for one of the specialities: lightly steamed oysters sprinkled with chopped scallions and dots of a paste of fermented black beans.

### JASPER'S *Eclectic*

240 Commercial St. (Lewis Wharf), North End. Map **12**D11 ☎523-1126 ▥ ⊙ ▥ Open for dinner only Tues–Sat. Closed Sun; Mon. **T** Aquarium (Blue Line).

In case anyone misses the point, the menu reads "Seafood Main Courses" and "Other Main Courses." For Jasper White, one of the most luminous of Boston's culinary stars, chooses to work with New England products and traditions, sifting them through a contemporary sensibility. He has even been known to offer a version of the regional boiled dinner, a classy echo of *pot au feu*. More typical are the skewered sea scallops with ham and scallions with wild rice fritters and mustard greens, and baked halibut brightened with spinach roulade and a saffron lobster sauce. A recent redecoration of the premises incorporated a display of hand-blown art glass, and Mr White took that opportunity to lower prices for most items. His glossy clientele is mostly over 35, well dressed and accustomed to this level of quality. The one distressing note in this otherwise harmonious picture is a rumor that the head man is threatening to move on to another enterprise: so call ahead.

### JIMMY'S HARBORSIDE *Seafood*

242 Northern Ave. (Pier 6 and Ramp St.), South Boston. ☎423-1000 ▥ ▱ ⊙ ⊙ ▥ Closed Sun lunch in summer.

Almost as famous as its neighbor, ANTHONY'S PIER 4, Jimmy's is slightly smaller, but has a similar harbor view and assembly-line feeding practices. The menu has more of an Italian cast, with scampi and pastas featured alongside standard seafood possibilities. Political junkies and the politicians they admire or at least hope to influence enjoy the robust bonhomie of the popular bar. Across the pier is the same owner's **Jimbo's Fish Shanty** (*245 Northern Ave.* ☎ 542-5600), without the view but with lower prices for similar food.

### JULIEN ☖ *Continental*

250 Franklin St. (Le Meridien hotel), Financial District. Map **12**F11 ☎451-1900 ▥ to ▥ ▱ ⊙ ⊙ ▥ Closed Sat lunch; Sun.

There is no grander gesture, no celebration better honored, than dinner in this glorious, towering space. It is the luxuriously appointed dining room of the hotel LE MERIDIEN (see pages 145–46), a former bank building whose directors stinted not one dollar in fashioning its Medici-like grandeur. The adjoining bar with the coffered ceiling was the room where they dispensed this largesse. The current management has been no less generous. High above the tables are five chandeliers of densely clustered crystals winking in the light. Bouquets of flowers release their gentle fragrances. Half-circle banquettes, upholstered wing chairs and Queen Anne sidechairs constitute the seating around the generously separated tables. Classically trained captains and servers, some of whom are French, bring gorgeously presented portions of such essentials as lobster salad and foie gras. As in every haute restaurant of breeding, diners are rarely sated until the last bite of dessert, so arrive prepared to start at the beginning and carry through, skipping not one delectable step. Lunches are briefer, less bountiful and cheaper, but no less carefully executed. Long may this Gallic outpost thrive.

### LEGAL SEA FOODS ♣ *Seafood*

35 Columbus Ave. (Park Sq.), Back Bay. Map **11**G9 ▥ to ▥ ▱ ⊙ ▥ Open daily for lunch and dinner. **T** Arlington (Green Line).

The guiding motto at this local chain is, "If it isn't fresh, it isn't Legal," and they stick to it. They serve food when it is done, not when the dishes for the entire table are ready. High volume and simple, virtually sauce-less preparations ensure that nothing lingers long in refrigerators or on the shelf. Add Legal's long-term popularity and moderate prices and it becomes clear why even what is a humdrum Monday evening for other restaurants is a barely controlled madhouse at its eight branches in the metropolitan area. They aren't small, either. The Columbus Avenue location, with its dining room, informal café, takeout, shipping and home-delivery functions takes up almost an entire city block. Still, reservations aren't accepted, and the only way to avoid a wait of up to an hour is to take any available seat in the bar. Good starters are the creamy clam chowder and smoked bluefish pâté. Main courses are broiled, baked, fried, or the wan "Cajun style." Preferred desserts are cheesecake, Key lime pie and Legal's own ice creams.

For some degree of tranquility — relatively speaking — try the Cambridge branch at **Kendall Square** (5 Cambridge Center, map **10**D7 ☎864-3400). The other Boston location is at **100 Huntington Ave.** (map **10**G8 ☎266-7775).

### LOCKE-OBER ⌂ Continental
3 Winter Place (between Washington and Tremont Sts.), Downtown Crossing. Map **12**F10 ☎542-1340 ▥ AE ◉ ⊙ VISA Closed Sat lunch; Sun lunch. **T** Park Street (Red or Green Line).

Find this restaurant off Winter St., a block E of Boston Common. The walls of this upper-crust sanctum almost sigh with the contentment that age and privilege can bring. Opened in 1875, it remained a refuge of financiers and politicians (of the proper sort) for nearly a century. They were primarily members of, or pretenders to, the Brahmin class, with degrees from the right universities and at least acceptable family pedigrees. They were also, until 1972, male. That's when, with a flutter of jowls and a heartfelt "humpff," women were allowed to enter the inner rooms. (There is still a private men-only club in back.)

The entry bar is mahogany and stained glass and leather, with a ceiling mural turned a tobacco brown, one imagines, by the tens of thousands of Coronas puffed industriously beneath it. Off it, to the right, is a handsome dining room with gleaming silver and brass that probably hasn't changed all that much in a century. Some effete parvenus huff that the food it serves is bland and predictable. It runs to unadorned oys-

ters on the half-shell, lobster bisque, broiled lamb chops and prime rib, differing mainly in price from the 1939 menu waiters like to present. So the naysayers are essentially correct — but they also miss the point.

### MARAIS ♣ Continental
116 Boylston St. (Charles and Tremont Sts.), Theater District. Map **11**F9 ☎542-7822 ▥ AE ◉ ⊙ VISA Open nightly for dinner only. **T** Boylston (Green Line).

This handsome new entry on the night scene captures the look and attitude of a Parisian Right Bank brasserie, with mahogany moldings and plenty of mirrors among the bleary photos of French music hall performers on the walls. Along one wall are quilted banquettes with tables covered with butcher paper, while the other has a long, long bar of pink marble leading back to an open kitchen with a woodburning brick oven. At a right angle are two more dining rooms. Prosperous intellectuals and glamourous foreigners make up much of the custom. The place is so chic it makes your teeth hurt, and most nights, the line of suppliants snakes down the block outside, fair weather or foul. Among the attractions are the stylish "premiers," dishes somewhere between appetizers and main courses that are inventive without being scary and are surprisingly inexpensive, considering they provide just-right pre-theater meals. They include such delights as duck leg confit with crusty disks of couscous and a sauce of orange and cherry; roasted figs stuffed with sausage; and calamari that avoids the deep-fried convention.

This is not to say all is well. The management has directed that persons who wish to eat at the bar first must surrender their credit cards, which are held hostage until the customer is ready to leave. In other words, they don't trust us, but we are expected to trust them. It is an irritating policy that seems to deter no one. Service is erratic, at best, the noise level extreme, and perhaps a third of the dishes are flops. And those lines get longer.

After 10pm, many seek entry to the **Esme** disco, in back of the restaurant. It carries on the theme nicely, closely resembling a pre-Great War Parisian bordello.

## MICHELA'S  *Italian*

*1 Athenaeum St. (between First and Second Sts.), Kendall Sq., Cambridge. Map 11D7* ▨ ⒜⒠ ⓢ ⓓ ▨ *Closed Sat lunch; Sun.* **T** *Kendall (Red Line), but then a long walk.*

Hot restaurants (and this one has sizzled for years) nearly always have a full set of affectations, some silly, others annoying. Michela's accepts reservations, but almost everyone is shunted to the bar to wait for their booked table. Once ushered into the dining area, that table proves to be large and at a comfortable distance from its neighbors. It is covered with white butcher paper, but is otherwise almost bare. A notice on the menu intones that they don't provide bread plates "in the Italian manner." The absence of salt and pepper, candles, flowers, or other decorations or amenities isn't explained. The waiter/waitress is called upon to deliver an extended recitation on the Italian region of origin of the current menu, about what kind of food it is, and finally, a list of the night's deletions and specials. A basket of chewy rolls and olive bread eventually arrives, with a small platter of extra-virgin olive oil in which to dip it. No butter.

But let's not be cranky. All the preceding commentary aside, the food is admirable, the staff coolly cordial, and no artificial standards of dress are imposed. *Fritto misto,* for one, elevates that homely dish to art, the edible innards of a small lobster very briefly exposed to hot oil, as is the nest of crispy escarole, the scallops, the clams. Similar updated thought is accorded to every dish that appears. *Osso bucco* and game dishes are more than merely safe choices, should they be available, and desserts are worth the probable ounces on the hips. Go with talkative friends, for dinner will extend beyond two hours as surely as the Tuscan sun sets in the West.

## MISTER LEUNG'S  *Chinese*

*545 Boylston St. (between Clarendon and Dartmouth Sts.), Back Bay. Map 11G8* ☎236-4040 ▨ *to* ▨ ⒜⒠ ⓢ ▨ *Closed Sat lunch; Sun lunch.* **T** *Arlington (Green Line).*

Several things we all expect of Chinese restaurants are absent in this belowground Copley Square venue. There are no golden dragons. No pagodas. No chopsticks (although they are available by request). The menu is in clear, understandable English. Waiters are in black tie, and they happily adjust orders to personal taste. The kitchen makes an effort to provide unlisted items. Black and white are the primary colors, with dozens of direct and diffused lights implanted in the ceiling, and baby spots trained on the bud in the glass vase on each table.

Dishes are similarly high-toned. *Gan bei* is a nest of short, thin threads of lighter-than-air seaweed that spends only seconds in bubbling oil. Crispy whole fish is sautéed quickly in Hunan sauce; *wan fu* lamb is cooked with port wine with minced pepper and scallions. If there is fault in these otherwise near-flawless concoctions, it is in the anemic seasonings. Items marked with an asterisk are supposed to be especially spicy: they aren't.

## MONTIEN  *Thai*

*68 Stuart St. (Tremont St.), Theater District. Map 11F9* ☎338-5600 ▨ *to* ▨ ⒜⒠ ⓢ ▨ *Closed Sun lunch.* **T** *Boylston (Green Line).*

For centuries, Thai cooks have borrowed and adapted from their neighbors, India and China, to formulate their own distinctive cuisine. There are more compelling versions than that preferred here, but not on this coast. It stands in quite nicely as a pre- or post-curtain choice, as it is only a few minutes from the major theaters and there is nearly always an available table. The bar and dining room strive for the dated ambience of a fading Manhattan piano bar, with black and white chairs and maroon carpeting. Thai food is known for its hot-hotter-hottest seasonings, although there are mild dishes, too. This menu signifies with two, one or no stars, the first of which should satisfy those who equate degrees of spiciness with tests of virility, and they can outdo one another by adding the optional sauces and powders that arrive on a trivet. Beef, chicken, pork, shrimp or scallops come with a choice of ten sauces and garnishes, a way to ensure that a meal includes vegetables, which is not always the case: "Red Sea," for example, is mostly deep-fried pieces of fish and shellfish. Service is smilingly attentive.

### OLIVES *Mediterranean*
*10 City Sq. (Main St.), Charlestown. Map 12C10* ☎*242-1999* ▥ ◉ ▨
*Open Tues–Sat for dinner only. Closed Sun; Mon.* **T** *Community College (Orange Line).*

People get quite irritable about this acclaimed storefront trattoria over the bridge in Charlestown. Few deny that the *nuova cucina* creations of Todd English are exceptional in nearly all their manifestations. While Italy is his principal source of inspiration, the energetic chef skips around the rim of the Mediterranean, improvising and re-inventing as he goes. A woodburning brick oven is a principal tool, and grilling and roasting by rotisserie help keep prices in the moderate range.

But there is a *but* — a big one, for many devoted restaurant-goers. At this writing, Olives serves only five meals a week — dinners — and they accept no reservations for parties less than six. Intense popularity ensures long lines and exasperating waits. Once inside, the clangor of 50 tight-packed diners has them cupping their ears to hear one another. The attentions of the rushed servers are wildly erratic and sometimes insolent. Whether this marvelous food is worth the attendant aggravation is the question.

Not far away is **Figs** *(67 Main St., map 12B10* ☎ *242-2229)*, Todd English's casual trattoria-cum-bakery for simple lunches and dinners of pizza and pasta.

### PARISH CAFÉ ♣ *Eclectic*
*361 Boylston St. (Arlington), Back Bay. Map 11F9* ☎*247-4777* ▥ Ⓐ ◉ ◎ ▨
*Open daily for lunch and dinner.* **T** *Arlington (Green Line).*

An intriguing concept/gimmick supports this casual spot near the Public Garden. The owners invited some of Boston's celebrity chefs to devise special sandwiches. Jody Adams (**MICHELA'S**), Jasper White (**JASPER'S**) and Lydia Shire (**BIBA**) were among them, and they came up with some dazzlers that redefine that humble food category. To select just one: smoked turkey, melted Gouda cheese and oily sun-dried tomatoes on a chewy, crusty baguette split down the middle. There are salads and regular entrées, too, but the sandwiches are the true stars, at least at lunch. At night, the minimally decorated two levels are transformed into a spirited singles bar. The managers have a good grasp on that formula — they also operate the **RATTLESNAKE BAR & GRILL** (see page 178), across the street.

### REDBONES ♣ *Barbecue*
*55 Chester St. (near Davis Sq.), Somerville* ☎*628-2200* ▥ *No cards. Open Tues–Sun for dinner only.* **T** *Davis (Red Line).*

The nearest rib shack as authentic as this is hidden in piney woods somewhere in Georgia. A cloud of tantalizing aromas envelopes every newcomer, arising from beef brisket and pork ribs slathered with barbecue sauce and slow-roasting over hot coals.

This is pick-up food, eaten with sleeves rolled up and napkins stuck in collars. People who have somehow been denied the guilty pleasures of true southern barbecue should make this a stop as important as Faneuil Hall. They can learn about hushpuppies (cornbread with scallions), fried okra (green pods integral to Cajun/Creole cooking), Louisiana catfish (marinated in pepper sauce, breaded in corn meal, plunged in hot oil). Damn the triglycerides and tear into slow-smoked pulled pork sandwiches, wood-grilled halves of chicken, or racks of baby back ribs with the flesh falling away at a loving look.

Just about everything comes with long-simmered beans and creamy coleslaw, of course. It's always crowded, and they don't accept reservations, but the wait in the adjacent bar isn't onerous, and downstairs there are dartboards, take-out packages that can be eaten right there, and a classic jukebox.

### ROCCO'S  *Italian*
*5 Charles St. South (Boylston St.), Theater District. Map 11F9* ☎ *723-6800* ▥ ▣
▣ ▣ ▥ *Open daily for lunch and dinner.*
**T** *Arlington or Boylston (Green Line).*
When it first opened at this convenient site near the Common and the Theater District, its menu was of the global persuasion. That certainly fitted the decor, which might be described, inadequately, as Italianate Colonial Post-Modern. Later, the managers decided to narrow the focus to northern Italian preparations. The result is hardly dogmatic, and there are a number of dishes never seen in Bologna. But pastas are among the best choices, as are seafoods and veal. The high-ceilinged room with its bank of large windows is a pleasant, sun-filled place in which to idle a lunch away. That's apt to be the pace, anyway, since the kitchen can be slow even when the room is half-full. After the office buildings and shops empty, the action shifts to the bar, and the tempo cranks up to high and stays there until long after theater curtains fall. All that in mind, Rocco's can be an agreeable choice any time from noon to midnight, and they don't treat eating and drinking as a religious experience.

### ST CLOUD  *Eclectic*
*557 Tremont St. (Clarendon St.), South End. Off map 10H8* ☎ *353-0202* ▥ *No cards. Open daily for lunch and dinner.*
**T** *Back Bay/South End (Orange Line).*
The crisp contemporary corner space, glass on three sides, points like a prow at the Boston Center for the Arts in the emerging South End. Ordinarily, a place that looks like this, with a menu like this, and especially with two or more waiters in ponytails, values its chicness over its presumed essential

function. St Cloud, however, manages to satisfy both needs. It *is* inclined toward such asterisked explanatory menu notes as "Items appearing beside a cloud are smaller portions" and "A combination of two or more can serve as a creative alternative to our single entrées." That's not to say that the suggestions aren't useful or that the results lack distinction and taste. *Penne arbiatta,* crab and corn fritters with spicy red pepper sauce, venison pâté, or smoked trout with buckwheat toast and wild greens are just the beginning. Follow that, perhaps, with lemon and ginger-glazed salmon with shrimp flan or bouillabaisse with aioli, and finish with sour cherry cobbler. At lunch, even the burger with roast potatoes impresses.

### SULTAN'S KITCHEN  ♣ *Middle Eastern*
*72 Broad St. (near Milk St.), Financial District. Map 12E11* ☎ *338-8509* ▢ ▣
*Open Mon-Fri 11am-5pm.* **T** *State (Blue or Orange Line).*
Fresh, tasty food at bargain prices make this a gratifying alternative to the usual run of franchised fast foods and bar grub. The owner is Turkish and identifies his offerings accordingly, although most diners will think of it as broadly Middle Eastern. There is a zippy humus, the chickpea dipping paste, falafel, several versions of shish kebab, grape leaves wrapped around rice, and *tabbouleh,* the cracked-wheat salad. Never mind origins. These versions are as good as any to be had in this part of the world, and far better than most. For proof, don't miss the marvelous curried lentil soup. The drill is to place an order at the street level, grab a beverage from the nearby cold case, and carry it all upstairs to the dining room. The tables there are bare, with salt and pepper in paper packets. No one cares about the lack of amenities and utensils, not with food this satisfying.

### TOSCANO  *Italian*
*41 Charles St. (Mt. Vernon St.), Beacon Hill. Map 11E9* ☎ *723-4090* ▥ *to* ▥ ▣
*Closed Sun.* **T** *Charles (Red Line).*

Soon after patrons are seated, a person with an untraceable accent comes to the table and undertakes a lengthy recitation of up to 12 appetizers, pastas and entrées, complete with Italian names, English translations, and details of preparation. It is a remarkable performance, deemed necessary by the manager to take into account ingredients that run out or are replaced during the course of the evening. In practice, diners' memories may crash and die around item six, but at least they can be assured that everything that emerges from the kitchen will be fresh and to order. Very good it is, too. Pasta is dressed, not drowned, the double-thick pork loin cooked to sublime tenderness. Recipes of Tuscany are much in evidence on the set menu, but the kitchen goes farther afield on its daily specials, where seafoods are more likely to prevail. People who seek bells and whistles and the latest pan-global stretches of gastronomic imagination are advised to look elsewhere. Those content merely with near-perfect renderings of the northern Italian canon are urged to make early reservations here. Have cocktails before arriving, for they sell only beer and wine.

## UPSTAIRS AT THE PUDDING  Eclectic
10 Holyoke St. (Massachusetts Ave.), Harvard Sq., Cambridge. Map 7B2
☎864-1933 ▥ ▨ ▥ ▥ Closed Sat lunch. T Harvard (Red Line).
Musical comedies featuring Harvard students, many of them in drag, have been a staple of Harvard's Hasty Pudding theatrical group since the last century. Their Greek Revival clubhouse is also used for lectures and meetings of fraternity alumni, and has a restaurant on its top floor. It is a spacious, two-story room with emerald green walls and posters from past Hasty Pudding shows. Pewter chandeliers supplement the illumination from candles in hurricane lamps; a table crowded with bottles functions as a service bar. Wooden chairs that might have been salvaged from a college cafeteria form the seating. It's the sort of place an undergraduate might take his mother and father on Parent's Day, assuming Dad was paying. The difference is the food, of a somewhat higher order than the sponsorship might suggest. Largely, but not slavishly, of the northern Italian persuasion, it is just good enough to be worth its price, but is well short of conversation-stopping. Typical are the six lightly broiled oysters with bits of pancetta and curls of lemon zest, as is the *pappardelle* with duck slivers. An inexpensive "rapido lunch" is served in five minutes. Dinner is more leisurely.

## UNION OYSTER HOUSE  Seafood
41 Union St. (Hanover St.), Faneuil Hall/Government Center. Map 12E11
☎227-2750 ▥ to ▥ ▨ ▥ ▥ ▥
Open daily for lunch and dinner.
T Haymarket (Orange Line) or State (Blue or Orange Line).
"Ye Olde" is the prefix to the name on its signs, only a partial affectation, considering it's been in business since 1826 and the building dates to 1714. The dining room gets by on atmospherics alone, which doesn't stop the tourist throngs (the restaurant is directly on the Freedom Trail). Better to leave the unexceptional meals to them and head instead to the raw bar in front, with its aged stone sinks and the man who deftly pries open fresh oysters and clams to order.

## WURSTHAUS  German/Continental
4 John F. Kennedy St. (Harvard Sq.), Cambridge. Map 7B2 ☎491-7110 ▥ to ▥ ▨ ▥ ▥ ▥ Open daily for breakfast, lunch and dinner. T Harvard (Red Line).
Yodelers and oompah bands occupy the sound system, and German and English brews are on draft. The highly conspicuous atmosphere is composed of high-backed wooden booths, shelves of Bavarian beer steins and Toby jugs of assorted famous people, and framed photos of noted customers. Even Frank Sinatra sent a letter, duly mounted. The menu persists in such notations as "served *mit* bread," a locution last amusing sometime around 1913. It is, however, a quiet stop for a

brew or a Wiener schnitzel when Harvard Square grows too frenetic. Sandwiches, sauerbraten, bratwurst and strudel are on offer, not expensive and not wonderful, but by no means unspeakable, either.

### ZUMA'S ♣ Tex-Mex

*North Market Building, Faneuil Hall Marketplace. Map 12E11* ☎*367-9114* ▢ ⬤ ▨ *Open daily for lunch and dinner.* **T** *Aquarium (Blue Line) or State (Blue or Orange Line).*

People who trouble themselves about authenticity can put Mexican cuisine out of their minds while in Boston. Instead, they must settle for mere taste and fun at any of the handful of admittedly frivolous Tex-Mex emporia. Zuma's stands out — slightly — from the general mediocrity of Faneuil Hall eateries, its menu careering from not-bad *enchiladas verdes* to okay *ceviche* to pretty-good mesquite-grilled tequila chicken. Most of the tourists (by day) and young singles (in the evening) who patronize the place appear to be more than content.

# Entertainments

## Boston by night

Indecision is probably the greatest obstacle to planning an evening out in Boston or Cambridge. All but the most bizarre tastes are accommodated, so it is possible to ease up to the night with tea dancing at the Ritz-Carlton, move on to sunset cocktails in a 33rd-floor aerie, then to dinner underscored by a tinkling piano, followed by ballet in the Theater District or a poetry reading near Harvard Square, wrapping up with an hour of honky-tonk blues. And afterward comes the realization that the surface has barely been dented.

Bostonians and Cantabrigians are devoted to their arts and entertainments, making it often necessary to obtain tickets well in advance, even as early as when reserving a hotel room. Many theaters accept credit-card orders from clients by telephone. Tickets are then mailed to the purchaser, or if too little time remains before the performance, they are held at the box office.

### TICKET AGENCIES

The telephone broker with the widest coverage of events is **Ticketron** (☎ 1-800-382-8080). Hours are Monday to Friday 9am–10pm, Saturday 9am–8pm, Sunday 10am–6pm. (That's the Eastern Time Zone, remember, if you are calling from a distance.) No refunds or exchanges are permitted.

A competing agency that provides a similar service is **Ticketmaster** (☎ 931-2000), and a third much-used broker is located at the **Out of Town** newsstand in the middle of Harvard Sq. (map 7 B2 ☎ 492-1900). Both of these handle stage shows, concerts and athletic (sports) events in and around the city. Their hours are Monday to Friday 9am–7pm, Saturday 9am–6pm.

Savings are possible, but you'll need to make the effort. A booth next to Faneuil Hall called **Bostix** (map 12 E11 ☎ 723-5181) sells half-price tickets for performances the same day, on a cash-only basis. These are leftovers, so they are rarely available for newly arrived hit shows or much-anticipated concerts. The agency also sells advance tickets paid for by cash or check, even for shows in other parts of New England and in New York. Opening hours for Bostix are Tuesday to Saturday 11am–6pm, Sunday 11am–4pm.

Brokers charge a fee for their services, of course, scaled to the importance of the event, but usually not too large.

**WHAT'S ON, AND WHERE?**
To find out what's on, look in the Calendar section of the Thursday edition of *The Boston Globe*, the Arts section of the weekly *Boston Phoenix*, or the "On the Town" pages of the monthly magazine, *Boston*. Hotel giveaway magazines *Panorama* and *Where* can be helpful, if it is remembered that they are primarily advertising vehicles.

In all listings in this chapter, addresses are followed by the name of the town or city if they are not in Boston itself: most are near the city limits and within reach of the MBTA public transport system.

# Performing arts

In its cultural quality and diversity, Boston has few peers in North America. There are over 40 theaters, concert halls and performance spaces to accommodate a rich diet of symphony, drama, opera, musicals, dance and jazz. Too much choice, not deprivation, is apt to be the problem. Even with a week in town, only a tasting is possible.

Free concerts are often sponsored by local banks and other businesses, especially in summer. Many of these are given at the open-air **Hatch Memorial Shell** on the Charles River Embankment, but they are also found in museums, university halls and public spaces such as **Faneuil Hall Marketplace** and **Copley Square**. Check the publications noted above.

**BALLET AND MODERN DANCE**
Premier among the several companies based in the Boston/Cambridge area is the much-heralded **Boston Ballet**. Among the others are the **Art of Black Dance and Music** and **Mandala**, which specializes in folk dances. Many major national and international troupes make Boston a regular stop in their annual travels, including **Alvin Ailey**, **Ballet Folklorico de Mexico**, **Twyla Tharp** and the **Mark Morris Dance Group.** Among the principal venues:

- **Boston University Theater**    264 Huntington Ave. Map **10**H7 ☎266-3918. Dance groups make appearances between stands by the resident repertory company.
- **Cambridge Multicultural Arts Center**    41 Second St., Cambridge. Map **11**C7 ☎577-1400. Frequent performances of ethnic music and dance in a building that also hosts art exhibits.
- **Emerson Majestic Theatre**    219 Tremont St. Map **11**F9 ☎578-8727. The college-owned 1903 theater includes dance in its varied programs of recitals and plays. It is one of several venues used by the **Dance Umbrella** organization.
- **Wang Center for the Performing Arts**    270 Tremont St. Map **11**G9 ☎542-3600. The superbly renovated former movie palace is home to the **Boston Ballet** and the presentations of a local organization known as **Dance Umbrella.** Visiting companies appear under the **Bank of Boston Celebrity Series** rubric (see opposite).

## CINEMA

Multi-screen theaters slavishly showing the current output of zillion-dollar Hollywood productions are no trouble to locate. But with its large, highly educated population of film buffs, opportunities to view art films or revivals of classics are abundant. While there aren't many conventional cinemas specializing in such films, those that exist are supplemented by programs at libraries, museums and universities. Their lifespans are unpredictable, however, and their programs subject to unannounced change, so check the newspapers or call ahead. Film houses that regularly present such fare include:

* **Brattle Theater**  40 Brattle St., Cambridge. Map **7B2** ☎354-3036
* **Coolidge Corner Cinema**  290 Harvard St., Brookline ☎734-3500
* **Loews Nickelodeon**  606 Commonwealth Ave.  Map **9G5** ☎424-1500
* **Somerville Theater**  55 Davis Sq., Somerville  ☎625-5700

Among those institutions with more-or-less regular showings or seasonal film festivals are:

* **Boston Film & Video Foundation**  1126 Boylston St. Map **10G6** ☎536-1540
* **Boston Public Library**  Copley Sq. Map **10G8** ☎536-5400
* **The French Library**  53 Marlborough St. Map **11F8** ☎266-4351
* **Harvard Film Archive**  24 Quincy St. Map **7B3** ☎495-4700
* **Institute of Contemporary Art**  955 Boylston St. Map **10G7** ☎266-5152
* **Museum of Fine Arts**  465 Huntington Ave. Map **9I5** ☎267-9300 ext.300
* **Wang Center for the Performing Arts**  270 Tremont St. Map **12G9** ☎482-9393

## CLASSICAL MUSIC

**Symphony Hall** *(301 Massachusetts Ave., map **10**H7 ☎ 266-1492),* with its superior acoustics, is home for both the **Boston Symphony Orchestra**, with its respected conductor Seiji Ozawa, and the **Boston Pops** orchestra. They share the year, with a September to April season for the Symphony, and for the Pops, April to June. In summer, the Pops bestow a week of free concerts upon the city at the Hatch Shell in the Charles River Esplanade. A chamber group of Symphony musicians makes appearances, as does the **Handel & Haydn Society**, a popular choral group.

No lover of serious music need feel deprived, no matter what time of the year. The annual **Bank of Boston Celebrity Series** sponsors music and dance at various locations around the city, often underwriting visits by major national and international artists. Local companies worth looking out for are the **Bach Society Orchestra**, the **Boston Conservatory Chamber Ensemble**, the **Pro Arte Chamber Orchestra of Boston**, the **Boston Baroque Orchestra** and the **Boston Classical Orchestra**.

**Jordan Hall** *(New England Conservatory, 30 Gainsborough St., map* **10**H6 ☎ *482-6661)* is an active venue that hosts various groups, from soloists to string quartets to chamber orchestras, as well as organizations participating in the Bank of Boston Celebrity Series. Other venues include the following:

- **Berklee Performance Center and Recital Hall** 136 Massachusetts Ave. Map **10**G6 ☎266-7455
- **Church of the Advent** 30 Brimmer St. Map **11**E8 ☎232-4540
- **The French Library** 53 Marlborough St. Map **11**F8 ☎266-4351
- **Sanders Theatre** Kirkland and Quincy Sts. Map **7**B3 ☎661-7067
- **Tsai Performance Center** 685 Commonwealth Ave. Map **9**G5 ☎232-9053

At the **Isabella Stewart Gardner Museum** *(280 The Fenway, map* **9**I5 ☎ *734-1359),* weekly concerts from September to May mostly feature chamber music and string quartets, with occasional solo pianists, providing a tempting opportunity to sample the unique atmosphere of this extraordinary monument to one woman's good taste. Soloists and small chamber groups perform frequently in the **Remis Auditorium** of the **Museum of Fine Arts** *(465 Huntington Ave., map* **9**I5 ☎ *267-9377, or 267-9300 for recorded information).*

## JAZZ AND BLUES

Even though it is most often heard in bars thick with smoke or as sanitized backdrop for Sunday brunches, America's purest musical art form deserves to be listed among the *corps de ballet* and chamber quartets. Jazz — from Dixieland to bebop to Fusion — is heard often in Boston and Cambridge, in restaurants and hotel lobbies and in parks, as well as murky cellars. Audiences hale from all age groups, unlike rock clubs, where anyone older than 30 is apt to feel like a fossil.

Big-name jazz in a concert-hall setting is often the program at **Berklee Performance Center** *(136 Massachusetts Ave., map* **10**G6 ☎ *266-1400),* which is a facility of the Berklee College of Music.

In June, a week-long jazz festival sponsored by *The Boston Globe* takes over spaces in or near museums and other landmarks for free concerts by combos and bands, with a headliner kicking off the festivities at the Hatch Shell on the Charles River Embankment. Clubs around the metro area supplement the menu with their own sessions.

For additional information, call the **Jazz Festival Hotline** *(*☎ *523-4047).*

A selection follows of clubs and bars that schedule jazz or blues groups on a regular, if not necessarily exclusive, basis. Some impose admission or cover charges. For current attractions, call the **Jazz Hotline** *(*☎ *787-9700).*

- **House of Blues** 96 Winthrop St., Cambridge. Map **7**C2 ☎491-2583. Actor Dan Aykroyd is one of the owners of this new club opened in 1992 near Harvard Square. The Sunday Gospel Brunch is a kick. Three sittings; book ahead. Variable cover charge. Food available.

- **Regattabar**   1 Bennett St., Cambridge. Map **7C2** ☎876-7777. Respectful audiences attend to polished performances in an intimate room of the Charles Hotel, Tuesday to Saturday.
- **Ryles**   212 Hampshire St., Cambridge. Map **8B4** ☎876-9330. This bi-level club on Inman Sq. usually has two different groups performing nightly. Mostly straight jazz, but veering over to blues or world-beat on occasion. Food available. Cover charge.
- **Scullers Jazz Club**   400 Soldiers Field Rd., Allston. Map **7E2** ☎783-0811. Imaginative scheduling ranging from duos to big bands makes tolerable the moderately long trip from downtown to this room at the Guest Quarters Suite Hotel. Cover charge.
- **Sticky Mike's**   Boylston Place. Map **11F9** ☎426-2583. On an alley full of clubs, these bands are good enough to stop conversation. Dancing is permitted. Open Wednesday to Saturday.
- **Wally's Café**   427 Massachusetts Ave. Map **10G6** ☎424-1408. This old-fashioned club has provided bargain jazz and booze to music lovers for more than 45 years. Open nightly. No cover.
- **Zachary's**   Colonnade Hotel, 120 Huntington Avenue. Map **10G7** ☎424-7000. Comfortable room for non-frenetic trios, quartets and singers. Dancing is permitted, and there are good wines by the glass. Open Tuesday to Sunday.

Other clubs prefer a more eclectic mix, presenting several kinds of music, including jazz. Possibilities include **Middle East Café** *(472 Massachusetts Ave., Cambridge, map 7D4* ☎*354-8238)* and **Nightstage** *(823 Main St., Cambridge, map 8D5* ☎*497-8200)*.

### OPERA AND CHORAL MUSIC

At the time of writing, the pre-eminent local company is the **Boston Lyric Opera Company**, in season from October to March, whose arena is the **Emerson Majestic Theater** *(219 Tremont St., map 11F9* ☎ *578-8727)*. The company is rumored to be seeking larger quarters.

The once esteemed **Opera Company of Boston**, led by Sarah Caldwell, fell upon hard times during the 1980s, as did its theater on lower Washington St., closed in 1990. Efforts to resuscitate both were continuing as of this writing.

The **Handel & Haydn Society**, a choral and instrumental ensemble, performs at various locations, including **Symphony Hall** *(301 Massachusetts Ave., map 10H7* ☎ *266-2378)* and **Jordan Hall** at the **New England Conservatory** *(30 Gainsborough St., map 10H6* ☎ *266-3605)*. **Boston Cecilia**, a chorus with origins in the 19thC, also uses Jordan Hall, among other places.

Watch out, too, for performances by the **Cantata Singers and Ensemble**, the **Spectrum Singers**, the **Masterworks Chorale** and **Chorus Pro Musica**.

### THEATER

In years past, Broadway-bound shows routinely trod the Boston boards to work out the kinks and flab. Often, the critics buried them where they stood, never to see the lights of Times Square. Or, the writers and directors tinkered with the scripts, stitched up the holes, and sent their babies off to try their wings. With the odd exception, the days of the Broadway tryout are gone, victims of economics, television and home video. Many of the old breed of lavishly rococo theaters are dark, never to open their doors again. Those that survive must make do with road-company versions of Broadway mega-hits and revivals, most of them necessarily featuring second-rank stars and stripped-down sets.

Yet pleasant, even exhilarating, nights of live theater are still happy possibilities. And notwithstanding dire predictions, new generations continue to strive for excellence in the provocative live performances of dozens of repertory and university companies, workshops in churches and hotels, and even community theater. There is dinner theater, too, but don't assume you will be moved or well-fed.

There are several stable venues, most of them presenting mainstream entertainments. In what remains of the theater district, from Boylston St. running s along Tremont St. *(map 11 F9-G9)*, there are six active venues:

- **Charles Playhouse**   74 Warrenton St. ☎426-5225. Two stages, one for traveling shows like *Ain't Misbehavin'*, the other occupied for years by the comic mystery *Shear Madness*.
- **Colonial Theater**   106 Boylston St. ☎426-9366. A classic 1900 theater in the grand tradition, superbly preserved, this is a prime showcase for touring companies of major shows, many of them revivals, such as *Annie Get Your Gun* and *Guys and Dolls*.
- **Emerson Majestic Theater**   219 Tremont St. ☎578-8727. Emerson College concentrates on study in the performing arts and communication (see WALK 4, page 84). While restoring this turn-of-the-century theater, it presents a mixture of entertainments, including but not confined to dance, music recitals, light opera and drama.
- **Shubert Theater**   265 Tremont St. ☎426-4520. The Shuberts of New York have kept this extension of their empire going for more than 80 years. Dramas and musicals are staples, the likes of *Six Degrees of Separation* and *A Chorus Line*.
- **Wang Center for the Performing Arts**   270 Tremont St. ☎482-9393. The founder of a now-defunct computer company helped underwrite the restoration of this glorious 1920s movie palace. It hosts local and visiting ballet and opera companies as well as dramas and musicals.
- **Wilbur Theater**   246 Tremont St. ☎423-4008. While smaller than most of the others, it retains much of its pre-World War I elegance.

Theaters in other parts of the city and across the river in Cambridge include:
- **BCA Theatre and Black Box Theatre**   539 Tremont St. Off map 10H8 ☎426-2787. South End's BOSTON CENTER FOR THE ARTS (see pages 95–96) has three performance spaces for usually experimental works. These two are the most active.
- **Boston University Theater**   264 Huntington Ave. Map **10**H7 ☎266-0800. Boston University sponsors the professional **Huntington Theatre Company**, which concentrates on serious classical and modern works. Its season here is September to June.

- **Loeb Drama Center**   64 Brattle St., Cambridge. Map **7**B1 ☎547-8300. Harvard University's non-profit **American Repertory Theatre** (ART) company has this as its principal home for Pinter, Shaw and lesser-known modern playwrights. Outreach programs have them in other venues for short runs, especially at the **Hasty Pudding Theatre** *(12 Holyoke St., Cambridge, map* **7***C2* ☎ *547-8300).*

- **Lyric Stage**   140 Clarendon St. Map **11**F8 ☎437-7172. Gloomy machismo from David Mamet and sophisticated light revues with the music of Cole Porter have occupied this stage.

Smaller stages are employed for comedies and dramas as well as revues and cabaret. They run the gamut from road productions of Off-Broadway plays to obscure experimental works by local playwrights. University and community theater groups are often surprisingly capable, if irregular and unpredictable. Check what's playing at the **Terrace Room** of the Park Plaza Hotel *(64 Arlington St., map* **11***G9* ☎*357-8384),* **Theatre Lobby** *(216 Hanover St., map* **12***D11* ☎ *227-9872)* and the **Triangle Theater Company** *(58 Berkeley St., map* **11***F8* ☎*426-3550).* The Thursday edition of *The Boston Globe* and the weekly *The Boston Phoenix* are sources of information about what's on.

# Nightlife

While it isn't yet one of those cities that hammers on toward dawn, Boston has loosened the laces on the corset considerably in recent years. Bars and clubs can stay open until 2am, and both in their number and diversity they should suit every taste. Our recommendations skim over the myriad possibilities, but they tend to be along streets or in neighborhoods that have other unlisted but equally attractive choices. Seek those out. And please understand that since owners and policies change abruptly, not every place we list will have survived the drying of this ink.

Except where noted below, casual dress prevails. The interpretation of what "casual" means is up to doormen and managers, and their brief can be ambiguous, even changing from night to night or hour to hour depending on how full or empty their rooms might be. At anything other than the tavern around the corner, it is often best, when heading out of an evening, to avoid jeans, shirts without sleeves or collars, athletic wear, heavy boots, and sneakers.

Establishments offering live entertainment usually, but not universally, impose admission or cover charges, collected at the door or added to the bill. Some also require a minimum amount of consumption, charging for two drinks or a specific dollar amount whether or not it is drunk or eaten. The drinking age is 21.

### BARS AND LOUNGES
The Hub has an abundance of pubs in every category to suit most transient tastes or needs: bars with views, for singles, for sports fans,

for enthusiasts of every kind of music, for beer-lovers, for everyone who comes from a culture that allows alcohol consumption and a few that don't. University students fill the rowdy brew pubs in and around Kenmore Square *(map 9 G5),* and in a city with more Irish people than Cork, Guinness and Harp flow freely. To ease selection, the suggestions below are squeezed into categories, which is not necessarily to imply that the establishments restrict themselves so readily.

### Bars with elevated viewpoints
The high places have a way of lifting the spirits, to coin a pun. The golden light washing over the city from a falling sun is unfailingly romantic, making the following three sky-high lounges ideal for the first or last night of a Boston visit. Better still, none of them imposes a cover charge.

* Highest of all is the **Top of the Hub** *(Prudential Tower, 800 Boylston St., map 10 G7* ☎ *536-1775),* on the 51st floor of the second-tallest skyscraper in Boston.
* The style-setter is the swank **Bay Tower Room** *(60 State St., map 12 E11* ☎ *723-1666),* on the 33rd floor of a downtown office tower, looking down at Faneuil Hall and over the harbor. Still wines and champagne are available by the glass. There is dancing to a live quartet Friday and Saturday, piano music the other nights. (See also WHERE TO EAT, page 155).
* People who aren't put off by rooms that revolve enjoy the **Spinnaker Italia** *(Hyatt Regency Hotel, 575 Memorial Drive, Cambridge, map 7 E2* ☎ *492-1234).* It's a full-service restaurant with a Northern Italian menu, but it is possible to simply sip a cocktail and take in the view across the Charles River.

### Bars with history
A city this old (as North American cities go) is bound to have a few oldsters among its roster of bars.

* On that list, **Jacob Wirth's** *(31 Stuart St., map 12 G10* ☎ *338-8586)* amounts to a required pilgrimage stop. It's old. German. Creaky. With a backbar black with age, and all of it dating from 1868. No hard liquor, and eat there only if famished.
* People go to **Locke-Ober** *(3 Winter Place, off Winter St.* ☎ *542-1340)* to connect, to "network," as they have since 1875. Politicians, power-brokers and the privileged meet and greet in the worn old tobacco-brown entry bar before going into the private club. Ordinary folk are welcomed, to a degree, if the men among them are wearing jacket and tie. (See also page 163.)
* But oldest of the old is surely the **Bell and Hand Tavern** *(45 Union St., map 12 E11* ☎ *227-2098),* still only a few steps off the Freedom Trail near Faneuil Hall. Hoist a flagon of ale in a room that is said to have been around since 1794. No doubt intervening alterations and assorted calamities have altered it beyond recognition, but it is a warming thought that Washington, Revere, John Hancock and two or three Adamses might have stood in the very same spot.

## Sports bars

No city exults more enthusiastically in its teams and athletes than Bean-town, whether at the university or professional levels. That means hardly a day passes without a televised contest of some sort, and fans crowd into the many sports bars to root for their favorites.

- Any list must begin with the **Bull & Finch** *(84 Beacon St., map 11 F9* ☎ *227-9605)*. Yes, it's the bar that inspired the long-running *Cheers* TV series. And no, the interior doesn't look like the one on the tube. Never mind. It's dark and woody and friendly, and whips up an exemplary Bloody Mary. Tourists and regulars mingle with little conflict, although the latter no doubt wish they had the place to themselves once again. (See also pages 103–4.)

- In the primped-up old COPLEY SQUARE hotel is **The Original Sports Saloon** *(47 Huntington Ave., map 10 G8* ☎ *536-9000)*. A classic of the genre, its walls are covered with photos of Boston's athletic greats: the Red Sox's Ted Williams, the Bruins' Bobby Orr, the Celtics' Larry Bird. Several TV monitors keep track of the current heroes, or pick up a stock-car race from Alabama if it's a day between seasons.

- Nearby, **Champions** *(110 Huntington Ave., map 10 G8* ☎ *578-0658)*, in the Marriott Copley Place hotel, has 18 monitors, sports memorabilia on the walls, and video games. When there isn't a game or match on-screen, a deejay spins the tops in pops.

- Athletes from local and visiting professional teams like to drop by **Daisy Buchanan's** *(240A Newbury St., map 10 G7* ☎ *247-8516)*, a fact not lost on their fans and groupies. On weekends, the management gives out free hot dogs.

- **Who's On First** *(19 Yawkey Way, map 9 H5* ☎ *247-3353)* is in the shadow of Fenway Park, home of the beloved but unlucky Red Sox. Baseball, obviously, is the sport *du jour*, but they make time for Monday Night Football and the NBA playoffs.

## Hotel bars

Most hotel bars are full of those out-of-towners too timid or too tired to venture far from their nests. A few, however, are inviting enough to bring in the locals, especially when such folk want to be able to hear themselves talk. All the following hotels feature in the HOTELS A TO Z, on pages 140–48.

- None of them gets more grand than the **Plaza Bar** in the COPLEY PLAZA hotel *(Copley Sq., map 10 G8* ☎ *267-5300)*. The ceiling is two floors high, heavy drapes and shutters keep lights low, tables are made cozy by enclosures, the bar is a beauty, and the man at the piano sings smooth renditions of Porter and Kern and reasonable requests. Jackets are required for men.

- The Hotel LE MERIDIEN in the Financial District is, appropriately, a converted bank. The board of directors didn't stint on their meeting room, with its high coffered ceiling and sumptuous detailing. It's now **Julien's Bar** *(250 Franklin St., map 12 F11* ☎ *451-1900)*, as gracious a prelude to dinner as might be imagined. To aid the mood, mellow jazz is sent rippling through the room Monday to Saturday.

- The **RITZ-CARLTON** (15 Arlington St., map **11** F9 ☎ 536-5700) doesn't give names to its bar nor its restaurant, but it has both. Jacket and tie are required, if only so the waiters won't be too much better dressed than the patrons. Think English manor house, with wingback chairs and a fireplace that is put to use whenever there's a nip in the air. This is also *the* spot for afternoon tea, with a harpist. A duo plays jazz and pop tunes for dancing Thursday to Saturday.
- The **FOUR SEASONS** (200 Boylston St., map **11** F9 ☎ 338-4400), the Ritz's principal rival, is not as old-world formal, but the staff in the spacious **Bristol Lounge** is, if anything, even more alert to patrons' needs. The large room looks out on the Public Garden. A fireplace is kept at work through the cold months, and the music of a piano or combo serves its unobtrusive purpose. There is afternoon tea daily, and an irresistible dessert buffet tempts during the post-prandial hours, Friday and Saturday.
- Conceding that the claim of the **OMNI PARKER HOUSE** (60 School St., map **12** E10 ☎ 227-8600) to be over a century old is a little shaky, the two bars look like they might have been around that long. Pols and execs are the principal tipplers in the **Last Hurrah** and **Parker's**. Both have music most nights and lay out complimentary bar snacks during happy hours.

### Bars with good eats

Speaking of food, there needs to be a category for bars where you can have a snack or a light meal. Most are attached to restaurants, as at **Biba**, the **Cottonwood Café**, **Marais**, **Mr. Leung's** and **Dalí**, all of which are described in the RESTAURANTS A TO Z, pages 154–68.

- A filling, inexpensive dinner can be had grazing through the "equatorial" offerings of the **East Coast Grill** (1271 Cambridge St., Cambridge, map **8** B4 ☎ 491-6568), which specialize in tropical fruits and fiery seasonings.
- **Small Planet** (565 Boylston St., map **11** G8 ☎ 536-4477) is a whole lot more fun than its predecessor, the Back Bay Bistro. Decorated with folk art and an attractive young crowd, it proffers such tasty tidbits as "Iroquois bean relish with blue cornchips" and "fried chicken and pork wontons." They are washed down with swigs of beer, drunk straight from the bottle.
- Not far away, the **Rattlesnake Bar & Grill** (382 Boylston St., map **11** F8 ☎ 859-8555) trumpets its "Food of the Americas," good enough for there to be often a short line outside waiting to get inside. Margaritas are the beverage of choice for edibles that have passed through the Tex-Mex screen on their way north. *Burritos* and *quesadillas* in appetizer portions are standouts.

### Brewery pubs

Those taverns that make their own ales and lagers, and a virtue of displaying the manufacturing process of same, are multiplying. The first three of the following serve simple but above-par pub grub, such as barbecued ribs and in-house sausages.

- Rows of stainless steel tanks are backdrop for the V-shaped bar at the **Boston Beer Works** *(61 Brookline Ave., map 9G5* ☎ *536-2337).* They produce almost chewy Beantown Nut Brown Ale and Boston Red Ale, among an expanding number of formulations.
- The **Commonwealth Brewing Company** *(138 Portland St., map 12D10* ☎ *523-8383)* has gotten itself a likely location, right in the path of thirsty basketball and hockey fans streaming out of home games at Boston Garden.
- The **Cambridge Brewing Company** *(1 Kendall Sq., map 10D7* ☎ *494-1994)* sets a party tone with live rock groups on Saturday nights.
- If all the above fail to satisfy the wandering Brit or international beer purist, **Cornwall's** *(510 Commonwealth Ave., map 9G5* ☎ *262-3749)* has 15 brands on tap, including such exotics as John Courage, Bateman's, Woodpecker, Harpoon and Pilsner Urguell, poured into Imperial (20-ounce) pint glasses.

### Irish bars

They range, in their abundance, from those that might have been lifted intact from Fleet Street in Dublin to those whose nods to authenticity consist largely of paper shamrocks on the mirrors and green beer on St Patrick's Day.

- In the former category, the pub of choice is **The Black Rose** *(160 State St., map 12E11* ☎ *742-2286).* Irish music nightly, Irish food, Irish beer, Irish coffee, Irish stories, Irish sentiments, Irish accents, and the lilt of Irish laughter . . . it's only been on the scene a little over a decade, but it seems forever.
- **Limericks** *(33 Batterymarch St., map 12E11* ☎ *350-7975)* comes close to the mark, too. On Friday and Saturday there is usually Irish music, sometimes mixed with other kinds, and Guinness and Harp are on tap.
- A newer entry is **Claddagh** *(Columbus Ave. and Dartmouth St., map 10G8* ☎ *262-9874),* in the South End. Sing-songs are common, fueled by Irish ales and whiskeys. On weekends, they bring in musical groups.
- Similarly, the **Purple Shamrock** *(1 Union St., map 12I11* ☎ *227-2060)* has live Irish music on weekend evenings, but doesn't go out of its way to imitate the original model.

### Singles bars

Even in these cautious times, singles bars are thriving. Discretion has noticeably toned down the predatory sensuality of such places, but people still want people. Young singles and the less-young-recently-detached flock to the score of bars and cafés located in and around Faneuil Hall Marketplace.

Efforts at distinctiveness aside, the most popular places follow essentially the same formula. They encourage casual but modish dress, discourage those who think tank tops and combat boots are the height of fashion, crank up the jukebox or the live rock, serve snacks that don't challenge common food prejudices, and pack the people in tight enough so they couldn't avoid meeting each other even if they wanted.

- Given those parameters, the leaders are **Cityside** (☎ 741-7390), **Frogg Lane Bar & Grill** (☎ 720-0610), **Cityside** (☎ 742-7390) and **Lily's** (☎ 720-5580), all in Faneuil Hall Marketplace *(map 12 E11)*.
- Nearby is **Houlihan's** *(60 State St., map 12 E11* ☎ 367-6377), with a dining room and dancing to recorded music.
- A little farther, and less frenetic, is **Michael's** *(85 Atlantic Ave., map 12 D11* ☎ 367-6425), in rooms with bare brick walls and ceiling beams. There are free hors d'oeuvres during happy hour.
- Over in Cambridge, the refurbished backroom bar of **Casablanca** *(40 Brattle St., map 7 B2* ☎ 876-0999) draws a slightly more sedate crowd reflecting a wider age-range than the Marketplace habitués.

## COMEDY AND CABARET

The 1980s enthusiasm for stand-up comedy has ebbed somewhat, inevitably cutting into the number of outlets for this type of entertainment. Those that have survived this thinning process seem strong enough to be around for years.

- Big names and up-and-comers who regularly work the comedy club circuit almost always make the **Comedy Connection** *(Faneuil Hall Marketplace, map 12 E11* ☎ 248-9700) their Boston stop. Judy Tenuta and the accordion that seems grafted to her chest are frequent callers. Open nightly; two shows on weekends. Reserved seating available.
- **Catch a Rising Star** *(30B John F. Kennedy St., Cambridge, map 7 C2* ☎ 661-0167) is one of a successful chain. Monday is improvisation night, Tuesday is "open mike" for all comers. Open nightly.
- **Nick's Comedy Stop** *(100 Warrenton St., map 11 F9* ☎ 482-0930) has a Theater District location that makes it a logical stop for an after-show giggle and drink. Richard Belzer has appeared. Open nightly.
- **Dick Doherty's Comedy Vault** *(124 Boylston St., map 11 F9* ☎ 267-6626) is beneath a restaurant in a former bank building. Cover charge.
- The **Back Alley Theater** *(1253 Cambridge St., Inman Sq., map 8 B4* ☎ 396-2470) has concentrated on improvisational groups. Open Thursday to Saturday.
- Satire and parody, often set to music, are the approaches of the teams appearing at the **Boston Baked Theatre** *(255 Elm St., Somerville* ☎ 628-9575). Call ahead before trekking to Davis Sq.
- **Stitches** *(835 Beacon St., map 9 G4* ☎ 424-6995) tends to stick to a schedule, with a risqué hypnotist one night, an audience-participation "dating game" another, and a music night still another.

## DANCE CLUBS

These haven't been called "discos" for some time, but to the uninitiated they look and sound pretty much as such places did 20 years ago. Certainly the music is just as ear-splittingly insistent, although of a wider variety of styles. These include, but are not limited to, techno-house, rave, world-beat, salsa, funk, metal, reggae, rap . . . much of which aging former disco-babies may find difficult to identify. To make oldsters feel at home and to catch the nascent wave of Seventies Revivalism, some clubs have taken to setting aside "Disco Inferno Nights."

Clothing codes are common, but unpredictable. One club will specify "jacket and shirts with collars" or "no jeans, no shorts, no sneakers," while another insists that no one in business attire is admitted. All this applies primarily to men, who are probably best advised to go in black, with a jacket. Empirical observation suggests that women can wear just about as much or as little of pretty well anything that they wish.

Thursday to Saturday are the big nights, of course, and lines start forming early. To avoid the possibility of exclusion by the watchdogs at the door, arrive by 9.30pm and nurse a beer until the action picks up. Admission/cover charges apply at most of the clubs suggested below; nearly all of them accept credit cards.

This is a volatile field, and what's hot this week can be arctic (or vanished) the next.

- **Avalon** *(15 Landsdowne St., map 9 G5* ☎ *262-2424)* has ample space for moving around as well as dancing, noteworthy in a neighborhood that has several clubs certain to dismay claustrophobes. Live bands frequently perform, with Top 40 and DJ choices in between sets, or instead. The crowd has a decided Euro-bent. Sunday is designated gay night. No food. Open Thursday to Sunday.

- **Axis** *(15 Landsdowne St., map 9 G5* ☎ *262-2437)*, cheek-by-jowl with Avalon, was decorated by someone with a favorite color: black. Almost everyone who shows up wears it, too. Strobes provide the illumination. Live bands are on some nights, with alternative, acid-house and their relations spun by disk jockeys the rest of the time. No food. Up one floor is a pool table and another dance floor. Open Tuesday–Saturday; Tuesday is often reserved for private parties.

- At **Cotton Club** *(965 Massachusetts Ave., map 7 C3* ☎ *541-0101)* rhythm and blues, rap and reggae prevail, both in deejay choices and when live groups perform. The balanced bi-racial crowd dresses well and knows how to party, moving between the two floors, which have different kinds of music.

- European and Latin American university students with money and time to burn make **M-80** *(969 Commonwealth Ave., map 9 G4* ☎ *254-2054)* a club of their own. The deejays play the kinds of music heard in such places back home in Milan and Caracas: house and its derivatives. Stylish clothes that cost a lot are more evident than funkier ensembles. Open Wednesday, Friday, Saturday.

- **NYC Jukebox** *(275 Tremont St., map 11 G9* ☎ *542-1123)*: think Elvis, ducktail haircuts, poodle skirts and doo-wop. Nostalgia is on the menu, served up to a preppie crowd that probably hadn't been conceived at the time. TV sets show black & white sitcoms of the era, a '54 Ford hangs over the bar, and the Wurlitzer jukeboxes play little that was heard after Lyndon Johnson assumed the Presidency. Open Thursday to Saturday.

- Groups of national reputation often appear at **Nightstage** *(823 Main St., Central Sq., Cambridge, map 8 D4* ☎ *497-8200)*, as do top regional bands and singers. Blues and jazz usually dominate, but other forms are also presented. Its popularity makes advance ticketing wise. Dancing. Open nightly.

- **Zanzibar** *(1 Boylston Pl., map 11 F9* ☎ *451-1955)*, on what is called "The Alley," a cluster of bars and clubs off Boylston St., is the most likely to attract visiting celebrities. In the past, they have included Stevie Wonder, Prince, Kevin Costner and Paula Abdul. The main rooms look like a West Indian island designed by Red Grooms. Up a flight are pool tables and VIP rooms. Open Wednesday to Saturday. Men are required to wear jacket *and* tie, which makes for a more mature crowd.

Other possibilities (but check first to be sure they're still in operation) are: **Avenue C** *(25 Boylston Pl., map 11 F9* ☎ *423-3832)*, **Man Ray** *(21 Brookline St., Cambridge, map 7 D4* ☎ *864-0400)*, **Narcissus** *(533 Commonwealth Ave., map 9 G5* ☎ *536-1950)* and **Venus de Milo** *(11 Lansdowne St. map 9 G5* ☎ *421-9595)*. Or you could just head for the single-block Lansdowne St., in the shadow of the Fenway Park stadium, or Boylston Place. There are more, above, below, or next to the ones mentioned above.


**POP/ROCK/FOLK**
This being a university town, the musical tastes of patrons aged 18 to 25 are those to which managers are predisposed. That means what is called "college" or alternative rock, raunchy rhythm and blues, and flat-out rock'n'roll. Folk music, much of it close kin to country, is another niche, presently enjoying a mild resurgence.

Name acts most often use arenas and concert halls — **Boston Garden**, **Jordan Hall**, **Berklee Performance Center**, **Wang Center for the Performing Arts**, even **Symphony Hall**. Summer is the busiest time, and the **Great Woods Concert Series** is the hot-weather hunting ground for star-seekers. It's near the juncture of Routes 140 and 495 in Mansfield, about one hour's drive to the s. Held on weekends from early June until early September, regular attractions have the luminosity of Sting, Tina Turner, Whitney Houston, Def Leppard, Elton John, B.B. King, Dwight Yoakam or the Beach Boys, to name a few who have appeared in the past. Call **Ticketmaster** *(* ☎ *931-2000)*.

Some of the clubs suggested below have dancing and dining, every night or on occasion, but their primary functions are drinking and listening. Unless otherwise specified, dress is casual.

- Many nighttime needs are met in the bar-restaurant-club **Johnny D's** *(17 Holland St., Somerville* ☎ *776-9667)*, on Davis Sq. The decent food is as eclectic as the music, which ranges from country to rock to blues to whatever. Small dance floor; music and food Tuesday–Sunday.

- Couscous and souvlaki aren't the reasons to go to the all-points music emporium **Middle East Café** *(472 Massachusetts Ave., Cam-*

*bridge, map 7D4* ☎ *354-8238 for reservations, 497-0576 for recorded info.).* Most predilections are served in its three rooms, from underground rock to blues to the international blends known as world-beat. The biggest space, downstairs, used to be a bowling alley; the café upstairs is used by acoustical performers. Open daily, 9am to after midnight.

• Singers and bands on the charge or on the comeback perform Wednesday to Saturday at **Paradise** *(967 Commonwealth Ave., map 9G4* ☎ *254-2053):* Cindy Lauper, for example. The club is primarily for concerts, but dancing is permitted late Saturday night. Sometimes there are comedians and small revues. Open Wednesday to Saturday and occasional other nights. It has been rumored that the club is to be closed and the space absorbed in an expanded **M-80** (see page 181).

• **Passim** *(47 Palmer St., Harvard Sq., Cambridge, map 7B2* ☎ *492-7679)* has roots deep in the folkie-hippie coffeehouses of the Woodstock Generation. Bonnie Raitt sang here in her early days. They have a gift shop, and a restaurant for light meals. Liquor still isn't served. Folk and bluegrass remain the staples, and a semi-big name sometimes drops by. Open daily: one show each weeknight, two Friday to Saturday.

• Rock, folk, country or blues shouters compete for attention every night at **The Plough and Stars** *(912 Massachusetts Ave., Cambridge, map 7C3* ☎ *492-9653),* a loud, jolly bar with an Irish tang. Brews from the Auld Sod are on draft; drinks are poured with a generous hand. Good no's and bad no's: no cover; no minimum; no reservations; no credit cards.

• **The Rathskeller** *(528 Commonwealth Ave., Kenmore Square, map 9G5* ☎ *536-2750)* has been known as "The Rat" to generations of college kids and tame ruffians. This raffish Kenmore Sq. beer hall pounds into the night from lunchtime to after midnight. Hardcore rock'n'roll shares the place with more cerebral, or at least less elemental, college rock. Live music Wednesday to Sunday, as a rule.

• Local and international rock bands, often of the underground variety, come with the decent Caribbean grub at **T.T. the Bear's** *(10 Brookline St., Central Sq., Cambridge, map 7D4* ☎ *492-0082).* Or grab a cue in the pool room. Low cover charges, as a rule. Open nightly.

Very many bars and restaurants offer live music once or twice a week. Among them are the **Cask 'n' Flagon** *(62 Brookline Ave., map 9G5* ☎ *536-4840),* a college bar with rock Thursday to Saturday during the academic year; **Zoots** *(228 Tremont St., map 11G9* ☎ *451-5997),* a funky tavern in the Theater District with R&B most Thursdays to Saturdays; **Loading Zone** *(150 Kneeland St., map 12G10* ☎ *695-0087),* barbecue and blues, in the Leather District; **Cecil's** *(129 South St., map 12G10* ☎ *542-5108),* an above-average restaurant with folk or rock on weekends; and **Christopher's** *(1949 Massachusetts Ave., Cambridge* ☎ *876-9180),* serving lunch and dinner daily, and acoustic folk or blues Thursday to Sunday.

# Shopping

## Something for everyone

Boston is not, boosterism aside, a "shopper's paradise." Not to other Americans, anyway. Little in the shops cannot be found in any of 50 other US cities. Most European and Asian visitors, on the other hand, will find that prices are quite low, even for products from their own countries, and that the 5-percent sales tax takes a far smaller bite than the VAT back home. (Unlike the VAT charged in most countries, however, the Massachusetts sales tax isn't refundable to foreign visitors.)

This isn't meant to discourage Americans from other regions. Those who regard shopping as a ritual diversion and essential element of any vacation will have no difficulty finding entire blocks and super-malls in which to spend hours browsing among stacks of antiques, racks of CD records, shelves of books and trays of jewelry.

### Where to head for

The first Boston shopping area that comes to most people's mind is Back Bay's **Newbury St.** and parallel **Boylston St.**, between Berkeley and Hereford Sts. *(map 10 G6 to 11 F9)*. Along these busy blocks are approximately 160 boutiques and designer outlets, emphasizing fashion and accessories but leavened with shops selling books, jewelry, crystal and porcelain, arts and crafts. **T** Arlington, Copley or Hynes Convention Center/ ICA (Green Line).

Second is **Charles St.**, an antiques row from Revere to Beacon St. *(map 11 E9)*. It can be conveniently combined with a sightseeing stroll through Beacon Hill, which it borders. **T** Charles/MGH (Red Line).

**Faneuil Hall Marketplace** *(map 12 E11)* inserts dozens of speciality shops and merchandise carts among its cafés and food stalls, with products ranging from T-shirts and costume jewelry to yuppie electronic toys. **T** State (Blue or Orange Line).

Not far away is **Downtown Crossing** *(map 12 F10)*, a traditional shopping district with the rival Jordan Marsh and Filene's department stores and 300 smaller satellite shops dealing primarily in mid-range goods. **T** Downtown Crossing (Red or Orange Line). A few steps away is the **Lafayette Place Mall**, which has yet to find its clientele.

The most successful indoor shopping mall is **Copley Place**, at the edge of Copley Square *(map 10 G8)*, with the pricey Neiman Marcus department store as its magnet and over 80 smaller, mostly upmarket shops. **T** Copley (Green Line).

Over in Cambridge, the relatively new **CambridgeSide Galleria,** opposite the Royal Sonesta Hotel *(map 11 C8),* has branches of Filene's, Sears, and another well-known area regional department store, Lechmere (pronounced "Leech-meer"). They are supplemented by more than 140 additional retailers. **T** A free shuttle service is provided from the Kendall Square station (Red Line).

The teeming **Harvard Square** shopping district fans out from The Coop, a small department store affiliated with the University. Most of the nearby shops cater to the interests of younger adults, including an amplitude of book and record stores and units of casual clothing chains. **T** Harvard (Red Line).

### When to go
As everywhere in North America, the best times for shopping are weekday mornings and mid-afternoons, the worst, lunch hours and weekends. Increasing numbers of stores, in tourist districts and shopping malls, are open Sunday afternoon, usually from noon–5pm. Many observe late closings at 8 or 9pm one or more evenings during the week — again, particularly those in malls.

The only holidays on which everything but convenience stores are sure to be closed are Thanksgiving, Christmas and New Year's Day. Larger stores use most other national holidays for sales.

### How to pay
Charge/credit cards are widely accepted, even in the smallest shops, although a minimum total amount is often stipulated. Travelers checks are *not* regarded as simply another form of money, and will not be accepted at all if they are drawn in a currency other than US dollars. Supplementary identification is often required. Personal checks from out-of-town banks are not welcomed, but individual managers can sometimes be persuaded to take them, with two or more types of identification, if the customer appears trustworthy.

### ANTIQUES
One of North America's oldest cities should be a bountiful source for antiques and collectibles, and indeed it is. The selection is broad, but bargains are few, except in that gray area between "old" and merely "used." The hunt usually begins on Charles St., at the foot of Beacon Hill, roughly between Revere and Beacon Sts. *(map 11 E9),* but Boylston and Newbury Sts. in Back Bay *(map 9 to 10, s of the river)* and Brattle St. in Cambridge *(map 7 B1-2)* are also fruitful.

While many dealers concentrate on narrow specialities, the casual shopper may prefer to browse in shops with stocks of broader range. With that in mind, here are some of the notable generalists:

- **Autrefois**  125 Newbury St. Map **11** F8  ☎424-8823
- **Bernheimer's**  52C Brattle St., Cambridge. Map **7** B2  ☎547-1177
- **James Billings**  74 Charles St. Map **11** E9  ☎367-9533

- **Boston Antique Cooperative**   119 Charles St. Map **11**F9
  ☎227-9810
- **Brodney Gallery**   811 Boylston St. Map **10**G7   ☎536-0500
- **Danish Country**   138 Charles St. Map **11**F9   ☎227-1804
- **Fleur de Lys**   52 Brattle St., Cambridge. Map **7**B2   ☎864-7738
- **Marcoz**   177 Newbury St. Map **11**G8   ☎262-0780
- **Marika's**   130 Charles St. Map **11**F9   ☎523-4520
- **Weiner's**   22 Beacon St. Map **12**E10   ☎227-2894
- **Wenham Cross**   179 Newbury St. Map **11**G8   ☎236-0409

## BOOKS AND RECORDS

A city with 300,000 high school, college and university students and the people needed to teach them can support almost limitless numbers of book and record stores. Here are only a few.

- **The Bookcellar**   1971 Massachusetts Ave., Porter Sq.,
  Cambridge ☎864-9625. Coffee and books and occasional poetry readings.
- **The Brattle Book Shop**   9 West St. Map **12**F10   ☎542-0210.
  Antiquarian books at a store with its roots in the early 19thC.
- **Briggs and Briggs**   1270 Massachusetts Ave. Map **7**B2   ☎547-2007. Records, cassettes and CDs in virtually all musical genres.
- **The Coop**   1400 Massachusetts Ave., Harvard Sq. Map **7**B2
  ☎499-2000. Begun as a cooperative by Harvard students in the 19thC, it has evolved into a midsized department store specializing in books, records and Harvard and MIT insignia gear.
- **Globe Corner Bookstore**   1 School St. Map **12**E10
  ☎523-5870. Travel books and maps, where Longfellow and his chums used to meet.
- **Goodspeed Bookshop**   7 Beacon St. Map **12**E10   ☎523-5970.
  Rare books, prints and autographs.
- **Harvard Bookstore Café**   190 Newbury St. Map **10**G7
  ☎536-0095. New titles to dawdle among, and indoor and outdoor tables with snacks and drinks.
- **New Words**   186 Hampshire St., Cambridge. Map **8**C5
  ☎879-5310. The world as seen and experienced by women.
- **David O'Neal Antiquarian Bookseller**   234 Clarendon St.
  Map **11**G8   ☎266-5790. First editions and rarities of several centuries.
- **Rizzoli**   Copley Pl. Map **10**G8   ☎437-0700. The unit of an Italian chain that specializes in gorgeous coffee-table volumes on art and architecture, but carries general-interest works as well.
- **Spenser's Mystery Bookshop**   314 Newbury St. Map **10**G7
  ☎262-0880. Mostly suspensers and whodunits under the name of Boston's favorite fictional detective.
- **Strawberries**   Downtown Crossing, map **12**F10   ☎482-5257
  and 30 John F. Kennedy St., Cambridge, map **7**C2   ☎354-632.
  Huge inventories of records and videos at nearly two dozen metropolitan locations.

- **Tower Records**    Massachusetts Ave. and Newbury St., map **10**G6 ☎247-5900 and 95 Mt. Auburn St., Cambridge, map **7**C2 ☎876-3377. The giant West Coast marketeer shakes up Boston. If they don't have it or can't get it, it may not be worth having.
- **Waterstone's**    Newbury and Exeter Sts. Map **10**G7 ☎859-7300. Three floors of over 15,000 titles in a century-old building.
- **Wordsworth**    30 Brattle St., Cambridge. Map **7**B2 ☎354-5201. Just about every new title anyone might want, and at discount.

## DEPARTMENT STORES
In many cities, this category of retailing is contracting. In Boston, they continue to thrive. Start at Downtown Crossing for a look at the first two listed below. All of these are open Sunday.

### FILENE'S
*426 Washington St., map* **12**F10 ☎*357-2100 and 100 Cambridgeside Place, Cambridge, map* **11**C8 ☎*621-3800.* Standard mid-priced stuff upstairs, a buying frenzy in the famous basement. In a tail-wagging-dog turnabout, **Filene's Basements** are now showing up all around the Northeast. The formula is well-known to Bostonians: 14 days after consignment down there, prices are marked down 25 percent; after 21 days, 50 percent; after 28 days, 75 percent. It's mostly seconds or fads that quickly fled, but higher-quality merchandise makes periodic appearances.

### JORDAN MARSH
*450 Washington St. Map* **12**F10 ☎*357-3000.* Glowering across the street at its biggest rival, Filene's, this strikes for a notch higher on the quality scale while remaining competitive. Well over a century on the retailing scene, it's now branching out beyond New England. If in town at Christmastime, stop by to see the elaborate **Enchanted Village**, a mockup of a late Victorian New England town.

### LORD & TAYLOR
*Prudential Center. Map* **10**G7 ☎*262-6000* . Upper-middle prices and quality and still just a bit stuffy, it gives much of its space to American-designed clothing for adults and children.

### NEIMAN MARCUS
*Copley Pl., 100 Huntington Ave. Map* **10**G8 ☎*536-3660.* Fattened up on Texas oil and cattle money back when Americans used a lot more of both, this is the first foray into New England. Home to high- and outlandishly-priced fashions and fantasy possessions, it has been known to peddle family-sized jet planes and exotic furs. The famous Christmas catalog is God's way of saying you have too much money.

### SAKS FIFTH AVE.
*Prudential Center. Map* **10**G7 ☎*262-8500.* Top designers, foreign and domestic, are featured in clothing for women, men, teenagers and children. The results are mostly conservative, but occasionally flashy.

## CLOTHING
Calvin Klein, Anne Klein, Ralph Lauren, DKNY, Perry Ellis . . . all are amply represented, as are the major European designers. Save time for the unknowns and lesser-knowns who have dozens of eye-catching Back Bay boutiques. Foreign visitors may want to stock up on genuine

American jeans and athletic gear, much cheaper here than they are in Kyoto or Cologne.

### LAURA ASHLEY
*83 Newbury St., map 11F8* ☎*536-0505 and 5 Bennett St., Cambridge, map 7B1* ☎*576-3690.*
You know who you are — you like floral prints and cottons and a few feminine frills, and you don't want to leave half a paycheck behind. You are, in other words, either a Laura Ashley woman or you are not.

### BANANA REPUBLIC
*201 Newbury St., map 10G7* ☎*267-3933 and 5 Bennett St., Cambridge, map 7B1* ☎*497-8000.*
The casual clothes were always well made, but now they are in simpler displays and with somewhat lower prices. That's probably due to major expansion after recent affiliation with The Gap chain. The temptation is to buy multiples of everything, which isn't really a bad idea.

### ALAN BILZERIAN
*34 Newbury St. Map 11F8* ☎*536-1001.*
The high arm-holes and fitted waists of these Italian suits, and their decidedly unpreppie accouterments, make this the place for men who wouldn't be caught dead in an Ivy League sack suit. Just the thing for that Concorde flight next week. For similarly high-style furnishings, try **Joseph Abboud** *(37 Newbury St., map 11F8* ☎*266-4200).*

### BONWIT TELLER
*500 Boylston St. Map 11G8* ☎*267-1200.*
Large, busy, but with a muted, genteel atmosphere. Women's fashions get most of the floor space, especially in sports and evening wear. Men aren't ignored, however, and both choose from a comprehensive range of American and European designers.

### BROOKS BROTHERS
*46 Newbury St. Map 11F8* ☎*267-2600 and 75 State St., map 12E11* ☎*261-9990.*
Always an Ivy League favorite for its largely unchanging natural-shoulder

fashions, Brooks has shaken off some of the cobwebs of late . . . just a bit.

### BURBERRYS
*Arlington and Newbury Sts. Map 11F9* ☎*236-1000.*
Famous rainwear and the cashmere-and-tweed country manor look from England, for both men and women.

### JASMINE
*37a Brattle St., Cambridge. Map 7B2* ☎*354-6043.*
For women who prefer a flair, a statement, not weird but not invisible, this might be the place. A total look can be achieved, from hat to hem, including bags and jewelry. For *simpatico* footwear, pop in next door at **Sola** *(37 Brattle St., map 7B2* ☎*354-6043).*

### BETSEY JOHNSON
*201 Newbury St. Map 10G7* ☎*236-7072.*
Women who work hard at staying fit know all about Betsey Johnson's youthful, often form-fitting or diaphanous creations. Others may wish to join a health club before dropping by. Appropriate accessories are available.

### LOOKS
*1607 Massachusetts Ave. Map 7A2* ☎*491-4251.*
Just slightly funky women's clothing and accessories at sensible, not discount prices. Helpful, friendly staff. Near Harvard Sq.

### LOUIS, BOSTON
*234 Berkeley St. Map 11G8* ☎*262-6100.*
Italian and English designers in an impressive 1862 building (see page 82). Men's and women's fashions, and a restaurant, too.

### J. PRESS
*82 Mt. Auburn St., Cambridge, map 7C2* ☎*547-9886 and CambridgeSide Galleria, Cambridge, map 11C8* ☎*255-2739.*
Where Harvards and Yalies and Princetonians have gone for ready-to-wear

and custom classics since Edward was on the British throne. At least as expensive as Brooks, maybe a little more.

## ROCHESTER BIG & TALL
*399 Boylston St. Map 11F8 ☎247-2727*
Perry Ellis, Charles Jordan, Bally and others provide stylish duds for the outsized male.

## ANN TAYLOR
*South Market Bldg., Faneuil Hall Marketplace, map 12E11 ☎742-0031; 18 Newbury St., map 11F9 ☎262-0763; 44 Brattle St., Cambridge, map 7B2 ☎864-3720.*
Quality business and casual wear for women, in silk, linen and other pure fabrics. All accessories, including shoes, for a one-stop shopping experience.

## JEWELRY
Several of the antique stores listed in this chapter, and most of the women's clothing stores mentioned, sell jewelry. Other than those, there isn't a lot of point in looking much beyond two places. The leader is **Shreve, Crump & Low** *(330 Boylston St., map 11F9 ☎267-9100).* They've been in the business since 1800, selling china to brides and watches to plutocrats. Aficionados of Steuben glass will find an extensive collection upstairs, and all jewelry and silverware is of the very highest order. The other place is a branch of **Tiffany's** *(Copley Pl., map 10G8 ☎353-0222)* in town, which is also good.

## MUSEUM STORES
While there is no shortage of souvenir and gift stores around town, mementoes and tokens of quality for the people back home are not as easy to unearth. Museum stores are an excellent source of thoughtful books, posters, calendars, even toys. Most of the goods for purchase reflect the interests of the museums in which the shops are located. Bargains are rare, but fortunately quality is not.

Be sure to stop for a look in the shops of the MUSEUM OF FINE ARTS, the ISABELLA STEWART GARDNER MUSEUM, the CHILDREN'S MUSEUM, the MUSEUM OF SCIENCE, the USS CONSTITUTION Museum in Charlestown Navy Yard, and the Peabody Museum at the HARVARD UNIVERSITY NATURAL HISTORY MUSEUMS.

# Recreation

## Boston for children

A few scraps of history go a long way with small people, who think the olden days ended about the time Ronald Reagan left Washington. The **FREEDOM TRAIL** might hold their attention, especially with those stops in graveyards and at the site of a "massacre." But after that, parents are apt to have their hands full with yawners and whiners and wanderers. Fortunately, Boston remains a family town, with many diversions of sufficient interest to keep both youngsters and adults distracted.

For more complete details, see SIGHTS A TO Z, where you should look out for the ✿ symbols, for things suitable for children. (There is a full list titled **YOUNG INTEREST** on page 91.) The Thursday "Calendar" section of *The Boston Globe* has listings of children's activities, as does the monthly *Boston* magazine.

### AQUARIUM AND ZOO
Right next to **FANEUIL HALL MARKETPLACE**, which can keep both kids and grownups fed and entertained for an hour or more, the **NEW ENGLAND AQUARIUM** stirs interest with the tanks of harbor seals and sea lions outside the doors. Inside, the centerpiece is a circular tank four stories high filled with the scary creatures that kids adore — sharks, a moray eel and other things with sharp teeth and black eyes. Outside is a barge with an enclosed pool for shows by performing dolphins and sea lions.

At some distance from downtown is the **FRANKLIN PARK ZOO**, best visited by car. While it doesn't qualify as a must-see, kids who haven't seen superior facilities elsewhere will enjoy it. There is a special children's section, suitable for the very young, with cuddly animals to pet.

### BOAT TRIPS AND RIDES
Offshore, to the SE, is the 28-acre **GEORGES ISLAND**, centerpiece of the **Harbor Islands State Park**. It has a 19thC fort that was used as a prison for Confederate prisons during the Civil War, and is said to be haunted. The island has opportunities for hiking, fishing, swimming and picnicking. Free shuttle boats from Georges Island take visitors to other islands in the vicinity.

Several companies (see page 56) offer a variety of harbor and whale-watching cruises and trips to Provincetown on Cape Cod. Most of them leave from **LONG WHARF** or **ROWE'S WHARF**.

And don't forget that the streetcars and subway trains of the MBTA are a treat for children who have never seen one.

## EVENTS AND ENTERTAINMENTS

The **BOSTON PUBLIC LIBRARY** has an extensive program for children, including storytelling, puppet shows and films. Call to find out about the week's activities.

Concerts for young people are regularly scheduled during the school year by the **Boston Symphony Orchestra**. Explanations are provided by the conductor, and the concerts can be proceeded and followed by tours of turn-of-the-century **SYMPHONY HALL**.

The **Greater Boston Youth Symphony Orchestras** ( ☎ *353-3348)* are composed of elementary and high school students drawn from schools throughout New England. Under the umbrella are two full-fledged orchestras and a number of smaller groups. They perform at various locations around Boston, December to June.

On Friday in summer, family films — classics and recent releases — are shown for free at the open-air **Hatch Shell** on The Esplanade beside Charles River.

## OBSERVATION POINTS

Apart from the restaurants atop the **Prudential Tower** and the building at **60 State Street**, which are too formal to keep younger children from fidgeting, there are several viewpoints that don't require them to sit still. Best of all, and highest, is the observatory of the **JOHN HANCOCK TOWER**, with a recorded commentary and a room with a model of Boston in 1775 that is used for a sound-and-light show about the events leading to the start of the American Revolution. A slightly different perspective and full 360° panorama is provided by the **Skywalk** in the **Prudential Tower**, one floor below the restaurant.

Some of that excess of youthful energy can be worked off on the 294 steps up the **BUNKER HILL MONUMENT**, the reward an unobstructed panorama of the harbor, the city and Cambridge.

One sky-nudging restaurant with food that kids like — pizzas and pastas — is the **Spinnaker Italia** atop the HYATT REGENCY (see page 176). Bonuses are the ride in glass-bubble elevators up the hotel atrium and the fact that the restaurant revolves, pretty exciting for unjaded youngsters.

For a complete list of high places described in SIGHTS A TO Z, see under **VIEWPOINTS** on page 91.

## MUSEUMS

Several museums go beyond merely accommodating young people: they directly serve them. Obviously, the **CHILDREN'S MUSEUM** was specifically created for them. In addition to the permanent participatory exhibits, each of them geared to different age groups, special shows are mounted every month or so. Puppetry, storytelling and buskers are among more traditional enticements, and a Climbing Sculpture with ramps and tunnels sets kids squealing with delight.

Next door is the **COMPUTER MUSEUM**, which isn't meant only for youngsters, but they tend to find the technology less intimidating than their parents might. There are more than 75 exhibits, one of them a giant walk-through computer.

Similarly, there is the MUSEUM OF SCIENCE, atop the Charles River Dam, with many interactive exhibits and a generator that creates real lightning bolts. Adjoining it is the **Hayden Planetarium**, with daily shows of celestial configurations as well as special laser displays set to rock music.

At the MUSEUM OF FINE ARTS, a Children's Room offers workshops intended to make the collections more accessible for ages 6–12. Poetry, acting and music are among the techniques employed *(for details and schedule* ☎ *267-9300 ext. 300)*. While at MFA, seek out the basement model ship display, nearly always a hit with the 8–14 set.

With that in mind, the USS CONSTITUTION **Museum** has a number of model ships, as well as some interactive exhibits related to Boston's nautical history.

### PARKS AND PLAYGROUNDS
Boston's Parks & Recreation department maintains scores of playgrounds around the city, many of them situated in parks that have attractions for adults as well as children. For information ☎727-7090.

Younger children seem fascinated by the duckling sculptures at the NE corner of the PUBLIC GARDEN *(map 11 F9)*, and a first trip to Boston isn't complete without a ride on the Garden's famous **Swan Boats**. Across the way, near the Beacon St. side of the BOSTON COMMON *(map 11 F9)*, the so-called Frog Pond serves as a wading pool and has nearby slides, sand pit and jungle gym.

On the river opposite Mass General Hospital *(map 11 D8-9)* is the **Charlesbank Playground**, with views of sailboats as well as swings, a slide and jungle gym. Farther upstream, in the vicinity of the **Hatch Shell** *(map 11 E9)*, is another similarly equipped playground, and still farther, by the lagoon, is a more elaborate structure for climbing and swinging.

### SHOWS AND THEATER
Presenting both new and long-beloved children's stories for almost 20 years in the metropolitan area, the **Puppet Showplace Theatre** *(32 Station St., Brookline* ☎ *731-6400)* is known for its productions of such classics as *Jack and the Beanstalk* and *Peter Rabbit*. It can be recommended for children five years and older: two shows on Saturday and Sunday during the school year, with extra weekday performances in July and August.

The **Boston Children's Theatre** *(93 Massachusetts Ave.* ☎*424-6634)* takes the educational aspect of its mission seriously. Take, for example, the production that traced the history of the Sioux Nation from the arrival of Columbus until the Battle of Wounded Knee. The underlying messages are made palatable by the fact that the performers, too, are children. In the mix, moreover, are such favorites as Hans Christian Andersen's *The Little Mermaid*. Performances are usually Friday evenings and Saturday and Sunday afternoons, with a mobile stage appearing in various locations in the summer. Admission charges for both are about the same as for a first-run film.

Circuses and the *Sesame Street Live* traveling show appear at the BOSTON GARDEN.

# Sports in Boston

Bostonians are avid followers of their university and professional teams in the major sports, to the point of inconsolable despair when the home teams lose and unrealistic fantasies of dynasties when they win. For all those beefy fans who engage in no more vigorous exercise than lifting beer bottles and bellowing at referees, however, there are surprisingly large numbers of active athletes. They are seen everywhere, running, cycling, rowing and skating, playing softball and touch football, flinging frisbees . . . . Here are some of the places to watch with the spectators and join with the players.

### BASEBALL
New Englanders and loyalists from other parts of the country tirelessly hang on to the hope that their Boston **Red Sox** will once again advance to the World Series. The last time they won the championship was in 1918, and they have been tantalizing and dismaying their fans ever since. They play in **Fenway Park** *(4 Yawkey Way, map 9 G5* ☎ *267-8661),* the oldest and smallest stadium in Major League Baseball. Some say it also has the warmest beer. The high left-field wall, dubbed the "Green Monster," challenges the most accomplished of home-run sluggers.

### BASKETBALL
Bill Russell and Larry Bird helped lead the Boston **Celtics** of the National Basketball Association to record numbers of championships. They are gone now, but the memories of their exploits live on at the **Boston Garden** *(150 Causeway St., map 12 D10* ☎ *227-3200 or 931-3100).* The arena creaks and sags and probably will be replaced soon, but it is redolent of the history of sports in The Hub. The season runs from October to May, and into June when the Celtics advance into the championship playoff series. Game times vary, so call ahead.

See also page 97.

### BOWLING
Two versions of bowling are common in the Boston area. Tenpin is the common, most familiar version, but candlepin, in which slightly taller, tapered pins are the targets of much smaller balls, is also popular. Among the facilities offering both games are the **Boston Bowl Dorchester** *(820 Morrissey Blvd., map 6 D4* ☎ *825-3800)* and **Lanes & Games** *(Route 2, Cambridge, map 5 B2* ☎ *876-5533).* **Ryan's Family Amusement** *(64 Brookline Ave., map 9 G5* ☎ *267-8496)* features only candlepin. All three have pool tables, as well.

### CYCLING
The city's streets are not inviting for cyclists. Recommended instead are the paths in the linear parks on both sides of the Charles River, where the greatest dangers come from rollerbladers, runners and the inevitable yapping dogs.

Bicycle rentals by the day are available at the **Community Bike Shop** *(490 Tremont St., off map 11 G9* ☎ *542-8623)* in South End: no credit cards. In Cambridge, rent through **Surf 'n' Cycle** *(1771 Massachusetts Ave.* ☎ *661-7659),* which does accept credit cards for the required deposit. Also in Cambridge, both the Royal Sonesta and Hyatt Regency hotels make bicycles available to their guests.

## FITNESS CENTERS
Many hotels offer exercise facilities, and these are the most convenient for visitors, avoiding the complications of locating health clubs willing to permit access to nonmembers. Look for the ♥ symbol in our hotel listings, pages 140–48. All the luxury hotels have at least modest equipment, and usually much more, as at the RITZ-CARLTON, the FOUR SEASONS and the BOSTON HARBOR. The largest fitness center, however, is that of the HYATT REGENCY CAMBRIDGE, with every exercise device that might reasonably be expected.

Even those hotels that don't have fitness rooms often have special arrangements with nearby health clubs. If those options aren't available, try the **Greater Boston YMCA** *(316 Huntington Ave., map 10 H6* ☎ *536-7800).* Members of other YMCAs pay a moderate fee, nonmembers somewhat more.

## FOOTBALL
Major-league professional football didn't come to New England until the 1960s. That team is now known as the **New England Patriots**, after moving to **Foxboro Stadium**, 25 miles s of Boston. They have experienced some success over three decades, but also more than their share of devastating failures.

The college version of the game is at least as diverting. Harvard is often a contender in the Ivy League, which includes as members Yale, Princeton and Dartmouth. Harvard's **Crimson** play at **University Stadium** in Allston *(map 7 D1* ☎ *495-2231).* The **Boston College Eagles**, in nearby Chestnut Hill *(* ☎ *552-3000),* have on occasion achieved national recognition on par with such powerhouses as Notre Dame and Miami.

## GOLF
New England has more than 700 golf courses, Massachusetts, more than 270. These include private, semi-private and resort courses, as well as public links. While there are no courses within the Boston city limits, several are open to the public in close-in suburbs.

For a list of the nearest courses and related information, call the **Massachusetts Golf Association** *(190 Park Rd., Weston* ☎ *891-4300).*

## HOCKEY
The glory days of Boston's professional hockey team, the **Bruins**, have begun to fade into misty memory. No doubt they will rise again, and the enthusiasm of their devoted followers is undiluted. They play in battered **Boston Garden** *(150 Causeway St., map 12 D10* ☎ *227-3200 or 931-3100),* which is in danger of replacement before the end of the

decade. University hockey teams engage one another in the February **Beanpot Tournament**.

## HORSE AND DOG RACING

**Suffolk Downs Racetrack** *(Route 1A, East Boston, map 6 B5* ☎ *567-3900)* has thoroughbred racing Wednesday to Monday during the season, early October to early June. One of the restaurants is situated above the finish line, and closed-circuit television sets dotted throughout the complex follow each race and post the results.

Grayhounds run at **Wonderland Park** *(190 VFW Parkway, Revere, map 6 B5* ☎ *284-1300)*, a short trip N of the city. There are nightly races at 7.30 and matinees Tuesday and Thursday at 1pm, year-round.

## ROWING

Rowing, in one-person sculls and crews of up to eight with coxswain, continues to be an extremely popular sport at the university level. The dammed and relatively tranquil Charles River is an ideal course, heavily used by crews from Harvard and other local universities in all but the coldest months. The major social event of the rowing year is the **Head of the Charles Regatta** *(* ☎ *727-9548)*, in mid-October, with more than 3,000 participants.

## RUNNING

The **Boston Marathon** is the oldest such race in the US, the central event of Patriot's Day, the third Monday in April. Starting at Hopkinton Common, it winds through the city on its traditional 26-mile, 365-yard course and finishes at Copley Place. Information about the Marathon and other running events can be obtained from the **Boston Athletic Association** *(* ☎ *236-1652)*.

Running continues as a popular form of exercise, the parks and pathways lining the Charles River being probably the most-used routes. Many hotels have jogging maps suggesting possibilities.

## SAILING AND BOATING

**Community Boating** *(21 Embankment Rd., map 11 E8* ☎ *523-1038)*, N of the Hatch Shell, has dozens of boats for rent and offers sailing instruction on the Charles from April through October. Rentals and sailing classes are also provided by the **Boston Sailing Center** *(54 Lewis Wharf, map 12 D12* ☎ *227-4198)*, on the Harbor.

For additional information on sailing in the metropolitan area, call the **Metropolitan District Commission** *(* ☎ *268-8556)*.

## SKATING

When temperatures are low enough, ice-skating is permitted on the lagoon in the Public Garden and on the Frog Pond in Boston Common. Although crowded, both are particularly convenient to most visitors. The Metropolitan District Commission *(* ☎ *727-9547)* maintains a number of other rinks around the area, open November to March, but most are in residential districts at some distance from downtown hotels.

In warmer weather, rollerskating and rollerblading are highly popular, especially along the paths of the riverside parks. Both ice skates and roller skates are rented by the **Beacon Hill Skate Shop** *(135 Charles St., map 11 F9* ☎ *482-7400),* which is handy to all the downtown sites mentioned.

## SKIING

New England's best ski resorts are 3–5 hours away, in the Berkshires and Vermont. In some years, they have snow into May. Less challenging, but far easier to reach, are the slopes of the **Blue Hills Reservation** *(Washington St., Canton, map 5 F3* ☎ *828-5090),* off Route 128, to the s of the city. It has snow-making equipment, so it is in operation even when city streets are clear.

The Metropolitan District Commission ( ☎ *891-6575)* operates a cross-country skiing school at the public golf course in Weston, on Park Road, w of Interstate 95, N of its intersection with Interstate 90. Skis are available for rent, and fees are payable for both lessons and trail use. They too have snow-making equipment. Call ahead for details.

## SWIMMING

Many Boston and Cambridge hotels have swimming pools; look for the ≋ symbol in our hotel listings, pages 140–48. There are many beaches around Boston Harbor, but those waters are notoriously polluted. Public pools can be very crowded and maintenance isn't always of a high standard. Alternatives to these are the swimming pools at the **Cambridge Family YMCA** *(820 Massachusetts Ave., map 8 D4* ☎ *661-9622)* and the **Central Branch YMCA** *(316 Huntington Ave., map 10 H6* ☎ *536-7800).*

## TENNIS

**Longwood Cricket Club** *(564 Hammond St., Chestnut Hill, map 5 D2* ☎ *731-4500)* isn't in a place called Longwood and cricket hasn't been played here in over a century. But its 27 grass and clay courts host the US Professional Tennis Championships every July.

Several private tennis clubs around the city have reciprocal agreements with clubs in other parts of the country. Check with your home club for details. Public tennis courts are maintained by both the Metropolitan District Commission and the Parks & Recreation Department at many locations around the city. Apart from the courts in Boston Common, which require permits for use, they are open to all comers.

For information about courts in Boston ☎ 725-4006; in Cambridge ☎ 349-6233. The handiest public courts to downtown are in **Charlesbank** *(*☎ *523-9746),* the park on the river near the intersection of Charles and Blossom Sts. *(map 11 D9).*

# New England

# Massachusetts

## Heart of New England

New England is thoroughly dominated by Massachusetts, as most natives of the state will cheerfully confirm. Geographically, it cuts through the heart of the region, from the Atlantic to the eastern border of New York State. Largest in population of the six New England states, Massachusetts' total of 5.7 million residents is nearly double that of Connecticut.

When the textile mills and factories that formed the backbone of its 19thC economy started moving south after World War II, the state converted itself, successfully in the main, into a center of hi-tech service industries. In doing so, it took full advantage of the brain power represented by such famed institutions as Harvard University and MIT and an envied network of private and state colleges and universities — as well as of the political savvy that has up till now produced four Presidents and nine Speakers of the US House of Representatives.

### HER INFINITE VARIETY

More to the point here, Massachusetts contains a multiplicity of diversions — cultural, historical, recreational — that can't be equaled by all its neighbors put together. Topography helps, and indeed, it underpins that awesome variety.

The coastal plain south of Boston provides miles of beaches and safe harbor for sailors, as do the long hook of Cape Cod and the islands to its south, principally Nantucket and Martha's Vineyard. In the west, the Berkshire Hills, while hardly as dramatic as the Rockies or the Alps, support several ski resorts with dozen of trails, and have been a summer retreat for generations of New Yorkers and Bostonians. And in between is the wide, billowing valley of the Connecticut River, which rises in northern New Hampshire and runs 407 miles to Long Island Sound.

### USING THIS CHAPTER

The historic maritime communities of the North Shore, above Boston, from SALEM TO CAPE ANN, the revolutionary towns of LEXINGTON AND CONCORD, and THE BERKSHIRES lend themselves to touring by car, and are treated accordingly in our proposed driving tours (which start on the opposite page).

Conversely, CAPE COD (page 216), MARTHA'S VINEYARD (page 220) and NANTUCKET (page 223), while equally rewarding, invite one to linger, settle in for a weekend, a fortnight — or the entire summer. We conclude this chapter with alphabetical gazetteers of all three coastal extremities, grouped on a town-by-town basis.

☎ The area code for the eastern half of Massachusetts outside the Boston metropolitan region is **508**. The area code for western Massachusetts is **413**.

# Massachusetts driving tours

## ROAD TO REVOLUTION: LEXINGTON AND CONCORD
*See map **2**F4. About 80 miles' round trip w of Boston. Allow one full day.*

Details are forgotten or disputed, but there is no doubt when and where the War for American Independence began. That conflict and its aftermath, of such profound consequence to the course of modern history, ignited on a misted April morning 17 miles out of Boston in the village of Lexington, Massachusetts. Before the day was over, the British regulars and American Minutemen had both tasted victory and suffered defeat, and the world was to learn of a new kind of warfare.

### The Battles of Lexington and Concord

A distillation of the events of the night of April 18, 1775 and the morning and afternoon of April 19 will prove useful in appreciating the excursion suggested in the following pages.

Tensions between the British troops garrisoned in Boston and the restive colonists had become increasingly virulent as the years went by. Anticipating the open conflict that seemed certain to come, the rebellious Americans had stockpiled munitions and military supplies in villages outside the city. The British General Gage heard about the stores in Concord, about 25 miles from Boston, and decided to set out secretly to destroy them. American spies learned of the plan and the route the British column was to take. With the lighting of the famous lanterns in Old North Church, Paul Revere and William Dawes rode off to alert the countryside and the rebel militia.

Chance decreed that two prominent American political leaders, John Hancock and Sam Adams, were spending that night in Lexington, on the road to Concord. Revere warned them in time to enable them to get away, but shortly afterwards was himself arrested. He and William Dawes never reached Concord, but along the way they had met Samuel Prescott, who completed the journey. In Lexington, a 77-strong force of Minutemen — members of the colonial militia who vowed to be ready to fight on short notice — gathered in a tavern on the Lexington village green to await the British column. When the 700 British regulars arrived at early dawn, their commanding officer ordered the Americans to lay down their arms. The Americans refused, and following a brief exchange of fire, 18 Minutemen lay dead or wounded. Not a single British soldier was injured.

Buoyed by their victory after a long night of marching in full battle gear, the British continued on to Concord. More rebel militiamen were assembling on Punkatasset Hill on the far side of the village. A British patrol was sent out to hold the Old North Bridge, which the Minutemen would have to cross to reach their main contingent in Concord. Hesitant at first, the Americans came down the hill to the bridge when they spotted smoke rising from the village. Convinced the British were burning their homes, they engaged the patrol at the bridge with the shots "heard round the world." Two Americans were killed, but 11 British regulars also fell, several of them officers. The British retired to rejoin the main force, and the rebels did not immediately press the advantage, as they were still outnumbered. Since the British had burned such stores as they were able to discover (in the event, it turned out to be only a small proportion), they were ordered to withdraw to Boston by the same way they had come. A British relief column of 1,000 men joined them at Lexington.

By then, early afternoon, the militia of farmers and tradesmen responding to the alarms and sounds of battle had swelled to an estimated 3,500 men. They lined both sides of what came to be known as "Battle Road," not out in the open, but protected by walls and trees. The British troops, many of whom had not slept, had already marched over 30 miles and still had to endure the gauntlet for 20 more. By nightfall, their casualties totaled 247. Only 89 Americans had been killed or wounded. The Revolution had begun.

**Points to remember**

The routes of battle and the villages involved survive today, as do many of the buildings and cemeteries. But Lexington and Concord aren't frozen in amber. They are thriving suburban communities whose residents respect the past but refuse to be slaves to it. Roads are crowded, and children and the elderly often cross without warning. For that reason, this excursion is best taken by at least two people, with the driver paying close attention to traffic and a passenger acting as navigator. Remember that state law stipulates that pedestrians have the right-of-way on crosswalks not controlled by traffic lights.

**Along Mass Ave. to Lexington**

Leave Boston or Cambridge driving NW on Massachusetts Ave., passing through Harvard Square in the direction of **Arlington**. Revere rode out on this road from Boston the night of April 18, 1775, several hours ahead of the British contingent. In the Arlington business district, watch for the church with the white cupola and bright blue roof.

At the next traffic light, over to the left is the c.1680 **Jason Russell House** *(7 Jason St.* ☎ *617-648-4300* 🖼 ✦ *compulsory: open Tues-Sat 2-5pm).* It is named after its occupant in 1775, who was killed in a skirmish with the British soldiers retreating after the battle at Concord. Visiting hours for the house are limited, and the interior is interesting although hardly compelling.

Continue along Massachusetts Ave. Shortly, in east Lexington, there is an intersection with Route 2A, from the left. Down 2A can be seen the entrance to the **Museum of our National Heritage** *(33 Marret Rd.* ☎ *617-861-0729* 💷 *open Mon-Sat 10am-5pm, Sun noon-5pm).* Operated by a Masonic order, it contains historical exhibitions and shows films, and sponsors activities related to early American history in the area.

Proceed again in the same direction along Mass Ave. Soon, also on the left, is the **Munroe Tavern** *(1332 Massachusetts Ave.* ☎ *617-861-0928* 📷 ✗ *compulsory: open mid-Apr to Oct 31, Mon-Sat 10am-5pm, Sun 1-5pm).* Dating from 1635, it is administered by the local historical society, and the docents are enthusiastic volunteers. Its moment in history also came late in the afternoon of April 19, 1775, when the British column took a break in their withdrawal to Boston to rest and treat their wounded. They shot the barman, who attempted to flee after pouring drinks for the officers. After the war, Washington made a brief visit to the tavern; a few mementoes of his stay can be seen.

## Lexington

Continue on Mass Ave., into Lexington proper. After the commercial district, a statue of a Minuteman stands atop a pile of rocks at the head of the triangular town green, or common, with the white **First Parish Church** facing it at the far side.

The man represented is Captain John Parker, a veteran of the French and Indian War, who is credited with uttering two of the most famous sentences of the war that was about to start. When word came of the imminent arrival of the column of British troops, he positioned his militia in front of the tavern on the green. A survivor of that day's events recalled decades later that Parker commanded: "Stand your ground. Don't fire unless fired upon, but if they mean to have a war, let it begin here!

Brave and foolhardy words, as such quotations often are. The Minutemen were outnumbered by more than ten to one. The British Major Pitcairn had apparently ordered his men not to shoot, but simply to disarm the rebels. He ordered the Minutemen to disperse. There is little agreement on what happened next, except for the result. Someone fired a shot. The far superior British force loosed several volleys and then charged with bayonets. Eight American militiamen were killed, another ten wounded. There were no reported British casualties.

Bear to the right (E) of the green. There is the **Buckman Tavern** *(1 Bedford St.* ☎ *617-862-5598* 📷 ✗ *compulsory: open early Apr-Oct 31 Mon-Sat 10am-5pm, Sun 1-5pm),* where Parker's men assembled to await the British column. The tavern was at the time already 85 years old. The costumed guides are often sprightly and highly knowledgeable. One purpose of the high bar, they might tell you, was to impose a proper drinking age. If a boy couldn't rest his chin on it, he was too young for rum. Tavern keepers kept track of pints and quarts of beverage sold by chalk marks on the wall, coining the expression, "Minding your P's and Q's." Among many artifacts of the period, some of the most intriguing are found in the kitchen, with its ingenious cooking implements.

Slightly behind the tavern is a **Visitors Center** *(1875 Massachusetts Ave.* ☎ *617-862-1450* 📷 *open June 1-Oct 31 daily 9am-5pm, Nov-May 31 daily 10am-2pm),* run by the local Chamber of Commerce, which contains a mildly informative diorama of the brief battle.

Continue down Bedford St., turning right on Hancock St. Coming up on the left is the **Hancock-Clarke House** *(36 Hancock St.* ☎ *617-862-5590* 📷 ✗ *compulsory: open mid-Apr to Oct 31 Mon-Sat 10am-5pm, Sun 1-5pm).* Hancock and Sam Adams were staying here the night Revere galloped up to warn them about the British advance. Among the objects on display are the brace of pistols carried by Major Pitcairn, who was the commander of the regulars who fired on the Minutemen at Lexington Green.

The Hancock-Clarke House, the Munroe Tavern and the Buckman Tavern are all run by the Lexington Historical Society, which offers a discounted combination ticket for all three.

**From Lexington to Concord**
Return to Bedford St. and turn right. This street carries Routes 4 and 225, heading toward Concord. Pick up Route 62, branching off to the left at the hamlet of Bedford. A sign declares that it is four miles to Concord. Where this road meets Monument St., turn right.

Shortly, on the right, is a parking lot for the **Old North Bridge battleground**, which forms part of the **Minute Man National Historical Park**. Walk across the street and down the path toward the bridge; there are explanatory plaques along the way. Note, on the other side of the field to the left, the **Old Manse** (Monument St. ☎ 508-369-3909 ▣ *✗ compulsory: open mid-Apr to late Oct Mon, Wed-Sat 10am-4.30pm, Sun 1-4.30pm)*. The grandfather of Ralph Waldo Emerson owned it, and watched the battle that morning from his window. His grandson lived there 60 years later, and Nathaniel Hawthorne eight years after that, so the house also has a literary history.

The obelisk at the near end of the bridge was raised in 1836, and a more celebrated statue of a Minuteman, long used on stamps and US savings bonds, stands at the other end. It was the first important commission of Daniel Chester French, who later sculpted the statue of Abraham Lincoln in his monument in Washington. He depicts a stalwart in a tricornered hat, musket at the ready, leaning on a plow with the other hand. The bridge itself, thrice-removed from the one that spanned the Concord River in 1775, was erected in 1956. It overlooks a placid scene of canoeists and kayakers.

The gravel path on the other side of the bridge curves up to a brick house on a low hill, the **North Bridge Visitor Center** (174 Liberty St. ☎ 508-369-6993 ▣ *open daily 8.30am-5pm)*. A belvedere in the garden overlooks the battleground and has a recorded description of the great events. Inside the house, built in 1911 and in itself of no great interest, there are exhibits of uniforms worn in the battle and a model of the battlefield. A short video program is shown.

**Concord**
Returning to the car, drive back down Monument Rd. into the center of Concord. The buildings around the historic town square merit exploration. In the center is a monument to Concord's Civil War dead, over to the left is the old **Hill Burying Ground**, which contains some veterans of the battle, and opposite the cemetery is the 1747 **Wright's Tavern**, now converted into shops, which was used both by the militia and the British as a headquarters on the day of the battle.

But depending upon what time of day it is and how hungry you feel, the building of greatest interest might be the one at the w end of the town square. See opposite . . . .

The 1716 **Colonial Inn** *(48 Monument Sq.* ☎ *508-369-9200* ▯ *to* ▯*)* claims to be the oldest inn in continuous operation in America. So it may be, but in a rambling structure like this with so many additions and alterations, the original occupants wouldn't recognize it. More important, it serves adequate food more or less continuously from breakfast through dinner, including afternoon tea. The comfortable rooms are priced according to season and whether they are in the main building or modern wing. Live entertainment of various kinds is provided every night in the pub.

Leaving the inn, take Lexington Rd. (Route 2A) exiting the E end of Monument Square. Soon, the road forks: bear right (on Route 2) for the **Concord Museum** *(200 Lexington Rd.* ☎ *508-369-9609* 📷 *open Tues-Sat, Mon holidays 10am-5pm, Sun 1-5pm, variable shorter hours Jan-Mar).* Over a dozen period rooms cover three centuries of Concord history; they include the study of Ralph Waldo Emerson. There are also Thoreau memorabilia and a lantern hung in the Old North Church, which sent Revere and Prescott off on their rides that night in 1775.

Continue on Route 2, which connects in about 20 minutes with Cambridge's Memorial Drive on the N shore of the Charles River.

## WITCHES, WARLOCKS AND WHALES: SALEM TO CAPE ANN
*See map 2F5 and route map overleaf. About 150 miles' round trip N of Boston.*
*Allow one long day minimum, but preferably two days, with an overnight stay.*

English settlement of **Massachusetts Bay** started several years before John Winthrop led his colonists into Boston. **Gloucester** was founded in 1623, **Salem** in 1626. They retain much of their early American maritime flavor, as do **Marblehead**, **Newburyport** and **Rockport**, and are still dependent on the sea for much that sustains them: sport and commercial fishing, boating, and tourism.

### The Salem witch hunts
For tens of thousands of visitors, the region's principal draw is "Witch City," Salem, the site of the notorious witchcraft trials of the early 1690s. Several young girls experienced convulsions and hallucinations, accusing dozens of men and women of witchcraft. Over 150 people were imprisoned, 19 were hanged, and one was slowly crushed to death under heavy stones. The tragic wave of mass hysteria has been a metaphor for subsequent episodes of unjustified persecution ever since, most notably the McCarthyism of the post-World War II years.

Salem exploits that brief but frenzied period of municipal history with aplomb, but don't expect too much in the way of scholarly detachment. Silhouettes of witches on broomsticks adorn shops selling sorcery supplies, cafés, taxis, the newspaper, even police cars. But remember too that Salem was one of the busiest ports in colonial America and inspired the novelist Nathaniel Hawthorne.

### When to go
Because it is so convenient to Boston and other New England cities, traffic in the oldest districts of these towns and villages can be immobilizing on weekends from late April to late October. Try to take the trip during the week.

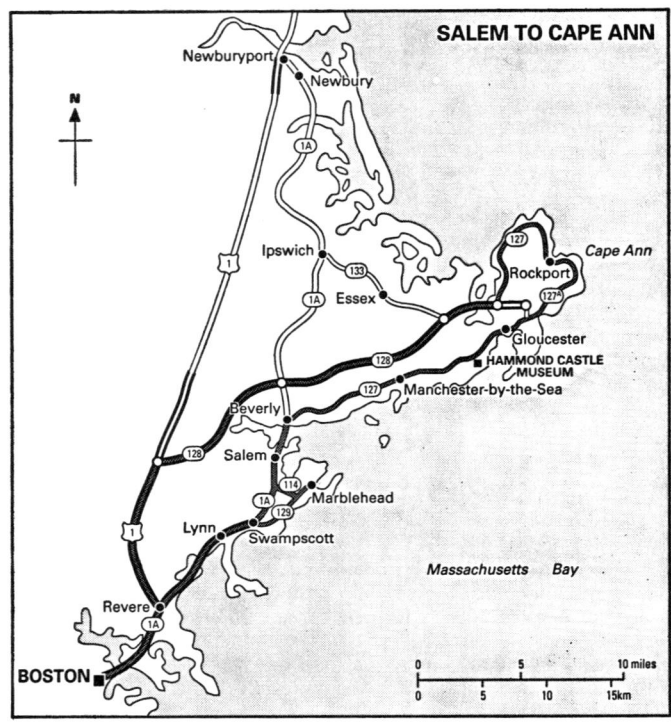

When planning to stay overnight in Rockport (a logical choice), bear in mind that it is a "dry" town. So if you want a drink, bring it with you.

**From Boston to Salem**

Take the Callahan Tunnel and Route 1A heading N toward **Revere** and **Lynn**. Expect little of scenic interest at first, heading on past the outlying urban dross of car-repair shops and fuel tanks. The road does pass the Wonderland grayhound racing track, which is open all year, should that be of any interest. Downtown Lynn won't long detain most travelers, but shortly thereafter, in **Swampscott**, pick up Route 129 toward Marblehead. This is Atlantic Ave., and at the point where it merges with Pleasant St. there is an information booth, which is open in the summer months.

Continue bearing right, heading toward the water. The seaside community of **Marblehead**, with its winding streets and large clapboard Georgian and Federalist houses packed together on small lots, is easily the loveliest on the North Shore. The large protected harbor on its eastern shore, and the harbor it shares with Salem, on the west, justify its claim to be the "Yachting Capital of America." From early spring through the fall, these waters are crowded with every kind of pleasure boat, from sloops to yawls to antique motor launches.

Marblehead rewards exploration on foot, so after driving through the town to make a reconnaissance, park in whatever space might become available. There are numerous shops for antiques and books, and galleries with paintings and crafts by local artists.

The unassuming seafood menu of the **Barnacle** *(141 Front St.  ☎617-631-4236 ▭ to ▥)* runs to cod and clams, fried, in chowder, or on pasta, plus sandwiches and salads. A greater virtue is its harborside setting and balcony, and the large windows from where there are views of the yachts tacking by.

Signs direct drivers out of Marblehead via Shore Drive and back onto Route 114. Turn right on 1A toward downtown Salem.

**Salem**

This city of 40,000 is the most popular destination on the North Shore, and the authorities provide helpful information for getting around. Green signs show the way to museums and historic sites, blue signs to downtown parking, and brown signs to the Visitor Center (see below). Large Victorian Gothic homes, some of which are bed-and-breakfasts, border the street entering the city. Follow the blue signs to the East India parking garage and leave the car there.

From the garage, on foot now of course, turn right, then right again into the pedestrian Essex St. Mall. On the left is a new building housing the **Peabody & Essex Museum** *(East India Sq.  ☎508-745-1876 ▰ open Mon-Sat 10am-5pm, Sun noon-5pm, closed major holidays ✗ available)*. Many regional museums might take lessons from these two floors of carefully mounted special and permanent exhibitions, with such thoughtful touches as portable cassette players that narrate the paintings and other objects on view. The focus is on Salem's maritime history, and the display includes model ships and fascinating collections of the exotic objects imported during three centuries of trade. Thankfully, the curators leave manifestations of Salem's brief period of witchcraft hysteria to others. The museum shop has some fine souvenirs.

Leaving the museum, turn left on Essex St. Mall. On the right, at the corner of a small plaza, is the **National Park Visitors Center** *(Museum Pl.  ☎741-3648 ▣ open daily 9am-5pm)*. Its exhibits and abundance of brochures make clear that Salem might easily occupy a long weekend. Attendants help point out the principal attractions. What visitors choose to visit must depend on time and interest, but the following should be given due consideration:

• **The House of Seven Gables**   54 Turner St. ☎508-744-0991 ▰ ▣ ✗ compulsory: open first Tuesday in September to June 30 daily 10am–4.30pm, July 1 to Labor Day 9.30am–5.30pm; closed major holidays and last two weeks in January. The historic site is in fact a complex of six buildings at the water's edge, dominated by the 1668 mansion (as it was in its time) that inspired Nathaniel Hawthorne's best-known novel. Guided tours are preceded by a slide-show presentation.

- **Salem Witch Museum**    Washington Sq. ☎508-744-1692 ▩
  Open July to August daily 10am–7pm; September to June daily
  10am–5pm. Closed major holidays. Every half-hour, sound-and-light
  presentations utilizing 13 dioramas illustrate, with not *too* excessive
  melodrama, the events of 1692–93. Be prepared for large crowds.
- **The Witch House**    310½ Essex St. ☎508-744-0180 ▩ Open
  March 15 to June 30 and first Tuesday in September to December 1
  daily 10am–4.30pm; July 1 to Labor Day daily 10am–6pm. Closed
  December 2 to March 14. The 1642 building, one of the oldest in
  New England, was the site of interrogations of many of the 200
  people accused of practicing witchcraft.

**The Witch House**,
Salem

- **Salem Maritime National Historic Site**    174 Derby St. ☎745-
  1470 ☒ Open daily 8.30am–5pm 𝒇 available. Restoration and
  maintenance of the core of the colonial waterfront are under the
  supervision of the National Park Service, shunning the commercialism
  that afflicts many Salem attractions. Available to view are 18th and
  19thC shops, warehouses, wharves, Customs buildings, residences,
  and a picturesque 1871 lighthouse that is still in service.

If time is short, a walk along the Essex St. Mall and parallel Lynde and
Front Sts. is pleasant, with a number of modern and restored buildings
with shops and eating places. A rapid tour of Salem can be made in
comfort: **Salem Trolley** *(191 Essex St.* ☎ *508-745-0004)* has buses
made up to resemble streetcars, in the manner of several Boston sightseeing firms. They make narrated tours of the city, leaving their depot
April to September daily, on the hour, between 10am and 4pm.

▤    Views of the harbor plus hearty
portions of simple seafood account for
the popularity of **Chase House** *(Pic-
kering Wharf* ☎ *508-744-0000* ▥ *).*

The brick-fronted **Lyceum Bar &
Grill** *(43 Church St.* ☎ *508-745-7665*
▥ *)* is on the street that lies one block
N of Essex St. Mall. Nicely prepared, not
too trendy victuals are served in either
a large dining room with high windows

or in the intimate bar-café.

🍷 ▤    More elegant dining is available in **Nathaniel's**, the dining room of
the Federalist-style **Hawthorne Hotel**
*(18 Washington Sq.* ☎ *508-744-4080*
▥ *to* ▥ *).* Convenient to Essex St. Mall
and most other attractions, it is the only
conventional hotel amid Salem's welter
of inns and motels.

## Cape Ann

Leave Salem on Route 1A heading N, picking up Route 127 in **Beverly** (paying close attention, for the turn is poorly marked). **Manchester-by-the-Sea**, about five miles on, is usually considered the beginning of Cape Ann. The road passes by handsome estates with ocean frontages, many of them converted to private schools and other purposes.

For an intriguing detour, keep a weather eye open for Raymond St., which exits the main road on the right. It goes down through the hamlet of Magnolia toward the shore, soon becoming Hesperus Ave. A startling structure, **Hammond Castle Museum** (*80 Hesperus Ave.* ☎ *508-283-7673* 📷 *open Wed-Sun and Mon holidays 10am-5pm* 🍴 *available*), stands on a cliff above the crashing water. Built by a wealthy inventor in the 1920s and incorporating parts of European castles, it contains secret passages and an organ with over 8,000 pipes. From the castle can be seen **Norman's Woe Rocks**, which figure in Longfellow's poem, *The Wreck of the Hesperus*. Continue on Hesperus Ave. as it rejoins Route 127, which is here called Western Ave.

Just before it crosses a channel into **Gloucester**, the road passes an information booth, open during the summer months. Shortly after, a statue of a fisherman in heavy-weather gear at the wheel of a boat signals emphatically that this was historically and still is a seafaring town. The harbor is home port to a large fishing fleet, as it has been since the early 17thC. Although there are few compelling reasons for visitors to pause in Gloucester, consider stopping for a meal or to watch the boats unloading the day's catch.

🍴 Typical of the waterfront seafood eateries are **Captain Courageous** (*25 Rogers St.* ☎ *508-283-0007* 💳 to 💳), which has an outdoor dining deck, and **Cameron's** (*206 Main St.* ☎ *281-1331* 💳).

For more elevated cuisine, there is **Bistro** (*2 Main St.* ☎ *508-281-8055* 💳 to 💳). Drop by and discover the kind of global cuisine that finds room on the same card for Mexican salsas, sweet potato focaccia and airy wontons. It is open for dinner only, from Tuesday to Sunday.

**Rockport**, which makes an attractive destination for an overnight stay, is about eight miles away on Route 127A, called Thatcher Road, which follows the coast (Route 127 is slightly shorter, but veers inland). On busy summer weekends, it's wise to park in one of the lots at the edge of the village and take one of the shuttle buses into town.

Down there, on a pier thrusting into the harbor, is a barn-red fishing shack with lobster floats hung on its walls and boats moored nearby. Residents call it *Motif #1* because it has figured in so many paintings by members of the local art colony. Several galleries sell oils and watercolors. Massive granite boulders strewn along the twisting shore explain the name of the village. Everywhere the eye falls are weathered shingled cottages and brick patios and, in season, clumps of blooming bushes, trailing vines and brightly-hued garden plots.

🛏 There are many inns and bed-and-breakfasts in and near Rockport. Probably the grandest of the lot is the **Yankee Clipper Inn** (*96 Granite St.*

☎ 508-546-3407 or 800-545-3699 ⬛). The main building is a Georgian-style mansion built in the early 1930s. Many of its rooms have balconies, and the dining room is on a glass-enclosed veranda. The cushion-like lawn, sectioned with flower beds, dips down to the craggy shore of Sandy Bay, looking across to Rockport center. Up on the road is the 1840 Bulfinch House, designed by the Boston architect in 1840, and a 1960 unit called the Quarter Deck, separated from the other two buildings, with suites with ocean views.

The family that runs the Yankee Clipper is also in charge at the **Ralph Waldo Emerson Inn** *(Philips Rd.* ☎ *508-546-6321* ⬛ *to* ⬛*)*.

## Inland from Cape Ann

Many visitors sleep late, lulled by the sound and smell of the sea. But try to leave by mid-morning, driving N on Route 127 as it hugs the shore, soon connecting with Route 128. This is a limited-access highway that quickly reaches Route 1, which returns quickly to Boston. Alternatively, if a few more hours are available, take 128 to Route 133 (Exit #14) w and then NW toward Essex and Ipswich.

**Essex** is best known for its unusually high number of antique stores and seafood restaurants, the latter featuring fried clams. **Ipswich** attracts visitors because of its dozens of 17th and early 18thC dwellings. If domestic architecture of that period is of interest, consider stopping at the Ipswich village green and strolling along the nearby blocks of East and South Main Sts. One of the oldest homes, which is open to the public, is the 1640 **John Whipple House** *(53 South Main St., Ipswich* ☎ *508-356-2811* ⬛ *open Apr 15 to Oct 31 Tues-Sat 10am-5pm, Sun 1-5pm, closed Mon and Nov 1 to Apr 14* ✗ *available)*. Ipswich also lends its name to a type of clam harvested in the area.

Route 133 merges here with Route 1A as it heads N. Stay on 1A. The maritime aspect of the land gives way for a time to orchards and chicken and dairy farms, but then salt marshes off to the right mark the village of **Newbury**. Not long after is **Newburyport**, on the Merrimack estuary. Here, Route 1A, now called High Street, is lined with many excellent examples of post-Revolution Federalist houses and the fashions that succeeded that era, including Classical Revival, Victorian Gothic and Queen Anne. Some interesting streets have even older buildings, and a coalition of public agencies and private groups has done an admirable job of rehabilitating the downtown commercial district.

Many visitors will want to park (it's easier here than in many of the towns visited along this route) and stroll along the waterfront promenade and past the shops in the restored brick rowhouses. Certainly a stop is warranted at the **Custom House Maritime Museum** *(25 Water St.* ☎ *508-462-8681* ⬛ *open Apr to mid-Dec Mon-Sat 10am-4pm, Sun 1-4pm; closed late Dec to Mar)*. The Greek Revival structure has model ships and exhibits relating to shipbuilding, which was responsible for the town's early prosperity.

≡ There are several promising restaurants in town, which prove trendy enough not to be boring but also conservative enough not to seem threatening to children. Among their number are **Scandia** *(25 State St.* ☎ *508-462-6271* ⬛*)* and **Ten Center St.** *(10 Center St.* ☎ *508-462-6652* ⬛*)*.

To return to Boston, pick up Route 1 heading s from downtown Newburyport. It is straight and fast and has few distractions.

## SHAKERS AND ARTISANS: THE BERKSHIRES
*See map 1F1–G1 and route map on page 213. About 350 miles' round trip w of Boston. Allow a minimum two days, preferably three.*

Once the frontier and the danger of Indian wars moved west, the Berkshires of Massachusetts became a magnet for intellectuals, writers, artists, and the wealthy of New York and New England. Two mountain ranges delineate the region, the western side of which is pressed up against New York, bordering Connecticut in the south and Vermont in the north. They are only hills, actually, the highest of them under 4,000 feet. But they enchant at every turning, with combes and vales channeling one sizeable river, the **Housatonic**, and cupping ponds and white villages in their folds.

No season is without its charms here, what with summer people coming for concerts at **Tanglewood** and idling evenings away at the lakeside to the thrum of crickets, weekenders driving slowly and gazing at the dazzling fall foliage, skiers tackling the slopes at the several resorts, and antique hunters trawling for treasures at auctions and in barns that range from chic to ramshackle. Stay for a fortnight or even a month and you'll hardly exhaust the possibilities. The driving tour suggested in the following pages seeks to provide little more than a taste.

### Famous residents
Berkshire County's multitude of admirers have included authors Herman Melville, William Cullen Bryant, Oliver Wendell Holmes, Nathaniel Hawthorne and Edith Wharton, abolitionist Henry Ward Beecher and African-American educator and writer W.E.B. DuBois.

Then there were the artists. Sculptor Daniel Chester French and popular illustrator Norman Rockwell had their studios near Stockbridge. Where artists go, the wealthy often follow. Hundreds of summer "cottages" — that is to say, mansions with dozens of rooms — were built in the late 19th and early 20thC for such plutocrats as Andrew Carnegie, who could live where he chose. As it happened, he died in Lenox, among his monied compatriots.

### When to go
Due to the many cultural events taking place on summer weekends in the Berkshires, room reservations are very difficult to obtain on short notice. Make plans at the earliest possible time. This applies to the foliage season, too, especially the middle two weeks of October.

When packing for a trip in July and August, do allow for the fact that summer nights in the Berkshires are often unexpectedly cool. April to May and September to October are unpredictable: warm and sunny one day, cold and wet the next. Snow and sleet are frequent from November to March. That's the reason why they invented mulled cider and hot buttered rum by the fireplace.

### The northern Berkshires
Leave Boston on Interstate 90 (a.k.a. the "Massachusetts Turnpike"),

bypassing Worcester and Springfield, two of the commonwealth's larger cities. Take Exit #1, which happens to be the last one in Massachusetts, and proceed N on Route 41.

In a little over nine miles is **Hancock Shaker Village** (★) *(Route 20, Pittsfield* ☎ *413-443-0188* ▨ ▣ *open mid-May to late Oct daily 9.30am-5pm, Apr 1 to mid-May and Nov daily 10am-3pm, closed Dec 1 to Mar 31* ✗ *available).* All by itself, it is sufficient reason for the journey. Led by an Englishwoman her followers called "Mother Ann" Lee, the Shakers established nearly a score of communities in several states in the early 1800s. Officially the United Society of Believers in Christ's Second Coming, the "Shakers" label was a reference to their ecstatic tremblings and movements at religious services. They lived communally but were celibate, and it may be inferred that this sublimated energy was channeled into their labors.

The Shakers are especially admired for their clean-lined furnishings, containers and tools, which anticipated Scandinavian Modern by over a century. Even very small original pieces sell for tens of thousands of dollars. Given their bedrock conviction regarding the means of procreation, it can't be surprising that the sect has all but died out. Only conversions and adoptions kept it going into this century, and there are no adherents left at this village, which became a museum in 1961.

Twenty restored buildings remain, equipped with the ingenious labor-saving contraptions and results of the Shakers' advances in horticulture and animal husbandry. Attracting much deserved attention is the round stone barn, which has a sculptural beauty far beyond its utility. Another building had running water, used both in cooking and for powering machines, decades before that became common. The Shaker motto, "Hands To Work, Hearts To God," is everywhere in evidence.

Drive E on Route 20 toward **Pittsfield**, a city of over 50,000 and the capital of the region. Admirers of Herman Melville may wish to make a somewhat complicated but short detour here. Turn right on Route 7, the city's main N–S street, then left (E) at Park Sq. on East St. Now turn right on Elm St. and right again on Holmes Rd.

Herman Melville wrote *Moby Dick* in the house he called **Arrowhead** *(780 Holmes Rd.* ☎ *413-442-1793* ▨ *open Memorial Day to Labor Day Mon-Sat 10am-4.15pm, Sun 11am-3.15pm; day after Labor Day to late Oct Thurs-Mon 10am-4.15pm, Sun 11am-3pm; closed late Oct to late May* ✗ *available).* He lived here from 1850 to 1863, during which period he became close friends with Nathaniel Hawthorne. Between two of America's greatest authors, what discussions must have transpired beside the large kitchen fireplace or in the study upstairs!

Leaving Arrowhead, turn right (S) on Holmes Rd. until it merges with Route 7 toward Lenox.

Pittsfield is the commercial and industrial center of the Berkshires, while the southern precincts of the region were and largely remain agricultural. When Carnegie and his monied chums came for the summer or to live out the twilight of their lives, however, they settled in and around **Lenox** and **Stockbridge**. Here they built their imperial "cottages," invariably large, with acres of manicured lawns and gardens, and often

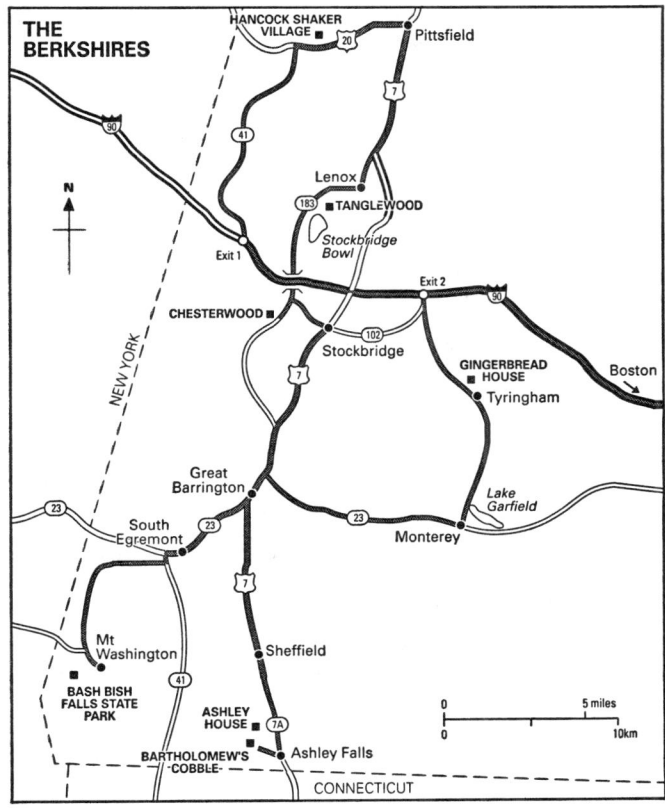

fabulously furnished, in the manner of the mansions these same people also commanded in Newport and Palm Beach. The names are a roster of the unimaginably rich of the late 19thC — the "Robber Barons" to some, paternalistic philanthropists to others: Vanderbilt, Westinghouse, Roosevelt, J.P. Morgan, Astor, Whitney, Hanna. Many of the cottages are inns now, echoing, in varying degrees, their years of glory.

**Blantyre** *(Route 20 and East St., Lenox, MA 01240* ☎ *413-637-3556* ▥▥ *closed Nov-Apr)* is intended to resemble a baronial Scottish castle, and performs its role quite magnificently. Rooms public and private are immense and luxuriously furnished. The dining room is memorable, and so indeed are

the prices. Pool and tennis are available.

Less costly possibilities in town are the **Gateways Inn** *(71 Walker St., Lenox, MA 01240* ☎ *413-637-2532* ▥▢ *to* ▥▥ *open all year)*, which has a popular restaurant, and the **Cliffwood Inn** *(25 Cliffwood St., Lenox, MA 01240* ☎ *413-637-3330* ▥▢ *to* ▥▥),*

213

which serves only breakfast. Even less expensive, but at no significant sacrifice to the visitor, is **Underledge** *(76 Cliffwood St., Lenox, MA 01240* ☎ *637-0236* 🎫 *)*; some rooms have working fireplaces, and breakfast is the only meal. The last two named above have no identifying signs out front.

Lenox is home to a number of renowned summer cultural events. Foremost among them is the concert season at **Tanglewood** *(ticket office: Tanglewood, Lenox, MA 01240* ☎ *413-637-1940)*. Seiji Ozawa conducts the Boston Symphony Orchestra from late June to Labor Day, while other ensembles and performers are given special concert dates. A large open-sided shed-like structure houses the orchestra. Tickets for inside seats tend to be sold out weeks ahead, but entry to the extensive grounds is cheaper and virtually unlimited (take a blanket). Watching the stars fill the velvet sky to the strains of Mozart is an experience not lightly forgotten. On the estate is a replica of the house in which Nathaniel Hawthorne wrote *The House of the Seven Gables,* and there are views of the Stockbridge Bowl, a large lake to the s.

Also in the area is Edith Wharton's former home, **The Mount** *(Plunkett St., Lenox, MA 01240* ☎ *413-637-1197)*, which has performances of both her works and of a fellow called William Shakespeare; the **Berkshire Performing Arts Center** *(40 Kemble St., Lenox, MA 01240* ☎ *413-637-4088)*, which invites performers in folk, jazz, blues and rock; **Jacob's Pillow** *(Route 20, Lee, MA 01238* ☎ *413-243-0745)*, which has a $2\frac{1}{2}$-month dance season; and the **Cranwell Opera House** *(17 Main St., Lee, MA 01238* ☎ *413-243-1343)*, which hosts the Berkshire Opera Company in July and August.

🍴 Several of the larger inns in Lenox, including **Blantyre** and the **Gateways Inn** *(see* 🔖 *above for both)*, the **Apple Tree Inn** *(224 West St.* ☎ *413-1477* 🎫 *)* and **Wheatleigh** *(Hawthorne Rd.* ☎ *413-637-0610* 🎫 *)*, serve well-prepared meals in formal settings.

More casual and accordingly less expensive are the **Church Street Café** *(69 Church St.* ☎ *413-637-2745* 🎫 *)*, an eclectic American bistro, and the **Cafe Lucia** *(90 Church St.* ☎ *413-637-2640)*, which serves inventive Italian specialities.

Taking leave of Lenox, drive w on Route 183, passing Tanglewood and the Stockbridge Bowl. In about four miles, watch for signs to the **Norman Rockwell Museum** *(Route 183, Stockbridge* ☎ *413-298-4100* 🎫 *open May-Oct daily 10am-5pm, Nov-Apr Mon-Fri 11am-4pm, Sat-Sun 10am-5pm)*. Few of his countrymen, at least those past the age of consent, are unfamiliar with the work of this beloved illustrator. Rockwell's covers for the *Saturday Evening Post* are classics of his craft, paeans to an America now largely lost. Art critics and proponents of modern art routinely condemned Rockwell as saccharine and sentimental. He, on the other hand, had nothing but kind words for the likes of Jackson Pollock and Willem de Kooning, and never pretended that he was anything more than a highly gifted illustrator. Thousands of his original sketches and paintings for his magazine covers and other works can be viewed in this large new (1993) building, which cost $4.4 million and replaced the former much smaller museum on Main St.

A little farther down Route 183, watch for the turnoff on the right to **Chesterwood** *(Williamsville Rd., Stockbridge* ☎ *413-298-3579* 📷 *open May 1 to Oct 31 daily 10am-5pm; closed Nov 1 to Apr 30)*. This was the home and studio of Daniel Chester French, the sculptor who specialized in public renditions of heroic figures, especially the Minuteman at the Old North Bridge in Concord, Massachusetts (see page 204), and the famous seated figure of Abraham Lincoln in Washington, DC.

French spent 34 summers here, in buildings designed by Henry Bacon, his friend and collaborator, who was the architect of the Lincoln Memorial. Some of French's less-known works bear at least passing resemblances to the sensual products of Auguste Rodin, although he has never received the same acclaim. Their lives were roughly parallel, and some of the nudes sculpted by French might have been influenced by the controversial Gallic sculptor.

Return to Route 183 and turn left. About a mile N, turn right on Route 102, which soon arrives in the center of Stockbridge. Main St. is lined with 18th and 19thC houses, most of them set well back from the street.

🕹 It's difficult to miss the **Red Lion Inn** *(Main St., Stockbridge, MA 02162* ☎ *413-298-5545* ▯▯ *to* ▯▯▯*)*. The biggest building in town spreads over a block, with a long front porch and room for more than 200 guests. The existing structure dates from 1896, with various expansions after that date, even though it looks older than that and in fact had its origins in the mid-18thC. The rooms have flowered wallpaper, brass bedsteads and, in some of them, canopied four-poster beds. There are three dining areas, ranging from formal enough for jacket-and-tie down to blue-jeans-relaxed. Most nights, there is live entertainment in the cellar tavern, the **Lion's Den**. Families are welcomed.

## The southern Berkshires

Pick up Route 7 heading s toward Great Barrington (at the w end of the Red Lion Inn). This passes the rocky outcrop of **Monument Mountain**, over to the w, and some unexceptional strip shopping malls to left and right.

Where Route 7 joins Route 23, there are choices to be made. To the right is the pleasant shopping town, **Great Barrington**, where the ingredients of a picnic can be purchased.

🍴 Picnics aren't everyone's cup of tea. If a sit-down meal is the preferred choice, two continental bistros in Great Barrington that attract much favorable attention are **La Tomate** *(293 Main St.* ☎ *413-528-3003* ▯▯ *to* ▯▯▯*)* and the **Castle Street Café** *(10 Castle St.* ☎ *413-528-5244* ▯▯ *to* ▯▯*)*.

Following Route 7 through town to Routes 23 and 41 through South Egremont leads eventually to **Bash Bish Falls**, a state park with a waterfall over 50 feet high and forest on all sides. Alternatively, continue due s on Routes 7 and 7A to the hamlet of **Ashley Falls**, named after a prominent 18thC citizen, to visit his home, the 1735 **Ashley House** *(Cooper Hill Rd.* ☎ *413-229-8600* 📷*)*. Adjacent to that property is **Bartholomew's Cobble**, a nature preserve with hiking trails wandering over glacial rock formations and past ferns, scrub and wildflowers.

A third choice, from the junction of Routes 7 and 23, is to turn left (E) on 23. **Monterey** is an appealing white village on this route. At its center, turn N on Tyringham Rd. It soon crosses a corner of Lake Garfield, and, in about ten miles, approaches an unusual building with a wavy shingle roof that recalls illustrations in books of fairy tales. Called the **Gingerbread House**, it now contains an art gallery. The same road soon approaches Exit #2 of Interstate 90, heading E to Boston.

A final detour makes a break on the drive back to Boston. Take Exit #9 off I-90 onto I-84, and look for Route 20 and signs to **Old Sturbridge Village** ( ☎ 508-347-3362 ⊠ *open late Apr to Oct 31 daily 9am-5pm, Nov 1 to late Apr Tues-Sun 9am-5pm*). The museum village comprises authentic 18th and early 19thC buildings brought here from locations around New England to simulate a town of the 1830s. Sheep graze on the common, tinsmiths and cobblers demonstrate their crafts, and costumed docents play the roles of various townspeople. A tavern serves simple, inexpensive lunches. Special events are scheduled in the village or near Sturbridge from April through the foliage season, including antique and crafts shows, sheep shearing, concerts and folk dancing.

✎ The experience can be extended with an overnight stay at the delightful 1771 **Publick House Inn** *(Rte 131, Sturbridge Common, Sturbridge, MA 01566* ☎ *508-347-3313* ▥*)*. There are three satellite buildings providing accommodation in addition to the original building, ranging from early Colonial style to motel-modern in their decor. Many of the rooms have four-poster beds; an outdoor pool and tennis facilities are provided.

Boston is merely an hour's drive away from Old Sturbridge Village.

# Cape Cod

*Map 2H5–G6.*

In profile, it resembles a flexed arm, with a clenched "fist" pointing back to the mainland. The long, narrowing peninsula thrusts east into the Atlantic from the southeastern corner of the state, angling abruptly to the north and embracing a large bay, a distance of 65 miles (105km). With the completion of a $17\frac{1}{2}$-mile canal at the base of the peninsula in 1914, Cape Cod met the textbook definition of an island, a fact that is beloved by trivia collectors.

English explorer Bartholomew Gosnold was the first European visitor, in 1602. The great schools of cod in the seas around the Cape inspired the name he chose. Today, tourism is the economic mainstay, but cranberry cultivation, boat-building and fishing remain important.

**FINDING YOUR WAY**

Be aware of some directional anomalies. The upper, north–south forearm is referred to as the **Lower Cape**, while the lower, or bicep, half is the **Upper Cape**. Got that? So, the Lower Cape is the location of a protected seashore administered by the National Park Service, and has fewer centers of population than the Upper Cape, where the primary tourist centers string out along the southern shore.

Route 6 is a major highway running s from Boston and through the center of the Upper Cape until it turns N into the Lower Cape, where it narrows to a scenic, if busy, road.

## WHEN TO GO
Summer is high season, for water sports, cycling, sailing, fishing, golf and tennis. Visitors more interested in contemplating the sea and the bird migrations of spring and fall can avoid the crowds and peak prices by visiting before Memorial Day (last weekend in May) or after Labor Day (first weekend in September). Most inns, motels, restaurants, museums and other attractions are closed during the winter months, so advance reservations are necessary at any time.

## BARNSTABLE
*Map 2H6. Postal zip code: 02630.*
Dating from 1637, this village has so far avoided the tacky commercialism that afflicts too many Cape Cod communities. It stands beside a protected harbor on the N shore of the Upper Cape, with a good beach at the satellite village of West Barnstable. This is one of several ports on the Cape for whale-watching cruises.

❧ **Ashley Manor** *(3660 Old King's Highway* ☎ *362-8044* ▥*)* takes the local laurels, with only six units, four of them suites, five with fireplaces, all with private bath — and at moderate tariffs that include breakfast. All this, in a building that retains much of the original 1699 structure. There is a tennis court.

➤ Another good buy is lunch or dinner at **Mattakeese Wharf** *(Barnstable Harbor* ☎ *362-4511* ▥*)*. The eclectic menu features pastas and seafood, and there are views of sailboats in the harbor.

## CHATHAM
*Map 2H6. Postal zip code: 02633.*
Settled in 1656, the town at the point of the "elbow" of the Cape retains its residential character, but is also a popular shopping center that has so far maintained rather higher standards of taste than some other tee-shirt-afflicted commercial districts. The **Chatham Light** is an obligatory camera subject, and there are boats to **Morris Island**, a barrier island to the E that is part of the **Cape Cod National Seashore**, and to **Monomoy Island** (s), a wildlife refuge.

❧ **Chatham Bars Inn** *(Shore Rd. and Seaview St.* ☎ *945-0096* ▥*)* is a venerable oceanside resort of considerable panache. It is matched in virtually every luxurious regard by the 104-room **Wequassett Inn** *(Pleasant Bay Rd., Chatham 02633* ☎ *432-5400* ▥*)*. Smaller, not as posh, the **Queen Anne Inn** *(70 Queen Anne Rd., Chatham* ☎ *945-0394* ▥ *to* ▥*)* dates to 1840, but has whirlpool baths in some of its 30 rooms.

≈ The **Queen Anne Inn** and **Wequassett Inn** *(see ❧ details above)* both have above-average dining rooms, open to the public. Less expensive, but satisfying, is the **Northport Seafood House** *(323 Orleans Rd. ☎ 945-9217 ▥ to ▥)*, which has entertainment most nights. An 1819 house is the setting for the expert continental edibles of **Christian's** *(443 Main St., Chatham ☎ 945-3362 ▥)*.

## FALMOUTH
*Map 2H5. Postal zip code: 02541.*

Quakers established the town in 1660 as a sanctuary from the persecution of the other religionists who colonized eastern Massachusetts (who had themselves been refugees from oppression). An 1842 **Friends Meeting House** survives from the Quaker era. On Falmouth Green are two adjacent 18thC homes that are open to visitors, the 1790 **Julia Wood House** and the 1794 **Conant House** *(both houses on Village Green ☎ 548-4857 ▣ open mid-June to mid-Sept Mon-Fri 2-5pm)*. A 1756 **Congregational Church** also faces the common.

Three miles away in **Woods Hole**, at the extreme southwestern corner of the Cape, is a cluster of celebrated scientific institutions, including the **Woods Hole Oceanographic Institution** and the **National Biological Service**. Ferries leave the port there and from Falmouth for Martha's Vineyard and Nantucket.

❧ The **Coonamessett Inn** *(Jones Rd. and Gifford St. ☎ 548-2300 ▥)* has rooms and suites in several buildings that are grouped around a central green. The oldest of them dates to 1796, and most have views of the inn's pond. The two restaurants of the inn are recommended for their highly competent renditions of the New England seafood repertoire.

## HYANNIS
*Map 2H6. Postal zip code: 02601.*

With one of the Cape's two airports, ferry service to Martha's Vineyard and Nantucket, and a railroad terminal that receives Amtrak trains on summer weekends, bustling Hyannis is the business and shopping center of the south shore of Cape Cod.

The recently opened **John F. Kennedy Museum** *(397 Main St. ☎ 775-2201 ▣)* celebrates the martyred young President's life, much of which was spent on the Cape. Quieter **Hyannisport**, not far from the center, is the location of the famed Kennedy Compound, where the President and his extended clan passed their summers when they were away from Washington. It isn't open to the public, but nearby **Craigville Beach** is. Look for it just off Route 28.

❧ Amid many undistinguished motels scattered around the town, an inevitable standout is **Tara** *(35 Scudder Ave. ☎ 775-7775 ▥ to ▥)*. This is a sprawling resort offering tennis, golf, and a fitness center with sauna and steam room. Rooms are somewhat bland, but then, not much time is spent in them.

## SANDWICH
*Map 2H5. Postal zip code: **02563**.*

Pilgrims established an outpost here in 1627 to trade with the Aptucxet Indians. Permanent settlement was begun a decade later, making this the oldest town on the Cape. The accomplishment for which it is most heralded is the type of lacy pressed glass that carries its name, which was mass-produced in a factory from 1825–88. The **Sandwich Glass Museum** *(129 Main St.* ☎*888-0251)* displays many examples of the products of the defunct factory, and a diorama of how it looked at its mid-19thC peak.

Of far greater scope and variety are the exhibits of the **Heritage Foundation** *(Grove and Pine Sts.* ☎ *888-3300* 🖼 *open mid-May to mid-Oct daily 10am-5pm)*. Its complex of buildings includes a replica of the round barn at Hancock Shaker Village, outside Pittsfield (see page 212), which contains a delightful collection of antique automobiles. Other buildings showcase such Americana as Currier & Ives prints, weathervanes, folk art, scrimshaw, a working 1912 carousel, and a collection of weaponry and miniature soldiers. Add the impressive garden and there truly is something here for everyone.

◆ **Dan'l Webster Inn** *(149 Main St.* ☎*888-3622* 🏨*)* is a replica of an 18thC house, but with all the modern gadgets, including cable TV in all bedrooms, and whirlpools in suites. There is live music and dancing to fill after-dinner hours; the inn has access to a health club and golf course; and there is a pool on the grounds. The restaurant is widely considered the best in town.

Or consider staying at the **Isaiah Jones Homestead** *(165 Main St., Sandwich 02563* ☎*888-9115* 🏨 *to* 🏨*)*, an antique-filled mid-19thC Victorian house. No children under 15 are allowed, and smoking isn't permitted on the property. A full breakfast is included in the very affordable rates.

## PROVINCETOWN
*Map 2G6. Postal zip code: **02657**.*

There is a land's-end, last-resort quality to this bustling village at the tip of the Lower Cape, similar to that of Key West at the southern end of the Eastern Seaboard. Its winter population of barely 3,500 swells to over 75,000 in summer, and those vacationers arrive in a party mood. They find many things that charm and some that appall, depending upon their state of mind. The mix includes large numbers of flamboyant gays, transvestites, latterday hippies, and artists. Summer evenings along Commercial St. are a riot of color and bizarre behavior, often amusing and rarely threatening.

The first Pilgrims anchored here in 1620, pausing to draw up and sign the Mayflower Compact, regarded as the first written document in the New World pledging its signers to democratic principles. Then they sailed on, across Cape Cod Bay to Plymouth, where they decided to stay. Their brief visit here is commemorated by a 252-foot **tower**, which can be ascended for a panoramic view of the Cape and Bay. Settlement of what was later to become Provincetown didn't occur until 80 years later.

A fishing settlement for most of its existence, Provincetown became quite prosperous in the 19thC, which explains the number of fine Victorian houses in the village. A former Methodist church contains the **Heritage Museum** *(Center and Commercial Sts.* ☎ *487-0666* ▨ *open mid-June to mid-Oct daily 10am-6pm).* Fishing and whale-watching cruises are prominent activities.

✧   There are hundreds of bed-and-breakfasts, guesthouses, motels and inns simple or luxurious to house the tens of thousands of summer people. None of them is exceptional, but then, few of them can be considered even moderately expensive. Three possibilities are the 1820 **Bradford Gardens** *(178 Bradford St.* ☎ *487-1616* ▢ *to* ▥ *)*, the **Fairbanks Inn** *(90 Bradford St.* ☎ *487-0386* ▢ *to* ▥ *)* and **Watermark** *(603 Commercial St.* ☎ *487-0165* ▥ *to* ▥ *)*. Breakfast is included at the first two.

≡   It seems that everyone winds up sooner or later at **Ciro and Sal's** *(4

*Kiley Court* ☎ *487-0049* ▥ *)*, despite the standard trattoria clichés. It would hardly have been out of place in Beatnik-era Greenwich Village, except that the pasta is al dente and it isn't always covered with tomato sauce.

Most of P-town's eateries specialize in seafood: **Front Street** *(230 Commercial St.* ☎ *487-9715* ▥ *to* ▥ *)* just does it better. The menu changes frequently, and includes game and beef.

For bargain fish, lobster and shellfish, book a table at **The Lobster Pot** *(321 Commercial St.* ☎ *487-0842* ▢ *to* ▥ *)*. Specialities are *bouillabaisse* and the distinctive San Francisco seafood casserole, *cioppino.*

## WELLFLEET
*Map* **2**G6. *Postal zip code:* **02667.**
Oyster fanciers may recognize the name of this town, which is given to a specific type of the bivalve. Harvesting oysters was the principal occupation of Wellfleet residents in the last century, along with codfishing and whaling. Tourism is important, but it is largely of the long-term variety, with few attractions for hit-and-run travelers. The village stands at the top of a fair-sized harbor halfway up the "forearm" of the Cape, a few miles from the dunes, wooded trails and isolated strands of the National Seashore.

≡   **Aesop's Tables** *(Main St.* ☎ *349-6450* ▥ *)* is open mid-May to mid-October. The 1805 house with several dining rooms is an appropriate setting for

eclectic American food, which concentrates on seafood and duck, with such *au courant* accompaniments as sun-dried tomatoes and balsamic vinegar.

# Martha's Vineyard

*Map* **2**H5.
It's certainly an unusual name for an island, but it's not one of recent origin. Two English explorers landed here in 1602. One of them, Bartholomew Gosnold, who visited and named Cape Cod on the same trip, noted the presence of wild grape-bearing vines and christened the island after his daughter.

The island lies south of the southwestern corner of Cape Cod, and is served by ferries from Wood's Hole, Falmouth and Hyannis, as well as through a small airport that accepts flights from Boston, New York and a few smaller New England cities. An appendage at the southwestern corner, nearly an island itself, has the principal scenic component: the **Gay Head Cliffs**, glacially-formed headlands that have the seductive capacity of changing colors as sun and clouds pass overhead. A state forest takes up a large portion of the interior, and there are over 50 smaller nature conservancies under various jurisdictions.

The eastern third of the island, where the three largest towns are located, is relatively flat, and one of the best public beaches runs along its rim, between Oak Bluffs and Edgartown. To the west are the more sparsely settled "up-island" districts. At the westernmost tip are the spectacular Gay Head Cliffs. Nearby is the hamlet of Gay Head, populated primarily by members of the Wampanoag tribe, who use the native clay to make pottery.

**MAKING THE MOST OF YOUR VISIT**
About 100 square miles (260sq.km) in area, the island is roughly triangular in shape, and all three corners can be reached by car in well under an hour from any other. It is therefore possible to tour the island on a day trip from Cape Cod, including the 45-minute ferry ride. But as is true of the Cape and Nantucket, this isn't a place to gobble up in a few hours. It rewards creative idleness and leisurely contemplation from the rickety porches of two-room rental cottages or the verandas of mansions of the rich and famous. Horseback riding and cycling are favored ways of getting around at a suitable pace. Sunning, swimming, fishing, golf, tennis, hiking and cycling are the predictable activities.

Visitors should be aware that most of the island — but not Edgartown and Oak Bluffs — proscribes the selling of alcohol.

## EDGARTOWN
*Map 2H5. Postal zip code: 02539.*
At the eastern tip of the island, Edgartown's harbor is wrapped around by **Chappaquiddick Island**. Its many stately homes are reminders of the profitable whaling days of the 19thC. Now, the boats that crowd the harbor are mostly pleasure craft, many of them spending the season cruising from Marblehead on down the coast to Florida. **North Water St.** is the center of the action, with its summer throngs supporting myriad shops, cafés and inns. Restored **Vincent House**, on Main St., was built in 1672, the oldest on the island and open to visitors.

☞ Pick of the litter of inns, most say, is the **Charlotte Inn** *(South Summer St.* ☎*627-4751* ⬜ *to* ⬜*).* It is in four different buildings, one of them dating back to 1705, clustered on a tree-lined street away from the hubbub of the shopping district. They are meticulously groomed and distinctively decorated with American and European antiques. The nearest beach for swimming is a long walk or short bicycle ride away. Breakfast is included in the room rate, and there's afternoon tea. The Charlotte Inn's restaurant, **L'Etoile** *(* ☎*627-*

*5187),* is widely regarded as one of the best on the island.

At the less expensive, folksier **Point Way Inn** *(Main St. and Pease's Point Way* ☎627-8633 ▥ *to* ▥), most of the private quarters have fireplaces, and some have balconies. Much of the inn's 1840s charm has been preserved, with walls of books and old photographs, and canopied beds with heaps of quilts. One of the owners is a passionate croquet player, who is ready to drop everything for a match.

🍴    A classy alternative to **L'Etoile** *(see* ❧ *above)* — even better, in some opinions — is **Warriners** *(Old Post Office St.* ☎627-4488 ▥ *to* ▥*).* It is elegant, eclectic, easier-going than its competition, and has two sections, one semi-formal and ambitious, the other casual; both satisfy.

But if those choices seem too dear or too serious, consider the **Wharf** *(Lower Main St.* ☎627-5187 ▥*)* or **Navigator** *(2 Lower Main St.* ☎627-4320 ▥*).* Both specialize in seafood.

## OAK BLUFFS
*Map **2**H5. Postal zip code: **02557**.*
In the last century and well into the present one, it was the custom of devout Protestants to gather as families in camps for revival meetings. This was true from New England to California, and often, tents were replaced by crude cabins, which in turn were replaced by houses . . . which accumulated into towns. That is the history of Oak Bluffs. While the original religious motivation is no longer evident, the rows of cottages remain, brightly painted and embellished with fancy Victorian gables and gingerbread scrollwork — a style sometimes known as Carpenter Gothic. Cars are not allowed to disturb the peace.

🍴    **The Oyster Bar** *(162 Circuit Ave.* ☎693-3300 ▥ *to* ▥*)* is the hands-down favorite Oak Bluffs eatery. Its decor of stamped-tin ceiling and splashy contemporary paintings reminds almost everyone of New York's SoHo, perhaps a little out of place amid all the local Victoriana. But it's frisky and fresh, with a marble raw bar for the eponymous bivalves and glistening-fresh seafood right off the boat. Only dinner is served.

## VINEYARD HAVEN
*Map **2**H5. Postal zip code: **02568**.*
The town has suffered its share of depredations, with a great fire in 1883 and ransacking by a British fleet during the Revolution. However, some handsome 19thC houses have survived, along Washington St. in particular, and the Daughters of the American Revolution operate a small but diverting **museum** on Main St. that contains objects brought back by whalers from foreign ports, as well as folk crafts and naive paintings. One provocative item is an engraved stone that some allege was left by Vikings who may have visited here over a thousand years ago.

On the way to and from the museum, there are many shops and cafés. One of them is **Crispin's Landing**, at the corner of Main and Union Sts., which contains the stalls of several craftspeople.

❧    Nonsmokers will like the **Thorncroft** *(278 Main St.* ☎693-3333 ▥*),* where lighting up the devil weed is prohibited. There are only 13 rooms, but most come with fireplaces, several with whirlpool baths, some with TV, all with at least a token antique or two, and often canopied four-posters. It has a compact dining room, and the beach is only a block away.

≕   Vineyard Haven isn't blessed with

many notable restaurants, hardly a problem on a compact island that enjoys many dining options. One possibility, though, is **Le Grenier** *(Upper Main St.* ☎ *693-4906* ▥*),* with a genuine French chef shaking the skillets. No gastronomic strides into the future for him: just the classics, well-executed.

# Nantucket

*Map* **2H6–I6.** *Postal zip code:* **02554.**

Another triangular island, Nantucket is only 14 miles across at its widest point. It lies about 30 miles due south of Upper (meaning "lower") Cape Cod, served by ferries from Woods Hole and Martha's Vineyard. There is also an airport near the south shore.

In the first half of the 19thC, Nantucket and Martha's Vineyard controlled over a quarter of the nation's whaling industry, an immensely profitable business for more than 150 years. It began to fade away when exploitation of oil reserves and electricity spelled the eventual end to the use of whale oil and rendered fat for illumination.

Nantucket slumbered for decades, slowly coming alive once again when it was developed as a tourist destination toward the turn of this century. Now, historic houses, intriguing museums and shops, and a salty, sun-bleached character keep both town and island engrossing for the duration of any stay.

In addition to the main town, which is also called **Nantucket**, make time to explore **Siasconset** (pronounce it "Sconset"), a village at the eastern corner of the island, which was discovered by artists at the end of the 19thC. Not far away is the **Sankaty Lighthouse**, with views of the ocean and cranberry bogs.

Camping is prohibited on the island, and cars, although permitted, are discouraged. Most of what there is to see lies within walking distance, and there are shuttle buses to popular beaches. Bicycles, mopeds and cars can be rented.

### Nantucket

The town holds a favored position on a harbor indented in the N shore, and it is the principal landfall and greatest attraction. The historic section of the town has scores of preserved and restored houses from the period of the island's greatest glory, especially along Main and Broad Sts. More than a dozen historic houses are made available to visitors, notably the **Jethro Coffin House** *(Sunset Hill* ☎ *228-1894* ▧*),* a 1686 saltbox on one of the town's many cobblestone streets.

**Hadwen House** *(96 Main St.* ☎ *228-1894* ▧*)* is younger, a Greek Revival manse erected in 1845 for William Hadwen. It is fully furnished with pieces from the middle decades of the 19thC. Hadwen was the owner of the factory, built at the same time as his house, which now contains the **Whaling Museum** *(Broad St.* ☎ *228-1736* 🎴*)*, where scrimshaw, a whaling boat and the tools of the seafaring trade are among the exhibits.

Two blocks away is Straight Wharf, where an old warehouse has been transformed into the **Museum of Nantucket History** *(* ☎ *228-3889* 🎴*)*. These sites, and several others, are operated by the local historical society. They sell comprehensive visitor passes that substantially decrease the total cost of admission, at least for people who intend to visit four or more of the properties.

⚓ A recently renovated 19thC facility called **Wauwinet** *(Wauwinet Rd.* ☎ *228-0145* 🎟*)* stands on an isolated finger of land surrounded by sea, sand and sky. It is superbly furnished with country antiques, all modern conveniences, and a keen sense of style . . . and is *very* expensive. In summer, a multi-night stay is required: money will need to be no object.

At the opposite end of the money scale, the 1765 **Carlisle House** *(26 North Water St.* ☎ *228-0720* 🎟*)* is almost cheap, especially as rates include breakfast. Principal sacrifices are that there are no bedroom phones or air conditioning. Some rooms have fireplaces.

For something in between, consider **Harbor House** *(3 South Beach St.* ☎ *228-1500* 🎟 *to* 🎟*)*. Essentially a motel, it has package plans that can include ferry fare and dinner, and breakfasts are also included off-season.

Some rooms have balconies or whirlpool baths; there is a heated pool and a restaurant.

🍴 **Le Languedoc** *(24 Broad St.* ☎ *228-2552* 🎟 *to* 🎟*)* has several rooms in its early 19thC building, including a lower-priced café serving lighter fare. Upstairs, pheasant and rack of lamb vie for diners' attention. At **21 Federal** *(21 Federal St.* ☎ *228-2121* 🎟*)*, an 1847 Greek Revival house, winning renditions of eclectic American recipes are the near-irresistible draw.

To offset the higher-than-average prices of Nantucket eateries, check out **The Brotherhood** *(23 Broad St.* 🎟 *)*. It strives, half successfully, for an English pub look. Sandwiches, burgers and chowders dominate the cards. Entertainment is provided most nights during season. They accept no credit cards and no reservations.

# Connecticut

## The Constitution State

The Native Americans who occupied the region called their life-giving river *Quinnehtukqut,* which translated as "the long tidal river." In the 17thC the European newcomers deemed that name a fine one for an embryonic colony, and anglicized it to "Connecticut." The river rises more than 400 miles north, near the Canadian border, separating New Hampshire from Vermont and cutting Massachusetts and Connecticut into two halves before emptying into Long Island Sound, an inlet of the Atlantic Ocean.

### A TALE OF FOUR RIVERS
Since the river was navigable well inland, the Dutch established a fort in 1633 at the site of the future city of Hartford. Adventurous members of the Plymouth Colony in Massachusetts established a trading post the same year at the present-day Windsor, a few miles farther upriver. Explorers from Massachusetts Bay recruited a large contingent of colonists from Cambridge, under the leadership of the Reverend Thomas Hooker, who arrived in 1636 and built their new village near the Dutch fort.

These encroachments were resisted by the Pequot tribe, but they were defeated in a brief war, and in 1639, the new towns along the river conjoined to establish the Connecticut Colony. As part of that process, they drew up the "Fundamental Orders," often claimed to be the world's first written constitution, which inspired the state's by-name, "The Constitution State."

Industries using water as a source of power, predominantly textile and arms manufacturing, developed in the 19thC along the Connecticut, Quinnipiac, Thames and Naugatuck Rivers. After World War II, many of those businesses migrated south, where they were less likely to be troubled by minimum wage requirements and other labor union demands. They left behind a number of economically depressed towns — Waterbury, Shelton and Meriden among them — that have yet to recover.

### CONTEMPORARY CONNECTICUT
Conversely, cities at the mouths of those four rivers have maintained a measure of prosperity, often due to enhanced tourism. Most visitors to the state are first attracted to the coastal towns, especially to **New London, Old Saybrook, Old Lyme** and **Mystic**, with its re-created 19thC whaling port. All of these lie along the southeastern shore of the state.

The undulating coastal plain of the state rises slowly as it climbs inland, especially in the northwest corner, where two mountain ranges, the Hoosac Mountains and Taconic Mountains, start their march into Massachusetts and Vermont. Here, though, there are no snow-capped peaks, and the **Litchfield Hills**, appealing as they undeniably are, reach heights of only around 2,000 feet.

Prominent institutions of higher education are the private Yale University in New Haven, Wesleyan University in Middletown, and Connecticut College in New London. The state university has its main campus in Storrs, in a rural area of the northeast section of the state. All of them contribute significantly to the cultural life of their communities.

## USING THIS CHAPTER
Several of the most important cities and towns are described in the following pages, starting with the two leading cities, HARTFORD and NEW HAVEN. The remainder of this section is grouped under two headings: THE SOUTHWEST EXURBS (Fairfield County, on the New York State border) and THE SOUTHEAST SHORE (the southeastern vacation area).

The chapter concludes with suggested driving tours of two of the state's most attractive recreational regions, the LOWER CONNECTICUT VALLEY and the LITCHFIELD HILLS.

☎   Connecticut's area code is **203**.

# The main cities

## HARTFORD
*Map* **1**H2.
State capital and largest city, Hartford is known to most outsiders as a center of the insurance industry, since 1794. As one of the earliest English colonies in North America, however, it profoundly influenced the course of domestic history. Most notable is the adoption, in 1639, of the Fundamental Orders of Connecticut, a document that was one of the first (*the* first, they are likely to say) to establish a government by the consent of the governed. That new tradition took firm root. When the royal governor-general of New England demanded the surrender of the liberal charter of the Connecticut colony in 1687, it was hidden from him in a hollow of an oak tree said to be more than a thousand years old. The tree, thereafter dubbed the Charter Oak, died in 1856.

Many celebrated Americans were born or lived in the city, including landscape architect Frederick Law Olmsted, financier J.P. Morgan, lexicographer Noah Webster and poet Wallace Stevens. Mark Twain, the acclaimed author of *The Adventures of Huckleberry Finn* and *Tom Sawyer,* lived in a wooded neighborhood w of downtown after his marriage in 1870. His large, fanciful Victorian residence is open to the public: the **Mark Twain House** (*351 Farmington Ave.* ☎ *525-9317* ▨ *✗ available*). It contains substantial Eastlake furnishings and much Tiffany glass, and within the grounds is his study, designed to resemble the pilot house of a steamer on his beloved Mississippi. The entrance fee includes admission to the far humbler cottage of Harriet Beecher Stowe, author of *Uncle Tom's Cabin.*

Several notable downtown buildings illustrate the architectural progression of the region since independence from England. One of the oldest that can be visited is the **Butler-McCook Homestead** *(396 Main St.* ☎ *522-1806* ▩ *),* which was continuously occupied by members of the same family from its completion in 1782 until 1971. Many of its furnishings were acquired by those several generations, including a collection of antique toys. Charles Bulfinch was the architect of the **Old State House** *(800 Main St.* ☎ *522-6766* ▣*)* in 1796, during the same period he was designing the gold-domed State House in Boston. Inside is one of the many portraits of George Washington by Gilbert Stuart.

The florid excesses of the post-Civil War period are flaunted with cheerful abandon in the **State Capitol** *(210 Capitol Avenue* ☎ *240-0222* ▣ *ƒ available),* completed in fantastical neo-everything style in 1879. The 20thC is amply represented by the glass-and-steel-tower headquarters of almost 50 insurance companies. Highest of them all, at over 500 feet, is the **Travelers Tower** *(1 Tower Sq.* ☎ *277-2431* ▣*).* Its observation deck is attained after a climb of 72 steps, but provides views of the city, suburbs and Connecticut River. Hours are restricted, so call ahead.

With all this, the one obligatory stop is the estimable **Wadsworth Atheneum** *(600 Main St.* ☎ *278-2670, open Tues-Sun 11am-5pm* ▩ *but* ▣ *on Thurs and Sat morning).* The nation's oldest public art museum retains most of the original building of 1842, nearly hidden by the many wings and additions. Particular strengths of its collections are paintings of the Renaissance and the 19thC French Romantics, and the broad survey of American arts, crafts and furnishings from the early Colonial period to the present. Examples of artists of the Hudson River School of landscape painting are particularly compelling.

❧ J.P. Morgan once lived in the Queen Anne Victorian mansion that is now **The Hotel at Goodwin Square** *(1 Haynes St., Hartford, CT 06103* ☎ *246-7500* ▥*).* Very probably he wouldn't be disappointed with the boutique luxury hotel it has become. 24-hour room service is available, and there is an exercise room with weight machines. **Piermont's**, the dining room, serves breakfast, lunch and dinner, while the bar has a piano player six nights a week.

Representatives of chains include the **Sheraton** *(315 Trumbull St., Hartford, CT 06103* ☎ *728-5151* ▥*)* and the **Ramada Inn** *(440 Asylum St., Hartford, CT 06103* ☎ *246-6591* ▥*).*

≡ **Brown, Thomson & Company** *(942 Main St.* ☎ *525-1600* ▥ *to* ▥*)* is a restaurant that makes the most of its location, a landmark 1877 Romanesque Revival building by H.H. Richardson, who designed Trinity Church in Boston. The interior fully meets expectations, looking like a place that Teddy Roosevelt would enjoy. Menu selections, however, bound around the world, making the customary stops for pastas, pizzas, and Cajun and Tex-Mex favorites.

Elegance is the keynote at **L'Americain** *(2 Hartford Sq.* ☎ *522-6500* ▥*),* where succulent contemporary cooking is on offer. A recycled industrial complex near Hartford Sq. provides the setting.

Sleekly old-fashioned **Carbone's**

*(588 Franklin Ave.* ☎ *296-9646* ▥*)* engages in tableside preparations and trots out such standards as *fettucine* *carbonara* and veal and seafood dishes that taste as delectable now as they did 30 years ago.

## NEW HAVEN
*Map 1H2.*

The city on Long Island Sound has its share of urban problems, but it is also home to **Yale University**, yet another distinguished member of the Ivy League group of renowned educational institutions. Its presence ensures a substantial cultural program, including jazz concerts on summer weekends and theatrical productions mounted by the respected **Yale Repertory Theater**.

On the university campus are the **Peabody Museum of Natural History** *(170 Whitney Ave.* ☎ *432-5050* ▨ *open Mon-Sat 10am-5pm, Sun noon-5pm),* which interprets its mission broadly, and the **Yale Art Gallery** *(111 Chapel St.* ☎ *432-0600* ▣ *open Tues-Sat 10am-5pm, Sun 2-5pm).* These days there are few tryouts in New Haven of Broadway-bound plays and musicals. However, the respected **Long Wharf Theatre** often initiates productions that eventually make the trip to The Great White Way. What's more, the refurbished **Shubert Theatre** hosts road company productions of hit shows.

At the waterfront are the re-created Revolutionary War **Fort Nathan Hale** and the Civil War **Black Rock Fort** *(Woodward Ave.* ☎ *787-8790* ▣ *✗ available),* both with excellent harbor views.

**West Rock Nature Center** *(Wintergreen Ave.* ☎ *787-8016* ▣*)* has exhibits of native wildlife; **East Rock Park** *(Orange St. and East Rock Rd.* ☎ *787-8021* ▣ *),* on the other side of the city, has a bird sanctuary, rose gardens, hiking trails and tennis courts. Both have picnic grounds. Near the Yale campus is the **New Haven Green**, set aside in 1638 in an example of very early city planning. Positioned around it are three churches opened in 1813 or '14.

✎ True bed-and-breakfast inns are not often found in downtown districts of large New England cities. But New Haven has **The Inn at Chapel West** *(1201 Chapel St., New Haven, CT 06511* ☎ *777-1201* ▥ *to* ▥*),* a Victorian beauty furnished with authentic antiques. Some of the ten rooms have fireplaces. Breakfast and afternoon tea are included.

No surprises, as they like to brag, at the **Holiday Inn** *(31 Whalley Ave., New Haven, CT 06511* ☎ *777-6221* ▥*),* but rates are quite reasonable and it's near the Yale campus. There is a pool.

🍴 New Haven is alleged by many to have the tastiest pizza in New Eng-

land. Test the claim at **Frank Pepe's** *(157 Wooster St.* ☎ *865-5762* ▢*).* No credit cards.

It is also insisted locally that the hamburger was invented in this city, at **Louis Lunch** *(261 Crown St.* ☎ *562-5507* ▢*).* They even know the year of the alleged invention: 1903. True or not, they produce an addictive version of America's favorite sandwich.

Leaving fast food aside, a theater district pseudo-brasserie of some note is **Bruxelles** *(220 College St.* ☎ *777-7752* ▥ *to* ▥*).* The menu is built around eclectic American fare rather than the traditional Belgian staples suggested by the name. Spit-roasted fowl are popular, as are the pastas.

# The southwest exurbs

**Fairfield County** snuggles up to the New York State border in the southwest corner of Connecticut. The fact that it is served by Metro North, the nowadays efficient railroad that radiates outward from New York City, makes it accessible to people who commute to the city for work and diversion. Most of the county, however, is over an hour away from Grand Central Terminal, making for daily round trips, including connections, of up to four hours and more. So was the term "exurbs" invented, referring to those bedroom communities beyond the suburban ring that surrounds the Big Apple.

The image associated with the county is one of contemporary country squires enjoying a privileged existence among manicured acres and beside shaded roads and tranquil village greens. That isn't inaccurate, for much of the county retains semblances of its New England roots. The picture is incomplete, though, for there are also several mid-sized cities strewn along the coast: **Stamford**, **Norwalk**, **Stratford** and **Bridgeport**, the last in such dire straits that the municipal government has considered filing for bankruptcy.

The following descriptions and recommendations highlight several places of touristic interest.

## GREENWICH
*Off map 1I1.*
Affluent Greenwich is the small city nearest New York. That proximity has meant a continual battle to avoid the grimmer aspects of metropolitan life, one that has been waged with considerable, if not complete, success. Two of the historic homes that can be visited were erected in the late 17thC — **Knapp's Tavern** *(243 East Putnam Ave. ☎869-9697 ◪)*, and, in the satellite hamlet of Cos Cob, the **Bush-Holley House** *(39 Strickland Rd. ☎869-6899 ◪)*. Both have limited, sometimes unpredictable hours, so call ahead.

❧▱ Let those dreams of a weekend escape from New York, only an hour's drive away, take fortuitous shape at the **Homestead Inn** *(420 Field Point Rd., Greenwich, CT 06830 ☎869-7500 ▱ to ▱)*. Built in 1799 and recently renovated, its rooms are decorated with flair and individuality, some of them with fireplaces. What's more, its **La Grange** dining room is top-rated in a wealthy town blessed with several very good restaurants: guests don't have to leave the premises — and may not wish to do so.

▱ Unbridled praise has been the enviable lot of **Jean-Louis** *(61 Lewis St.* ☎622-8450 ▱ to ▱) since the day it opened. The French owner-chef and his wife, who is the maîtresse d', don't stint in any regard. They regale their clients with choices of his innovative *créations* and impeccable *classiques*. This may well be the best restaurant in Connecticut, and it is small, so it is advisable to reserve well in advance.

But Jean-Louis isn't unique in its class. It is hard-pressed for the crown by several other accomplished restaurants, including **La Grange** *(see ❧ above)* and **Bertrand** *(253 Greenwich Avenue ☎661-4459 ▱)*, whose redoubtable chef honed his skills at New York's honored Lutèce.

## NEW CANAAN
*Map 1I1. Postal zip code:* **06840**.

Prosperous though its residents are, this handsome town N of Stamford is known as an artists' colony. That is due to the presence of the **Silvermine Guild Arts Center** *(1037 Silvermine Rd.* ☎ *966-5617* ▨ *)*, which incorporates a school of the arts, studios, and three galleries in which regular exhibitions are mounted.

☞ There are two lodging places in town that are within a short walk of each other, **The Maples Inn** *(179 Oenoke Ridge Rd.* ☎ *966-2927* ▢ *to* ▨ *)*, in a large turn-of-the-century house, and the 1740 **Roger Sherman Inn** *(195 Oenoke Ridge Rd.* ☎ *966-4541* ▢ *)*.

## RIDGEFIELD
*Map 1I1. Postal zip code:* **06877**.

No town in Connecticut has a more imposing main street, with its large estate houses standing well back on lush expanses of lawn beneath ancient towering shade trees. Times Square seems very far away. In 1777, the eventual traitor to the patriot cause, Benedict Arnold, commanded American troops in a battle with the Redcoats. The **Keeler Tavern** *(132 Main St.* ☎ *438-5485* ▨ *)* was already there, and an English cannonball is still embedded in one of its walls. The tavern has been restored and period furniture installed.

A major attraction is the continuously improving and ever more ambitious **Aldrich Museum of Contemporary Art** *(258 Main St.* ☎ *438-5485* ▨ *)*. While the large sculptures standing around the lawn can be viewed anytime, the hours of the clapboard museum itself fluctuate by season and according to the rotating exhibitions held there.

☞ ≡ Chefs, fortunes and owners change, but Ridgefield's inns manage to stay on a remarkably even keel. Cream of the crop for decades, **Stonehenge** *(Routes 7 and 35* ☎ *438-6511* ▢ *to* ▨ *)*, just seems to keep improving, even after the discouragement of a recent fire. Out front is a pond with mute swans, ducks and geese; for human water-splashers there's a pool. Rooms are in three separate buildings, which are of varying sizes and decor. Breakfast and the morning newspaper are delivered to each room. The menu in the dining room is fairly traditional, but lightened.

Ridgefield's oldest inn (1799) is **The Elms** *(500 Main St.* ☎ *438-2541* ▢ *to* ▨ *)*, with pleasant rooms and a competent dining room. A third possibility, the **West Lane Inn** *(22 West Lane* ☎ *438-7323* ▨ *)*, provides lodging and continental breakfast only, and is associated with the **Inn at Ridgefield** *(* ☎ *438-8282* ▨ *)*, which serves meals of the continental variety.

## WESTPORT
*Map 1I1. Postal zip code:* **06880**.

Where artists go, it seems, lawyers and stockbrokers inevitably gather, driving up prices so the artists can't stay. That was, in large measure, the story of this attractive seaside community, where commercial art and advertising are the creative crafts now practiced. It enjoys a sweeping arc of beach on Long Island Sound and straddles the Saugatuck River. The **Westport Playhouse** *(25 Powers Court* ☎ *227-4177* 🔲 *)* is a summer theater that mounts productions of professional caliber.

🗇 ➤ The **Westport Inn** *(1595 Post Rd. East* ☎ *259-5236* 🎛 *)* has plenty to offer: an indoor pool, sauna, restaurant and exercise room.

Other possibilities are the 19thC **Inn at Longshore** *(260 South Compo Rd.* ☎ *226-3316* 🎛 *)*, with a large swimming pool and water views, and the **Cotswold Inn** *(76 Myrtle Ave.* ☎ *226-3766* 🎛 *)*.

➤ **Café de la Plage** *(233 Hillspoint Rd.* ☎ *227-7208* 🎛 *)* has a pleasant situation that overlooks the strand on the Sound. For traditional French fare, *haute* division, the odds-on favorite is **La Chambord** *(1572 Post Rd. East* ☎ *255-2654* 🎛 *)*, while fans of Italian classics will want to reserve at the small, stylish **Da Pietro** *(36 Riverside Ave.* ☎ *454-1213* 🎛 *)*.

# The southeast shore

The lion's share of the tourist dollars left behind in Connecticut are gathered up in the southeastern quadrant of the state. This is especially true since the explosive success that attended the 1993 opening of a gambling casino on an Indian reservation in **Ledyard**. But even before that, the re-created whaling port and aquarium at **Mystic**, down in the corner near Rhode Island, was the preferred destination of travelers from New York, Boston, and other parts of New England.

So far, that section of coastline, and the **Thames River** that defines its western edge, have largely avoided the "kitsch *und* dreck" that afflicts similar regions along the East Coast. The result is a near-perfect family vacation destination, with enough sugar-coated history to let parents feel virtuous and enough shopping to sate even those who think they can never get enough.

## GROTON
*Map 1H3. Postal zip code: 06340.*
Ever since it was founded in 1705, the settlement on the Thames produced generations of fishermen and seafarers. The presence of the Electric Boat company and a large submarine base sustain that reputation, even if the future looks uncertain after recent cutbacks on military spending. *Nautilus,* the world's first nuclear submarine, was launched here in 1954 and is still based at this port. The **USS Nautilus Memorial/Submarine Force Library & Museum** *(Route 12 and Crystal Lake Rd.* ☎ *449-3174* 🔲 *)* celebrates that achievement, with hands-on periscopes, a replica of a control room, and the Revolutionary War progenitor of the submarine, the *Turtle,* among other exhibits.

Thames cruises on the *River Queen* and *River Queen II* pass the *Nautilus* and any other vessels that happen to be in port. The trips vary in length and time of departure, with dinner and musical outings among the options ( ☎ 445-9516), leaving from the dock at the Thames Harbour Inn (see below).

Ramparts remain from the Revolutionary War **Fort Griswold** (*Monument St. and Park Ave.* ☎ 445-1729 ☎), now the centerpiece of a state park. In 1781, 800 British troops under the command of the turncoat Benedict Arnold attacked the fort, which was defended by 140 rebel militiamen. They were beaten back several times, but finally prevailed, and the Americans surrendered. The victors had lost 200 soldiers, the defenders only three. Accounts of the ensuing massacre are unclear as to motive or provocation. It is undisputed, however, that between 75 and 85 of the rebels were slaughtered as soon as they had laid down their arms. Among the victims were their commander, Colonel William Ledyard, and two black freemen. A 134-foot obelisk commemorates the event.

🔦 River cruises depart from the dock at **Thames Harbour Inn** (*193 Thames St.* ☎ 445-8111 ▥). In the inn itself, refrigerators are standard equipment, and 20 of the rooms have kitchenettes.

## LEDYARD
*Map 1H3. Postal zip code: 06339.*
Few people outside the region had even heard of this rural village and its Mashantucket Pequot reservation before January 1993. Recent court rulings and an 1988 act of Congress have made it possible for sovereign Indian tribes, no matter how small, to operate gambling casinos on their lands. They can do so even in states which strictly control or forbid gambling. Now, the Mashantucket Pequot tribe's new and highly modern **Foxwood Casino** ( ☎ 572-0731) is open around the clock and has proved a phenomenal success. Roulette, craps, blackjack and slot machines are providing millions of dollars for the housing of formerly indigent Mashantuckets, job training, comprehensive health care, and university educations for their children. By the time these words are published, a new hotel and second casino may have opened.

## MYSTIC
*Map 1H3. Postal zip code: 06355.*
There are ample reasons to make time for a weekend visit to this shipbuilding town on Long Island Sound, which has its origins in the 17thC. Paramount is **Mystic Seaport** (*50 Greenmanville Ave.* ☎ 572-0711 ☎ *open July-Aug daily 9am-8pm, May-June and Sept-Oct 9am-5pm, Nov-Apr 9am-4pm*). It is a comprehensive museum village of 17 acres, with period houses and shops, a functioning shipyard, costumed docents, a maritime museum, tall-masted 19thC whalers and clippers, and more than 400 other craft. Large schooners depart the Seaport on cruises lasting one to three days.

A close second in appeal is the **Marinelife Aquarium** (*55 Coogan Blvd.* ☎ 536-3323 ☎ *open July to first Mon in Sept daily 9am-6pm, rest of Sept to June daily 9am-4.30pm*). More than 6,000 fish and other aquatic creatures are displayed in 50 exhibit areas. Of special interest are the penguins and the only beluga whales in captivity in New England. Seals, dolphins and sea lions perform hourly.

Nearby **Olde Mystick Village** *(Coogan St. and Route 27* ☎ *536-4941* 🖂 *open Mon-Sat 10am-5.30pm, until 8pm in summer, Sun noon-6pm)* makes a stab at re-creating an early 18thC farm village, but its overt purpose is shopping, not contemplation of the past. And two historic homes deserve visits, the 1717 **Denison Homestead** *(Pequotsepos Rd.* ☎ *536-9248* 🖼) and the 1770 **Whitehall Mansion** *(Route 27* ☎ *536-8845* 🖼).

An enjoyable side trip E along Route 1A hugs the shore and arrives after five miles in the picturesque village of **Stonington.** Random exploration beyond the small business district leads to the **Old Lighthouse Museum** *(7 Water St.* ☎ *535-1440* 🖼), which contains an intriguing collection of artifacts relating to the maritime past of the region.

🐦🍴 **The Inn at Mystic** *(Routes 1 and 27* ☎ *536-9604* 🖳 *to* 🖳*)* combines comfortable motel units with a Georgian-style mansion. (The motel rooms are cheaper.) Guests have access to a pool, tennis court, and a dock. Here too is the highly regarded restaurant, **FloodTide** *(*☎ *536-8140* 🖳*)*, where preparations tend to fall under the "conservative continental" rubric.

🍴 One of the better deals of the many middle-ground eateries is the "quick bites" menu at **The Steak Loft** *(Olde Mystick Village* ☎ *536-2661* 🖳*)*. In Stonington, **Noah's** *(113-115 Water St.* ☎ *535-3925* 🖳*)* is an ingratiating place for any meal of the day; no credit cards, though.

## NEW LONDON
*Map 1H3. Postal zip code: **06320**.*

Whalers, fishermen and maritime traders made this colonial settlement one of the most prosperous ports in New England. It was created in 1646, not long after the establishment of the Connecticut Colony, and is the home of the US Coast Guard Academy. An old mill that was built in 1650 for Governor John Winthrop, one of the founders, still exists, under the bridge at Mill St. and State Pier Rd.

The town's oldest home is the 1678 **Joshua Hempsted House** *(11 Hempsted St.* ☎ *443-7949* 🖼), next to the 1759 **Nathaniel Hempsted House** *(same address and* ☎*)*. The Federalist **Deshon-Allyn House** *(613 Williams St.* ☎ *443-2545* 🖂) was built in 1829 and was the home of a well-to-do sea captain. **Monte Cristo Cottage** *(325 Pequot Ave.* ☎ *443-0051* 🖼) was the childhood home of the Nobel Prize-winning playwright Eugene O'Neill.

Ferries leave New London for the offshore **Fishers Island**, Orient Point (New York) and Block Island (Rhode Island). Whale-watching cruises on the *Sunbeam Express* *(*☎ *443-7259)* leave from a dock near the Niantic River Bridge in the nearby village of Waterford.

🐦 Forgive the overly cute name, for the **Queene Anne Inne and Antiques Gallery** *(265 Williams St.* ☎ *447-2600* 🖳*)* delivers fair value in its converted turn-of-the-century house. Much of the period furniture (and accessories) is for sale. Hearty breakfasts and afternoon tea are included. Most, but not all, of the ten rooms have private baths.

Entirely conventional, the downtown **Radisson** *(35 Governor Winthrop Blvd.* ☎ *443-7000* ▥▢*)* does have an indoor pool, restaurant and fitness room, and is near both the Amtrak railroad station and Interstate 95.

☰ Settle for the atmosphere of **Ye Olde Tavern** *(345 Bank St.* ☎ *442-0353* ▥▢*)*, its rooms festooned with photos, maritime objects and assorted arcania collected since its opening at the end of World War I. Steaks, chops and seafood come in routine preparations.

# Connecticut driving tours

## SHANTEYS AND SEAFARERS: LOWER CONNECTICUT VALLEY

*See map 1H2–3 and route map opposite. About 110 miles SW of Boston, 175 miles NE of New York. Allow two days minimum.*

This river has provided livelihood, power and sustenance since the earliest colonists waded ashore in 1635 at the site of Old Saybrook. They started building boats almost immediately, and that was a major industry for a century before the Revolution. Schooners plied the West Indies sea lanes with lumber, grain and rum. Coastal packets carried produce and livestock from Maine to Maryland. Oystermen made their forays from here. By the mid-19thC, steamships crowded with vacationers were a common sight: they still are.

Not one of its towns is without interest, from **Old Lyme** to **Essex** to **Chester** to **East Haddam**, nor are they more than 15 minutes from their neighbors. Although it is a compact area, it can handily occupy every waking minute of a long weekend. Inns and shops there are aplenty. Sunfish and ketches dance on the waters and swing gently at moorings in protected harbors. A wisp of show-business glamor is imparted by a venerable riverside theater that has often been the scene of pre-Broadway tryouts. There is even a castle glowering down from the brow of a high round hill, adding a momentary Rhineland flavor.

### Points to remember

The starting point of this itinerary, **Old Lyme**, is reached via I-95 from both Boston (about $1\frac{1}{2}$ hours) and New York ($2\frac{1}{2}$–$3\frac{1}{2}$ hours, depending upon traffic). Make reservations before setting out on weekends or during the fall foliage season in early to mid-October, or be prepared for disappointment in the form of a second-rate motel likely to be miles from the most beguiling centers and attractions. There will be opportunities for fishing, hiking, picnicking and water sports, so plan and pack accordingly.

### Old Lyme

Leave Boston on Interstate 93 and take I-95 S through PROVIDENCE, Rhode Island (see page 247). After crossing into Connecticut, I-95 passes N of STONINGTON and MYSTIC and then goes through GROTON and NEW

LONDON, every one of them towns that deserve and reward detours if time permits (see pages 231–33). The I-95 joins the Connecticut Turnpike, then continues w to **Old Lyme**. Take Exit #70 onto Lyme St. (on Route 156).

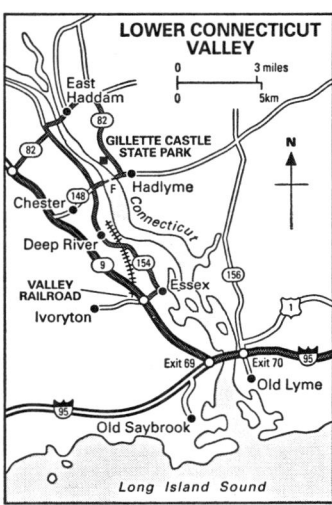

This is the main street of a quiet village that was at one time a thriving shipbuilding center. By the late 19thC, that business and its supporting merchant trade had all but disappeared. Then it was that artists discovered the community's charms, and by the end of the first decade of this century, many of the painters who came to be known as the "American Impressionists" had visited Old Lyme. They were encouraged and even offered shelter by the daughter of a local sea captain. She transformed her late-Georgian mansion into an artists' colony, where her guests often repaid her support with paintings instead of money. The oldest part of the **Florence Griswold House** *(96 Lyme St.* ☎ *434-5542* 🖼 *open June-Oct Tues-Sat 10am-5pm, Sun 1-5pm; Nov-May Wed-Sun 1-5pm)* dates from 1817. Today, its period rooms reflect the history of the region in artworks and furnishings.

🐟 🚊 Two good inns bracket the museum and are reason enough to linger. Cool and spare to the glance, the **Old Lyme Inn** *(85 Lyme St., Lyme, CT 063712* ☎ *434-2600* 🔲 *to* 🔲*)* has commodious bedrooms, each with a four-poster or "cannonball" bed and love seat or rocking chair, mostly Victorian. They have phone, clock radio and private bath, but no TV. Breakfast is included in room rates. Four of the dining rooms are stiffly formal for some tastes, but the fifth compensates with a grand old back bar and walls hung with sportfishing prints and

paraphernalia. A guitarist plays there weekend nights.

Not far away, the **Bee and Thistle Inn** *(100 Lyme St., Old Lyme, CT 063712* ☎ *434-1667* 🔲 *to* 🔲*)* is more a folksy clutter of antiques and collectibles of no specific period. Only two of the 11 rooms must share a bathroom. The core building was built in 1756 and the grounds back up to the Lieutenant River, a tributary of the Connecticut. Only children over 12 are accepted.

The kitchens of both inns are professional and imaginative, although service can be amateurish.

## Essex

Leave Old Lyme on I-95, cross the Connecticut River and then take the first exit (#69) N to Route 9, which is a limited-access road. At the second exit on 9 (#3), take Route 154 N and follow signs to **Essex**, on the w side of the river.

Main St., lined with shops and historic houses, leads directly to the harbor and its flotillas of pleasure boats. On the way, it passes one of the oldest continuously operating inns in the nation:

☜ ☎ Cosseting travelers since 1776, the **Griswold Inn** *(36 Main St.* ☎ *767-1776* ▢ *to* ▢*)* is the very heartbeat of the riverside town, a short walk away from everything. The Griswold rambles over a sizable part of downtown Essex — an annex here, a bungalow there, and wings and additions hither and yon. Its public rooms are encrusted with ship models, marine memorabilia, old paintings and cruise posters, and Currier & Ives prints of steamships and side-wheelers. In the lobby, a fire blazes on the flimsiest of excuses and the people never stop coming and going, at least from 6am to midnight. They surge through for happy hour in the **Tap Room**, where someone is always pounding on the upright piano or bellowing sea chanteys, and for satisfying, if unadven-

turous, American meals in the meandering dining rooms. The Sun Hunt Breakfast buffet is special.

A few miles w, in nearby Ivoryton, the **Copper Beach Inn** *(46 Main St., Ivoryton, CT 06442* ☎ *767-0330* ▢ *to* ▢*)* stands in sharp contrast to the jolly, rumpled Griswold. It is studiously correct, with not one hair out of place. Built for an ivory importer in the late 19thC, the main building has airy, romantic rooms upstairs, while guests who want 1990s convenience with their rustication are advised to choose one of the newer rooms in the detached carriage house. There's television, but no telephones. Children must be over six years old. Meals in the dining room are delicate arrangements of artistry and refinement: dinner only, from Tuesday to Sunday.

Essex is irresistible to walkers. A systematic way to explore it is by going first to the foot of Main St. Over to the left, a former warehouse is now occupied by the **Connecticut River Museum** *(Steamboat Dock* ☎ *767-8269* ▨ *open Tues-Sun 10am-5pm; shorter hours vary by demand in winter)*. There were steamboat services operating on the river by 1823, according to the exhibits within this engaging museum. Two floors of ship models, paintings and maritime artifacts tell the story from the shipbuilding era that began in 1733 through the days of oceanic trade and commercial fishing. Essex once had nine boatyards. The first warship of the Revolution, the *Oliver Cromwell,* was built here in 1775, causing retribution by the British during the War of 1812.

Try to pick up a walking map of Essex: they are usually available at the museum. Strolling back up Main St., real estate agencies appear to outnumber all other enterprises, but nonetheless there are many interesting structures. At #51 is the **Robert Lay House,** built about 1730 and probably the oldest building in town. Diagonally across the street, at #42, is the only slightly younger **Noah Tooker House,** a Colonial with a central chimney, owned by a boat-builder. Next door, at #40, is the imposing brick Federalist **Richard Hayden House.** The owner was a prominent merchant and shipbuilder. In 1814, British marines raided Essex and burned 28 boats, including Hayden's entire fleet and holdings. He died soon after, still young, a broken man.

A quietly exhilarating alternative means of transportation is the **Valley Railroad** *(1 Railroad Ave.* ☎ *767-0103* ▨ *)*, with a station on the road between Essex and **Ivoryton**. Antique carriages drawn by a vintage steam engine chuff from Essex to just beyond **Deep River**, a sleepy hamlet five miles NW. An optional extension of the excursion transfers passengers to a replica of a classic riverboat for a one-hour cruise. Connections are made with the railroad for the return to Essex. Call for the daily schedule, which fluctuates by season, and to inquire about special trips, including dinner rides and the Halloween mystery tour.

## Chester and Hadlyme

When leaving Essex, proceed N on Route 154 through Deep River, following signs into **Chester**. Apart from its Colonial and 18thC architecture, the attractive village is catnip for those who regard shopping as a prime form of recreation. Around the central intersection of Route 154 and 148 are several antique, gift and crafts stores. One to seek out is **Artisans** *(1 Spring St.* ☎ *526-5575)*, a co-operative displaying the selected works of regional craftspeople. Nearby are **Ceramica** *(36 Main St.* ☎ *526-5575)*, a dealer in quality Italian majolica and glassware, and **One-of-a-Kind** *(21 Main St.* ☎ *526-9978)*, specializing in silverware and country furniture.

Seafood is as fresh as the morning at **Fiddler's** *(4 Water St.* ☎ *526-3210* ▯▯*)*, a fact that keeps the small, neat eatery full at lunch and dinner. Lobster rolls are a signature dish.

Two blocks away is one of the most honored restaurants in the valley, **Restaurant du Village** *(59 Main St.* ☎ *526-5301* ▯▯ *to* ▯▯▯*)*. What looks like a transplanted Provençal bistro — flowers and a few watercolors make up most of the decor — provides a backdrop for delectable terrines, seafood cassolettes, *escargot en croûte* and supernal *pot-au-feu*. Only dinner is served, Tuesday to Sunday.

From Chester, take Route 148 E down to the eight-car ferry to **Hadlyme**. The service (but not the ferry) has been in place since the late 1700s, operating April to November. The trip across is short but pretty, dominated by the castle high on the opposite shore.

Turn left off the ferry, following signs up into **Gillette Castle State Park** *(67 River Rd., Hadlyme* ☎ *526-2336* ▨ *open late May to mid-Oct daily 10am-5pm)*. William Gillette was an actor and playwright who grew rich through his theatrical portrayals of Sherlock Holmes. The idiosyncratic castle he built at the summit of this 190-acre property bears little resemblance to its alleged Norman inspiration. But it is fascinating all the same, for Gillette's misbegotten million-dollar caprice, completed in 1919, is full of odd little notions. The dining-room table, for example, slides on metal tracks to save space. . . in the 24-room residence of a widower! In addition to the baronial living room, there is a replica of the #221B Baker St. stage set in which he made his fortune. On the grounds are picnic facilities, and there are lovely river views.

## East Haddam

Exiting the park, turn N on Route 82, arriving soon in **East Haddam**. Another shipbuilding town, it enjoyed its greatest prosperity in the decades after the Civil War, when packed steamboats from New Haven, New York and other East Coast ports ferried vacationers to the river resort hotels.

Entertainment was provided at the **Goodspeed Opera House** *(Goodspeed Landing, East Haddam, CT 06423* ☎ *873-8668* ▨*)*, which opened in 1877. Dominating the shore, the six-story Victorian theater is the tallest structure for miles. After a long period of decline, near-destruction and nick-of-time restoration, it has lately been packing in the audiences just as it did with early productions of *Factory Girl* and *All is not Gold that Glitters.* Professionally staged musical revivals are the usual fare. A number of original productions have made the long step from here to Broadway. The season is April to December.

To return to New York or Boston by Interstate 95, follow Route 82 w across the bridge at East Haddam and turn s on Route 9.

## STONE FENCES AND THE NEW GUARD: THE LITCHFIELD HILLS
*See map 1G1–H1 and route map opposite. About 150 miles w of Boston, 90 miles N of New York. Allow two days minimum.*

Few rural regions within the orbit of New York City have remained free of soulless shopping malls and voracious housing developments that destroy what they came to appreciate. That alone makes the Litchfield Hills region, with its peaceful forests, silvered lakes and tumbling streams, a treasure to be savored before human rapacity overwhelms it.

Artists have known about it for over a century, and the well-to-do followed on their heels, building lakeside and hilltop houses large enough to contain four-generation families for long idle summers in the days before machine-chilled movie theaters and central air conditioning. An unhurried pace still prevails in the hamlets cupped in cool green valleys. Wealthier artisans, diplomats and executives have lately arrived, but they are of that sub-variety of the privileged and celebrated classes that prefers a low profile — at least when it suits them. So have these hills retained their gentility and soothing demeanor.

### When to go
They are best combined with a visit to **THE BERKSHIRES** (see pages 211–16), as a weekend escape from New York, or as a stopover on the way from Boston to New York and points south. The ideal times are May through October, to take advantage of the excellent fishing along the **Housatonic River**, boating and water sports on **Lake Waramaug**, cycling on country lanes and hiking up forested hills. The fall foliage season is special, usually arriving in these parts in the weeks on either side of Columbus Day. That's on October 11, and lodgings must be secured far in advance. Fortunately, these hills have many full-service inns, bed-and-breakfasts, and some motels.

Note that most inns in the area require a two-night minimum on weekends. That hardly counts as deprivation. . . . In summer, there are opportunities for swimming and frequent picnic grounds, so pack and plan accordingly.

### The northern Litchfield Hills
Leave Boston via Interstate 90, driving w. After passing **Springfield** in about 1½ hours, take Exit #3 and go s on Route 202 to **Westfield**. Pick up Route 20 w and then Route 23 w, passing through the pretty villages and resort areas of **Big Pond**, **Otis** and **Monterey** on the way to **Great Barrington**, the principal shopping center of the southern Berkshires.

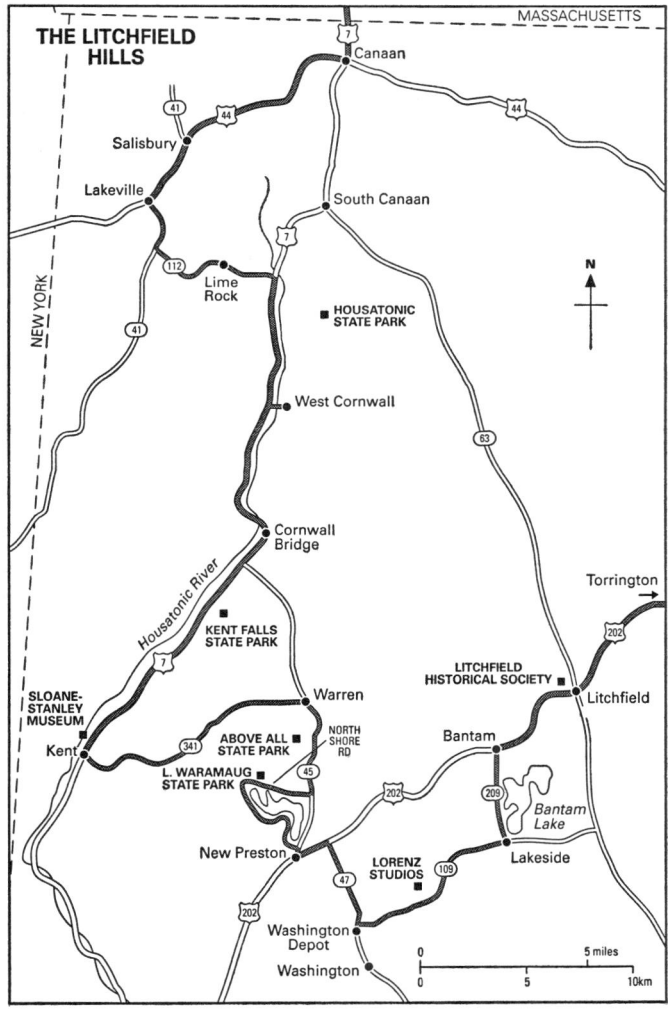

Pick up Route 7 and follow it s through Great Barrington toward Connecticut. After crossing the state line and entering the busy, unprepossessing town of **Canaan**, turn right (w) on Route 44 toward **Salisbury**.

Many small farms border the road, many of them concerned with growing sweet corn. The ears ripen in the latter part of August, and are best eaten within an hour or two of picking. That's a fact to keep in mind at dinnertime, perhaps in concert with a hefty Maine lobster and a glass of fruity Connecticut Chardonnay. Yes, they make wine in these parts, and while the Napa and Gironde Valleys needn't fear the competition — yet — the local pressings are quite satisfying on a soft summer evening.

Enter the business district of Salisbury at the juncture of Routes 41 and 44. On the right is one of the area's longest-lived inns:

✎ ⇌ The fortunes of **The White Hart Inn** *(The Village Green, Salisbury, CT 06068* ☎ *435-0030* 💷*)* have fluctuated wildly over the decades. For now and the immediate future, prospects are decidedly upbeat. The former gift store, which was a notable past mistake, has been removed to accommodate sitting areas and three new restaurants. Wicker furniture fills the long front porch, and chintz has not been spared in the redecorated bedrooms, which also have private baths, cable TV, telephones and air conditioning.

Alternatively, a few blocks down on the left is the brick-fronted **Ragamont Inn** *(Main St.* ☎ *435-2372* 💷*)*, with several comfortable rooms in the main building and a newer annex, as well as an accomplished dining room. The Ragamont doesn't take credit cards.

After the small commercial district, Route 44 continues into the contiguous village of **Lakeville**. Take Route 41 when it branches left (S) off Route 44. Soon, on both sides of the road, is the campus of **Hotchkiss**, a distinguished preparatory school.

Turn left (E) on Route 112. After horse farms and nurseries, the road enters **Lime Rock**, a modest village with quirky Victorian homes, known primarily for its auto racetrack. It has hosted Formula One events as well as less elitist truck competitions. Connecticut resident Paul Newman is known to show up. The season is April to October. For information ☎ 1-800-722-3577.

Shortly after Lime Rock, turn right (S) on Route 7. The hills are steeper here, and covered with the dense stands of the **Housatonic State Forest**, most of which is old, first-growth trees. In under four miles, a sign abruptly appears on the left pointing to **West Cornwall**.

Make that turn, immediately arriving at the entrance to a one-lane, wooden covered bridge, one of the few surviving in the state. Drive carefully across and into the small village. Incorporated in 1740, West Cornwall exemplifies the image many people hold of rural Connecticut, and has avoided boutique-ification. One agreeable stop on the short main street is the **Cornwall Bridge Pottery Store**, on the right. Its wares include sturdy, often quite large stoneware bowls and urns, carved wood pieces and some esoteric gourmet items. If it's time for lunch, there is a likely prospect across the street:

✎ **Freshfields** *(Route 128, West Cornwall* ☎ *672-6601* 💷 *to* 💷*)* occupies an old house beside a millstream. Nothing on the American menu startles, but most of it satisfies, especially at these fair prices. Sunday brunch is popular.

Leave West Cornwall by the bridge, turning left (S) on Route 7. On the left, the **Housatonic River** is now in full view. Broad, shallow and swift, it serves little commercial purpose and isn't attractive to boaters. That leaves it to anglers on the hunt for the elusive trout. Their cars are parked alongside the road as they wade out into the chill stream debating how to present just the right dry fly in the precise eddy sheltering the legendary lunker. More often than not, they return to shore with empty creels, but a day in such a place as this is never a waste.

At **Cornwall Bridge**, not much more than a wide spot in the road, Route 7 crosses the river and continues in a SW direction toward Kent. This is hardly a thrill-a-minute byway, it must be admitted. Throughout this itinerary, farm stands are pretty big attractions, and hand-painted posters announce church pancake breakfasts, chili cook-offs and fire-fighter festivals.

### The southern Litchfield Hills

But soon, on the left, is the **Kent Falls State Park**, with picnic grounds and a pleasant, non-arduous hike to a vantage over the cascade of the same name. Farther down Route 7, on the right, is the entrance to the **Sloane-Stanley Museum** *(☎ 927-3849* ▨ *open mid-May to Oct Wed-Sun 10am-4.30pm)*. Eric Sloane was an artist and writer who created a popular series of books, still in print, that illustrated and explained pioneer woodworking tools and skills. The small museum contains exhibits of those early implements. Also on the grounds is the ruined Kent Iron Furnace, a remnant of the early 18thC period when iron ore was discovered in the area.

The business district of **Kent** has a number of crafts stores, galleries and mostly unassuming restaurants. Consider pausing for a stroll or a bite.

⊐ Dual functions are served by the **Milk Pail** *(Route 7* ☎ *927-3136* ▥*),* which serves American food and displays the works of local artists.

Turn left on Route 341 toward **Warren**, noting that 341 soon turns left again. This passes **Above All State Park**, whose highest peak is a not especially arresting 1,470 feet. A number of Connecticut vineyards are located in this vicinity.

Turn left (S) on Route 45. In about three miles, watch for the street on the right, **North Shore Rd.** It has signs announcing Lake Waramaug State Park, The Inn at Lake Waramaug and Hopkins Inn. The next street on the right is Hopkins Rd. Turn into it and go up the hill. At the top, on the right, is another road that leads to the **Hopkins Vineyard** *(Hopkins Rd.* ☎ *868-7954* ▣*).* Tours and tastings are offered daily from May to December, and on Friday to Sunday from January to April.

✎⊐ Four inns occupy prime locations around the lake, none more favorable than the **Hopkins Inn** *(Hopkins Rd., New Preston, CT 06777* ☎ *868-7295* ▥ *to* ▥▥*),* opposite the red barn that is the tasting room of the Hopkins Vineyard. (The inn and winery are under separate ownership.)

The inn's main building dates to 1847, vaguely Classical Revival in style, with the usual subsequent extensions to back and side. Rooms are available, but the inn is known most fondly for its dining. The menu is continental, with light Austrian touches, especially on the dessert table. Warm-weather dining is enjoyable on the large patio. No credit cards.

Proceed past the front of the inn on what is now called Bliss Rd. It descends to join once again the North Shore Rd. Turn right. Another inn is just ahead:

✍ ⇌ It may look like just another 19thC farmhouse sprawling without plan over its wooded slope. On the contrary, although **The Inn at Lake Waramaug** *(North Shore Rd., New Preston, CT 06777* ☎ *868-0563* ▥ *to* ▨ *)* grew without much predetermination, it contains a hidden indoor pool and a tennis court, and has canoes, a private beach, and a large pontoon boat that makes sightseeing cruises around the lake. Many of the rooms have fireplaces.

Down by the lake, the **Boathouse** café provides casual meals under umbrella tables on a wooden deck.

North Shore Rd. hugs the shore. At the far NW corner of the lake, take the left turn that continues to follow the shoreline. Right there is **Lake Waramaug State Park**, with a swimming beach, canoes and paddleboats for rent, a log cabin snackbar, and picnic tables and campsites standing among the trees.

Keep bearing left, following the edge of the lake. Many of the large shingled houses along the southern shore date from the decades fore and aft of the turn of the century, when four-generation families spent not just a week or two but the entire summer here. Big lawns and wide verandas are standard, and many of the houses have satellite cottages or boathouses directly on the water.

Continue around the lake to the intersection next to the village beach (which is restricted to residents, by the way). Turn right into **New Preston**, which has undergone a measure of gentrification in recent years, acquiring in the process a well-used restaurant and several antique stores. Drive through the village to the junction with Route 202 and turn left (E). After $1\frac{1}{2}$ miles, take the right turn onto Route 47. This leads s to **Washington Depot**, a small retail center.

Turn left on Route 47, which goes up a hill to the town of **Washington**, whose chief historical distinction lies in its claim to be the first municipality to have adopted the name of the first President. More important, it has a lovely town green surrounded by a church and white clapboard houses with black or green shutters. Since it has received only slight publicity, the green remains much as it was a century or more past. Continue past the green and down the hill. On the left is the entrance to a hostelry that might well prove the most memorable stop on this tour:

✍ ⇌ At one time owned by The Gunnery, a prestigious boarding school, the **Mayflower Inn** *(118 Woodbury Rd., Washington, CT 06793* ☎ *868-9466* ▨ *)* has been elevated to a new plateau of rarefied country glamor by owners who could afford to do what needed to be done. The grounds are meticulously and thoughtfully landscaped with the merest hint of Oriental order, the kitchen staff is amazingly adept, and the bedrooms are fulfilled fantasies of what New England inns might be but too rarely are. Five buildings comprise the complex, all in the Dutch Colonial style, with hipped gambrel roofs. Apart from the fitness club, activities include a heated pool, hiking trails and tennis. Children under 12 aren't welcome, and smoking is discouraged.

After a surely reluctant departure, turn right (S) on Route 47, back up the hill through Washington and down to Washington Depot, in order to pick up Route 109 heading E. After a few miles, note, on the left, a farmhouse and collection of outbuildings identified as the **Lorenz Stu-**

**dios**. It has some decidedly nontraditional outdoor sculptures standing around the property. Farther on, turn left (N) on Route 209, toward Bantam. This passes **Bantam Lake**, heavily used for recreation, and enters the town of **Bantam**, which won't detain many travelers. Turn right (E) on Route 202.

Ignore the outlying dross of service stations and small strip malls on the approach to **Litchfield**. Considered by many to be *the* essential New England town, photogenic Litchfield is built around its large **Green**, which is surrounded by stately homes. In fact, a bit of trickery has been worked here. Many of those handsome houses were built during the Victorian era, and at one time they looked it. But over the last two decades of the 19thC and the first of the 20th, their occupants undertook to remodel the buildings so they would resemble earlier Colonial styles. That ambitious transformation was complemented by a design for the Green executed by the firm of Frederick Law Olmsted, who was born in Connecticut, and is famous for his Central Park in New York and the Emerald Necklace in Boston.

🚇 For a snack or a stroll, bear right of the Green toward the row of mostly brick retail establishments. Look out for the **Litchfield Food Company** *(The Green* ☎ *567-3113),* which allows a possible stop for an inventive sandwich or a selection of coffees and gourmet food items.

Litchfield was the site of the nation's first law school. That establishment counted among its distinctions the dubious honor of graduating Aaron Burr, who later killed Alexander Hamilton in a duel and was accused of trying to carve his own country out of Florida or Louisiana. Near the center of The Green, where Routes 63 and 202 intersect, is the **Litchfield Historical Society** *(East and South Sts.* ☎ *567-4501* 🎫 *open Mar to mid-Oct Tues-Sat 10am-4pm, Sun noon-4pm; mid-Oct to mid-Dec, Sat 10am-4pm, Sun noon-4pm).* Portraits and memorabilia relating to the town's past are exhibited, and there is also a substantial reference library.

🍴🚇 For a meal or an overnight stop in the Litchfield vicinity, consider the **Tollgate Hill Inn** *(Route 202, Litchfield, CT 06759* ☎ *567-4545* 💳 *to* 💳💳*).* About two miles beyond the Litchfield Green, on the left, the inn is comprised of several barn-red buildings, including a 1745 tavern. The 20 rooms and suites are variously fur-nished and equipped, with queen- to twin-sized beds; some have fireplaces, refrigerators and VCRs, and all have private bath, air conditioning and cable TV. Market availability dictates the menu in the romantic dining room, but shellfish pie is the favorite speciality. On some weekends, traditional jazz is showcased.

To return to Boston or other destinations in northern New England, follow Route 202 through **Torrington** to Route 8 heading N. After **Winsted**, turn E on Route 20, continuing to **Granby**. From there, turn N on Route 202, in about 15 miles picking up Interstate 90 E to Boston. If traveling on to southern Connecticut or New York City, take Route 254 S to limited-access Route 8, in the direction of **Waterbury**.

# Rhode Island

## The smallest state

The longest official name, "The State of Rhode Island and Providence Plantations," belongs to the smallest and most densely populated of the 50 states. Italian explorer Giovanni da Verrazano is believed to be the first European to sail into what came to be called Narragansett Bay, after the Indians who lived there. He thought the large island in the bay resembled Rhodes, in the Aegean Sea.

Roger Williams fled from the Massachusetts Bay Colony, where he was persecuted for his belief in absolute religious freedom and the separation of church and state. He established a colony here, in which Jews, Quakers, Catholics and non-Puritan Protestants were among the earliest settlers. In the tide of rising sentiment favoring resistance to English authority, Rhode Island was at the forefront, declaring its emancipation two months before the signing of the Declaration of Independence.

When the Industrial Revolution finally arrived in America, Rhode Island was among the first states to embrace the new technologies. Diverse manufacturing, especially in textiles, reinforces Rhode Island's logical position as a maritime center, for much of the state is wrapped around the bays and harbors adjoining **Narragansett Bay**. Through those fortunate circumstances, many of its citizens became markedly prosperous, and state capital **Providence** grew in the 19th century into one of the wealthiest and largest cities in New England.

**Newport**, in particular, is notable for its rows of large estates and extravagant mansions erected in the palmy days before World War I and the institution of the personal income tax. Recreational sailing continues to be a preoccupation. For most of this century, challenge races for the America's Cup races were held in these waters. Yacht clubs ring the bays and islands, and pleasure craft registered in ports all along the East Coast make anchorage here from April to October. Saltwater sportfishing is a particular draw for vacationers on **Block Island**, which stands offshore 13 miles out in the Atlantic.

☎   Rhode Island's area code is **401**.

# The main attractions

## BLOCK ISLAND
*Map 2I4. Postal zip code: 02807.*

Dutch explorer Adrian Block made landfall on the island in 1614, but the first European settlers did not arrive until 1661. They were, in the main, farmers and fishermen, but smugglers and pirates also found the island hospitable. So did salvagers, who stripped the scores of wrecked ships that foundered in fogs and storms which unexpectedly blow up in these climes.

Seven miles long N to S and $3\frac{1}{2}$ miles wide, the island has rugged cliffs plunging into the sea, fine beaches, acres of wildflowers, hundreds of freshwater ponds and small lakes, and a great salt bay nearly cutting it in two. In the late 19thC, tourism became important to the economy, and large Victorian cottages and hotels were erected along the shores. By strict regulation and alert enforcement, the island has avoided most of the less appetizing aspects of commercial development. Camping is prohibited, for example, as is shell-fishing without a license, which is not always easy to obtain.

Among the points of interest are the **National Wildlife Refuge** and its inoperative but picturesque lighthouse at the extreme N end, the 185-foot-high **Mohegan Bluffs** on the S shore, and **Crescent Beach** on the E. There is a small airport, and ferries connect the island with Providence and Newport as well as New London, in Connecticut, and with Montauk, at the end of New York's Long Island. Bicycles and mopeds are the preferred modes of transportation, and can be rented at shops near the dock. Hotel reservations must be made well in advance for the short summer season.

♥ ⇌ Consensus clearly favors the **Hotel Manisses** *(Spring St.* ☎ *466-2063* ▥*)* for both dining and lodging. Given the name of the island used by the tribe that once inhabited it, the 1870 Victorian structure is kept up-to-date without sacrificing its antiquarian allure. Buffet breakfast is included in the admittedly hefty room rates. Some rooms have Jacuzzis. The restaurant smokes it own meats and fish and has a flourishing vegetable and herb garden. It is closed November to mid-April, and open only Saturday and Sunday from mid-April to late May.

The same owner-managers operate the neighboring **1661 Inn and Guest House** *(Spring St.* ☎ *466-2421* ▥*)*. Here too breakfast is included. A few rooms share baths, but some of the others have private whirlpools. It is closed from mid-November to mid-May.

⇌ Less expensive but satisfying meals are on hand at the spirited **Harborside Inn** *(Water St.* ☎ *466-2836* ▥*)*, near the ferry docks. Its terrace is a justly popular gathering place. Mostly simple beef and seafood dishes are what is on offer here.

## NEWPORT
*Map 2H4. Postal zip code: 02840.*

Few cities its size (the population is under 30,000) can flourish a social history and architectural heritage as sumptuous as this. Founded in 1639 by visionaries who anticipated basic tenets of the Constitution more than 150 years before it was conceived, Newport has been a refuge of America's de facto aristocracy since the smoke of the Civil War cleared away. The super-rich and the merely wealthy made it a regular stop on their seasonal itineraries, erecting faux châteaux and Italianate palazzos by the score. The fabulous fortunes of Astors and Vanderbilts and their brethren were committed to the cause, and such celebrated architects as Stanford White and William Morris Hunt were commissioned to conjure the fantasies in marble and velvet. Since few of their descendants and contemporary potentates can afford to sustain such extravagantly luxurious properties, with their platoons of servants, gardeners, workmen and service people, many of the palatial buildings are open to a wondering public.

Two districts are of particular interest. Despite the efforts of the British Army, which destroyed much of the town during the Revolution, remnants of the Colonial era survive, most of them clustered downtown, near the N end of the main harbor. Among them are the following major points of interest:

- **Hunter House** *(54 Washington St.* ☎ *847-1000* 🖾*)* was built in 1748.
- The **Wanton-Lyman-Hazard House** *(17 Broadway* 🖾*)* dates from about 1675.
- The Quaker **Friends Meeting House** *(29 Farewell St.* 🖾*)* was built in 1699.
- The **Touro Synagogue** *(85 Touro St.* ☎ *847-4794* 🖾*)*, opened in 1763, is the oldest in the US.
- Walking tours of the Colonial district start at the **Newport Historical Society Museum** *(82 Touro St.* 🖾*)*, next to the **Seventh Day Baptist Meeting House** *(83 Touro St.* 🖾*)*, which was built in 1729. Among the above buildings, all those without a telephone number share the common ☎846-0813.

The other district of major interest is **Bellevue Ave.**, running s from downtown, which contains many of the 19thC mansions that are open to view. Combination tickets are available for all the Bellevue Ave. mansions using ☎847-1000. The following are among the most prominent along that boulevard and its intersecting streets (several have no assigned street number):

- The 1852 **Chateau-sur-mer** *(Bellevue Ave.* 🖾*)* has a fetching toy collection.
- Caroline Astor's **Beechwood** *(580 Bellevue Ave.* ☎ *846-3772* 🖾*)* has actors in costume serving as docents.
- The Gothic Revival **Kingscote** *(Bowery St.* 🖾*)* was built in 1839 to a design by Richard Upjohn, who was responsible for over a dozen churches in New York City alone.
- The Vanderbilts' enormous Italian Renaissance Revival palace, **The Breakers** *(Ochre Point Ave.* 🖾*)*, has 70 stunning chambers.
- **The Elms** *(Bellevue Ave.* 🖾*)* is notable for its extensive gardens laid out according to formal French precepts.

Newport hosts numerous yacht races and tennis tournaments each year. In summer there are jazz and folk music festivals.

🐚🗣 Get in the Newport mood in the 1874 mansion that is now **The Inn at Castle Hill** *(Ocean Drive* ☎*849-3800* 🔲 *to* 🔳*)*. The hilltop location confers fine views of the bay. Much of the furniture is original. Bedrooms vary substantially in size and accouterments, and not all of them have private baths, which accounts for the wide range in rates. There are separate cottages, and the dining room serves all meals. Children must be 12 or older.

While it could be just about anywhere, the **Newport Marriott** *(25 America's Cup Ave.* ☎*849-1000* 🔲 *to* 🔳*)* is fitted out with all the conventional hotel comforts, as well as an indoor pool, racquetball courts and a health club. Rooms with harbor views are more expensive.

🗣 Ambiance is the reason to go to the **White Horse Tavern** *(Marlborough and Farewell Sts.* ☎*849-3600* 🔲 *to* 🔳*)*, said to be the oldest tavern in the US. Parts of the building date to 1675. It is far more memorable than the food, which runs to standard meat and seafood dishes.

The elite meet to greet and eat at the stylish **Black Pearl** *(Bannister's Wharf* ☎*846-5264* 🔳*)*. Diners can choose from the informal tavern, the dressy Commodore's Room or the outdoor café. Next door, attracting a similarly upmarket crowd, is the **Clarke Cooke House** *(Bannister's Wharf* ☎*849-2900* 🔳*)*. Several dining areas vary in ambition and degrees of formality, but men must wear jacket and tie.

Reservations are strongly advised or required at all three of the restaurants mentioned above.

## PROVIDENCE
*Map 2G4.*

In 1636, Roger Williams, arguably America's first civil libertarian (see page 244), left Boston and founded what became Rhode Island's state capital and eventually New England's second largest city. Its most dramatic growth came during the booming 19thC decades of maritime trade and industrialization. Enlightened development policies have preserved many buildings from its three centuries of existence.

Especially blessed is the **College Hill** historic district. Set back from the busy commercial district bordering the Providence River, its most impressive byway is Benefit St., bordered by residences reflecting origins from Colonial times to the post-Civil War "Gilded Age."

Among the houses on Benefit St. open to visitors are a 1786 Georgian beauty, the **John Brown House** *(Power and Benefit Sts.* ☎*331-8575* 🔳*)*, which now functions as a small museum, and the 1707 **Governor Stephen Hopkins House** *(Hopkins and Benefit Sts.* ☎*884-8337* 🔳*)*, which is named after a resident who was both a signer of the Declaration of Independence and frequent state governor. John Quincy Adams and George Washington were among its distinguished visitors.

On the w side of Benefit St. is the respected **Rhode Island School of Design**, while to its E is the campus of **Brown University**, founded in 1764 and now an innovative member of the Ivy League of illustrious private universities.

The **Providence Preservation Society** *(21 Meeting St.* ☎*831-7440)* provides $1\frac{1}{2}$-hour audiotape walking tours, and in June sponsors tours of homes not normally open to visitors. Shoppers with an historical turn of mind will no doubt be keen to explore **The Arcade** *(65 Weybosset*

*St.* ☎ *272-2340),* a Greek Revival shopping mall opened in 1828 and still functioning according to its original purpose.

✎   Early Art Deco in many of its details, the 1922 **Omni Biltmore** *(Kennedy Plaza, Providence, RI 02903* ☎ *421-0700* ▥ *to* ▥*)* has enjoyed a costly renovation, bringing it into line with all but the most expensive modern hostelries. Guests have access to a nearby health club.

Very similar in size and amenities, but minus the gloss, the local **Holiday Inn** *(21 Atwells Ave., Providence, RI 02903* ☎ *831-3900* ▥ *to* ▥*)* adds an indoor pool to its list of enticements.

Those who prefer the coziness of a bed-and-breakfast are almost certain to enjoy a stay at the **Old Court Inn** *(144 Benefit St., Providence, RI 02908* ☎ *751-2002* ▥ *to* ▥*).* It is in the handsome College Hill district and near the 1762 Old State House. The 1863 inn is a former rectory, with furnishings of the period. Buffet breakfast is provided.

≊   **Al Forno** *(577 South Main St.* ☎ *273-9760* ▥ *to* ▥*)* takes the gastronomic laurels, according to informed opinion. Its food is Cal-Ital, with wood-fired grills of designer pizzas, meats, and fowl redolent with fresh herbs. No smoking is allowed, only dinner is served Tuesday to Saturday, and they don't accept reservations, so a wait can be anticipated, especially on weekends.

Most of those limitations are avoided at **Hemenway's** *(Old Stone Sq. and South Main St.* ☎ *351-8570* ▥ *to* ▥*).* Seafood is paramount, much of it imported from other US regions and foreign waters, but with an emphasis on New England fabrications. Outdoor dining is available in good weather.

# Vermont

## Essential New England

We learn much about the craggy topography and rural character of Vermont from the fact that marble, granite, maple syrup and dairy products are its primary exports. For many Americans, it is the quintessential New England, distilled in the national consciousness into a portrait of laconic natives, covered bridges, halcyon hills, and white clapboard inns on sedate village greens. Its ancient worn mountains are verdant or snow-covered or, for too brief a time in early October, ablaze with crimson and gold. Short but glorious summers are the reward — for the year-round residents, at any rate — for stoical sufferance of the long, hard winters. Skiers from all over the Northeast and Middle Atlantic coast make Vermont a regular destination six months a year, and the state's expertise in keeping its roads clear make the farthest corners accessible even in deepest January.

With about 16 percent more land area but less than 10 percent the population of Massachusetts, to its south, Vermonters have ample elbow room. Only four towns have more than 10,000 residents, and the capital, **Montpelier**, is not one of those. The largest city is **Burlington**, with fewer than 38,000 inhabitants. It lies on the shore of **Lake Champlain**, a beautiful body of water that forms much of the western border with upper New York State.

The eastern boundary with New Hampshire is delineated by the **Connecticut River**, which rises near the edge of the province of Québec, Canada. Running north and south is the spine of the **Green Mountain** range, much of which is a national forest. The mountains also contain more than 30 ski areas, including **Stratton**, **Bromley**, **Stowe**, **Haystack** and **Killington**.

Permanent settlement came later than other parts of New England, for the region was contested first by the British and French and later by claims to the territory from New York and New Hampshire. Ethan Allen and his militia, the Green Mountain Boys, provided the rebellious colonies with one of their earliest, most decisive, victories over the British when they captured Fort Ticonderoga in 1775. Cannon taken there were transported all the way to Boston, helping the Continental Army persuade the British to evacuate that city. After a brief period as an independent republic, Vermont joined the union of the 13 original states in 1791. In the following decades, it established itself as one of the most egalitarian, the first to ban slavery and to allow universal suffrage for men.

Apart from the state university, centered in Burlington, Vermont's best-known educational institutions are the small and highly selective Middlebury and Bennington Colleges. Cultural events — symphony concerts, opera, and Shakespeare and other theatrical festivals — are held at various locations, especially in Burlington and during the summer.

☎   Vermont's area code is **802**

For more than 140 years, **covered bridges** have been synonymous with New England, and nowhere more so than Vermont. Today, some 840 of them survive in the region, just half the number present 45 years ago. This one is at **Arlington**, ten miles N of Bennington in sw Vermont.

# Southern Vermont

## BENNINGTON

*Map 3E1. Postal zip code: **05201**.*

Ethan Allen and his Green Mountain Boys were among the most effective military units in the colonial cause, first against the French, then the New York claimants to Vermont, and finally the British. They were headquartered in this attractive town, which served as a supply depot during the Revolution. In 1777, the British launched an attack to capture those stores, but were thwarted by the militia under General John Stark.

The town has a sizable historic district of colonial and post-Revolutionary domestic architecture, and the progressive (and very expensive) Bennington College. One prominent landmark is the **Bennington Battle Monument** *(15 Monument Circle* ☎ *447-0550* ▨ *open Apr-Oct daily 9am-5pm),* an 1891 obelisk 306 feet high, commemorating General Stark's victory over the British in the battle of 1777. An elevator takes visitors to an observation deck, from which there are views of the mountains and meadows of three states. Another landmark is the **Old First Church** *(Monument Ave.* ▧ 𝒇 *available, open June Sat-Sun 9am-5pm, July-Oct daily 9am-5pm),* dating from 1805. In the adjoining burial ground are the remains of poet Robert Frost and the soldiers who fell in the 1777 battle.

Exhibits of artifacts, crafts and manufactured goods relating to the daily lives and heritage of Vermonters are displayed at the **Bennington Museum** *(West Main St./Route 9* ☎*447-1571* 📷 *open Mar-Nov 9am-5pm)*. Among the highlights are a luxury 1925 automobile, and paintings by "Grandma" Moses, who took up paint and brush at age 70 and continued until her death at 101. Her naive depictions of New England life enjoyed considerable popularity.

❧ ╍  Housed in a Georgian-Revival mansion, **Four Chimneys** *(21 West Rd.* ☎*447-3500* 🏷*)* is noted especially for its restaurant, with a carefully executed continental menu. Its dozen bedrooms have TV and air conditioning, and rates include breakfast. Tennis is available. They close for two weeks in early spring and late fall. It is advisable to reserve ahead.

## DORSET
*Map 3E1. Postal zip code: 05251.*
Vermont specializes in postcard-perfect rural villages. This one, ringed by the gentle Green Mountains of the southern part of the state, is one of the most memorable. Its first prominent industry was quarried marble, which is so abundant in the area that the village's sidewalks are made of that material. To the s of town on Route 30 is the **J.J. Hapgood Store** *(Main St.* ☎*824-5911 open daily)*, an 1827 emporium that is, in effect, a living museum, complete with "penny" candy and locals trading gossip around the stove.

During the summer months, a professional company mounts plays at the local theater.

❧ ╍  The **Dorset Inn** *(Church St.* ☎*867-4455* 🏷*)* declares that it is the oldest inn in continuous operation in Vermont. It doesn't rest on that claim, however, not with two tennis courts, a pool, sauna and nearby ski trails, as well as a hard-working kitchen. Its principal competition is **Barrows House** *(Route 30* ☎*867-4455* 🏷*)*, which has similar virtues and facilities.

## GRAFTON
*Map 3E2. Postal zip code: 05146.*
A photogenic collection of restored and preserved houses and churches, the formerly prosperous mill and soapstone-quarrying town has been returned to its post-Revolutionary appearance. Greek Revival is the predominant style.

❧ ╍  **The Old Tavern at Grafton** *(Main St.* ☎*843-2231* 🏷 *to* 🏷*)* is an historic site by virtue of its age (1801) and, with its restaurant, bar and diverse lodgings, a center of community activity. Among its most distinguished guests have been Henry David Thoreau, Nathaniel Hawthorne, Daniel Webster and Ralph Waldo Emerson. The bedrooms are furnished with appropriate 19thC reproductions and antiques, including some four-poster beds; they have private bathrooms, but no TV, telephones or air conditioning. Breakfast is included. Cross-country and downhill skiing are available, and there is a pond for swimming, as well as two tennis courts.

## LUDLOW
*Map 3D2. Postal zip code:* **05149**.
In the shadow of the **Okemo Mountain Ski Resort and State Forest**, Ludlow has a functioning cheese factory that is the oldest in the country.

❧ ⇌　The Victorian residence of a former Vermont governor has been resuscitated as **The Governor's Inn** *(86 Main St.* ☎ *228-8830* ▥*)*. It dominates in a town with more than its share of country inns, especially in its dining room. The eight bedrooms, all with private baths, are decorated with antiques and authentic-to-the-period accessories. Rates fluctuate according to season, and usually include both breakfast and dinner, as well as afternoon tea. Closed April and May. No room phones. Smoking is not allowed.

⇌　Eclectic food, mostly American, but with international digressions, is purveyed in a choice of dining areas at **Nikki's** *(44 Pond St.* ☎ *228-7797* ▥ *to* ▥*)*. Selections, which include satay and steak *au poivre*, are complemented by an excellent wine cellar.

## MANCHESTER
*Map 3E2. Postal zip code:* **05254**.
Along with the neighboring village of **Manchester Center**, this is the heart of one of New England's premier resort regions. **Stratton** and **Bromley Mountains** attract avid skiers from throughout the northeast in winter. But the clean, crisp streams and rivers of Vermont are magnets for anglers, too, evidenced by the presence of the **American Museum of Fly Fishing** *(Seminary Ave. and Route 7A* ☎ *362-3300* ▨*)*. It displays rods and tackle once owned by Dwight Eisenhower, Winslow Homer and Ernest Hemingway.

　　**Hildene** *(Route 7A* ☎ *362-1788* ▨*)* was the summer residence of Abraham Lincoln's son, Robert, and is now open to the public. Cultural activities, including exhibitions, recitals and films are presented at the **Southern Vermont Art Center** *(West Rd.* ☎ *362-1405* ▨*)*.

❧　Mostly, the heavily-advertised resort hotel **Equinox** *(Route 7A* ☎ *362-4747* ▥ *to* ▥*)* lives up to its own claims. Its many facilities include tennis courts, 18-hole golf course, indoor and outdoor pools, fitness center with sauna and steam room, and in winter, nearby downhill and cross-country skiing. The oldest section of the constantly upgraded complex dates to the 18thC, although much of it has a late Victorian look.

　　More intimate possibilities are the **1811 House** *(Route 7A* ☎ *362-1811* ▥ *to* ▥*)* and the 1850 **Reluctant Panther Inn** *(West Rd.* ☎ *362-2568* ▥*)*. Their rates include breakfast, and each has access to some recreational facilities.

## MARLBORO
*Map 3E2. Postal zip code:* **05344**.
The tiny college named after the small village in which it is located is home to a famous chamber music festival, which is held on weekends from mid-July to mid-August. Tickets must be reserved well in advance *(*☎ *254-2394)*. Marlboro is eight miles w of **Brattleboro**, in the SE corner of the state.

## NEWFANE
*Map 3E2. Postal zip code: 05345.*
The principal draw in this pretty but otherwise drowsy village is the **Four Columns Inn** (see below). A few miles N on Route 30 is the **Scott Covered Bridge**, the longest in Vermont. Flea market fans will want to be around on Sundays in summer and fall, when a monster sale of collectibles and salable flotsam takes place on several acres slightly N of the green.

One of New England's most celebrated inns, the gracious and accomplished **Four Columns** *(230 West St.* ☎ *365-7713* 🎫*)*, stands on Newfane's delightful village green. The 16 rooms and suites of the Greek Revival main structure and its modern annex are comfortably furnished with antiques, telephones, air conditioning and private baths, but no TV. An excellent dining room features New American cooking.

# Central Vermont

## KILLINGTON
*Map 3D2. Postal zip code: 05751.*
With only a handful of people comprising the permanent population, Killington is known neither for architecture nor history, but for its more than a hundred downhill ski runs and an aerial tram said to be the world's longest ski lift. It stays in operation all year, so nonskiers can enjoy the ride and sweeping vistas of mountains and rolling countryside.

**Inn of the Six Mountains** *(Killington Rd.* ☎ *422-4302* 🎫 *to*🎫*)* is a full-service 4-season resort, nearly as busy in the warmer months as in winter. Skiing, yes, but hiking, cycling, golfing and year-round swimming, too. The fitness center has sauna and whirlpool.

Quieter, smaller, but with some of the same facilities and a more ambitious restaurant, the **Vermont Inn** *(Route 4* ☎ *775-0708* 🎫*)* maximizes its early 19thC origins without sacrificing 20thC amenities. No TV in rooms, but a pool, sauna, tennis, and nearby golf and skiing.

## MIDDLEBURY
*Map 3C1. Postal zip code: 05753.*
One of New England's most prestigious liberal arts colleges shares the name of this, its hometown. The college sponsors the noted Bread Loaf Writer's Conference and is highly regarded for its foreign-language programs. Attractions include the **State Craft Center at Frog Hollow** *(Route 7* ☎ *388-3177* 📷*)*, housed in an old mill and offering exhibits by scores of native craftspeople, and the **Sheldon Museum** *(1 Park St.* ☎ *388-2117)*, an early 19thC dwelling chock-full of antique furniture, kitchen implements, crockery, clocks and toys.

Parts of the **Swift House Inn** *(25 Stewart Lane* ☎ *388-9925* 🎫*)* date from 1815. The rooms have antiques, quilts and four-posters; some of them have fireplaces and whirlpool baths. Continental breakfast is included; the dining room features an eclectic American menu.

## MONTPELIER

*Map 3C2. Postal zip code: 05602.*

State capital since 1805, Montpelier is a town of fewer than 9,000 souls. Many of those citizens are involved in government, and the principal sight is the 1849 **State House**, with its unmistakable gold dome.

☎ ≈ The presence of telephones, TV sets, air conditioning and private bathrooms cannot be assumed in all country inns. But **The Inn at Montpelier** *(147 Main St. ☎ 223-2727 ▯▯ to ▯▯)* provides them, and at reasonable prices. Some rooms have fireplaces and desks as well as antiques. Two restored early 19thC structures constitute the inn, which incorporates one of the capital's most popular restaurants. A bountiful buffet breakfast is included.

≈ An intriguing dining experience can be had at **Tubb's** *(24 Elm St. ☎ 229-9202 ▯▯)*. Not only is the restaurant installed in an old jailhouse, but it serves as a training ground for students of the New England Culinary Institute, which produces many of the nation's top chefs.

## WOODSTOCK

*Map 3D2. Postal zip code: 05091.*

One of the earliest Vermont settlements, Woodstock was made a county seat shortly after its founding in 1761. Apart from a few mills on the **Ottauquechee River**, it managed to prosper without much industry. Many early to late 19thC residences remain, some of which constitute a large historic district. Walking tours leave from the information booth on the village green *(☎ 457-2450).* Three covered bridges cross the river, one of them built only 20 years ago. The mountains that rise to either side of the Ottauquechee have almost 30 downhill ski runs as well as cross-country trails.

☎ ≈ **Woodstock Inn** *(14 Village Green ☎ 457-1100 ▯▯ to ▯▯)* is more resort than conventional inn. Ten tennis courts, golf and two pools are the central recreational features, with downhill skiing only five miles away.

**Charleston House** *(43 Pleasant St. ☎ 457-3077 ▯▯ to ▯▯)* is a rehabilitated 1835 building furnished, for the most part, with antiques. The rooms are compact. Full breakfast is included in the tariff.

≈ Gourmands are tempted to dine every night of a long Woodstock stay at **The Prince and the Pauper** *(24 Elm St. ☎ 457-1818 ▯▯)*. Here, sophisticated eclecticism is the theme that rules the menu and the kitchen, and the candlelit dining room enhances that experience. Dinners are fixed-price and entirely reasonable for what is proffered.

# Northern Vermont

## BURLINGTON

*Map 3B1. Postal zip code:* **05401.**

Vermont's largest city commands a strip of **Lake Champlain** frontage in the NW quadrant of the state, about 100 miles s of Montréal. Its cultural life is enhanced by the presence of the **University of Vermont**, founded in 1791, the same year the state joined the union. In July and August, the campus is the site of Mozart and Shakespeare festivals. In June there is a jazz festival at various venues.

Several ferries ply the waters of the 125-mile lake, providing pleasant passages that surpass mere transportation. One of them travels between Burlington and Port Kent in New York State from mid-May to mid-October ( ☎ *864-9804),* taking cars and passengers. Alternatively, there are cruises from **Perkins Pier** on a replica of an old-fashioned paddlewheel steamer, during the day, at sunset, and for dinner ( ☎ *862-9685).*

Several parks offer lake vantages, including one named after Revolutionary War hero Ethan Allen, who had a home here part of his life, and **Battery Park**, named after the guns that defended Burlington from British warships in the war of 1812.

But the major attraction in the area is the **Shelburne Museum**, seven miles to the s in the cluster of villages sharing the name, next to Route 7 ( ☎ *985-3346* ▧ *open mid-May to mid-Oct daily 9am-5pm).* It has extensive exhibits of Americana of every variety in 37 buildings on 45 acres, with collections of folk arts and crafts, farm equipment and carpenter tools, housewares and kitchen devices, and furniture and accessories from over three centuries of Vermont life. But that summary barely scratches the surface. Also on the premises are an early 20thC side-wheel steamship, a lighthouse, a covered bridge, a blacksmith's forge, a jail, a complete country store, more than a hundred carriages, and a miniature circus with thousands of hand-carved figures. With all this, frequent demonstrations, and a restaurant and shop, much of an entire day can be fruitfully occupied.

⌁ Lake views, an indoor pool and an executive level mark the **Radisson** *(60 Battery St.* ☎ *658-6500 ▥ to ▦)* as the city's closest approximation of a luxury hotel.

Less expensive, but with similar facilities, the local **Holiday Inn** *(1068 Williston Rd.* ☎ *863-6363 ▥)* has two pools, one indoor, and an exercise room. It's in South Burlington, near the airport.

 Blessed with at least five area restaurants that go to considerable expense and effort to pique their interest and appetites, Burlingtonians have an enviable dilemma. Should they drive down the road to the **Café Shelburne** *(Route 7* ☎ *985-3939 ▥)* for high-minded French edibles, or to **Francesca's** *(Route 7* ☎ *985-3373 ▥)* for bargain pastas and veal dishes? Or stay in town to take in Creole-Cajun delights at the **Bourbon Street Grill** *(213 College St.* ☎ *865-2800 ▥),* the piquant-to-blazing Asian treats at **Five Spice Café** *(175 Church St.* ☎ *864-4505 ▥),* or the restless culinary explorations of **Deja Vu Café** *(185 Pearl St.* ☎ *864-7917 ▥ to ▦)*

Truth to tell, they can't go wrong with any of these.

## NORTHEAST KINGDOM
*Map 3B3–C3.*
Authoritative explanations for the origin of the name are elusive, but the three counties in the far northeast corner of the state bear the label proudly. Beauty must have been the central criterion, for this is a landscape of silvery lakes, tumbling streams, billowing meadows and embracing mountains.

**St Johnsbury** is the largest town, but several villages lying to its north are of greater interest, especially on driving tours during the immensely popular fall foliage season, which occurs in late September most years, but spills over into October. Especially picturesque are **Peacham**, **East Burke**, **Barnet**, **Cabot** and **Craftsbury Common**.

For both lodging and food, few establishments in the Kingdom equal St Johnsbury's **Rabbit Hill** (*Lower Waterford, VT 05848* ☎ *748-5168* ▥ *to* ▥). Rooms are in a turn-of-the-*last*-century structure, which first started operating as an inn between the Revolution and the War of 1812. Creative cooks make dinner in the dining room an event to be cherished.

## STOWE
*Map 3B2. Postal zip code: 05672.*
**Mount Mansfield** is the tallest peak in Vermont, and the village at its base is an irresistible location for a winter resort. An aerial tram and several chair lifts take skiers and summer sightseers to the top. The resort touches a state forest and park, which offer hiking, swimming, fishing and picnicking.

A skiing center of Stowe's renown has no shortage of lodging possibilities, of every sort. No doubt the most famous is the **Trapp Family Lodge** (*Trapp Hill Rd.* ☎ *253-8511* ▥), owned by members of the family immortalized in a film, *The Sound of Music*. There are three swimming pools, a fitness room and, of course, skiing.

**Topnotch At Stowe** (*Mountain Rd.* ☎ *253-8585* ▥) is a full-fledged resort with all-season recreational facilities serving interests from mountain cycling to hydrotherapy, from dancing to live bands. Two pools, 12 tennis courts, horse trails and fitness center.

Ski resorts are given to alpine themes and conceits, so at least one restaurant serving fondue is inevitable. **Swisspot** (*Main St.* ☎ *253-4622* ▥) fulfills that obligation, adding such related munchables as quiche, bratwurst and pastas, neatly representing the four gastronomical regions of the country of inspiration. Prices are exceptionally reasonable for a resort town.

Updated American recipes are the thrust of **Stubb's** (*Mountain Rd.* ☎ *253-7110* ▥), which uses Vermont products wherever possible.

# New Hampshire

## The Granite State

Emblazoned on automobile license plates is the motto of the Granite State, "Live Free or Die." The words of a Revolutionary War patriot, they have come to be regarded as emblematic of the state's tradition of rock-ribbed conservatism and spirit of resolute independence.

That image has been buttressed by the all but routine election of Republican politicians since the Civil War and the vitriolic editorial pronouncements of the *Manchester Union Leader* newspaper published in Manchester, the largest city. Since the early 1970s, however, that perception of rugged rural individualism has been diluted. The fact that the state imposes no sales or personal income taxes inevitably attracted refugees from "Taxachusetts," to the south. Urbanites from Boston and its satellite communities brought their own ideologies with them to larger industrial cities near the border, notably **Nashua, Concord, Portsmouth** and **Manchester**.

On maps, the state appears as a virtual mirror image of Vermont, with the diagonal slash of the **Connecticut River** that delineates their common border. The two neighboring states are nearly equal in area, but due to the expanding population centers in the south, New Hampshire has twice as many residents, a total that recently sailed past the one million mark. Unlike its neighbor, it has a short frontage on the Atlantic Ocean, but otherwise, they share a similar topography. The **White Mountains** of the Appalachian range run down the middle, their highest peaks clustered in the north-central part of the state. **Mount Washington**, at 6,288 feet, is the tallest. (By contrast, Mount Mansfield, Vermont's highest, is only 4,393 feet.)

With the multiple opportunities available for skiing, camping, hiking and rock-climbing, the mountains are one of two primary recreational resources. The other is **Lake Winnipesaukee**, the largest of several bodies of water constituting the Lake Region in the heart of the state. Ringed around with hills, it is one of the most scenic districts of New England, a magnet for water skiers, windsurfers and sailors.

John Adams had the first land grant, and he named the colonial tract after the English county, or shire. At first, the territory incorporated what are now Maine and Vermont. Puritan settlers from Massachusetts Bay arrived in the 1630s. Over the next 150 years, control shifted repeatedly, with disputes flaring successively with the Crown, Massachusetts and New York before it took its present form as the ninth state to sign the

Constitution in 1766. Distinguished past residents of New Hampshire included the poet Robert Frost and Mary Baker Eddy, founder of the Christian Science church.

☎    New Hampshire's area code is **603**.

# Southern New Hampshire

## CONCORD
*Map* **4E4**. *Postal zip code:* **03301**.
The state capital is on the **Merrimack River**, which rises in the Lake Region, to the N. It is famous for its granite quarries and has been an industrial center since well before the Civil War.

The nation's largest state legislature meets in the oldest **State House** *(25 State St.* ☎ *271-2154* 🖾 *open Mon-Fri 8am-4.30pm).* Around the corner is the **New Hampshire Historical Society** *(30 Park St.* ☎ *225-3381* 🖾 *open Mon-Sat 9am-4.30pm, Wed until 8pm),* with a library and exhibits relating to state and regional history.

Time should be made for a visit to the **Canterbury Center,** 15 miles N on Route 132 or Interstate 93. A Shaker community was established there shortly after the Revolution. The hardworking adherents to Mother Ann's demanding faith were known for their simple but beautiful furniture and agricultural innovations. Since they observed celibacy, the only way they sustained a living presence was through conversion and adoption. Few Shakers are left, and this village has been made into a working **museum** *(288 Shaker Rd.* ☎ *783-9511* 🖾 *open May-Oct Mon-Sat 10am-5pm, Sun noon-5pm; Nov-Dec and Apr Fri-Sat 10am-5pm, Sun noon-5pm).* There are crafts demonstrations, costumed docents, and a restaurant serving food derived from authentic Shaker recipes.

✇    While there are no exceptional lodging choices in the immediate Concord area, the **Ramada Inn** *(172 Main St.* ☎ *224-9534* 🕮*)* provides standard hotel–motel comforts, and has an exercise room.

➟    For no readily apparent reason, Concord has *two* good Mexican restaurants, **Tio Juan's** *(1 Bicentennial Sq.* ☎ *224-2821* 🕮*)* and **Hermanos Cocina Mexicana** *(6 Pleasant St.* ☎ *224-5669* 🕮*).* Both are lively and fun, with very tasty semi-authentic dishes that include *chimichangas* and *taquitos.* Prices are kind to travel budgets. Tio Juan's is housed in a former police station.

## MANCHESTER
*Map* **4E4**.
Belying New Hampshire's rural image, its largest city has scores of light-to-medium industries, many of them producing textiles, clothing or electronics. Manchester's **Currier Museum of Art** *(192 Orange St.* ☎ *626-4158* 🖾 *open Tues-Wed, Fri, Sat 10am-4pm, Thurs 10am-9pm, Sun 2-5pm)* has a surprisingly sophisticated collection of Euro-

pean and American paintings and sculpture, from the Renaissance to the recent past. One important part of the museum's holdings is the small **Zimmerman House**, designed by Frank Lloyd Wright, and there are frequent special exhibitions.

Standard motels and hotels provide most lodgings in this river city near the Massachusetts border, including a downtown **Holiday Inn** *(700 Elm St., Manchester, NH 03101* ☎ *625-1000* ⅢⅢ *to* ⅢⅢ*)* and a **Howard Johnson** *(298 Queen City Ave., Manchester, NH 03102* ☎ *668-2600* ⅢⅢ *to* ⅢⅢ*)*.

For an experience that speaks far more of New England, there is the **Bed-** **ford Village Inn** *(2 Old Bedford Rd., Bedford, NH 03102* ☎ *472-2602* ⅢⅢ *to* ⅢⅢ*)*, a few miles s on Route 101. All the accommodations in the converted barn are of luxurious order, with four-poster beds, whirlpool baths and some fireplaces. The restaurant, in another building of the former farm, lives up to the same high standards, starting with an unusually large wine cellar.

## PORTSMOUTH
*Map 4E5. Postal zip code: 03801.*
Settled in 1623, this small but beguiling city was New Hampshire's capital for almost a century and is the state's only true seaport. Its nautical tradition is undergirded by the presence of the **Portsmouth Naval Shipyard**, established in 1800 in Kittery, Maine, on the opposite shore of the **Piscataqua River**. It was the site of the signing of the treaty that ended the Russo-Japanese War in 1905, after a peace conference convened there by Theodore Roosevelt.

Several historic districts and streets preserve the city's architectural heritage, with three centuries of restored houses and commercial structures. First among these is **Strawbery Banke** *(Hancock and Marcy Sts.* ☎ *433-1100* 📷 *open May-Oct 10am-5pm)*, the original waterfront settlement, which is now a ten-acre living museum with over 40 buildings. The oldest dates from 1695, and others include the mansions of merchants and wealthy sea captains. A number are still undergoing rehabilitation, while crafts demonstrations and exhibits detailing colonial life are offered in those open to the public.

Outside Strawbery Banke, a popular walking tour connects six more houses that welcome visitors, most of them built in the early decades of the 18thC. Maps are available from the **Chamber of Commerce** *(500 Market St.* ☎ *436-1118)*.

A short, pleasant day trip can be made to the attractive village of **New Castle**, about four miles to the SE and accessible by bridge. In addition to its many pre-Revolution houses, it has a fort that has guarded the river entrance since 1808. The village was built upon the remains of British fortifications first erected in the 1630s.

**Sise Inn** *(40 Court St.* ☎ *433-1200* ⅢⅢ *to* ⅢⅢ*)* tucks its Victorian self harmoniously into the city's historic district. Unlike many inns, it supplies cable TV, VCRs and an exercise room. Somehow cozier, and less expensive, the **Martin Hill Inn** *(40 Islington St.* ☎ *436-2287)* is only a short walk from the district. Of two buildings dating from the mid-19thC, the "Guest

House" is marginally the more private and spacious. Breakfast is included.

≈ Books all over the place justify the name of **The Library** (*401 State St.*

☎ *431-5202* ▥ *to* ▥), located in a former downtown hotel. The kitchen skips around the globe for inspiration, with dishes from Asia to Europe and stops in between.

# Central New Hampshire

## HANOVER
*Map 3D3. Postal zip code:* **03755**.
**Dartmouth College** opened here six years before the Revolution, part of its intended purpose being to educate young Native Americans. The town on the Connecticut River has been dominated by the prestigious Ivy League institution ever since — much to its benefit, for most of its uncommonly rich cultural life is provided by the college's **Hood Museum of Art** (☎ *646-2808* ▣ *open Tues-Fri 11am-5pm, Sat and Sun 9.30am-5pm)* and the **Hopkins Center** (☎*646-2422)*, which hosts art exhibitions, concerts and theatrical productions throughout the year. The two stand next to each other on the campus. **Dartmouth Row** is composed of four brick buildings from the earliest years. Daniel Webster was an alumnus, and his 1780 **student cottage** is open to the public.

In **Cornish**, 15 miles s of Hanover, are the house and studio of a noted 19thC sculptor, the **Saint-Gaudens National Historic Site** (*Route 12A* ☎ *542-5802* ▨ *open mid-May to Oct daily 8.30am-4.30pm).* He created the Shaw Memorial, opposite Boston's State House. On the grounds are a formal garden and a gallery exhibiting contemporary artworks. Nearby is the longest **covered bridge** in the US, built in 1866 and spanning the Connecticut River to connect Cornish with Windsor, Vermont.

♋ ≈ Part resort, part motel, **Hanover Inn** (*Main and Wheelock Sts.* ☎*643-4300* ▥ *to* ▥) is owned by Dartmouth College and stands on the campus. Guests have access to tennis, golf and a health club, with downhill skiing only ten minutes away. Parts of the building date to the Revolution, but most gadgets and conveniences are provided. Book well ahead for major college events, especially football games and graduation ceremonies. The **Ivy Grill** dining room is surprisingly expert.

≈ Classical French cuisine is alive

and well at **D'Artagnan** (*13 Dartmouth College Highway* ☎ *795-2137* ▥), and few big-city rivals can match these stylish victuals. The setting is an 18thC inn with beamed ceiling. It's in **Lyme**, ten miles N on Route 10. Advance booking is a must, especially as it serves lunch only on Sunday and is closed entirely on Monday and Tuesday and for a total of four weeks in March and December.

A more modest but entirely acceptable alternative in Hanover is the **Café la Fraise** (*8 West Wheelock St.* ☎ *643-8588* ▥).

## NEW LONDON
*Map 3D3. Postal zip code:* **03257**.
**Colby-Sawyer College** is the principal "industry" of this comely town

within easy reach of **Lake Sunapee** and the **Ragged Mountain** and **King Ridge** ski areas.

☙ ◿ A recent change in ownership has improved the already agreeable **New London Inn** *(Main St.* ☎ *526-2791* ▥ *to* ▦*).* The late 18thC inn is in the center of things, all the more reason to stop for a meal from the creative young chef. Breakfast is included in the room rates.

## SUNAPEE
*Map 3E3. Postal zip code: 03782.*
Hills and uplands surround lovely Lake Sunapee, and a state park provides access to its shore for swimming and picnics. A favorite excursion on the ten-mile-long lake is on the **M/V *Mount Sunapee II*** *(Sunapee Harbor, off Route 11* ☎ *763-4030* ▨ *mid-May to mid-Oct).* Cruises among its islands and past the large turn-of-the-century summer cottages take 1½ hours. Alternatively, sunset dinners afloat are the pleasant option provided by the **M/V *Kearsarge*** *(Sunapee Harbor* ☎ *763-5477* ▨ *mid-May to mid-Oct).*

☙ ◿ **Dexter's Inn & Tennis Club** *(Stagecoach Rd.* ☎ *763-5571* ▥ *to* ▦*)* enjoys a pastoral setting. Combining the virtues of inn and resort, it has peaceful lake vistas, a pool and three all-weather tennis courts. Modified meal plans are obligatory for overnight guests. Closed November to April.

**Seven Hearths** *(Old Route 11* ☎ *763-5657* ▦*)* has a pool, and views of the lake and mountains. No tennis, but its kitchen has an edge because of its imaginative menu and praiseworthy execution. Breakfast is included in room rates. The main structure dates from 1801.

## WOLFEBORO
*Map 4D4. Postal zip code: 03894.*
Wolfeboro is the biggest of the many villages and towns on **Lake Winnipesaukee,** New Hampshire's largest. Vacation homes have risen on its shores since *before* the Revolution, underlying its claim to be the oldest summer resort in North America. Day trips in the immediate area can take in the charming villages of historic **Wakefield Corner, Alton Bay** and **Center Ossipee**, on the lake of the same name.

Several excursion boats offer cruises of varying duration. Clearly the most prominent is the **M/S *Mount Washington*** *(* ☎ *366-2628* ▨ *late May to mid-Oct),* which takes a leisurely 3-hour-plus route stopping at Wolfeboro, Alton Bay, Center Harbor and Weirs Beach.

Rail buffs may prefer a ride on the **Winnipesaukee Railroad** *(* ☎ *528-2330* ▨ *end of May to mid-Oct),* which runs between Meredith and Lakeport. Vintage coaches are used on the scenic one- or two-hour journeys. Special excursions are scheduled for Thanksgiving and during the Christmas season.

☙ ◿ The oldest part of the rambling **Wolfeboro Inn** *(44 North Main St.* ☎ *569-3016* ▥ *to* ▦*)* dates to 1812, but additions and renovations have expanded it well beyond the original structure. The old tavern is delightfully atmospheric, and it and the two dining rooms are warmed by several fireplaces. Food selections are conventional but well prepared. Bedrooms have cable TV and air conditioning. There is a beach on Lake Winnipesaukee, and boats, canoes and bicycles are available to guests.

**⊒** A venturesome menu of decidedly eclectic orientation is offered at **The Bittersweet** (*Route 28* **☎** *569-3636* □ *to* □□). The chef has a sure hand with seafood and reworked regional recipes. Cheaper snacks and light meals are available in the lounge; the Sunday buffet brunch is a treat.

# Northern New Hampshire

## DIXVILLE NOTCH
*Map 4B4. Postal zip code: **03576**.*
Every presidential election year, New Hampshire holds the first primary election of the long quest to gain the nominations of the two major political parties. And minutes after midnight that February day, the handful of eligible voters of Dixville Notch cast their votes, bringing them their quadrennial dose of the media spotlight. For the rest of the time, the residents must content themselves with one of the most ravishingly scenic settings in New England, including the aptly named **Lake Gloriette**.

Passes through the White Mountains are called "notches," and this hamlet, at an elevation of 1,871 feet, is located at the northernmost notch. Nearby **Table Rock** proffers views taking in parts of three states and the Canadian province of Québec. The **Balsams Wilderness Ski Area** (*Route 26* **☎** *255-3400* **⊠** *open late Nov-Apr)* has one run of two miles.

**⟲ ⊒** Resort living in the grand 19thC manner is the gratifying mission of **The Balsams** (*Route 26* **☎** *255-3400* □□). Prices are high, but they include three meals a day during summer, or breakfast and dinner in cooler months. To round out a full day of golf, skiing, tennis, skating, hiking, cycling and/or swimming, take to the dance floor after dinner. Dining is at near-gourmet levels, despite the large numbers of people that are served. Jackets are required at dinner, and reservations are imperative for non-guests. Closed April 1 to May 15 and October 15 to December 15.

## FRANCONIA
*Map 3C3. Postal zip code: **03580**.*
About 12 miles N of the pass with which it shares its name — **Franconia Notch** — this resort village is lively for 12 months a year. Among its handy skiing locales are the **Bretton Woods Ski Area** and **Cannon Mountain**, which has an aerial tram that operates in warmer months. **White Mountain National Forest**, about 8 miles SE on Route 18, has more than a thousand miles of hiking trails, including a long section of the **Appalachian Trail**, which runs from northern New England to the Deep South.

An early conference of the yet-to-be-born United Nations was held in 1944 at **Bretton Woods**, about 20 miles E. **Mount Washington** looms above the resort area — a cog railroad makes 3-hour round-trips to the summit — and the ski center on Route 302 has both cross-country and downhill trails.

**Profile Lake**, near Franconia Notch, provides the best vantages to view the **Old Man of the Mountains**, a craggy 40-foot formation that resembles a human face viewed from the side. Some early viewers insisted it was Thomas Jefferson. About five miles farther S is **The Flume**, a narrow rock canyon with a dramatic tumbling stream. Trails, bridges and staircases wind back and forth and over the chasm.

The **Franconia Inn** *(Easton Rd.* ☎*823-5542* ▥ *to* ▥*)* has a mid-19thC ambiance and late 20thC recreational facilities. The latter include a heated pool, cross-country trails, tennis, and nearby golf and downhill skiing. No room TV, phones or air conditioning. No pyrotechnics in the dining room, either, but capable renderings of the conservative menu. Closed April to mid-May.

Another possibility is the **Sugar Hill Inn** *(Route 117, Sugar Hill* ☎*823-5621* ▥*)*, a few miles W of Franconia. Rooms in the late 18thC farmhouse and six cottages are attractively furnished with quilts and antiques. During busy periods, guests must take dinner on the premises, but even then, rates are quite reasonable. Reserve ahead, for it is closed in April and between Thanksgiving and Christmas.

## JACKSON
*Map 4C4. Postal zip code: 03846.*
A resort village since the last century, Jackson is only a few miles S of the exceptionally scenic **Pinkham Notch** district. The pass is formed by **Wildcat Mountain**, which has an aerial tram, and **Mount Washington**, at 6,288 feet the state's highest peak, with a steep road winding all the way to the top. Near the notch is **Glen Ellis Falls.**

Jackson proper has a covered bridge and several grand resort hotels surviving from a more stately era. In summer, children are enraptured by the pretend village and rides of **Story Land** *(at Glen, on intersection of Routes 16 and 302* ☎*383-4293* ▩ *open mid-June to early Sept daily 9am-6pm, Sept to early Oct on Sat and Sun only 10am-5pm).* In winter, there is skiing at **Black Mountain,** which is only three miles N *(Route 16B* ☎*383-4490* ▩*).*

Settle in at **Christmas Farm Inn** *(Route 16B* ☎*383-4313* ▥ *to* ▥*)* and stay awhile. Several 18thC buildings comprise what amounts to an historic village, including a jail and a church. Understandably, the individual rooms vary in size and decor. Some have whirlpool baths and TV. On site are a pool and sauna; golf and downhill skiing are available.

The restaurant follows trendy transglobal conceits and includes "nutritionally correct" dishes.

**Eagle Mountain Resort** *(Carter Notch Rd.* ☎*383-9111* ▥ *to* ▥*)* is one of the venerable hotels of decades past, restored and fully functional. Golf, skiing, tennis and fitness center.

Celebrated New York architect Stanford White designed in 1895 what are now the **Inn at Thorn Hill** *(Thorn Hill Rd.* ☎ *383-4242* ▥*)* and **The Inn at Jackson** *(Thorn Hill Rd.* ☎ *383-4321* ▥*),* right next door. Full breakfasts are included in the reasonable room rates.

## NORTH CONWAY

*Map 4C4. Postal zip code:* ***03860.***

Known primarily as a winter resort, within short drives of five ski areas, North Conway has its share of summer attractions, too. One of these is the **Conway Scenic Railroad** *(Route 16* ☎ *356-5251* ▧ *open mid-June to late Oct for daily trips, early May to mid-June for trips on Sat, Sun only),* which departs from a restored late 19thC station on one-hour rides through the valley.

🏌 ⚒ Golfers are pleased to learn that the new **Hale's White Mountain** *(West Side Rd.* ☎ *356-7100* ▥*)* has an 18-hole course that draws the attention of golf magazines and professionals across the nation. Other facilities include tennis courts, pool, fitness center, cross-country and hiking trails. Another possibility is the **Red Jacket Mountain View** *(Route 302* ☎ *356-5411* ▥*),* essentially similar, but without the golf.

⚒ **Scottish Lion** *(Route 302* ☎ *356-6381* ▥ *to* ▥*)* is a bed-and-breakfast inn, too, but locally known primarily as a restaurant. It should come as little surprise that featured specialities have their origins in the Scottish Highlands: they include oatcakes and game pie.

## CONVERSION FORMULAE

| To convert | Multiply by |
|---|---|
| Inches to Centimeters | 2.540 |
| Centimeters to Inches | 0.39370 |
| Feet to Meters | 0.3048 |
| Meters to feet | 3.2808 |
| Yards to Meters | 0.9144 |
| Meters to Yards | 1.09361 |
| Miles to Kilometers | 1.60934 |
| Kilometers to Miles | 0.621371 |
| Sq Meters to Sq Feet | 10.7638 |
| Sq Feet to Sq Meters | 0.092903 |
| Sq Yards to Sq Meters | 0.83612 |
| Sq Meters to Sq Yards | 1.19599 |
| Sq Miles to Sq Kilometers | 2.5899 |
| Sq Kilometers to Sq Miles | 0.386103 |
| Acres to Hectares | 0.40468 |
| Hectares to Acres | 2.47105 |
| Gallons to Liters | 4.545 |
| Liters to Gallons | 0.22 |
| Ounces to Grams | 28.3495 |
| Grams to Ounces | 0.03528 |
| Pounds to Grams | 453.592 |
| Grams to Pounds | 0.00220 |
| Pounds to Kilograms | 0.4536 |
| Kilograms to Pounds | 2.2046 |
| Tons (UK) to Kilograms | 1016.05 |
| Kilograms to Tons (UK) | 0.0009842 |
| Tons (US) to Kilograms | 746.483 |
| Kilograms to Tons (US) | 0.0013396 |

### Quick conversions

| | |
|---|---|
| Kilometers to Miles | Divide by 8, multiply by 5 |
| Miles to Kilometers | Divide by 5, multiply by 8 |
| 1 meter = | Approximately 3 feet 3 inches |
| 2 centimeters = | Approximately 1 inch |
| 1 pound (weight) = | 475 grams (nearly $\frac{1}{2}$ kilogram) |
| Celsius to Fahrenheit | Divide by 5, multiply by 9, add 32 |
| Fahrenheit to Celsius | Subtract 32, divide by 9, multiply by 5 |

# Clothing sizes chart

## LADIES
### Suits and dresses

| | | | | | | |
|---|---|---|---|---|---|---|
| Australia | 8 | 10 | 12 | 14 | 16 | 18 |
| France | 34 | 36 | 38 | 40 | 42 | 44 |
| Germany | 32 | 34 | 36 | 38 | 40 | 42 |
| Italy | 38 | 40 | 42 | 44 | 46 | |
| Japan | 7 | 9 | 11 | 13 | | |
| UK | 6 | 8 | 10 | 12 | 14 | 16 | 18 |
| USA | 4 | 6 | 8 | 10 | 12 | 14 | 16 |

### Shoes

| | | | | | | |
|---|---|---|---|---|---|---|
| USA | 6 | $6\frac{1}{2}$ | 7 | $7\frac{1}{2}$ | 8 | $8\frac{1}{2}$ |
| UK | $4\frac{1}{2}$ | 5 | $5\frac{1}{2}$ | 6 | $6\frac{1}{2}$ | 7 |
| Europe | 38 | 38 | 39 | 39 | 40 | 41 |

## MEN
### Shirts

| | | | | | | | |
|---|---|---|---|---|---|---|---|
| USA, UK<br>Europe, Japan | 14 | $14\frac{1}{2}$ | 15 | $15\frac{1}{2}$ | 16 | $16\frac{1}{2}$ | 17 |
| Australia | 36 | 37 | 38 | 39.5 | 41 | 42 | 43 |

### Sweaters/T-shirts

| | | | | |
|---|---|---|---|---|
| Australia, USA, Germany | S | M | L | XL |
| UK | 34 | 36-38 | 40 | 42-44 |
| Italy | 44 | 46-48 | 50 | 52 |
| France | 1 | 2-3 | 4 | 5 |
| Japan | | S-M | L | XL |

### Suits/Coats

| | | | | | |
|---|---|---|---|---|---|
| UK, USA | 36 | 38 | 40 | 42 | 44 |
| Australia, Italy,<br>France, Germany | 46 | 48 | 50 | 52 | 54 |
| Japan | S | M | L | XL | |

### Shoes

| | | | | | | |
|---|---|---|---|---|---|---|
| UK | 7 | $7\frac{1}{2}$ | $8\frac{1}{2}$ | $9\frac{1}{2}$ | $10\frac{1}{2}$ | 11 |
| USA | 8 | $8\frac{1}{2}$ | $9\frac{1}{2}$ | $10\frac{1}{2}$ | $11\frac{1}{2}$ | 12 |
| Europe | 41 | 42 | 43 | 44 | 45 | 46 |

## CHILDREN
### Clothing

UK

| | | | | | | |
|---|---|---|---|---|---|---|
| *Height (ins)* | 43 | 48 | 55 | 60 | 62 | |
| *Age* | 4-5 | 6-7 | 9-10 | 11 | 12 | 13 |

USA

| | | | | | | |
|---|---|---|---|---|---|---|
| *Age* | 4 | 6 | 8 | 10 | 12 | 14 |

Europe

| | | | | | | |
|---|---|---|---|---|---|---|
| *Height (cms)* | 125 | 135 | 150 | 155 | 160 | 165 |
| *Age* | 7 | 9 | 12 | 13 | 14 | 15 |

## What readers from all over the world say:

• "We could never have had the wonderful time that we did without your guide to *Paris*. The compactness was very convenient, your maps were all we needed, but it was your restaurant guide that truly made our stay special . . . . We have learned first-hand: *American Express — don't leave home without it*." (A. R., Virginia Beach, Va., USA)

• Of Sheila Hale's *Florence and Tuscany*: "I hope you don't mind my calling you by your first name, but during our recent trip to Florence and Siena [we] said on innumerable occasions, 'What does Sheila say about that?' " (H.G., Buckhurst Hill, Essex, England)

• "I have visited Mexico most years since 1979 . . . Of the many guides I have consulted during this time, by far the best has been James Tickell's *Mexico*, of which I've bought each edition." (J.H., Mexico City)

• "We have heartily recommended these books to all our friends who have plans to travel abroad." (A.S. and J.C., New York, USA)

• "Much of our enjoyment came from the way your book *(Venice)* sent us off scurrying around the interesting streets and off to the right places at the right times". (Lord H., London, England)

• "It *(Paris)* was my constant companion and totally dependable . . . . " (V. N., Johannesburg, South Africa)

• "We found *Amsterdam, Rotterdam & The Hague* invaluable . . . probably the best of its kind we have ever used. It transformed our stay from an ordinary one into something really memorable . . . . " (S.W., Canterbury, England)

• "Despite many previous visits to Italy, I wish I had had your guide *(Florence and Tuscany)* ages ago. I love the author's crisp, literate writing and her devotion to her subject." (M. B-K., Denver, Colorado, USA)

• "We became almost a club as we found people sitting at tables all around, consulting their little blue books!" (F.C., Glasgow, Scotland)

• "I have just concluded a tour . . . using your comprehensive *Cities of Australia* as my personal guide. Thank you for your magnificent, clear and precise book." (Dr. S.G., Singapore)

• "We never made a restaurant reservation without checking your book *(Venice)*. The recommendations were excellent, and the historical and artistic text got us through the sights beautifully." (L.S., Boston, Ma., USA)

• "The book *(Hong Kong, Singapore & Bangkok)* was written in such a personal way that I feel as if you were actually writing this book for me." (L.Z., Orange, Conn., USA)

• "I feel as if you have been a silent friend shadowing my time in Tuscany." (T.G., Washington, DC, USA)

## What the papers say:

- "The expertly edited American Express series has the knack of pin-pointing precisely the details you need to know, and doing it concisely and intelligently." (*The Washington Post* )

- "*(Venice)* . . . the best guide book I have ever used." (*The Standard* — London)

- "Amid the welter of guides to individual countries, American Express stands out . . . . " (*Time* )

- "Possibly the best . . . guides on the market, they come close to the oft-claimed 'all you need to know' comprehensiveness, with much original experience, research and opinions." (*Sunday Telegraph* — London)

- "The most useful general guide was *American Express New York* by Herbert Bailey Livesey. It also has the best street and subway maps." (*Daily Telegraph* — London)

- " . . . in the flood of travel guides, the *American Express* guides come closest to the needs of traveling managers with little time." (*Die Zeit* — Germany)

## What the experts say:

- "We only used one guide book, Sheila Hale's *AmEx Venice*, for which she and the editors deserve a Nobel Prize." (travel writer Eric Newby, London)

- "Congratulations to you and your staff for putting out the best guide book of *any* size *(Barcelona & Madrid)*. I'm recommending it to everyone." (travel writer Barnaby Conrad, Santa Barbara, California)

- "If you're only buying one guide book, we recommend American Express . . . . " (*Which?* — Britain's leading consumer magazine)

- "The judges selected *American Express London* as the best guide book of the past decade — it won the competition in 1983. [The guide] was praised for being 'concise, well presented, up-to-date, with unusual information.' " (News release from the London Tourist Board and Convention Bureau)

# Index

- Museums, historical houses, churches and other sights located in towns *outside* Boston and Cambridge are listed with the town name: for example, Beechwood, Newport, 246.
- Page numbers in **bold** type indicate main entries.
- *Italic* page numbers indicate illustrations and maps.
- See also the LIST OF STREET NAMES on page 282.

# List of street names

- Listed below are all streets mentioned in the text that fall within the area covered by our color maps **7** to **12**.
- Map numbers are printed in **bold** type. Some smaller streets are not named on the maps, but the map reference given below will help you locate the correct neighborhood.

**A**corn St., **11**E9
Appian Way, **7**B2
Arlington St., **11**F8–G9
Ash St., **7**B1
Athenaeum St., **11**D7
Atlantic Ave., **12**D11–G11
Avon St., **12**F10

**B**atterymarch St., **12**E11
Beach St., **12**F10–G11
Beacon St. (Boston),
  **9**H3–**12**E10
Beacon St. (Cambridge),
  **7**A3–**8**B4
Belvedere St., **10**G6–H7
Bennet St., **7**B1–C2
Berkeley St., **11**F8–G8
Blossom St., **11**D9–E9
Bowdoin St., **12**E10
Boylston Pl., **11**F9
Boylston St., **9**H4–**11**F9
Brattle St., **7**B1–2
Brimmer St., **11**E8–F9
Broad St., **12**E11
Broadway, **7**B3–**10**D7
Brookline Ave., **9**I3–G5
Brookline St., **7**F3–**8**D4

**C**ambridge Parkway,
  **11**C8–D8
Cambridge St. (Allston),
  **7**E1–2
Cambridge St. (Boston),
  **11**E9–**12**E10
Cambridge St.
  (Cambridge), **7**B2–C8
Cambridgeside Pl., **11**C8
Canal St., **12**D10
Cardinal Medeiros Ave.,
  **8**D5–C6
Causeway St., **12**D10
Central Sq., **8**D4

Central Wharf, **12**E11–12
Charles St., **11**D9–F9
Charles St. South,
  **11**F9–G9
Charlestown Br., **12**D10
Chatham St., **12**E11
Chelsea St., **12**B10–C10
Chestnut St., **11**E8–F9
City Sq., **12**C10
Clarendon St., **11**F8–G8
Clark St., **12**D11
Clinton St., **12**E11
Commercial Ave.,
  **11**D7–C8
Commercial St.,
  **12**C11–E11
Commonwealth Ave.,
  **9**G3–**11**F8
Congress St.,
  **12**D10–G12
Congress St. Br., **12**F11
Constitution Rd., **12**C10
Copley Sq., **10**G8
Court St., **12**E10
Cross St., **12**D10–11

**D**alton St., **10**G7–H7
Dartmouth St., **10**F7–H8
Divinity Ave., **7**A3–B3
Dock Sq., **12**E11
Dorchester Ave.,
  **12**F11–G11
Dunster St., **7**B2–C2

**E**liot St., **7**C2
Embankment Rd.,
  **11**E8–F8
Essex St., **12**F10–11
Exeter St., **10**F7–G8

**F**airfield St., **10**F7–G7
Farwell Pl., **7**B2

Federal St., **12**E11–F11
The Fenway, **9**H4–**10**H6
First St., **11**C8–D8
Fitzgerald Expressway,
  **12**D10–G10
Forsyth Way, **10**I6
Franklin St., **12**F10–E11
Fruit St., **11**D9

**G**ainsborough St.,
  **10**H6–7
Garden St., **7**A1–B2
Gloucester St., **10**F7–G7
Green St., **7**C3–**8**E5
Grove St., **11**D9–E9

**H**ampshire St., **8**B4–D6
Hancock Pl., **11**G8
Hancock St.,
  **11**E9–**12**E10
Hanover St., **12**E10–D11
Harrison Ave.,
  **12**F10–G10
Harvard Br., **10**E6–F6
Harvard Sq., **7**B2
Hawthorn St., **7**B1
Hereford St., **10**F6–G7
Holyoke St., **7**B2–C2
Hudson St., **12**G10
Hull St., **12**C10–D11
Huntington Ave.,
  **9**I5–**10**G8

**I**ndia St., **12**E11
Inman Sq., **8**B4

**J**ohn F. Kennedy St.,
  **7**C1–B2
Joy St., **11**E9

**K**endall Sq., **10**D7
Kenmore Sq., **9**G5

Kirkland St., **7**B2–**8**A4
Kneeland St., **12**G10

**L**afayette Pl., **12**F10
Landsdowne St., **9**G5
Lewis Wharf, **12**D11–12
Linden St., **7**C2
Long Wharf, **12**E11–12
Longfellow Br., **11**E8
Louisburg Sq., **11**E9
Lynde St., **11**E9

**M**cKinley Sq., **12**E11
Magazine St., **7**E3–**8**D4
Main St., **12**B10–C10
Marlborough St.,
 **10**G6–**11**F8
Marshall St., **12**E11
Mason St., **7**B1
Massachusetts Ave.,
 **7**A2–**10**I7
Memorial Dr., **7**B1–**10**E7
Milk St., **12**E10–11
Moon St., **12**D11
Mt. Auburn St., **7**B1–C3
Mt. Vernon St., **11**E9
Museum Rd., **9**I5
Museum Wharf, **12**F12

**N**ewbury St., **9**G5–**11**F8
Newton St., **10**H7–H8
North Sq., **12**D11
North St., **12**D11–E11

Northern Ave., **12**F12
Northern Ave. Br.,
 **12**F11–12

**O**tis St., **12**F10
Oxford St., **7**A2–B2

**P**alace Rd., **9**I5
Park Sq., **11**G9
Park St., **12**E10
Parmenter St., **12**D11
Pearl St., **12**E11–F11
Pilgrim Rd., **9**I3–H4
Pinckney St., **11**E9
Plympton St., **7**C2
Portland St., **12**D10
Post Office Sq.,
 **12**E11–F11
Prince St., **12**D10–11

**Q**uincy St., **7**C2–B3

**R**evere St., **11**E9
Richmond St.,
 **12**D11–E11
River St., **7**E2–D4
River St. Br., **7**E2
Rowe's Wharf, **12**E11–12

**S**t James Ave., **11**G8–9
Salem St., **12**D11
School St., **12**E10
Second St., **11**C8–D7

Sleeper St., **12**F12
Smith Ct., **11**E9
Snowhill St., **12**C11–D11
Soldiers Field Rd.,
 **7**C1–**9**F3
South St. (Boston),
 **12**F10–G10
South St. (Cambridge),
 **7**C2
State St., **12**E10–11
Storrow Dr., **9**F3–**10**F8
Stuart St., **10**G8–**11**F9
Summer St.,
 **12**F10–G12

**T**remont St.,
 **10**I7–**12**E10

**U**nion St., **12**E10–11

**W**alnut St., **11**E9
Warrenton St., **11**F9
Washington St. (Boston),
 **12**E10–G10
Washington St.
 (Cambridge), **8**A4–6
West St., **12**F10
Willow St., **11**E9
Winter Pl., **12**F10
Winter St., **12**F10
Winthrop St., **7**C2

**Y**awkey Way, **9**G5–H5

# American Express Travel Guides

*spanning the globe....*

**EUROPE**
Amsterdam, Rotterdam
  & The Hague
Athens and the
  Classical Sites
Barcelona, Madrid &
  Seville
Berlin, Potsdam &
  Dresden
Brussels
Dublin
Florence and Tuscany
London
Paris
Prague
Provence and the
  Côte d'Azur
Rome
Venice
Vienna & Budapest

**NORTH AMERICA**
Boston and New
  England
Los Angeles & San
  Diego
Mexico
New York
San Francisco and
  the Wine Regions
Toronto, Montréal &
  Québec City
Washington, DC

**THE PACIFIC**
Australia's
  Major Cities
Hong Kong & Taiwan
Singapore &
  Bangkok
Tokyo

*Clarity and quality of information, combined
with outstanding maps — the ultimate in
travelers' guides*

## KEY TO MAP PAGES

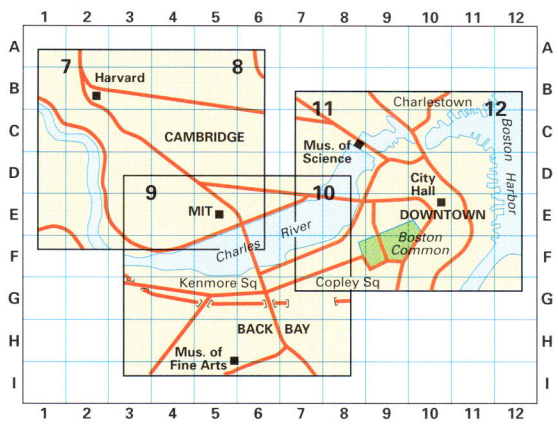

## KEY TO MAP SYMBOLS

### City Maps

Major Place of Interest

Other Important Building

Built-up Area

Park

Cemetery

Church

Synagogue

Hospital

Garage / Parking Lot

Information Office

Post Office

Police Station

MRT Station

Adjoining Page No.

### Environs/Area Maps

Place of Interest

Wood or Park

Cemetery

Limited-access Highway

Other Divided Highway

Main Road

Secondary Road

Other Road

Interstate Highway

US Highway

State Highway

Ferry

Railroad

Airport

International Boundary

State Boundary

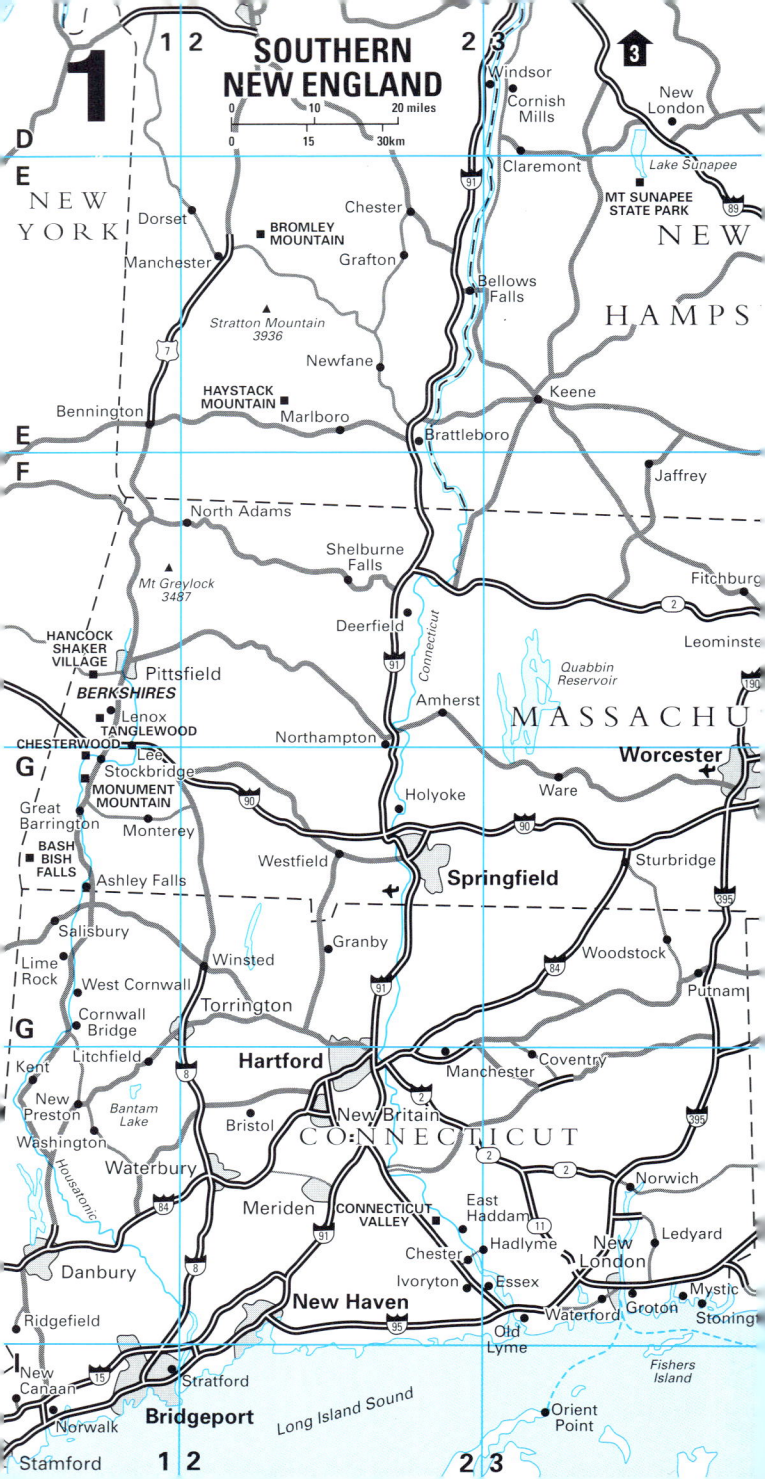

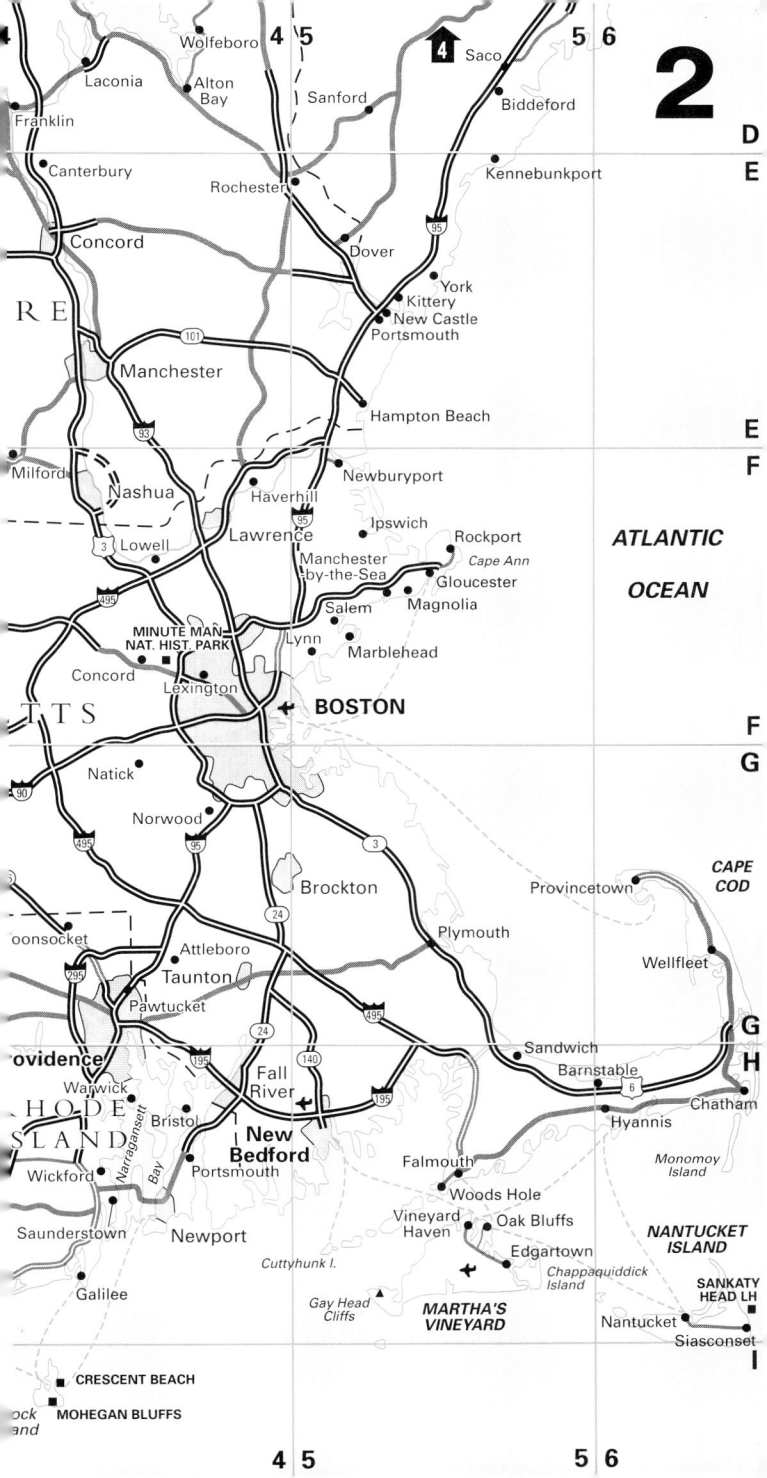

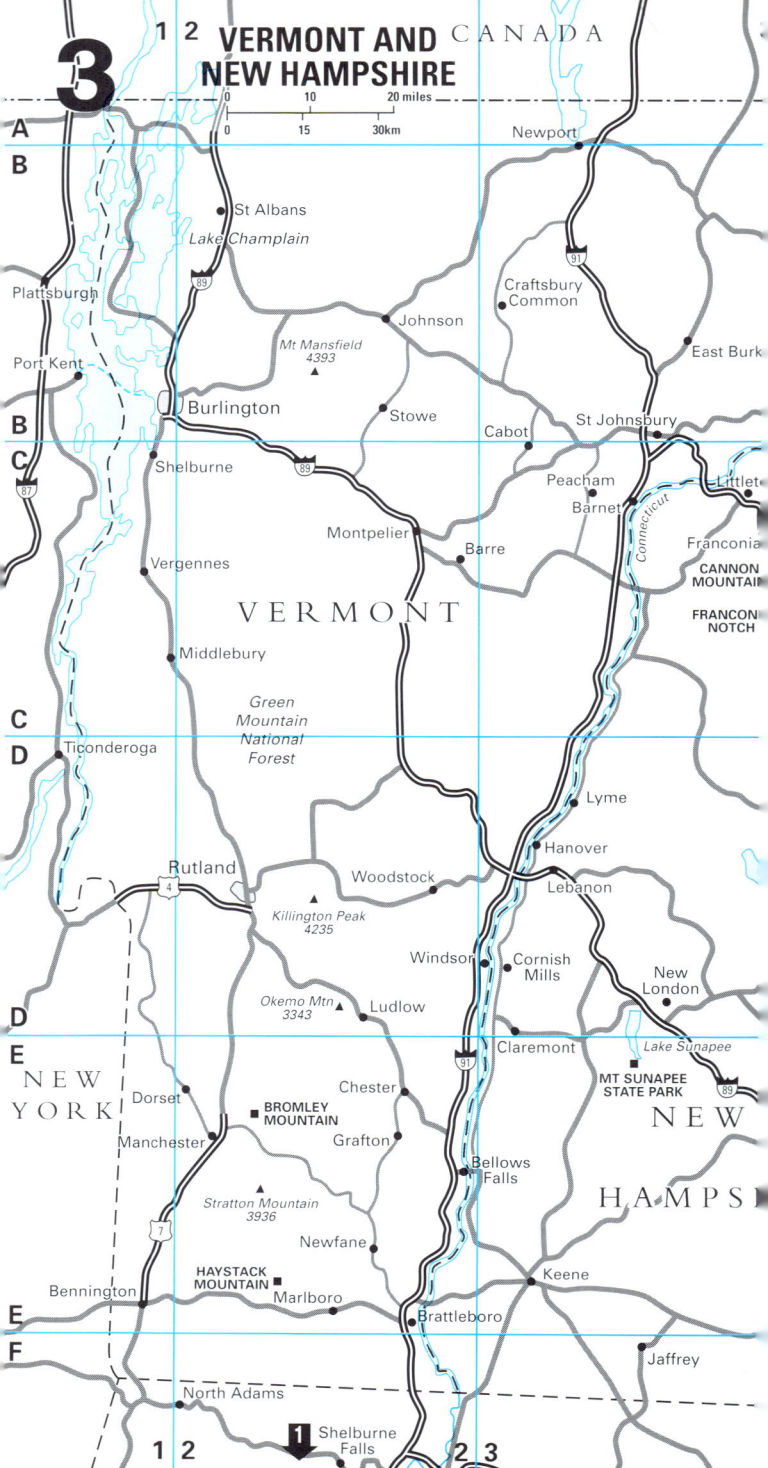

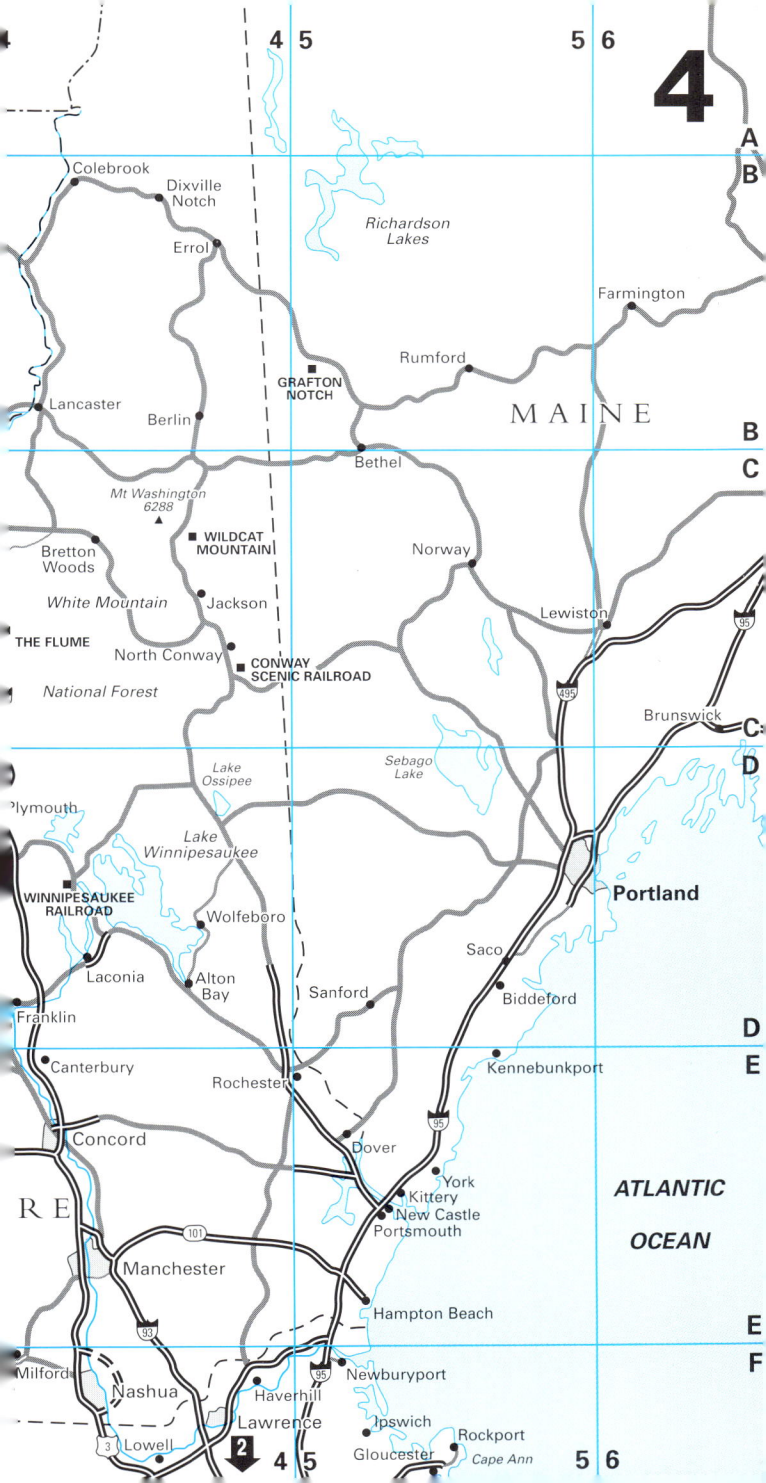

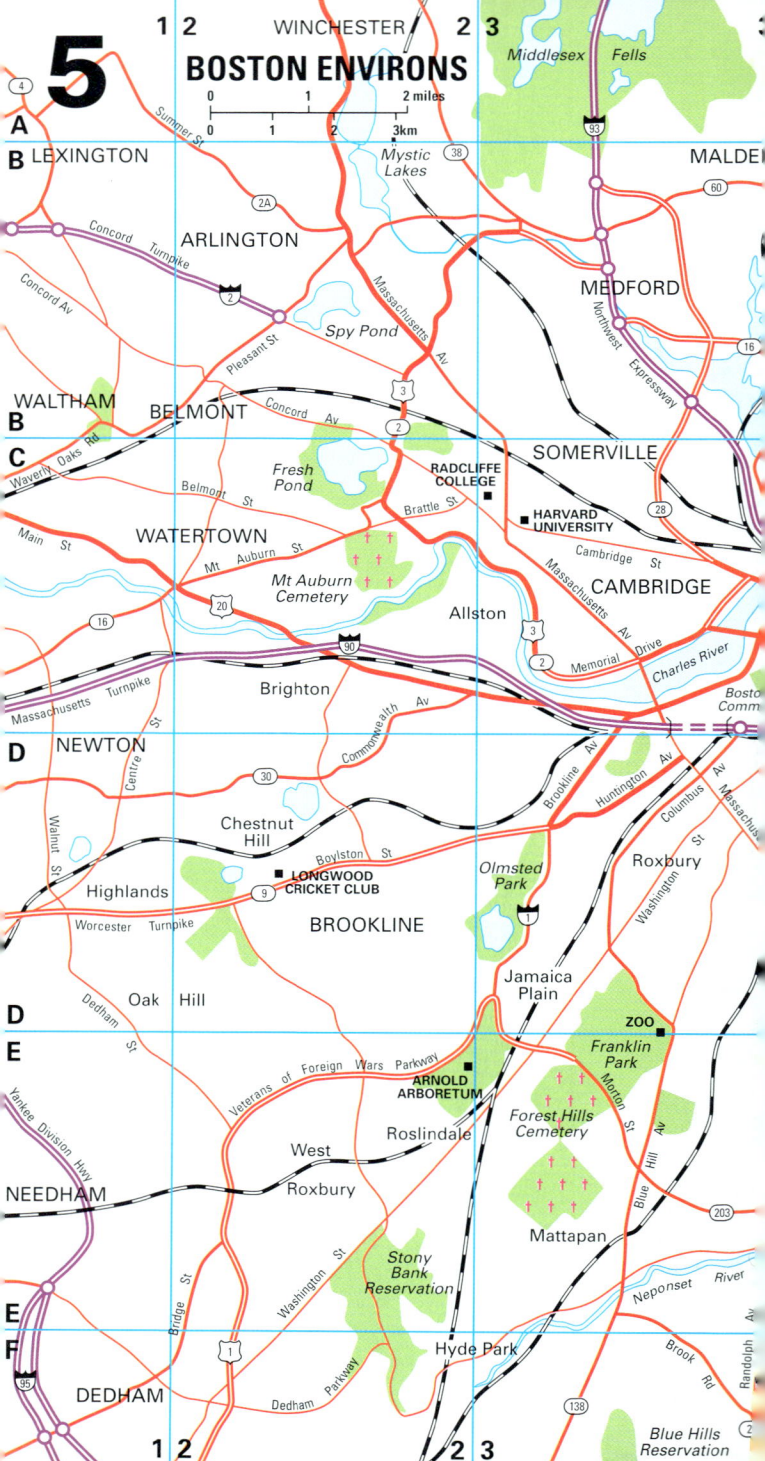

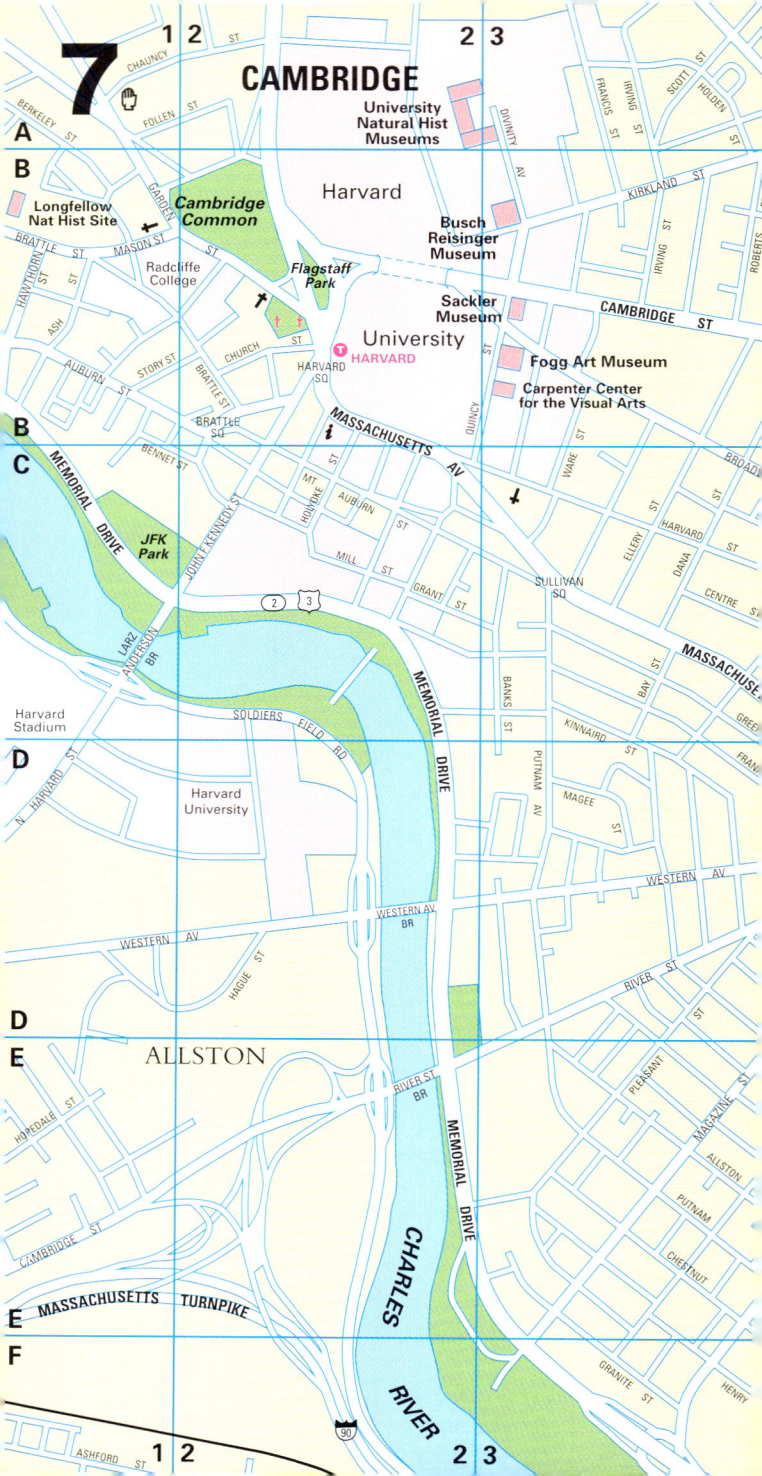

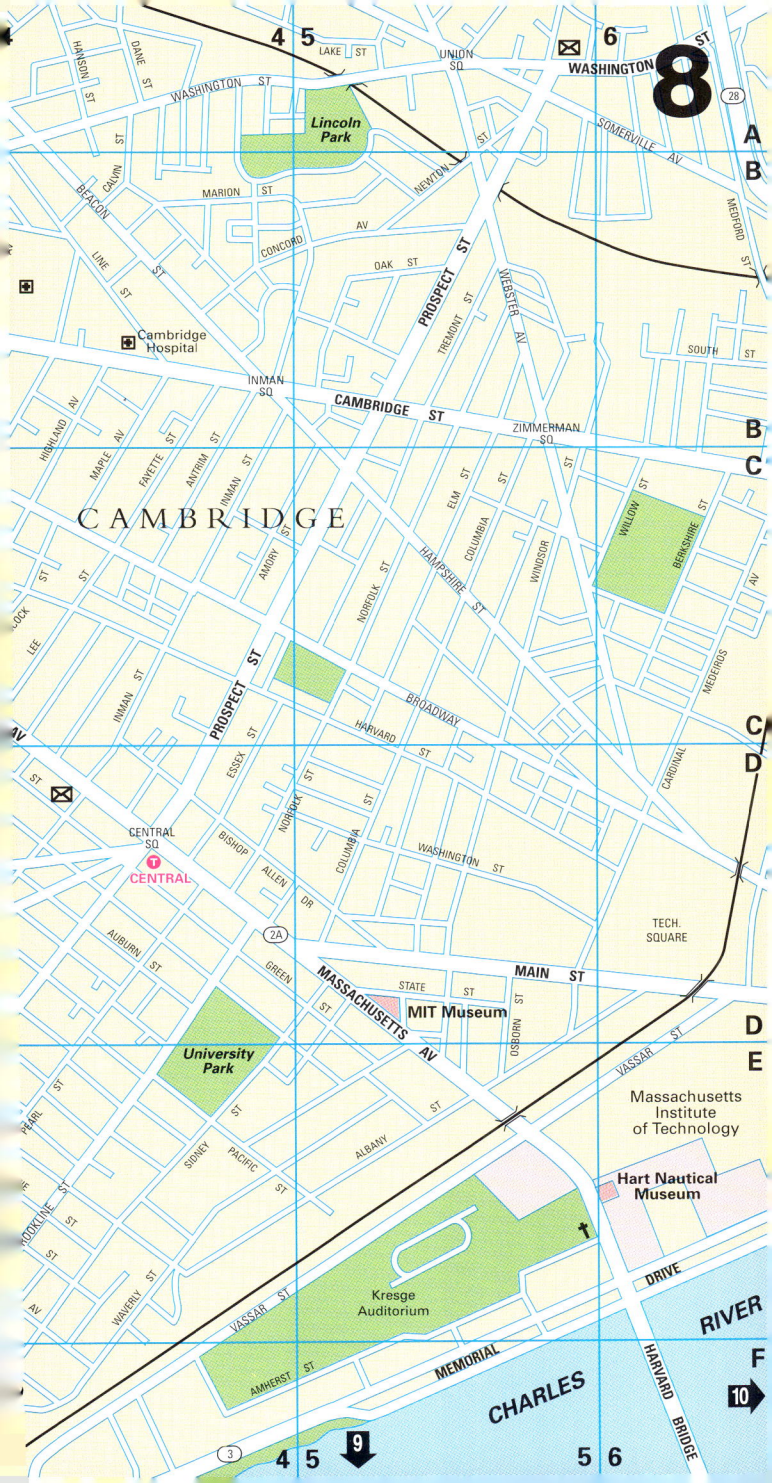

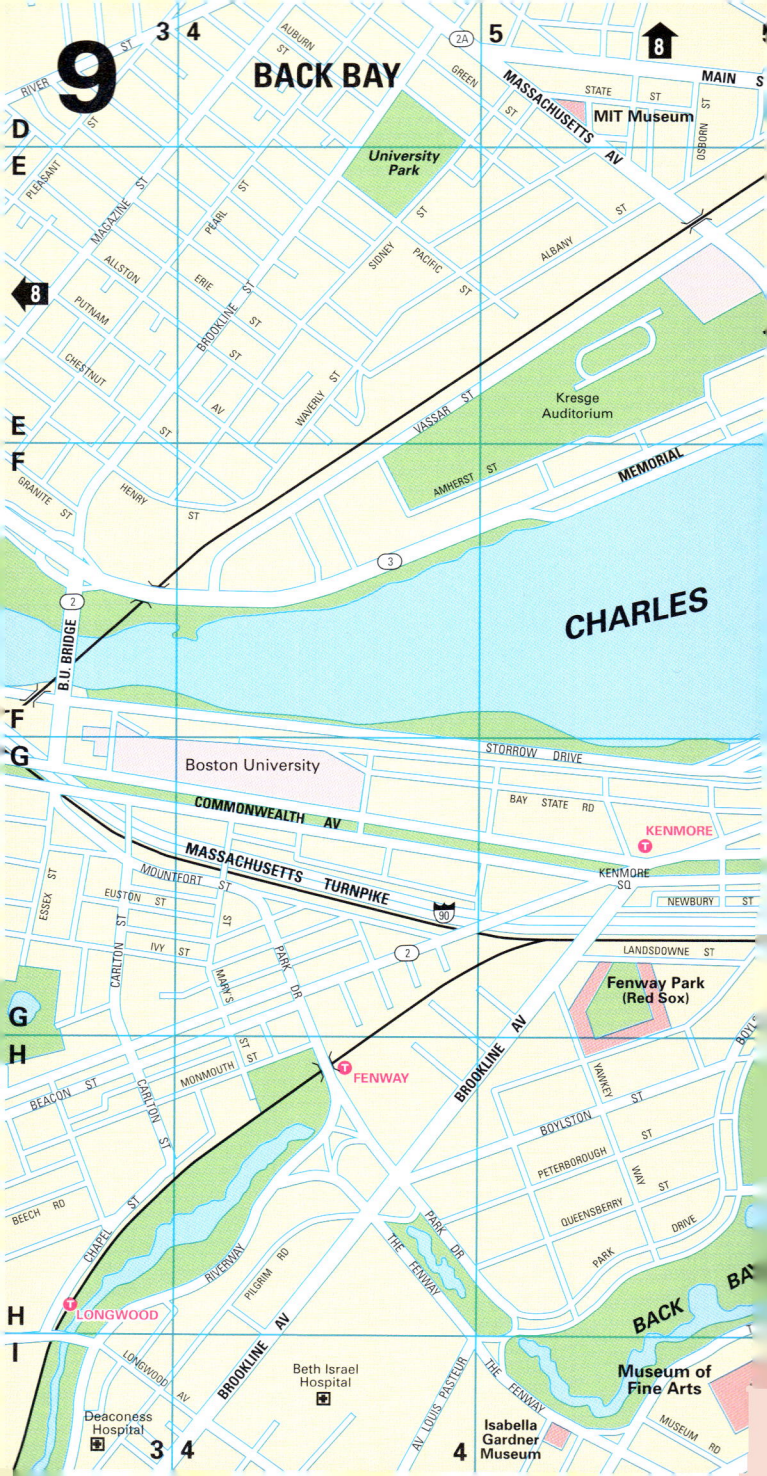

**9**

RIVER ST

AUBURN ST

GREEN ST

2A

MASSACHUSETTS AV

STATE ST

OSBURN ST

MAIN S

**BACK BAY**

**8**

D

MIT Museum

E

University Park

PLEASANT ST

MAGAZINE ST

PEARL ST

SIDNEY ST

PACIFIC ST

ALBANY ST

ALLSTON

**8**

PUTNAM

ERIE ST

BROOKLINE ST

CHESTNUT

AV

WAVERY ST

VASSAR ST

Kresge Auditorium

E

F

GRANITE ST

HENRY ST

AMHERST ST

MEMORIAL

3

**CHARLES**

2

B.U. BRIDGE

F

G

**Boston University**

STORROW DRIVE

**COMMONWEALTH AV**

BAY STATE RD

**KENMORE**
T

**MASSACHUSETTS TURNPIKE**

ESSEX ST

EUSTON ST

MOUNTFORT ST

CARLTON ST

IVY ST

MARY'S ST

PARK DR

90

KENMORE SQ

NEWBURY ST

2

LANDSDOWNE ST

**Fenway Park
(Red Sox)**

G

H

BEACON ST

CARLTON ST

MONMOUTH ST

T **FENWAY**

BROOKLINE AV

YANKEY

BOYLE

BOYLSTON

BEECH RD

CHAPEL ST

RIVERWAY

PILGRIM RD

PARK DR

THE FENWAY

PETERBORDUGH

QUEENSBERRY

WAY ST

PARK DRIVE

H

T **LONGWOOD**

**BACK BA**

I

LONGWOOD AV

BROOKLINE AV

Beth Israel
Hospital

AV LOUIS PASTEUR

THE FENWAY

**Museum of
Fine Arts**

Deaconess
Hospital

Isabella
Gardner
Museum

MUSEUM RD

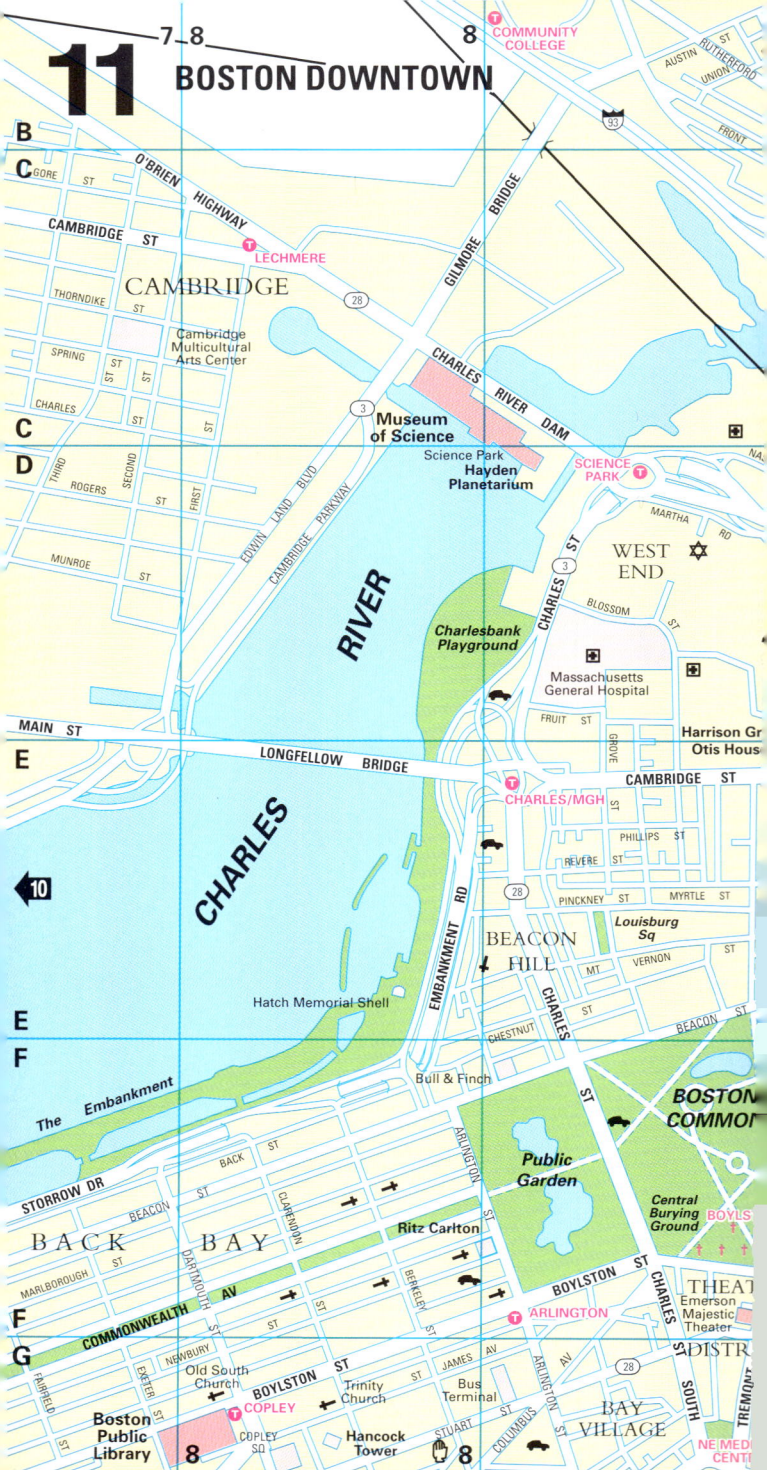

COMMUNITY COLLEGE

AUSTIN

RUTHERFORD

UNION ST

93

FRONT

B

C GORE ST

O'BRIEN HIGHWAY

CAMBRIDGE ST

LECHMERE

GILMORE

BRIDGE

THORNDIKE

ST

CAMBRIDGE

28

SPRING

ST

Cambridge Multicultural Arts Center

CHARLES RIVER DAM

CHARLES

ST

CHARLES

ST

3

Museum of Science

C

NA

D

THIRD

ROGERS

SECOND

FIRST

ST

EDWIN LAND BLVD

CAMBRIDGE PARKWAY

Science Park
Hayden Planetarium

SCIENCE PARK

MARTHA RD

MUNROE

ST

WEST END

3

BLOSSOM

ST

CHARLES ST

RIVER

Charlesbank Playground

Massachusetts General Hospital

MAIN ST

FRUIT ST

GROVE

Harrison Gr
Otis Hous

E

LONGFELLOW BRIDGE

CHARLES/MGH

CAMBRIDGE ST

PHILLIPS ST

REVERE ST

CHARLES

10

EMBANKMENT RD

28

PINCKNEY ST

MYRTLE ST

Louisburg Sq

BEACON HILL

MT

VERNON

Hatch Memorial Shell

CHESTNUT

CHARLES ST

BEACON

E

F

Bull & Finch

The Embankment

BOSTON COMMO

STORROW DR

BACK

BEACON

BACK

ST

CLARENDON

ST

Public Garden

ARLINGTON

ST

Central Burying Ground

BOYLS

BAY

Ritz Carlton

DARTMOUTH

AV

BERKELEY

ST

CHARLES ST

THEAT
Emerson Majestic Theater

MARLBOROUGH

ST

BOYLSTON ST

F

COMMONWEALTH

AV

ARLINGTON

ST DISTR

G

NEWBURY

EXETER

FAIRFIELD

Old South Church

BOYLSTON ST

COPLEY

Trinity Church

JAMES AV

Bus Terminal

STUART

COLUMBUS

AV

28

SOUTH

TREMONT

BAY VILLAGE

NE MEDI
CENTI

Boston Public Library

8

COPLEY

Hancock Tower

8

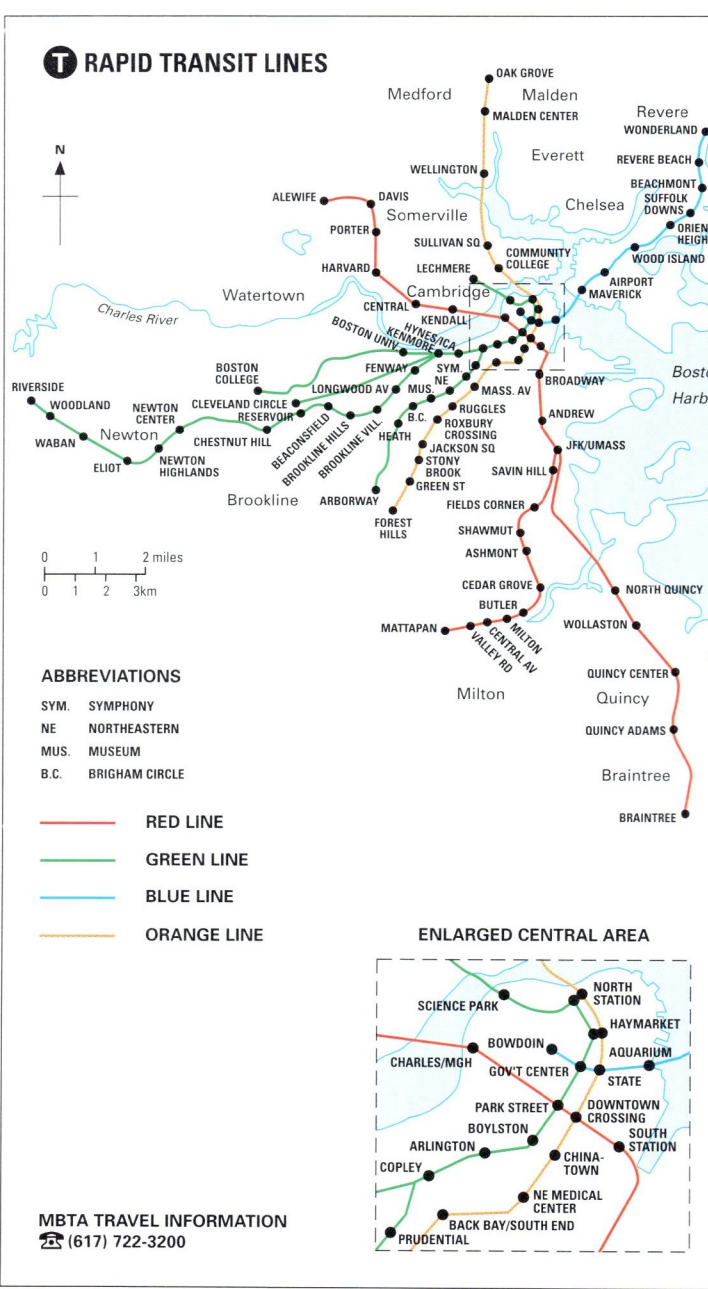

# 🚇 RAPID TRANSIT LINES

N

Medford
Malden
OAK GROVE
MALDEN CENTER
Revere
WONDERLAND
Everett
REVERE BEACH
BEACHMONT
SUFFOLK DOWNS
Chelsea
ORIENT HEIGHTS
WOOD ISLAND
AIRPORT
MAVERICK

WELLINGTON

ALEWIFE
DAVIS
Somerville
PORTER
SULLIVAN SQ
COMMUNITY COLLEGE
HARVARD
LECHMERE
Watertown
Cambridge
CENTRAL
KENDALL
HYNES/ICA
Charles River
BOSTON UNIV.
KENMORE
BOSTON COLLEGE
FENWAY
SYM.
NE
MASS. AV
BROADWAY
Boston Harbor
RIVERSIDE
WOODLAND
NEWTON CENTER
CLEVELAND CIRCLE
RESERVOIR
LONGWOOD AV
MUS.
B.C.
RUGGLES
ANDREW
WABAN
Newton
CHESTNUT HILL
BEACONSFIELD
BROOKLINE HILLS
BROOKLINE VILL.
HEATH
ROXBURY CROSSING
JACKSON SQ
JFK/UMASS
ELIOT
NEWTON HIGHLANDS
STONY BROOK
GREEN ST
SAVIN HILL
Brookline
ARBORWAY
GREEN ST
FIELDS CORNER
FOREST HILLS
SHAWMUT
ASHMONT
CEDAR GROVE
NORTH QUINCY
BUTLER
MATTAPAN
MILTON
CENTRAL AV
VALLEY RD
WOLLASTON
Milton
QUINCY CENTER
Quincy
QUINCY ADAMS
Braintree
BRAINTREE

```
0     1     2 miles
0   1   2   3km
```

## ABBREVIATIONS

| | |
|---|---|
| SYM. | SYMPHONY |
| NE | NORTHEASTERN |
| MUS. | MUSEUM |
| B.C. | BRIGHAM CIRCLE |

——— RED LINE
——— GREEN LINE
——— BLUE LINE
······ ORANGE LINE

## ENLARGED CENTRAL AREA

NORTH STATION
SCIENCE PARK
HAYMARKET
BOWDOIN
AQUARIUM
CHARLES/MGH
GOV'T CENTER
STATE
PARK STREET
DOWNTOWN CROSSING
BOYLSTON
SOUTH STATION
ARLINGTON
CHINA-TOWN
COPLEY
NE MEDICAL CENTER
BACK BAY/SOUTH END
PRUDENTIAL

**MBTA TRAVEL INFORMATION**
☎ (617) 722-3200